D1591121

DEMOCRACY IN CHINA

DEMOCRACY IN CHINA

The Coming Crisis

JIWEI CI

Harvard University Press

Cambridge, Massachusetts, and London, England 2019

First printing

Library of Congress Cataloging-in-Publication Data

Names: Ci, Jiwei, 1955– author.
Title: Democracy in China : the coming crisis / Jiwei Ci.
Description: Cambridge, Massachusetts : Harvard University Press, 2020. |
    Includes bibliographical references and index.
Identifiers: LCCN 2019014446 | ISBN 9780674238183 (alk. paper)
Subjects: LCSH: Democracy—China—History—21st century. | Democratization—
    China—History—21st century. | Legitimacy of governments—China—History—
    21st century. | Zhongguo gong chan dang.
Classification: LCC JC423 .C56736 2020 | DDC 320.951—dc23 LC record available at
    https://lccn.loc.gov/2019014446

Contents

Preface   vii

Introduction: A Prudential Approach to Democracy   1

PART ONE   **The Legitimation Crisis**   33

  1 Legitimacy and Performance   35
  2 The Question of Regime Perpetuation   70

PART TWO   **The Democratic Challenge**   99

  3 The Case for Democracy   101
  4 Democracy and the Self-Protection of Society   156
  5 Contradictions and Arrested Transitions   195
  6 Democratic Preparation   252

PART THREE   **The International and Hong Kong Dimensions**   309

  7 Democracy at Home and Legitimacy around the World   311
  8 Two Systems, One Democratic Future   333

Concluding Reflections   370

Notes   383
Index   415

Preface

We live in extraordinarily challenging times for democracy. In China this challenge takes the form not of democracy's oligarchic capture, as in America and to a lesser degree in Europe, but of democracy's seeming loss of value or relevance even before its arrival. I have written this book to show that democracy has never been more necessary for China than it is today—not so much on the strength of its normative appeal as because of its indispensability for political stability in the foreseeable future. There is no better way of hinting (for this is all I can do at this point) at such indispensability than by suggesting that China has already developed a substantial degree of democracy. Hence the title of the book, in one of its meanings.

But this is true only if one hastens to add that four decades of reform have created a largely democratic *society* without a complementary democratic *polity*. This mismatch—between an increasingly democratic ethos in China's society and the still exclusively vertical character of its political life—raises legitimation challenges that cannot be met indefinitely without democratization, or so I shall argue in this book. Insofar as this line of argument is indebted to Alexis de Tocqueville (among others), the title I have chosen for the book contains a none-too-subtle echo of Tocqueville's classic work on democracy in America.

Not unlike one strand of Tocqueville's thought, mine is an essentially prudential argument for democracy (in terms of democracy's necessity, given China's circumstances) rather than a normative one (in terms of democracy's moral appeal, regardless of its necessity). This is not a kind of argument that is commonly made today with reference to China—at least not, to the best of my knowledge, with the explicitness, comprehensiveness, and attention to its full implications that I have attempted to bring to it. I felt compelled to renew and enrich this argument by calling attention to an unprecedented legitimation crisis looming on the horizon, a crisis whose moment of uncontainable eruption is uncertain yet whose signs are nowhere more evident than in the drastic political tightening of society. Inasmuch as this tightening prevents all airing of crisis consciousness in public, the crisis itself takes on an extra dimension: democracy is being given the least attention, with a virtual moratorium on open discussion of it, at a time when it is more necessary, in a prudential sense, than ever before. I would not have bothered to undertake the present intellectual exercise, however, if I did not believe that the coming crisis has as its proverbial double an opening and opportunity. Thus the subtitle of the book connotes as much cautious hope as foreboding. For the same reason, the book itself is a quest, in roughly equal measure, for understanding and for an idea of a solution.

The first opportunity to systematically try out some of the main ideas in this book came when I was invited by Tim Scanlon and Mathias Risse to give a series of lectures at Harvard University in November 2015. The proposal for this visit originated with Tim, to whom I owe an inexpressible gratitude not only for the invitation but also for the meticulous care with which he planned the whole series of lectures. Mathias played an essential role throughout, as gracious host and thoughtful organizer, and in other ways that made the visit possible and such an intellectually rewarding experience. My philosophical engagements with them during the two weeks at Harvard were among the most enjoyable and instructive I have ever had. I am also grateful to Tim and Mathias, and to Lucy and Kozue, for their touching hospitality.

The lectures, which were not all directly related to China, were given at the Fairbank Center for Chinese Studies, the Safra Center for Ethics, the Department of Government, Harvard Law School, and the Department of Philosophy. My thanks go to Mark Eliot, Danielle Allen, Michael Rosen, William Alford, and Tim Scanlon, respectively, for hosting these lectures; to Iain Johnston and Stephen Angle for serving as commentators on two of these occasions; and to the audiences for their instructive feedback. While at Harvard, I also had the pleasure of engaging in stimulating discussions with Eric Beerbohm, Loubna El Amine, David Estlund, Helen Haste, Eske Møllgaard, May Sim, Anna Sun, David Der-wei Wang, Daniel Wikler, Peter Zarrow, and, especially, Jane Mansbridge, who went out of her way to offer challenging criticisms and constructive suggestions that I found extremely helpful.

I have presented earlier versions of parts of some chapters at the National University of Singapore, the University of Oxford, the University of Hong Kong, Hong Kong University of Science and Technology, and Seoul National University. I wish to thank—as hosts or commentators—Eric Beerbohm, Nick Bunnin (to whom additional, special thanks are due for help and support over many years), Christian Daniels, Paul Flather, He Baogang, Johannes Hoerning, Nomi Claire Lazar, Mathias Risse, and Jieuwh Song.

I have benefited enormously from discussions with friends and colleagues: Stephen Angle, Stefan Auer, Daniel A. Bell (as a good-humored challenger to my views), Joseph Chan (especially on democracy in Hong Kong), Chang Xiangqian, Albert Chen, Chen Jian (to whom I convey my belated thanks for his generosity), Martin Chung, Cui Zhiyuan, John Dunn (a source of inspiration on democratic theory), Fan Ruiping, Johannes Hoerning, Huang Yong, Jiang Dongxian, Sungmoon Kim (on Confucian democracy), Stefanie Lenk, Li Chenyang, Liang Zhiping, Liu Antong, Liu Qing, Mang Ping, Marco Meyer, Haig Patapan, Shang Zheng, Shu-mei Shih, Quinn Slobodian (on neoliberalism), Hans Sluga (including on the Occupy movement in Hong Kong), Billy So (on modern Chinese legal culture), Wu Fen, Xu Chenggang, Felix Yeung, Zhao Tingyang, and Zhou Lian. As the wide spectrum of positions of those listed here attests, none of these colleagues or friends is responsible in any way for the views expressed in this book.

Thanks are also due to the anonymous readers for Harvard University Press. I do not remember ever making such extensive revisions in response to comments from peer reviewers as I have done for this book. The depth of my appreciation, not least of the most challenging comments, is reflected in this very fact.

It gives me special pleasure to thank Kathleen McDermott, my editor at Harvard, whose admirable professionalism and steady guiding hand I have come to fully appreciate only with the passage of time, and Mihaela Pacurar, also of Harvard University Press, for editorial assistance rendered with a nice human touch. For the book's production stage I could not have wished for a better team to work with: Cheryl Hirsch as a superbly understanding and effective production editor, and Ashley Moore as an exemplary copy-editor, to both of whom I am most grateful. For additional textual improvements, I sincerely thank Gail Naron Chalew.

DEMOCRACY IN CHINA

Introduction

A Prudential Approach to Democracy

A MAJOR SHIFT in intellectual opinion has occurred in China, and to some degree even in the world at large, regarding the relevance and appropriateness of democracy under China's current circumstances and given its tradition. I am tempted to call this shift a sea change, given its swelling proportions and potentially far-reaching consequences. To get some sense of how difficult it has recently become to make a case for democracy in China, I begin by attending briefly to this important shift.

Not the least interesting aspect of this change is the way in which events in China have interacted, even dovetailed, with broader trends in the world, creating and sustaining a climate of opinion through mutually reinforcing causes. And not the least unexpected beneficiary of the resulting climate of opinion, including for the first time a broad swath of international opinion, is a set of forces denying democracy's relevance and suitability for China—indeed, paradoxically, for a China that is witnessing an inexorable democratization in its ethos, its organization of production and consumption, its structure of human interaction and familial relations; in a word, in its entire society, as distinct from its political system. All of this is thanks, in no small measure, to democracy's vicissitudes abroad.

Multiple developments of global significance have conspired in the past few decades to bring about a major downward reassessment of democracy. First (to name just a few), the ascendance of neoliberalism in the 1970s in the context of capitalist accumulation problems helped overturn the postwar balance between democracy and capitalism massively in favor of the latter, as epitomized by the skyrocketing fortunes of the much-resented "1 percent." Then the US-led invasion of Iraq in the wake of September 11 gave the lie once again, in the full glare of international public opinion, to what had always been a precarious belief in democracies' supposed love of peace. It was not long before a human-made disaster of a different variety struck—namely, the financial crisis of 2008. After years of scandalously deregulated private debt and financialization, this global crisis, with its epicenter at the heart of the democratic capitalist world, ushered in an age of stagnation and austerity that has since, along with the migrant crisis and the increasingly manifest polarizing effects of globalization and digital technology, caused a severe backlash in the form of populism. A mood of panic has set in throughout the Western world that has not been seen since the Great Depression.

It is one of the more depressing ironies of our age that developments such as these seem to have hit democracy the hardest. To be sure, democracy is marked, in the case of all modern Western states, by its imbrication with capitalism and, in the case of America, by its additional, ongoing project of empire. It is also true that democracy is vulnerable to erosion and even takeover by oligarchy or bureaucracy. The rise of the network society has not helped either, giving rise to a further crisis of democracy, in the form of media politics and scandal politics, specific to the information age.[1] Still, that democracy should bear the brunt of the reputational damage rather than capitalism or empire or the new plutocracy or the network society speaks volumes about the political hermeneutics of our time. The upshot, especially since the financial crisis and the rise of populism, has been little short of a global devaluation of democracy—the resurfacing especially among the elite of what Jacques Rancière has called "the hatred of democracy" *(la haine de la démocratie)*. It is almost as if capitalism or empire or oligarchy could be restored to vigor and virtue with a cutback on democracy or even its replacement.

In the meantime, China has done more than any country outside the "free world" to confirm this harsh verdict on democracy. It had embarked on its own economic reform at roughly the same time that Margaret Thatcher launched her neoliberal makeover of Britain, in both cases with global repercussions. Since then China has been steadily rising and is now the world's second-largest economy and already the largest in terms of purchasing power parity. It has also become the highest contributor to global economic growth, although the continuation of this role is being made more uncertain by an apparently heightened American determination to put China in its place. Needless to say, China has accomplished these feats in spite of not being a democracy—nay, according to much of Western intellectual opinion, as well as China's own, precisely *because of* this Chinese characteristic. Much as democracy is being blamed for not a few of the West's ills, so the lack of it is credited with China's spectacular rise. But what is China, positively, if it is not a democracy? In some contexts, it is taken unflatteringly to be a communist dictatorship or an authoritarian regime. In the present context, however, China is an enviable meritocracy. It has earned this title by virtue of its supposedly unbroken Confucian tradition and on the strength of its current performance, the latter backed up with a corresponding official legitimating discourse. In the eyes of many, instead of the apparently moribund democratic capitalism, China now features a meritocratic capitalism led by the Chinese Communist Party (CCP), combining the best of both worlds, thereby not only bringing efficiency and long-term vision but also conferring a well-deserved legitimacy.

This is in essence what has been called the China model. Never mind whether the meritocracy in question is communist or Confucian, because the important feature is not its form but meritocracy itself, which carries a potentially universal appeal. If only the cadres of capitalism (to use Immanuel Wallerstein's apt way of putting it) in the West could learn from this model and exercise leadership with fewer constraints from democracy and greater reliance on sheer moral and executive merit!

One important reason why meritocracy is supposed to confer legitimacy is the (quasi-democratic) belief that, given the choice between meritocracy and democracy, most people in China would settle for meritocracy. How does one know? Well, because meritocracy delivers the goods and the Chinese people clearly care about those goods—both their frenetic production and their equally frenetic consumption. Because, also, meritocracy is part of the Confucian tradition, now increasingly taken for granted as a still-living tradition, and thus the Chinese are simply expected to favor meritocracy.

But what exactly is the empirical evidence for these lines of reasoning—more than one hundred years after the fall of the last imperial (Confucian-Legalist) dynasty, with Confucianism either ignored or discredited for most of the intervening decades? It has to be the fact, above all, that there is now barely a murmur heard in or from China supporting democratic transformation, or the autonomy of civil society, or constitutionalism, or even the vaguer project of political reform. This *is* a fact. What is not adequately noted, however, is that this fact, in turn, has its primary cause in the officially imposed moratorium on the very discussion of such topics, including in academia and civil society, the latter barely surviving. Those who used to urge political reform, especially democratic or constitutional reform, are effectively silenced, as are those who belonged to the once-influential so-called liberal camp *(ziyoupai)*, the term itself having virtually gone out of circulation and acquired the uncanny feel of a distant memory. The entire intellectual-political field is now confined to an exceedingly narrow (even by the CCP's own standard in the reform era) spectrum of opinion, with meritocracy, whether communist or Confucian, occupying a precious segment of it. This is one crucial reason why the doctrine of meritocracy looms so large in today's China—larger than at any time since 1949. One does not recall a single period since the start of reform four decades ago— with the exception of June 4, 1989, and its immediate aftermath—when there has been such a dearth or even absence of contestation of political opinions. This is not a relatively spontaneous phenomenon but a thoroughly politically engineered one, created and sustained by the Repressive State Apparatus.

It is necessary to mention the term with which the Repressive State Apparatus is paired by the French Marxist philosopher Louis Althusser: the Ideological State Apparatuses. It is a defining feature of this famous distinction that Althusser always speaks of the Ideological State Apparatuses in the plural. As he explains, "While there is *one* Repressive State Apparatus, there are several Ideological State Apparatuses. This difference is important." On the one hand, "the state apparatus that we are identifying as repressive presents itself as an *organic whole;* more precisely, as a *centralized* corps that is *consciously and directly led* from a *single centre.*" On the other hand, "it is a different story with the *Ideological* State Apparatuses. They exist in the plural and have a relatively independent material existence."[2] A sure sign of this relative independence is that the Ideological State Apparatuses are left alone even when they say things that the Repressive State Apparatus does not want to hear—even when, as Althusser puts it, "they . . . 'grate' on certain occasions, terribly."[3]

Although Althusser is here performing an anatomy of the liberal state, such as France, he is also laying bare the nature and operation of ideology as such. In France, as in liberal states in general, the Ideological State Apparatuses (the church, schools, trade unions, the family, culture, entertainment, the media, and so on) "are objectively distinct, relatively autonomous, and do not form an organized, centralized corps with a single, conscious leadership."[4] Herein lies the meaning of their plurality: plurality makes possible ideology as ideology, which in turn is constitutive of much of what we typically think of as freedom. If the lack of freedom may be defined as the overly obtrusive presence of the Repressive State Apparatus, it may also, by the same token, be defined in terms of the absence of ideology, which in turn can be defined in terms of the singularity of the Ideological State Apparatus, itself now revealed as a contradiction in terms in the singular form. For unless the Ideological State Apparatuses exist in the plural, as Althusser rightly insists *as a matter of definition,* the apparent organs of ideology come under the conscious, open, direct, and complete control of the Repressive State Apparatus; they become the latter's mere appendages and are *known* to be such. Thus these organs are made to operate against their own supposedly *ideological* (as distinct from repressive) logic, and, in this way, they cease to be ideological altogether.

This is largely the condition in China today. Unlike France, China has not several Ideological State Apparatuses but only one, for all the different institutions that are designed to perform an ideological function are centrally controlled and devoid of even relative autonomy. Indeed, these institutions are all supposed to bear the Communist Party as their surname *(xingdang),* as it were, according to one official form of words. The upshot is profound and hugely consequential: the nonexistence in China today of ideology in any strict, meaningful, and effective sense, or, put differently, its degeneration into propaganda known as propaganda. Those who remember the days when the Ideological State Apparatuses were able to "'grate' on certain occasions, terribly"—Althusser's litmus test for ideology—will know what this means and what has been lost.

This state of affairs, more airtight than at any time in recent memory, has rendered the support for democracy barely audible in China today. But inaudibility does not mean nonexistence—why else would the intensified operation of the Repressive State Apparatus be necessary?—and it is only by the false and convenient equation of the two that the illusion has been created that China, meaning not only the CCP but also the people at large, neither needs nor desires democracy. This is one of the most amazing and pernicious illusions coming out of China today. It is all the more deleterious to the degree that it is taken up by Western intellectuals and politicians and projected back onto China, in what one may call a new (political) orientalism.

The projection may be carried out unknowingly and from time to time even out of an otherwise admirable cultural respectfulness and political modesty. But it is also sometimes conducted by those who seem intent on interpellating China as the nondemocratic other in order to highlight the China threat—one posed by an authoritarian regime *and* culture to democratic America and the democratic West as a whole. Such interpellation seems to please some but alienate many others, creating in China and the Chinese people a new enemy that the United States, among others, seems to need for its own political and strategic purposes. As America in particular gets tougher on a China thus interpellated, many Chinese will demand an equally tough response and, whatever their political views, will come to hate America in return for the latter's increasing disapproval of China. When they thus learn or relearn to detest America, by reputation still the paradigmatic democracy in the world, some of them may well come to hate democracy by association, thus conforming to and confirming the new American and Western image of China as the nondemocratic other. The resulting damage will be inestimable, whether this new image is meant to be a compliment or a curse.

A vicious circle is thus being formed, with an all-encompassing Repressive State Apparatus silencing all democratic sentiments and aspirations, from which the inference is innocently or knowingly drawn of the absence of such sentiments and aspirations. This inference is, in turn, reinforced by the authoritarian-meritocratic discourse coming out of China until it hardens into conventional wisdom and, in that form, is projected back onto China in the manner of a self-fulfilling prophecy—all of this happening in an intercultural setting in which respect for (political) difference merges imperceptibly with a new and ever so subtle (political) orientalism.

There is one illogicality, however, that will not go away despite this vicious circle. If China is really what its new domestic and international image makes it out to be, with a culturally ingrained lack of desire for democracy complemented by the impressive recent track record of meritocracy as practiced by the CCP, why are we witnessing a dramatic escalation of the already formidable presence of the Repressive State Apparatus? Whence the need for heightened repressive measures when no one can reasonably argue that such measures are welcomed by the Chinese people, least of all to buttress politico-cultural beliefs whose very existence would suffice to make such measures, in their current scope and intensity, unnecessary in the first place?

The Continuing Relevance of Democracy for China

Most signs indicate that the CCP is more confident of itself—of its path, theory, (political) system, and culture, in the party's own parlance—than ever before, with an unabashed assertion of political entitlement that sweeps all before it. *Most* signs, I say, but not all, in that it is reverting to palpably intimidating practices of thought control and stability preservation that until recently were thought to have been permanently left behind. This revival of measures created in Mao Zedong's time of domestic and international revolutionary class struggle is giving rise to a level of fear—of being visibly out of line and its consequences—unseen since the fateful year of 1989 and its immediate aftermath. That such emergency-like measures are deemed necessary at all betrays, in turn, a level of fear on the part of the CCP itself that also has not been seen since 1989.

Whence this latter fear? After all, to use its own latest terminological inventions,[5] the party has been highly successful in producing among an extremely large segment of the population an ever-rising sense of fulfillment *(huodegan),* happiness *(xingfugan),* and security *(anquangan).* Of these, *huodegan* comes first and stands out—a newly minted term meaning not quite "fulfillment" (as in the official translation) but, literally, the sense of "acquisition," with a subtle yet unmistakable emphasis on livelihood issues, on tangible things and the fulfillment such things can bring. It is not a sense of fulfillment in its broad meaning, then, but a sense of essentially acquisitive and sensuous fulfillment. Still, what is there for the CCP to fear from the population if, as is hardly deniable, it is creating an ever-higher level of such fulfillment, combined with a corresponding sense of happiness and security? What is left to be desired whose haunting absence could spell trouble in such otherwise auspicious circumstances?

One lack immediately springs to mind, and that is a sense of agency (*zhutigan*, my term, not the party's): the sense of being free as individuals and as members of civil society and of being citizens with a credible role in shaping the life and destiny of the political community. This sense of agency is conspicuously absent from the CCP's self-professed list of achievements and future goals—a fact highlighted rather than contradicted by occasional vague references to undefined "democracy." I am not concerned at this point to make any normative argument in support of such agency but only wish to suggest a diagnostic hypothesis: having omitted to provide for an adequate sense of agency, the CCP cannot be sure whether the population, if set individually and politically free, would support or oppose its rule. It is this uncertainty that leaves the CCP in constant fear, and all signs indicate that this fear is as distracting and debilitating as the CCP is otherwise strong and confident. Which means that even the party itself implicitly acknowledges the existence of conditions in China that give many people reasons to desire a greater sense of agency, including through democracy, and that therefore democracy has lost none of its relevance for China, despite a deafening silence on the subject. It means also that, until the CCP is willing and able to cater to the desire for agency, including through democracy, its regime cannot be truly secure and therefore it cannot be truly confident. The party's assertion of the so-called four elements of confidence, although backed up by formidable power, also conjures up a specter of weakness, unwittingly drawing attention to its Achilles heel. Only a reasonably credible sense of agency for ordinary people, with democracy and freedom as its necessary conditions and forms of expression, can dispel this specter.

It follows that all that has been accomplished in the cause of "the great rejuvenation of the Chinese nation" does not dispense with the need—in the interest of China's own social and regime stability—for democracy as an essential part of a sense of agency on top of, and distinct from, the already substantially achieved sense of acquisitive and sensuous fulfillment. This point can be reinforced by invoking the CCP's own Marxist heritage, in that Karl Marx was unquestionably a democratic thinker seeking to move beyond the bourgeois democratic revolution rather than merely opposing it.

The Need for a New Type of Argument

It is one thing to show that the question of democracy is still relevant for China and quite something else to address the question intelligently and with balance and good sense. I, for one, have found the task anything but easy. Now that I have made some progress that I believe is worth sharing as an interim report, as it were, please bear with me as I take the first step, in this introduction, to present a line of thought that differs significantly from the conventional wisdom on the topic. This request is especially needed because the case I make for democracy in China is not chiefly normative, as such arguments usually are, but essentially prudential.

I use three building blocks to structure my argument for the necessity and possibility of democracy in China. These blocks are, first, a distinction between the prudential (need-based) and the normative (value-based) approach to democracy; second, close attention to the nature and implications of what I see as an impending legitimation crisis; and, third, a justification of democracy that proceeds from social circumstances to political regime. As I deploy them, these blocks will build an essentially prudential case for democracy in China by demonstrating the need for democracy given the country's specific conditions today.

If need provides the impetus to invention (and bringing about a workable democracy in any country does require invention), it does not by any means guarantee success. In the case of China, in particular, the challenges are enormous, and thus a further component of my avowedly prudential case for democracy involves confronting these challenges and considering how best to meet them. This, then, is a fourth building block.

I want to put these building blocks in preliminary action here to give the reader a sense of how they work together to produce a coherent argument. Indeed, for the book as a whole, my goal is to make the argument not only coherent but also compelling. So compelling, that is, that the parties concerned, including the CCP, will have no good reason to reject its plausibility as a prudent assessment, first, of certain crisis tendencies in China's political status quo and, second, of democracy's much-needed contribution to counteracting such tendencies. In this context, a compelling argument is not one that is necessarily correct but one that has to be sufficiently plausible to merit serious consideration. This standard is high but not impossibly so, and I do not pursue it out of misplaced self-confidence but only because the stakes are so high. That the stakes are so high and one should therefore err on the side of caution is itself part of my argument. For this reason, the argument will not serve any useful purpose unless it is plausible enough to give an intellectual jolt to what seems a prevailing complacency about the status quo.

I do not believe for a moment, of course, that this will be anything but an uphill struggle, as I am aware of the difference between the parties concerned having no *good* reason to reject the plausibility of my case for democracy and having no reason at all to do so. One source of difficulty that is particularly worth mentioning is that while I must try to persuade every reasonable reader of the plausibility of what I say, in some places of my argument I will need to convince specific parties, such as the CCP, ordinary Chinese citizens, and international players or concerned parties of various kinds. This latter need arises whenever a particular set of actors has an exceptional stake in the matter under discussion and will understandably have the greatest difficulty accepting my judgment if it happens to diverge from theirs. Precisely for this reason, however, it will be all the more important to try to convince them, because, given their exceptional stake, their beliefs and actions are likely to be especially consequential.

There is an obvious sense in which the CCP happens to be both the most important actor to address and the most difficult one to convince. It should come as no surprise that this sense pervades my argument. However, the argument itself is put together as an exercise in public reason, not as an adjunct to political action in the narrow sense. Accordingly, this book is not targeted at any particular audience but is meant for every reader who is interested in understanding China's political condition and political future and what China's political developments may mean for the world at large. While my awareness of the multiple parties with whom I need to engage in an imaginary dialogue has given the book a corresponding multiplicity of voices and even sympathies, my aim is to produce a distinctive case for democracy in China that will hang together as one coherent and compelling argument accessible to every interested member of the Chinese and global public sphere.

In constructing such a case, it is essential to make an honest attempt to suspend partisanship (to the degree possible), in the interest of providing a reasonably objective diagnosis and reasonably dispassionate prognosis.

Gaining a grip on China's complex political situation and thinking construc-tively about its uncertain political future are difficult enough, and one does not need to create further obstacles by taking sides on intensely normative issues, important as they are, where doing so is not strictly necessary for the diagnostic and prognostic task at hand. With regard to the CCP, I will be candid and unreserved for diagnostic and prognostic purposes but will re-frain from purely moral judgment. I will approach the West in a similar spirit, mutatis mutandis, especially with regard to Western democracy and attitudes toward China and the CCP. At stake are difficult issues over which reason-able people could all too easily disagree and that therefore make good-faith and fair-minded discussion especially necessary. I will thus do my level best to avoid partisanship, and I hope the reader will find the results, including the effort itself, positive rather than irritating and will set me right where such effort is unsuccessful or, with respect to particular matters, misguided in the first place.

The Best Case for Democracy in China
Is a Prudential One

It is all too easy, even today, to argue in favor of democracy, either in gen-eral or with particular reference to China. Since the end of World War II and especially since the end of the Cold War, democracy has become a so-called essentially contested concept.[6] As such, it signifies a major political value or virtue to which no regime can long afford not to lay a claim in one way or another; the only sustainable option open to a regime in its right mind is to contest democracy's meaning rather than to disown democracy altogether. For all its failures and flaws, some arguably irredeemable, and all the bad things done in its name, this special normative status of democracy is not going to change in the foreseeable future. There is a sense, then, in which it is unnecessary to try to make the *normative* case for democracy—as distinct from a particular understanding or design thereof. Up to a certain point, the justificatory task is accomplished—or preempted—by the very political mood or ethos of our world.

In another sense, however, this more or less taken-for-granted case for democracy is rather insufficient. For one thing, democracy may be very fine in theory—in either unrealistically utopian normative philosophy or starry-eyed popular imagination—but much less so in practice.[7] For another, what once was or seemed achievable in practice may well be receding from our present range of realistic possibilities, with the result that today's democracy is not very fine in either reality or prospect.[8] To put it bluntly, our age of radically accentuated globalization has not been a very auspicious time to make a normative case for democracy that is at once inspiring and plausible—one that goes much beyond whatever broad consensus lies in democracy as an essentially contested concept. Given this state of affairs, there seems no better balance to be struck than that suggested by John Dunn's judicious counsel: "An ingenuous attitude towards democracy is a discredit to any modern citizen. But a settled hostility towards it will always involve, under careful inspection, a substantial measure of ingenuousness towards some other human grouping, and one which will necessarily over time prove *at least* equally deserving of distrust."[9]

Being unnecessary in one sense and insufficient in another, the typical, normative case for democracy will not serve my purpose. My purpose is to make an effective case for democracy in China, the kind of case that, if well made, could help create or enhance a distinct set of incentives to bring about democracy in a sober and effectual manner. I believe the only way to make such a case for China today is to make a prudential one, showing that China badly needs democracy in order to avoid grave outcomes rather than to bring about better ones than are currently possible, where the grave outcomes have to do with the basic necessity of social and regime stability rather than, as it were, normative luxuries. In other words, the main reason for having democracy in China is that democracy is our best bet for effectively responding to current and especially impending legitimation challenges, or so I shall argue, rather than that China would be much better off, normatively or otherwise, if it were to opt for democracy even though it does not strictly need to. What is important about this reason is that, while it does not imply any denial of democracy's normative appeal, it will not rely on any such appeal—except for its empirical efficacy. It shuns any thought that democracy is such a (normatively) wonderful thing—either in theory or in any actual exemplars—that we must have it in China, too.

A prudential case for democracy, then, is not concerned, at least not primarily, with the (Aristotelian) question of the best regime. It is concerned, rather, with what is likely to be the most stable and durable regime under the given historical circumstances, as subject to, and aided by, only distinctly un-demanding moral constraints. Whereas the question of the best regime is a general one unrestricted by time and place, the prudential question is most appropriately posed and answered for a particular time and place. Thus, the prudential case for democracy I will be making is specific to China: it is a response to the question of what is likely to be the most stable and durable regime under the circumstances in which China now finds itself.

Thus construed, the prudential case for democracy in China is invulner-able, say, to Joseph Schumpeter's debunking of what he calls the classical theory of democracy based on the notion of popular sovereignty literally un-derstood as self-government, on the one hand, or to any persuasive demon-stration of Western democracy's serious failings in any regard other than re-gime stability, on the other.[10] By the same token, the prudential case deflects the vexed question of what "genuine" democracy is, as well as the unneces-sarily distracting question of whether democracy, once certified as "genuine," is a universal value. The only goods at stake in the prudential case are legiti-macy in a (Weberian) de facto or sociological sense, or hegemony à la An-tonio Gramsci, and the resulting social and regime stability. What is required to deliver these goods need not be so-called genuine democracy, whatever that may mean, but only a plausible and sustainable semblance of democracy, defined as whatever is reasonably regarded as more or less consonant with China's present social conditions. To this end, the prudential case for democ-racy works at the level of what Niccolò Machiavelli calls "the effectual truth of the thing," rather than "the imagination of it."[11]

At this level, we need a scrupulous and sensible assessment of whether and, if so, why democracy is really needed in China, and of what democracy may reasonably be expected to do for China, without exaggeration or moral grandstanding. This will, in turn, require an honest, unbiased assessment of the CCP's strengths and vulnerabilities. It is an important fact of the party's rule that the main threat it faces does not come from organized opposition, which is not permitted, nor from powerful interest groups waiting for the right moment to show their true political colors, for the most powerful such groups are, on balance, beneficiaries of the current system and would face an uncertain future if things were to change. Therefore, to appreciate the CCP's vulnerabilities, we must look instead at powerful tendencies within *Chinese society* and ask whether some of these tendencies make a truly formidable legitimation crisis almost impossible to avoid, leaving open various risky political scenarios if effective measures are not taken to prevent them. We must then ask whether democracy will not have to be one of these measures, given the party's vulnerabilities, as well as powerful tendencies in Chinese society, and whether, to give democratic change a realistic chance of success, the CCP will not have to play a crucial and leading role in the process, given its strengths. In seeking answers to such questions, our object is the "effectual truth" of democracy, and our chief impediment the ever-present temptation to fantasize about democracy.[12]

This does not mean, however, that a prudential case for democracy has no use for normative considerations. Indeed, such considerations are essential, if only because democracy must take one form or another, not least in its relation to capitalism, as we shall see, and it is impossible to be indifferent to the normative grounds and implications of so consequential a choice. I will therefore allow myself to cross the line between the normative and the prudential freely, leaving it to the reader to assess the (implicit) rationale and the advisability of my moves. More precisely, then, I will be presenting an essentially prudential case, not a purely prudential one. The latter is neither necessary nor sufficient and would be unduly restrictive while serving no useful purpose.

I describe my case for democracy as *essentially* prudential because there is no doubt in my mind that normative considerations will fall into their proper place only within the parameters of a successfully conducted prudential case for democracy, in two senses: first, that they will kick in only after the prudential case for democracy is established, and, second, that they should continue to be informed and constrained by prudential considerations. In other words, we have to demonstrate the sheer necessity of democracy in order to get the case for democracy decisively off the ground, and thereafter we will still need to maintain a scrupulous sense of reality as we go about figuring out how democratic change may come to positive fruition in the real world.

This is not to suggest that a prudential case for democracy, duly freed from overly idealistic normative complications, will be easy to make. By definition, a prudential case speaks to the self-regarding concerns of the parties involved, with other-regarding concerns filtered through and assimilated to the self-regarding ones, at least in the first instance. As such, a prudential

argument seeks to make self-regarding concerns more rational or "enlightened," or, if necessary, to trigger self-regarding concerns where they did not
previously exist or only existed in inchoate form. The point is always to present to the parties involved reasons for action that they could not *rationally*
reject—or, to put it more mildly (this is quite good enough for our purpose),
they had better not reject—from their *prudential* point of view. Since we are
talking about rational or enlightened self-regarding interests, it is improbable that a well-made prudential case for democracy would fail the test of
the parties' normative concerns should such concerns be active as well. Thus
a successful prudential case for democracy may also be expected to be one
that the parties involved would have little good reason to reject from their
normative point of view.

One must not assume that the parties involved have a complete convergence of self-regarding interests (nor, for that matter, of normative considerations) when it comes to democracy. There is, however, a prudent way of maximizing the convergence, and that is to accept the necessity of, and make the
best of the possibility of, working within the parameters of the existing balance of power. As far as China is concerned, especially with regard to democratic change, there can be no doubt that the balance of power overwhelmingly favors the CCP. For this reason alone, a successful prudential case for
democracy must, first and foremost, be one that the party could not, on balance, rationally reject in the light of its self-regarding interests.

The matter is complicated, however, by the changing nature of the balance of power between the CCP and the citizenry. Indeed, an unprecedented
degree of volatility will be introduced into this balance in the event that
the party decides, and is known to have decided, to embark on democratic
change. However much support it may be able to win for such a historic
decision, should it be made, the party will from that point on be bound to
gradually lose the firm grip on power that is available, however temporarily,
only to an uncompromising defender of the status quo. In making my prudential case for democracy, of course, I will suggest that the status quo will
actually, in due course, cease to be defendable—without excessive cost. But
this does not change the fact that a politically reforming CCP cannot be
indifferent to whether it will have an important role to play in a democratic
China it will have helped bring into being. I believe, on prudential grounds,
that this (as yet only imagined) understandable desire on the part of the

party must be respected and given a good deal of room. It is at this point, among others, that any prudential argument for democracy in China must be addressed just as much to the citizenry. For unless the citizenry responds prudently to the CCP's democratic initiatives, it could well compromise or even doom such initiatives given the party's continuing desire for power, as well as its vulnerabilities. The only prudent way of accomplishing orderly and effective democratic change is to try as much as possible to work with the CCP rather than against it. Unless the populace adopts this prudent approach, the party will be discouraged from developing a reasonably positive disposition toward democracy. And unless the CCP is aided rather than hindered in acquiring such a disposition and in accomplishing a task that is already difficult enough, China may well experience very dark days in the not too distant future.

Needless to say, it is not part of this prudential argument that democracy is bound to come to China in one form or another, for it is not part of this argument that the parties involved will actually be prudent. The argument consists rather in showing that grave consequences will follow if China does not democratize and do so with well-conceived and well-executed preparation. It is intended to drive home these consequences in order to foster the realization that it is in the interest of all concerned, not least the CCP as by far the most decisive actor, to avoid such consequences and to take bold and prudent measures to this end before it is too late.

Simple as its basic logic is, I do not expect such a prudential case to be at all easy and straightforward to make. In fact, the task is harder still because various international actors will have some impact as well, and their prudence or lack of it will make a far from negligible difference. What I do not doubt for a moment, however, is that this is the kind of case for democracy in China that urgently needs to be made. To this end, I will present democracy as the broadly positive yet patently less than perfect political value and institutional practice that it is. It is only by approaching democracy with a sober view of its advantages and liabilities—both in general and with particular reference to China—that we will have a reasonable chance of making the kind of case for democracy in China that is urgent and potentially consequential. It is a case for democracy that even the CCP could neither rationally nor reasonably reject without serious qualms, or so I believe, because the case would remain strong despite all the reservations, both prudential and normative, that one could plausibly have about democracy. To borrow a figure of speech from the title of John Dunn's 2014 book on democracy, I want to make the case for democracy without falling under its spell.[13]

Finally, it is worth noting the growing belief that the fundamental political challenge of our digital age is presented by technology—with its profound, unprecedented implications for the totality of human life, including the political—rather than by overtly political matters such as democracy.[14] While there is an element of truth in this view, I doubt that the challenge created by the so-called fourth industrial revolution will simply overtake that of democracy, considered in itself, as far as the foreseeable future of China is concerned. One of the ways in which China stands out is precisely the fact that, for all its involvement in IT, AI, robotics, and so on, and for all their impact on its society, China remains stuck with the yet-to-be-surmounted challenge of coming up with a reasonably dependable formula for regime stability and perpetuation. My prudential argument for democracy is a response to this distinct and independently daunting challenge.

The Looming Legitimation Crisis

I have said that the prudential case for democracy in China consists in showing that China badly needs democracy in order to stave off the potentially disastrous consequences for social and regime stability of trying in vain to indefinitely maintain the status quo. Such consequences, if and when they materialize, will amount to an extremely severe legitimation crisis that threatens not only the rule of the CCP but also the stability of an entire country that has been made to depend exclusively on this rule.

Regarding a political system, I am happy to accept the notion that if it is not broken, it would be a bad idea to try to fix it (beyond improving it), especially to the extent of replacing the system. After all, changing a political system is fraught with risks even under the best of circumstances. I am also prepared to concede that the Chinese political system is not broken. Why fix it, then? Because we have reason to fear that it is going to be broken in the foreseeable future—broken in the sense of experiencing a potentially fatal legitimation crisis.

This takes us into the territory of prognosis. There is no reason to shy away from prognosis, despite its notoriously large room for error. The reason to face up to the need for prognosis is rather more compelling. For all political action, not least when it is prudentially motivated, involves an element of conjecture about the future, as well as some interpretation of the past, and the same is true of intellectual reflection on political action.

To assess the likelihood of a legitimation crisis in China, it is crucial to determine what kind of legitimacy the CCP still enjoys. To formulate the problem in this way is not to beg the question—whether the party *is* currently enjoying any legitimacy—but to proceed on the right kind of assumption. Since my aim is to show an *impending* legitimation crisis, in the sense either of something new or of something old becoming worse, it is only reasonable and prudent to give the CCP the benefit of the doubt. Let us assume, then, although this happens also to be my considered view, that the CCP still commands a quite considerable degree of legitimacy. The crucial question is, What kind of legitimacy?

It has become more or less received wisdom that what the CCP still commands is essentially performance legitimacy (or performance-based legitimacy). Yet, this assessment is seriously mistaken and indeed is a dangerous view to hold if it turns out to be false. As long as we subscribe to this assessment, we are led to believe that it is an open question how long the CCP's legitimacy will last. For it will simply be a question of how good the CCP's future performance turns out to be—and of the continuous interpretation of what counts as good and relevant performance.[15]

Contrary to this view, I hold that the CCP still enjoys a reasonably high degree of legitimacy in the much stronger sense of the *right to rule*, which is the mandate not only to perform but also, more fundamentally, to occupy the position (of authority) from which to perform. It is, if you will, the party's equivalent of the Mandate of Heaven. If one were to ask an authoritative ideological spokesperson of the CCP what this mandate is, or where it comes from, one would surely be told that it comes from 1921 and 1949 and that, however it may be described, Mao plays an indispensable part in it—always has and always will. There can be no doubt about it: the mandate springs from the launching of the communist revolution (1921) and its first decisive success (1949), although neither term—*communist* or *revolution*—is explicitly used very much. Thus the CCP sees itself as still enjoying a lingering legitimacy that is inextricably linked to its communist revolutionary past. This self-assessment is quite correct.

I would like to suggest that it is only because of a substantial remnant of the old communist revolutionary legitimacy that the CCP's good performance in the reform era can serve to enhance it. Let us not be distracted by quibbling about what good performance is and how good it has been. The important thing is to pin down what exactly the party's supposed good performance has been doing for, or in relation to, its legitimacy. I want to suggest that what we are witnessing is *legitimacy enhancement through good performance*—that is, the enhancement of the CCP's mandate to rule, as rooted in its communist revolutionary past, through current performative success in the form of economic growth, rising individual prosperity and national power, and so on. The question immediately arises as to how such legitimacy and such performance can be yoked together—one of many questions I will address later. For now, the crucial point is that legitimacy enhancement can take place only if there is still sufficient legitimacy left for good performance to enhance. And let us not forget that the CCP, by virtue of being the *Communist* Party, can have no other publicly avowable source of legitimacy than the one bound up with its communist revolutionary past. Suppose this source of legitimacy runs dry and the legitimacy ceases to exist. What then? Presumably there can still be good performance of sorts, in terms of economic growth, rising living standards, and so on: what people generally mean when they speak of *performance legitimacy*. But upon reflection this does not really hold up. For, under the conditions hypothetically stipulated (that is, the disappearance of legitimacy), what good performance can achieve is no longer legitimacy enhancement, because there is no legitimacy left to enhance in the first place, but only *amelioration of a lack of legitimacy*. Legitimacy is not improved; it is only made to matter less. Thus performance *legitimacy* would be a misnomer. But, much more importantly, is it true that a thorough *lack* of legitimacy can be caused to matter so little as not to place a regime in mortal danger? The CCP would be the first to agree that one cannot rule a country on a long-term basis by means of amelioration of the lack of legitimacy. This is plainly not a good idea. Suppose this line of reasoning is correct so far, pending more detailed argument and exposition in Chapters 1 and 2. Grant, in other words, that what the CCP is doing right now is legitimacy enhancement through good performance, on the assumption, of course, that there is still considerable legitimacy left. It follows, decisively, that the key question to be confronted next is how long this lingering legitimacy can last, rather than merely how long good performance can last. The second question is important in its own way, but far less so than the first.

In response to the first, key question, it would be difficult to turn away from the well-grounded fear that the CCP's lingering legitimacy will be all but completely exhausted by the time of the next leadership succession, whenever that is, or soon thereafter. To be sure, the current leadership is the most powerful and most confident at least since Deng Xiaoping. And all signs indicate that it is exerting a degree of control over the country—not least over ideology, over institutions of education, over what people say and write—reminiscent of the Mao era. My point here is not to appraise this development but simply to suggest that, like it or not, this will be an impossible act to follow for Xi Jinping's successor, who, significantly, as of now, is nowhere in sight. With the communist revolutionary legitimacy completely spent, Xi's successor will face unprecedented difficulty in keeping intraparty factionalism under control and maintaining the CCP's all-important intraparty legitimacy. In the country at large, Xi's successor will find it a no less insurmountable challenge to muster the will to crush another June 4 if preventive measures fail. And, of course, the more this will is lacking and known to be lacking, the more likely preventive measures are to fail. In the face of these vulnerabilities, no amount of good performance by itself will suffice. A new kind of legitimacy will be needed.

It is needed right now, because China also needs democratic preparation, to be discussed in Chapter 6, and the current leadership is the only one with the power and leisure to undertake it. It will be too late if it is left to the next generation of leaders, who will be much weaker and will also be much closer to the impending legitimation crisis. That is why it is necessary to fix the political system *before* it is broken.

Democracy as the Only Appropriate Way to Fix the Political System

It is not by accident that fixing the current one-party system requires democracy. Thanks to the four-decade-old reform, and therefore thanks also to the CCP itself, China has become a democratic society—a democratic *so-*

ciety (in the sense of the eradication of a fixed social hierarchy, as in an aristocracy, or of fixed class distinctions, as in Mao's China, and their replacement with what Alexis de Tocqueville calls "equality of conditions") as
distinct from a democratic *political* regime. A strong dynamic is thereby set
in motion that is succinctly captured by Charles Maier, writing about the
history of democracy in the nineteenth and twentieth centuries:

> Why could not democracy [as a political regime] simply be resisted? . . .
> The reason was that society itself was evolving democratically. *Political
> forms followed changes in social structure.* If, as Tocqueville . . . claimed,
> all history tended towards the destruction of aristocracies, there could
> be no long-term societal barrier to a government of and by the people. . . .
> In 1859 Mill argued similarly, "There is confessedly a strong tendency
> in the modern world towards a democratic constitution of society, ac-
> companied or not by popular political institutions." . . . The point, how-
> ever, was that *they would be so accompanied.* Political forms would tend
> in the long run to recapitulate social trends.[16]

Such is the dynamic unleashed by the democratic constitution of society, itself an unstoppable trend in the modern world!

If we invoke Protagoras, the first philosophical defender of democracy, as I
will do in Chapter 3, we will be able to add to democratic society two further
elements: a democratic epistemology in which every person is allowed to
speak and reasons alone are supposed to carry the day, and a democratic conception of virtue that treats every citizen as capable of learning to contribute
to a shared civic life.[17] All of these we already find in China to a substantial
degree: democratic society, democratic epistemology, and a democratic conception of virtue. Indeed, China is fast acquiring one more democratic trait,
which may be called a democratic conception of the good: the idea that every
man or woman is capable of deciding for him- or herself what the good life
is, subject only to reasonable and reasonably permissive laws.

We can fold all of these democratic traits into a larger notion of democratic society and say that just such a society is what China already has today
to a degree both entrenched and progressing. The only thing missing is a
democratic *political* regime. This is clearly a case of a nation's collective existence being split against itself—that is, democratic in almost all significant

respects except a single, isolated one, that of government or system of rule. No wonder the political regime—the odd one out, as it were—is not stable and has to devote a disproportionate amount of energy and nervous energy, not to mention personnel and financial resources, to maintaining stability *(weiwen)*.

What is so good about democracy then? Not that it is good, strictly speaking, but only that it is more fitting. It may not be *better* than all other regime types in the abstract, but given a democratic society that is here to stay, a democratic political regime is definitely *better fitting*. And because it is better fitting, it makes a society—an already largely democratic society—more governable. So, to cut a long story (to be detailed in Chapter 3) short, my arguments for democracy in China boil down to two: first, the argument from fittingness and, second, the argument from governability. In the light of these arguments, only a democratic political regime has a chance of maintaining a legitimate and stable government in the context of a democratic society. Given that it is manifestly a democratic society today, China has already taken the first step, an irreversible first step, whether by design or by default. Therefore, in the interest of a legitimate and stable political order, it has no choice but to take the second.

Four Daunting Challenges

This does not mean that it will not be easy to mess up in taking the second step. To imply, as I have just done, that a democratic political regime is only one step away from a democratic society, already in existence, is not also to imply that this one step will be free of the most daunting challenges. Far from it. In practice, as distinct from concept, it will have to be one long, possibly very long, step.

This brings me to the other half of my prudential case for democracy in China. The first half of my case, as the reader will recall, is a matter of demonstrating the sheer necessity of democracy for today's China, of making clear why China stands in dire need of democratic change in order to stave off a paralyzing legitimation crisis in the foreseeable future. It makes sense to outline this part of my case first, because the opposite view has many adherents, and especially because the enormity of the democratic challenge can be properly appreciated only in the light of the unavoidable necessity of democracy. Now that I have laid out the reasons supporting the necessity of democracy, I must complete my case by proceeding to the difficulty of responding appropriately to this necessity. As I see it, there are at least four daunting challenges, each of which is important to surmount and none possible to avoid.

FIRST CHALLENGE. The first challenge has to do with the place and role of the CCP in China's potential passage to democracy. Whether one likes it or not, the party is by far the most powerful political force in China. Indeed, other than its minor, compliant allies, it is the only legally permitted political force, certainly the only political force that has ruled China, and hence has gained any experience of ruling, since 1949. It is safe to say that, as things stand, the party alone is capable of initiating political change in China and making its execution reasonably smooth and orderly. For any political change even to get off the ground, therefore, the party must see the need for it and be willing to undertake it. This is all the more emphatically true of democratic change, in that such change would alter the very status and power of the CCP and the stakes could not be higher. It would be naïve and utterly irresponsible to believe that the party could simply be swept aside as part of a largely orderly, if not entirely peaceful, turn to democracy. Given the stakes involved, there is no compelling reason to expect that the CCP will let itself be swept aside—which would mean nothing less than ending up in the "dustbin of history"—without reacting in ways that would seriously, even fatally, damage the prospect of an orderly democratic transition.

Even if we suppose, for the sake of argument, that the CCP does somehow, under pressure, exit the stage without too much fuss, there is just as obvious a dearth of reasons to expect that an alternative political force or coalition of forces will be able to step into the breach and, after an initial period of regrouping and trial and error, act with greater moral authority and political sagacity than the party ever did, with regard to democratic change or anything else. After all, the CCP has not given any potential political force the remotest opportunity to gain experience and maturity or acquire the civic virtues and sheer toughness and resourcefulness needed to govern a political behemoth like China. Put another way, it has not given China a chance to be held together as a reasonably peaceful and prosperous country by any political force other than itself. Against this background, to imagine China's orderly passage to democracy without assigning a positive role to the party is at best a leap in the dark—not a good strategy given the enormity of the stakes.

To avoid such a scenario, it would require that the party act voluntarily to initiate democratic change, having seen the dire necessity of democracy in the face of a looming legitimation crisis. It would also require that the ordinary citizens of China develop a positive and patient disposition toward a reforming CCP, giving full credit where credit is due and, as it were, rewarding the CCP with an important, even a leading, role in a democratic China, at least initially.

The indispensability of the party for an orderly democratic transition is the result of a historical contingency. The CCP is itself largely responsible for this contingency—for creating and maintaining China's excessive political dependence on itself—but this does not change the fact of the matter. It can only impinge on our moral assessment of the fact, which also does not change the fact itself. From a prudential point of view, this fact alone matters.

SECOND CHALLENGE. Another upshot of the same historical contingency, one for which the CCP is equally responsible, is that individual Chinese citizens and Chinese society as a whole have been kept under compulsory moral tutelage by the party. They have been effectively prevented from acquiring any independent moral agency, agency that is attributable to their own initiative, individual and collective, and over which the CCP does not have the prerogative of guidance and control. This compulsory moral tutelage worked well enough when, under Mao and in the early stages of the post-Mao reform, China was a tightly organized, collectivistic society, with top-down control of all aspects of life, including the moral. What has happened since is the gradual but, by now, quite thorough dismantling of the Maoist, totally organized form of life. Yet, for reasons to be explained in the main body of the book, the CCP has not seen fit to let go of its control over the moral life of individuals and society, nor to do what it takes to adapt the manner and content of its moral guidance to the actual, ever more bourgeois reality of the brave new China. The predictable result is a deep and protracted moral crisis in reform-era China, which finds the most visible expression not only in rampant official corruption but also, in the country at large, in a widespread lack of respect for moral norms and the law.

A grave problem in its own right, this moral crisis is also a major cause for worry as far as democratic change is concerned. For in the absence of a basic level of individual and societal moral maturity (the latter meaning the moral maturity of civil society), it is hard to imagine the unhampered emergence of the minimal level of civic virtue that is necessary to give a burgeoning democracy a reasonable chance to work. Today the CCP alone stands between China and even worse moral chaos, just as it alone keeps political disorder at bay. Having single-handedly prevented individual and societal moral maturity, only the party is capable of keeping the lid on the Pandora's box, morally and politically speaking. Until the lock and key are handed over to, or shared with, a more or less independent civil society and a relatively mature citizenry, China is simply not ready for the passage to political democracy.

What China sorely needs, then, is *democratic preparation,* meaning all that it takes to create a basic level of individual and societal moral maturity and a reasonable degree of respect for the law. Only by being thus prepared will citizens of a future democratic polity no longer depend so heavily on the CCP for a semblance of moral agency. And only in this way will they be able, in the absence of the guiding and controlling hand of the party, to act in concert with a reasonable degree of initiative, responsibility, and effectiveness. This second major challenge confronting China's shift to democracy is daunting enough in its own right. It is made even more daunting by the fact that any success in meeting this challenge will depend on the CCP soberly perceiving the need for democratic preparation, which, in turn, is contingent on the CCP perceiving the need for democratic change and deciding to pursue such change in the first place.

THIRD CHALLENGE. Imagine a positive scenario in which the CCP perceives the need for democratic change, decides to take the plunge, and then has the prudence to undertake democratic preparation before completing the passage to political democracy. Even in this extremely propitious scenario, there is the distinct risk that, as the party has become known to think the better of holding on to its current monopoly of power and to favor a more fitting regime yet to be achieved, it may suffer a weakening of its centripetal capacity. Were this to happen, it would create, among other dangers, unprecedented opportunities for all separatist tendencies to suddenly expand and try their luck in more confident and aggressive ways than ever before. Since China has no shortage of political and geopolitical adversaries and since it will not become the most powerful country in the world anytime soon, it will be an open question whether, in such a scenario, domestic separatist forces will not receive encouragement and even aid from foreign powers keen to take advantage of a less united and cohesive China. Even the very possibility of some such scenario is enough to constitute a distinct, and distinctively daunting, challenge for China's passage to democracy. It is a reminder that China's successful democratic change is predicated on its ability to hold a vast country, with its ethnic diversity and territorial integrity, together—and that this is dependent not only on the domestic balance of forces but also on the international environment at large. What we know for sure is that, if this challenge is not well handled, there will be no confident and orderly transition to democracy—in all probability, no transition to democracy at all.

It is part and parcel of this challenge that, historically, China has largely not had the kind of values, institutions, and composition of social and political forces that are responsible for the stable democratic order in the modern, especially contemporary, West.[18] In other words, democracy is deeply foreign to the Chinese tradition of conducting public affairs, and this profound *politico-cultural* fact is not changed by China's new equality of conditions, which signals the presence of a democratic *society*. Nor, however, will this politico-cultural fact be able forever to prevent the increasing equality of conditions from propelling China toward political democracy except at the cost of progressively reduced governability. It is undeniable that, at least to some degree, the socioeconomic reality on the ground and the politico-cultural tradition in the soil, as it were, are pulling in opposite directions. This mismatch makes China's democratic challenge all the more daunting and democratic preparation all the more necessary.

It is in keeping with the just-noted absence of democratic theory and practice in the Chinese tradition that I will not be able to draw on that tradition to make my case for democracy in China today. Thus I will be discussing a present-day Chinese reality—a democratic society—without being able to use a homemade, Chinese discourse to make sense of it, and this is even more true when I then argue for unimpeded progress from this social reality to a democratic political regime befitting it. In the latter case especially, I will have to draw heavily on the theoretical and historical understanding of democracy developed in, of course, those places where democracy has figured prominently, if always problematically and contentiously. This, then, is not a matter of intellectual choice or affective preference but one rooted in the plain facts of the matter—namely, the presence of strong social conditions, and of the correspondingly strong need, for democracy in China today, on the one hand, and the lack of significant historical precedents and major intellectual resources in the Chinese tradition, on the other. I see little harm and mostly benefits, especially under these circumstances, in learning from the theory and practice of democracy in the West, provided that one is mindful of negative lessons as well as positive ones—not least the lesson that, in the final analysis, democracy can only grow out of, and in response to, the real and pressing needs and challenges presented by a society itself.

FOURTH CHALLENGE. The fourth challenge differs from the first three in being less purely prudential and containing an irreducibly normative component. Nevertheless, as I conceive of it, this challenge is also prudential to a substantial degree, and it certainly bears on the other challenges, especially the first one.

What is at issue in this challenge is the relationship between democracy and capitalism. This is a tough challenge in any modern democracy, and it is hard to think of a large democracy today that is truly exemplary in this regard. It should come as no surprise that the challenge is even more daunting for a country like China whose democratic political forces are much weaker than its capitalist economic ones. What is noteworthy about China in this regard is that the socioeconomic dynamic unleashed by the reform is now pushing the country simultaneously toward a political democracy and a more purely capitalist economic order. This simultaneity is itself nothing out of the ordinary, but it may well become an extraordinary menace because of the gross asymmetry in power between a capitalist class eager to weaken or, better still, capture the state for their corporate interests given the chance, on the one hand, and ordinary citizens seeking a real increase in political participation, on the other.

It is also worth noting that we are living in an age in which neoliberalism is reshaping democracy to the point where democratic institutions have increasingly degenerated into the handmaidens of corporations, legitimating the latter much more than counteracting them in the interest of society. The rich and powerful everywhere in the world today openly aggrandize themselves at the expense of society, only in different ways.[19] China is far from immune to the neoliberal influence, its reform having coincided almost exactly with neoliberalism's rise and eventual conquest, to different degrees, of all Western democracies. Xi Jinping has gone out of his way to distance the CCP under his leadership (with its own distinct idea of supply-side reform) from neoliberalism, but this does not change the fact that neoliberal orthodoxy has become the mainstream understanding among the extremely powerful Chinese economic and financial elite of the correct relationship between the state and the free market. If this massive neoliberal infiltration into Chinese political consciousness makes itself felt in China's process of democratic change, as it well might, we have reason to fear that the consequence will be a democracy utterly subservient to capitalism.

My worry is not exactly that a newly established Chinese democracy will be no better than today's democratic capitalism in the West, itself a pale shadow of, say, European social democracy in its heyday or the New Deal in America. What I fear is rather that, lacking long-standing democratic institutions for neoliberalism to try to roll back, as in Europe or America, China after its democratic transition could turn into such a capitalist morass as to make neoliberal capitalism in the West look positively socialist. If we are not careful, this may well be the fate of China's democratic transition, leaving many, possibly hundreds of millions, to wonder about the point of democratic change. That is why balancing democracy against capitalism will be no less daunting a challenge than the first three. Because failure in this regard may fatally undermine popular support for democracy, even to the point of prematurely dooming the newborn democracy, meeting this challenge is also a prudential necessity.

It so happens that such an eventuality would spell the end not only of any prospects of a remotely bracing democracy but also of the CCP as a potentially preeminent political force in a democratic China. For this if for no other reason, the party, if and when it sees fit to set China on the path toward political democracy, will have a vested interest in seeing to it that China's democratization does not become conflated with the shrinkage of state power in favor of the free market. Given the state of the Chinese economy and public opinion, and given the current global ideological environment, it may be too much to expect the party to be the first to reverse the supposedly counterintuitive logic whereby the wealthy retain their dominance even in a democratic system with universal suffrage. Yet there is reason to hope that the CCP, once the democratic transition is under way, will, if only for its own credibility as a self-professed left-wing party, try to ally itself more with democratic forces than with corporate interests. Indeed, the formation of such an alliance, as well as the active promotion of social justice, will have to be an integral part of democratic preparation, in addition to the cultivation of individual and societal maturity, if the CCP is to find an important role for itself, still with its supposedly Marxist-inspired identity, in a democratic China.

This is not a prediction, nor a pious normative wish. It is straightforward prudential reasoning about a hypothetical scenario in which the CCP has taken the plunge in favor of democratic change yet made up its mind not to give up its political preeminence but rather to maintain it in a new way consistent with the norms of a democratic polity. We have thus come full circle, with the intelligibility of every other challenge and any possible success in meeting them depending on the surmounting of the first and foremost challenge. In this context, it is entirely appropriate to wish the party well with respect to its *rational* self-regarding interests.

In perusing the more detailed arguments in the eight chapters that follow, readers can orient themselves by remembering that everything that is said in this book contributes either to demonstrating why China stands in urgent need of democratic change or to illuminating what the chief challenges are and what the appropriate responses might be. Not every chapter is devoted to only one task or the other, and most mix these tasks together, sometimes more or less imperceptibly.

The book falls into three parts, the first part showing that a looming legitimation crisis calls for an urgent and prudent response, the second arguing that the only fitting and effective response will be meaningful democratic change of one kind or another, and, finally, the third dealing with the international and Hong Kong dimensions of China's democratic challenge.

Chapters 1 and 2 set the stage for the book's argument for democratic change by showing that the problem of legitimacy is far from resolved even under what appears to be an exceptionally strong leadership delivering what seem to be extremely impressive economic and other performances. Chapter 1 explains what political legitimacy is, why so-called performance legitimacy cannot deliver what legitimacy uniquely can and is therefore, strictly speaking, not legitimacy, what it takes to secure legitimacy, and why the current Chinese arrangement has not secured it, thereby leaving wide open the possibility of a devastating legitimation crisis. Chapter 2 then examines the presence of this possibility in the various crisis tendencies already afflicting the CCP, which have the distinct potential for causing grave political problems in the near future, especially for turning the next leadership succession into an unprecedented challenge to regime continuation.

The second part of the book, comprising Chapters 3–6, presents my response to the looming legitimation crisis, arguing for the dire need for democracy and at the same time showing the formidable challenges and complications involved in meeting this need, and hence the simultaneous need for prudence. Chapter 3 represents my concentrated attempt to hammer home why only democracy can help China avoid a paralyzing legitimation crisis—why, to put it more strongly, only democracy can save China. Chapter 4 shows why democracy is necessary in order to shield individuals and communities in China's new capitalist society from the worst effects of a market economy left entirely to its own devices. As the reader will recall, this figures also as the fourth challenge confronting China's progress to democracy.

Lest we see the necessity of democracy in China and the resulting challenges as simple and straightforward at least in theory, whatever the practical difficulties, Chapter 5 provides a conceptual narrative of the complex transitional and contradictory character of China's current moral and political condition. The picture that emerges is one in which the necessity of democracy is intrinsically bound up with the challenge of answering it, with both springing not from some exogenous logic or normativity but from internal dynamics that render the course of democratic change anything but simple and straightforward. The reader will find in this chapter—taken together with Chapters 3 and 4 and, to a lesser degree, Chapter 1—the closest thing in the book to a systematic set of theoretical reflections on democracy, although I present these reflections for the most part with close reference to

China. My aim, in addition to the main task of shedding light on China, is to give an account of democracy in which some of democracy's crucial connections—such as with liberty, equality, morality, power, capitalism, unity, and the good—can fall clearly into place. For this reason, my entire undertaking may also be viewed as, in part, an exercise in democratic theory embedded in a discussion of China.

Chapter 6 further spells out the plea for working with the CCP rather than against it in going about democratic change. It is also complementary to Chapter 4 in putting forward the idea of democratic preparation. Its significance may be expressed by saying that the argument for democracy in China translates, for the present and immediate future, into an argument for democratic preparation.

Part III of the book discusses the additional complications deriving from the international and Hong Kong factors that may help or hinder China's democratic change. Chapter 7 addresses the relevance and potential impact of international factors, arguing, on the one hand, that China cannot expect fully to resolve the domestic legitimation crisis unless it makes significant progress in enhancing its legitimacy around the world, and vice versa, and, on the other, that political and ideological hostility toward China's (nominally) communist system is unlikely to help the democratic cause.

What is happening in Hong Kong vis-à-vis (mainland) China is a particularly instructive case in point, because Hong Kong is both part of China and subject to a political arrangement that grants it a special status and identity somewhat apart from China. In Chapter 8 I discuss both democracy in Hong Kong and Hong Kong's impact on democracy in China. In certain important respects, Hong Kong is representative of the democratic challenge that China faces in regions of the country that are granted or promised a high degree of autonomy. This is an added reason for giving Hong Kong a substantial place in this book; another reason is that, of all the regions in this category, Hong Kong is the one I happen to know best. It is also worth emphasizing that democracy in Hong Kong and its impact on Chinese democracy are so closely connected that this dual topic deserves relatively comprehensive treatment in its own right.

I bring the book to a close with reflections that provide a concluding perspective. I will first confront the possibility—ruled out in theory by my account of legitimacy in Chapter 1 but nevertheless deserving a final look—that the Chinese Dream, as performance legitimacy in its most comprehensive and elevated form, might arrest the momentum toward democracy inherent in China's social conditions. This is a possibility that defies the ordinary dynamic of sociopolitical change and whose effective life span coincides with that of Xi Jinping's leadership. This means that the unprecedented challenge to regime continuation at the time of the next leadership succession will remain unaltered.

Finally, I allow myself the luxury of speculating on the circumstances, however improbable, in which what I have said in this book would turn out to be wrong—not merely wrong in some detail or with regard to timing but wrong in its main thrust and thus as a whole. Such circumstances concern in particular the very close link between the democratic fortunes of China and America, as well as the power relations between them. I pursue this speculation out of a humility that, given my desire to be forthright wherever appropriate, may not have been evident in my main argument, but also in keeping with an important belief that informs this book. It is the belief that democracy depends for its advent and success in a country at least as much on fortunate circumstances, both domestic and international, as it does on whatever prudential and normative merit it may have.

PART ONE

The Legitimation Crisis

CHAPTER ONE

Legitimacy and Performance

SOME FOUR DECADES into the still ongoing "reform and opening up" (*gaige kaifang*) and nearly seventy years after the founding of communist rule, China has an awe-inspiring list of achievements to its credit, not least to the credit of the Chinese Communist Party (CCP). Although this is by no means the only list, there is little doubt that communist China as a whole has been an overachiever, surpassing even its own wildest realistic dreams. Yet, communism aside, one long-overdue task remains unaccomplished: the establishment of a political order, communist or otherwise, that can be counted on to reproduce itself over time without the permanent specter of subversion or collapse. Nowhere is this elusive goal better captured than in a Chinese phrase fondly used by official media and the CCP leadership: *changzhi jiu'an*, loosely translatable as "enduring order and lasting stability." China is today no nearer this goal than it has been since the fall of the last imperial dynasty in 1911 or since the party's seizure of power in 1949. If truth be told, neither 1911 nor, despite claims to the contrary, 1949 has turned out to be the Chinese equivalent, let alone continuation, of 1789—the inauguration of the bourgeois democratic revolution that Karl Marx, for one, both lauded as necessary and progressive and sought to move beyond for being radically incomplete.

Meanwhile the task of bringing about *changzhi jiu'an* has become more urgent than at any time since 1949 and especially since the start of reform in the late 1970s. The most important domestic event for China in the next ten to twenty years will be a sharp fall in the political authority of the party-state.[1]

In 2029, China will be celebrating the eightieth anniversary of the founding of the People's Republic. By then, if not sooner, the power of its revolutionary past to impart legitimacy to the CCP will have all but exhausted itself, with no one around who has played any part in the revolution itself and with only an aging, largely inactive, and fast-depleting number of later generations who carry even secondhand memories of the revolution. A distance of eighty years, or four generations, will have effectively dispelled the aura of successful revolutionary violence, with its unique ability to inspire awe and command obedience, to naturalize and even consecrate power. A new source of legitimacy must be found, a new account of the normative origin of power provided. The revolutionary legitimacy of the CCP will need wholesale replacement in the same way that the imperial legitimacy rooted in the Mandate of Heaven did in 1911.

It is no secret that the communist teleological-revolutionary legitimacy[2] of the CCP has been steadily declining since well before the death of Mao Zedong and especially since the launch of the economic reform by Deng Xiaoping—the latter signaling nothing less than the abandonment of the revolution as both telos and means. So far, however, this fall in one source of political authority has apparently (for we have yet to figure out exactly what has been going on) been made up for by a dramatic rise in another—that is, the great success of the party-state in creating economic growth, higher standards of living, and, later, the much more complicated phenomenon known as national pride. The result is the effective maintenance of the party-state's authority on a rather different basis, or so it seems: not so much its normative appeal as its sheer performance, its ability to deliver the goods. The goods have been coming thick and fast for nearly three decades, although they have been far from equitably shared and have come at incalculable human and environmental cost. This apparent compensatory mechanism—the shifting from one leg (legitimacy) to the other (performance) instead of walking on the twin legs of legitimacy *and* performance—has all along been dogged by the improbability that the extraordinary times of recent decades will continue indefinitely.[3] As a matter of fact, such times, characterizing as they do the earlier developmental phase of a so-called newly industrializing economy, seem already to have come to an end. The current leadership is trying to cool expectations by referring to this rise in China's economic challenges as the New Normal, and to transform ambitions by sublimating the individual desire for prosperity into the collective dream of national rejuvenation. More-over, to its credit, and by force of circumstance, the CCP leadership has fi-nally embarked on the paradigm shift from high-speed growth to high-quality growth, in an attempt to move beyond a growth model overtaken by the country's own success and to move up the international value chain. This very shift means that economic performance is no longer a matter of growth per se but one of successful upgrading and rebalancing—an even taller order than growth itself. Indeed, Chinese leaders themselves have acknowledged, openly and with a fitting sense of gravity, the sheer newness, as well as enormity, of the challenges ahead. If they show no sign of counting on any easy and pre-dictable surmounting of such challenges, no one else has more reason to. Bar-ring unforeseen improvements in the global economy, it is thus safe to say that China's economic performance potential has passed a point of no return: no more dramatic growth, and hence no more dramatic boost to legitimacy from this source. Prudence dictates, especially given what is at stake, that we err on the side of caution rather than confidence. In any case, the point is not that China's economy is not doing reasonably well but rather that we are gradually approaching (or must prudently project) a situation in which walking on one leg—the compensation by *extraordinary* performance for weak legitimacy—will no longer suffice when the leg that has so far carried China has become considerably weaker. But as we know all too well, China has become overreliant on this leg precisely because the other one, the old revolutionary legitimacy, was showing signs of terminal wear and tear. This other, hitherto hobbling leg cannot simply be pressed back into service as in the past.

Within the next ten to twenty years, then, communist China will be facing a crisis of political authority the likes of which it has never experi-enced before. It is only a matter of time before the party-state will no longer be able to draw at all on the legitimation potential of its revolutionary past as a basis for its authority. And it is also only a matter of time before it will no longer be able, even in the face of further waning legitimacy, to rely so lopsidedly and headily on performative success as a complementary source of prestige and authority. The compounding of a legitimation crisis by per-formance problems will be all the more daunting in that performance has come to cover not only economic growth but also such other tough items as social justice, official corruption, and, with an ever-rising profile in public consciousness and expectations, food and vaccine safety and an unpolluted environment. This *double* shortfall—in both legitimacy and performance—or, put another way, a weakening of both legs at the same time, is one that the CCP has never faced before, and it must be dealt with in ways the party has never had to contemplate before. Unless it is handled by such extraordinary means as are adequate to the challenge and handled in a timely fashion, China's future could be bleak indeed. There is no need to rule out the possibility of a rosier scenario—of performance, not legitimacy—coming true. Countless predictions have been made, positive, negative, and anywhere in between. All these may be set aside in favor of two simple truths: that we cannot know for sure, not even remotely in this case, and that it is imprudent to base regime authority and political stability solely or even primarily on the uncertain fortunes of the economy. Unless there is a high probability of a positive scenario, it would be reckless to rely on it to save the day. And we have not even considered the potentially shattering implications of the demise of communist teleological-revolutionary legitimacy—assuming a reasonably good level of performance and hence largely *regardless of* performance.

June 4, 1989, and the Rise of Performance Legitimacy

I have been speaking of legitimacy and performance as two alternative sources of political authority as if they were clear and largely unproblematic categories. They are *not,* and we must now delve deeper into what they mean and how they are related in the context of reform-era China. Especially problematic and requiring clarification is the notion that performance can contribute to political authority in such a way that the result deserves to be considered a distinct kind of legitimacy—namely, *performance legitimacy.*

To understand the importance of performance and the rise of performance legitimacy, we must go back to the legitimation crisis that led to the events of June 4, 1989, and was, in turn, exacerbated by them and their aftermath. June 4 signaled two things: a deepening of the legitimation crisis involving the CCP's revolutionary past, and a new discontent with the party-state's purely economic performance. The students' invocation of the deceased Hu Yaobang—the former CCP general secretary known for his exceptional willingness, in the interest of reform, to move away from aspects of the party's revolutionary past—spoke volumes about the nature of the legitimation crisis. At the same time, the students were reacting, and understood themselves to be reacting, to changes in the Chinese economy that seemed to have little directly to do with legitimacy. Chief among their grievances, shared by society at large, was a set of what have since come to be called livelihood issues *(minsheng wenti)*—namely, a spate of unprecedented price rises that had started to cause panic among the general public. These two sets of concerns—with the legitimacy of the CCP's mandate as rooted in its revolutionary past and with the "performance" of an economy in the process of being reformed—came together in an irrepressible outpouring of public resentment of official corruption and the loud and clear call, spearheaded by the protesting students, for democracy. The students may not have had a clear idea of what they were after or, as a later complaint has it, even what democracy was. But in joining together the twin concerns in their protests, they were nothing if not prescient—a harbinger of things to come and of a problematic that is still with us.

The CCP, for its part, first had to deal with the immediate challenge to its legitimacy, indeed to its very survival. It did so by violently putting down the student-led democracy movement and then launching a nationwide ideological campaign aimed at restoring its legitimacy, at least a semblance of legitimacy in the form of the complete absence of resistance, even verbal resistance. It was not without internal division at the highest level of the party, nor indeed without moments of mortal danger, that Deng was able to muster the determination and the sheer military force to crush the students' "rebellion." But when all is said and done, we must see in Deng's decision and its successful execution what must have been a very substantial degree of *intraparty* legitimacy. Had this legitimacy been even higher, there would undoubtedly have been less division and less hesitation than we later heard about. But the very fact that the CCP was able to put down an extremely popular movement with the open and determined use of deadly force is indicative of a level of intraparty legitimacy, and hence unity, that must have been very considerable indeed. And it is worth noting that the CCP's intraparty legitimacy has always mattered even more than its legitimacy in the country at large. In a way, from the very fact of a high level of intraparty legitimacy, we may even infer the belief among the more powerful members of the CCP at the time that the party still enjoyed a substantial degree of legitimacy in the country at large. This belief was to be proved entirely correct by subsequent developments, but not before the CCP had gotten around to addressing the second of the students' grievances—namely, those directed at livelihood issues and hence at the economy as a whole.

This second prong of the CCP's response to June 4 took the form, especially, of Deng's famous southern tour in 1992 to revive the economy and the sinking fortunes of the party in the wake of the national and international shock of 1989. Everyone knows what happened after Deng's initiative, and it would be no exaggeration to say that the reform got its second lease on life—and what life! From that point on, the party started to pursue economic growth with unprecedented determination and freedom from dogma and, some would say, at all cost. We have since witnessed not only rapid economic growth culminating in China's rise to the status of the world's second-largest economy but, more importantly for our purposes, a renewed legitimacy for the party. Thus, not only has the students' second concern been effectively addressed, but their first grievance, having to do with the basis of the CCP's legitimacy, has also receded. And the latter is due as much to genuine popular approval of the CCP as to the deterrence effect of June 4. Since this rejuvenated legitimacy has a lot to do with economic growth and with efficient performance in general, it is thought by many to be a brand-new kind of legitimacy. What else could it be but performance legitimacy?

What Is Performance Legitimacy?

But what exactly is performance legitimacy? It is sometimes also called performance-based legitimacy, making it explicit that the legitimacy in question is a function of good (meaning, mostly, efficient) performance, or performative success, and nothing else. In the Chinese case at hand, this notion usually seems to carry the implication that performance legitimacy is all that the CCP has enjoyed since 1989 and all that is needed. In other words, the implication is that performance legitimacy has been a *comprehensive substitute* for the CCP's old teleological-revolutionary legitimacy, and that, as such, it has been *independently effective* and, indeed, very much so.

The picture becomes more complicated when performance legitimacy is paired with the other, more standard kind of legitimacy in the distinction between input legitimacy and output legitimacy. Performance legitimacy is output legitimacy—what a regime is able to deliver in the shape of visible goods, which is amenable to assessment *after* the delivery. By contrast, input legitimacy is a regime's title to state power, an already warranted position from which it will then be able to try to deliver what it intends to deliver. For the CCP, the title, or mandate, even today still comes from whatever is supposedly contained in its name (*gongchandang*, communist party), or else its name would have outlived its usefulness and deserved to be abandoned for something else. More on this later, but for now it is necessary to take up a question that concerns the relation between input and output legitimacy and is prompted by this very distinction. In the Chinese case, the question takes this specific form: What is the nature of the relation that has existed since, say, 1992 between the so-called performance legitimacy newly gained by the CCP and the party's old teleological-revolutionary legitimacy? This question, in turn, gives rise to further questions—or different ways of raising what is essentially the same question. How much of the old teleological-revolutionary legitimacy is left, or, how strong is it today? Does it even matter how much is left and how strong it is, and why? Is so-called performance legitimacy a sufficient basis of political authority? Is it independent or dependent, and if the latter, on what is it dependent? Is de facto power—the sheer fact of being in power and being powerful enough to maintain that power, at least for the time being—enough to provide a starting point, a prior position of authority, for performance legitimacy? Or is legitimacy—that is, input legitimacy—necessary to create the starting point for performance legitimacy—that is, output legitimacy—to get off the ground?

Before we address such questions, some clues provided by the CCP itself are worth noting. True, the CCP may have been pursuing economic growth at all cost, but at the same time it has been guarding its links to the revolutionary past—to 1921 and 1949 and the Long March (literally and metaphorically) in between—with even greater jealousy and determination. True, the CCP has been using performative success to strengthen its position, but it has never given any indication of doing so as a *substitute* for its old communist revolutionary legitimacy; otherwise it would not have needed to care so much about the latter. True, the CCP is giving the Chinese Dream a teleological substance—"the great rejuvenation of the Chinese nation" (replacing the earlier emphasis on individual prosperity and happiness)—that seems to have nothing explicitly communist or revolutionary about it, but it has done everything possible to place the Chinese Dream in the context of 1921 and 1949 and to render the party essential, rather than merely contingently useful, to its realization.[4] "Stay true to the original aspiration" (*Buwang chuxin*) is the party's foremost exhortation to itself, tirelessly highlighted at the nineteenth party congress and ever since. Whatever one may say to draw attention to the subtle or not-so-subtle reinterpretation of "the original aspiration," even more telling is the emphatic reference to this aspiration as the *original* one. True, the CCP, in pursuing economic growth and other performance goals, has turned China into what, in many respects, looks like a capitalist society, but it has also stuck to its public self-understanding as a communist party presiding over a socialist market economy, with the result that it has acquired a double identity, neither component of which is less important or defining than the other. One could go on in this vein, but this is already enough to suggest that the proposition that the CCP's performative success, amounting to performance legitimacy, has served as a substitute for its old communist revolutionary legitimacy is one that the CCP would be the first to reject. And I believe the party would be entirely correct in doing so.

This implies, of course, that the CCP still believes it enjoys to a considerable degree its old teleological-revolutionary legitimacy, or else what is no longer serviceable would be ripe for substitution or radical adjustment. In this too I think the party is entirely right, although the exact degree of legitimacy in question is hard to gauge and must be left open to debate. Recall what I said earlier about the CCP's intraparty legitimacy and its dependence on (the perception of) wider legitimacy in the country at large and vice versa. I said all that with reference to the strength of the CCP's position during and after June 1989. I believe the same kind of strength is enjoyed by the party today. Simply put, all signs indicate that the CCP today still possesses a sufficiently strong combination of intraparty legitimacy and wider legitimacy in the country to maintain a reasonable degree of unity and cohesion and keep potentially fatal factionalism at bay, and to maintain the deterrence effect of June 4 against any similar uprising. This deterrence effect, created by the actions of the CCP leadership in 1989, is dependent for its continued efficacy on the perceived or imagined will on the part of the CCP leadership *today* to prevent or, if necessary, suppress a repeat of June 4. There is every reason to believe that this will is indeed strongly present, which is not to say that it is necessarily *overwhelmingly* present (it was not so even at the time of Deng); hence the importance of prevention. And the will to thwart and crush all opposition is, in turn, a function of perceived intraparty legitimacy, itself indicative of perceived wider legitimacy around the country. Were things otherwise or perceived otherwise, China simply would not be as stable as it is today. On the other hand, were the CCP's legitimacy, intraparty and beyond, even higher than it actually is and, more importantly, enduringly so, China would not need to devote such a large amount of resources and so much nervous energy to maintaining stability or, more bluntly put, to preventing another June 4.

This is where the CCP stands in its own estimation of its legitimacy, or so we can reasonably infer. It derives a great deal of confidence from its performative success domestically and, increasingly, also in the international arena, though not without ominous pushback from the United States in particular. And it undoubtedly believes that all this performative success does something positive for its legitimacy; this is one crucial reason why it has been pursuing economic growth with such abandon. Yet good performance by itself does not speak to the party's distinctive history and self-understanding, and, just as important, it cannot serve as a basis, discursive or psychological, for the sheer will to put down all opposition. For these purposes, legitimacy—in a sense that is stronger than and qualitatively different from so-called performance legitimacy—is called for. That is why the CCP is hanging on for dear life to its communist revolutionary legacy, however necessary and expedient it may have found it to finesse the interpretation and presentation of this legacy.

If we pay close attention to the CCP's own words and, especially, deeds, we will be left in little doubt that the party believes, first, that legitimacy (as distinct from so-called performance legitimacy) is even more important than performance (or performance legitimacy), and, second, that the party still enjoys a substantial amount of legitimacy. If, as a matter of its public self-understanding and self-presentation, the CCP takes its own legitimacy so seriously, then we must do so as well in order to understand how the party operates and intends to operate. If, as a matter of self-estimation, the CCP still considers itself to be in possession of a considerable, if precarious, level of legitimacy, then we must, in assessing its present and future, give it some benefit of the doubt.

The Importance of the Right to Rule

It so happens that I agree with both the CCP's self-understanding and its self-estimation. Recall, however, my earlier prognostic concern that in the foreseeable future the party may well suffer an unprecedented legitimation crisis comprising a double shortfall in legitimacy and performance at the same time. Not only is this prognosis not in conflict with the party's self-understanding and self-estimation, it is actually based entirely on my agreement with both of the latter. Indeed, from the CCP's own words and deeds, it would be all too easy to infer a sense of crisis on its part that is not so different from mine, although there is no need to insist on this point.

The important thing is that the legitimation crisis I am talking about is not yet staring China in the face. It is coming but still in the distance. If the current leadership is betraying an exceptionally acute sense of the possibility of just such a crisis, through its unprecedented anticorruption campaign and its firm yet anxious tightening of ideological and security controls, it is just as definitely evincing a degree of confidence, however qualified, that has not been seen at least since Deng. It is one thing to say that a formidable crisis will emerge unless effective measures are taken to prevent it and something else to assess whether the crisis has already arrived. The unprecedentedly grave legitimation crisis under discussion has definitely not arrived; far from it.

To say this is to believe, as I do, that the current leadership is still enjoying, to a substantial degree, the mandate to preside over China—or legitimacy in a bona fide sense. This mandate is what we may call the *right to rule,* and the leadership's confidence is nothing but part of the larger political fact of the CCP's still broadly acknowledged right to rule. This right must not be reduced to performance legitimacy. It is true, of course, that since the close of the Mao era and especially since the honeymoon of Deng's reform came to a definitive end in 1989, the party has been increasingly relying on economic growth and rising prosperity to maintain public support for or acquiescence in its continuing rule. In this context, performance is a matter of largely economic success, with its widely (if inequitably) distributed benefits, and so-called performance legitimacy is the political acceptability that thereby accrues to the CCP. This is all very well except that performance legitimacy is not legitimacy strictly construed, if only because whatever political acceptability is conferred by performative success *alone* would not be able to underwrite the legitimate threat and use of state violence, including to put down June 4 or to preempt its recurrence.

The right to rule includes, above all else, the title to employ force in the interest of rule and of self-preservation, and this title goes well beyond mere performance legitimacy. As such, the right to rule pertains to government *(tongzhi)* in its strict and basic sense as distinct from governance *(zhili)*. Government in this sense includes the right to prevent and suppress opposition— such opposition as would undermine the political order if left unchecked. And this derives, in turn, from the right to be in power—and thereby to be in legitimate possession of the means of violence—in the first place. By contrast, governance is only about managing differences and conflicts within more or less stable parameters already established through government, as well as delivering other public goods. It is thus a matter of carrying out responsibilities, hence of performance, whereas government is the *prior* right to occupy the position that confers such responsibilities, as well as to carry them out—and to use violence, if necessary, both to keep itself in this position and to discharge its responsibilities. Government or, strictly speaking, the *right* to govern (or to rule) is alone "*ex ante* effective in legitimating decisions,"[5] and hence it alone amounts to legitimacy in the fundamental sense of (prior) authorization. Governance is secondary to and parasitic on government, and, by the same token, performance is secondary to and parasitic on legitimacy.

It is worth mentioning in passing Jürgen Habermas's distinction between legitimacy as a lifeworld concept and performance (steering) as a system concept. Within Habermas's framework, to believe that so-called performance legitimacy can be a substitute for legitimacy proper would be to confuse or conflate the lifeworld and system. Performance legitimacy, strictly speaking, pertains to system—the result of successful steering of the economy. Legitimacy proper, on the other hand, has to do with the lifeworld—that is, with communicating subjects who must be convinced (by good arguments) rather than bought off (with material benefits such as rising living standards). There is thus a huge, qualitative difference between legitimation deficits and steering deficits.[6]

It is also worth briefly bringing in the concept of sovereignty.[7] It would suffice to point out the closeness in meaning between the right to rule and

sovereignty to realize how far so-called performance legitimacy falls short
of what is required by the CCP and of what is indeed claimed by it. For what
the CCP claims for itself, and still enjoys to a substantial degree (as I am arguing), is what is in effect sovereignty of the party, as expressed in the language of a species of popular sovereignty that is mediated by the CCP's constitutionally stipulated exclusive representative function. By this standard,
performance legitimacy is not enough and not what is needed first and foremost. The exclusive right to rule, or sovereignty—that which authorizes the
uniquely legitimate use of state power—is what the party needs and claims;
in other words, legitimacy in its fundamental and integral sense. Compared
to this, so-called performance legitimacy is secondary and derivative, involving only what is (well) done with what must be antecedently and independently authorized in the first place, although it contributes to legitimacy
proper in ways that I shall discuss presently.

This distinction between the right to rule and performance legitimacy is
crucial for any reliable diagnosis of the political strength of the party today
and for any plausible prognosis of how long this strength is likely to last. For
analytical purposes, performance legitimacy is best used as a descriptive notion, a notion applied from a third-person, observer perspective to the
reality of the political relation between the CCP and the populace. In the present context, the right to rule is to be taken in exactly the same descriptive
sense. Thus, by using the phrase *right to rule,* I do not intend here to make a
first-person, reflective, normative judgment but only to render a third-person,
empirical assessment of whether the party actually enjoys—that is, is sufficiently widely acknowledged to have—the right to rule.

It makes a world of difference whether one views the current political
standing of the CCP vis-à-vis the populace chiefly in terms of performance
legitimacy or the right to rule. From a diagnostic point of view, as we shall
see, the difference boils down to, first, whether the party really enjoys much
legitimacy in the first place and, second, what exactly the party is doing when
it copes with legitimation problems by ostensibly relying on performative success. With regard to the second issue, it will turn out that both performance
legitimacy and the right to rule are partially present in the current political
relationship between the CCP and the populace. Even so, it is still useful, indeed essential, to draw the distinction in order to capture the complexity of
the relationship and especially to be alert and attentive to the ever-evolving

balance between performance legitimacy and the right to rule and its profound implications. In the meantime, this brings me to the matter of prognosis.

From a prognostic point of view, the difference between the two perceptions of the political standing of the CCP vis-à-vis the populace is more immediately obvious, so I can briefly state it. If, or insofar as, the CCP is relying on performance legitimacy, its political future will depend on whether it will be able to maintain its performative success, at what level, and for how long—the only other significant variable being what happens to be the popular understanding of performative success at any given time and how successfully the party is able to shape it. On the other hand, if, or insofar as, the CCP is still largely enjoying the right to rule, then the crucial question is whether and for how long it will be able to keep fresh and plausible the conditions for this right to rule. Depending on which prognostic approach is adopted, one will be looking for different signs to see how well the party is doing and at what point, if any, it will encounter exceptionally challenging, even insurmountable, legitimation problems. Depending on this choice as well, one will either view Xi Jinping's speech at the nineteenth party congress as a highly significant and potentially highly impactful attempt to shape the popular understanding of what properly counts as performative success in what is now called the new era—that is, the Xi era—or view it as both this *and* an extraordinarily determined renewal of the CCP's claim to the right to rule.

I happen to favor the second prognostic approach, as well as the diagnostic approach that goes with it—in keeping with the CCP's own self-understanding and self-estimation. I hasten to add that there is an element of truth in the other approach too, and yet, as we shall see, this is the case only if the so-called performance legitimacy is viewed as complementary to, indeed parasitic on, a substantial degree of the right to rule. Without this proviso, as I will try to show, the very notion of performance legitimacy will cease to make much sense even diagnostically, let alone for prognostic purposes.

Now, those who prefer to work with the notion of performance legitimacy precisely in the absence of this proviso may well object that, diagnostically, I am attributing to the CCP more legitimacy than it really has—that is, more bona fide legitimacy in the sense of the right to rule. They may go on to suggest that I seem to be hinting, by way of an implicit prognosis, that the party may well be able to hang on to its political supremacy indefinitely. Paradoxically, however, it is their diagnosis that is more open to such prognostic implications. For if the CCP is able to rely effectively and exclusively on performance legitimacy, and has been for quite some time, there is no reason why it cannot continue to do so indefinitely other than the highly contingent one that a reasonably high level of performance may not be forthcoming. The strongest conclusion supported by an awareness of such contingency is that performance legitimacy is without guarantee, but then, by the same token, the discontinuation of performance legitimacy can be no more certain, in principle. Moreover, performance is a flexible notion, subject to official (as well as popular) reinterpretation and reshaping, and therefore performance legitimacy must be treated as flexible as well. This adds to the contingency already noted, with the result that it is doubly contingent how well and for how long the CCP will be able to maintain a reasonably high level of performance and hence a reasonably high level of performance legitimacy. Performance legitimacy, if such it is, may grind to a halt anytime but could also last a very long time indeed, with manageable ups and downs along the way. Although this lack of certainty either way would be enough to set one's prudential instincts going, the prognosis based exclusively on performance legitimacy is hardly a definitely pessimistic one.

I am, needless to say, not competing to see who can deliver the more negative prognosis (or diagnosis, for that matter). The point is not to be negative but to be accurate—to have a conceptually reasonably precise basis for a prognosis (or diagnosis) along the right lines. In this spirit, let me put forward what happens to be a more negative prognosis. It is based on my diagnosis, according to which the CCP is still enjoying the right to rule, to a substantial degree, and that is the main reason why it has been able to preside over China with the stability and the economic and other achievements for which it is correctly credited—and indeed to allow its performative success to help enhance its legitimacy in the first place. Now, in the light of this diagnosis, the principal determinant of the CCP's foreseeable political future is what happens to those conditions that have served as the basis of its right to rule. As I will spell out presently, there is reason to think that those conditions, which have been gradually deteriorating in the reform era, will weaken drastically and precipitously in the foreseeable future—that is, once the present party leadership has effectively (not only nominally) left the political stage.

What thus lies in store for the party, and for the country at large, is an unprecedented legitimation crisis with the distinct potential to shake to its foundations the CCP's right to rule. When this happens, my hypothesis goes, no amount of performative success or performance legitimacy will be able to compensate, and the only effective substitute will have to be a new basis for the right to rule. To spell out this line of reasoning, we must look more closely at the nature of the relation between performance and legitimacy.

Enhancement of Legitimacy versus Amelioration of a Lack of Legitimacy

I have argued that performance legitimacy is not really legitimacy in the sense of the right to rule, where "the right" signifies (normative) title or warrant and "to rule" involves the comprehensive exercise of power well beyond mere performance and governance. This does not mean that performative success cannot contribute in a significant way to legitimacy—that is, legitimacy properly so called. In the present case, the key to such a contribution lies in the CCP's ability to create a narrative that makes it possible to hitch its performative success to whatever remains of its old teleological-revolutionary legitimacy. That is why successive leaderships of the party since Deng have been careful to retain the totemic status of Mao in their legitimation discourse. That is why they are hanging on to the original name of the party despite the noiseless evaporation of communism from the CCP's doctrine and agenda, the occasional lip service notwithstanding, just as they are refusing to let go of Marxism as still supposedly the underlying theoretical basis and guidance for what is happening in China today, including all of its performative success. And that is also why they, and the propagandists in their employ, never tire of linking the achievements of the Deng-initiated reform (the so-called second thirty years) to the accomplishments of the Mao-led earlier phase of communist rule (the so-called first thirty years), and, of course, linking both to the Marxist-inspired revolutionary struggles whose success led to the founding of the People's Republic of China in 1949. It is of the highest ideological and symbolic significance that the current CCP leadership's grand objectives are framed in terms of two "one hundred years"—the first one hundred years reaching all the way back to 1921, the year that saw the birth of the CCP, and the second one hundred years dating from 1949.[8] It is because of their supposedly uninterrupted link to 1921 that China's achievements by 2020 will be thought possible and be what they are, in meaning and significance, and the same is true of the even bigger accomplishments that China is projected to have secured by the year 2050. Indeed, without the jealous guardianship of the party's links to these two great beginnings, the loci of "the original aspiration," there would be no 2020 or 2050 to speak of—and no CCP to speak of at either of these future times.

For all its social, economic, and even political transformation in the reform era, then, the CCP remains unshaken in its official self-understanding and public identity in terms of its communist revolutionary origins. This is because it is from its founding moment alone that even today's CCP still derives *all* of its right to rule, all of its legitimacy in the strict sense. Of course, performative success matters, but in a way that is legitimacy enhancing only when interpreted as having its place and meaning in the longer, larger teleological-revolutionary master narrative. (This is why the occasional, somewhat abashed reference to a communist future cannot be avoided altogether even as China is fast becoming a billionaires' paradise.) To contribute to legitimacy, performative success needs a goal, a point of reference, a political agent with a definite identity, and all of these are provided by this master narrative. Conversely, for the master narrative to retain its relevance today, to be a living narrative, it must unceasingly renew itself, and this requires, among other things, a new kind of performance. The economic reform, whose upshot is now insistently called the *socialist* market economy, is but part of the latest chapter of the CCP's master narrative. Another part is "the great rejuvenation of the Chinese nation," whose nature and meaning is supposedly "socialism with Chinese characteristics for a new era" (the name given to Xi Jinping Thought), rather than mere nationalism, if only by virtue of its being led by the party. In this context, what is called performance or performance legitimacy as if it were something independent or freestanding is actually nothing but a sign of the successful renewal of the master narrative—the communist revolution's new lease on life in a new era. Nothing seems more natural, in this master narrative, than the reinvigorated or reinvented communist revolution feeding on, and manifesting itself in, a new kind of performance fit for the twenty-first century.

Whether, and to what degree, performance can be thus hitched to legitimacy and thereby contribute directly to it is a complicated matter. Given the communist revolutionary tenor of the CCP's legitimacy, which cannot be removed without also eviscerating the legitimacy itself, and given the quasi-capitalist thrust of the Chinese economy and way of life today and hence of what counts as performative success, it should come as no surprise if such linkage does not happen smoothly and with anything approaching universal credibility. The CCP definitely has its work cut out for it. But it would be naïve to dogmatically rule out all room for some kind of belief sufficient to achieve a measure of success in hitching genuinely appreciated performance to some vaguely endorsed legitimacy. Much depends on the interpretative ingenuity of the party, not least in making a plausible move from a distinctive teleological-revolutionary agenda to the much more general and increasingly depoliticized one of "the great rejuvenation of the Chinese nation." Much also depends on the goodwill and credulity of the populace, which in turn is affected by how well aggregate performative success translates into substantial and widespread benefits for individuals and communities. Above all, the CCP must be taken to still boast a substantial amount of legitimacy, to begin with, to which performative success can be hitched. The more the party succeeds in updating its master narrative and making its links to the revolutionary legacy plausible, the better able it will be to channel performative success into a renewed right to rule instead of leaving it unassimilated and freestanding.

Insofar as performative success has served to shore up the CCP's right to rule—that is, its legitimacy in the strict sense—it can only have done so along the lines just sketched. Otherwise, performance would come across as freestanding, in which case it would not bestow or enhance the right to rule, the title to exercise power, in all the customary senses associated with rule and power. Otherwise, to be more precise, performative success would not be able to count as such within the CCP's own master narrative, and no legitimating consequences would accrue to the party as the performer. Only when performative success contributes to legitimacy in an internal, organic way—that is, via a reasonably credible master narrative—does it deserve to be called performance *legitimacy*. But then there will be no need for a separate category of *performance* legitimacy, because all legitimacy is dependent on success in some kind of performance that is fit to be incorporated into some legitimation discourse.[9] What defines a particular instance of good performance is whether it is *internally* related to legitimacy—that is, by lending itself to assimilation into the master narrative constructed around the legitimacy in question. Only performance that meets this standard is potentially legitimacy enhancing. Any other performance can bear on legitimacy only in an external, ad hoc manner and hence with only limited efficacy; more on this in a moment.

The distinction between performance and legitimacy remains a useful one, however, allowing for the possibility that performance can indeed be disconnected from legitimacy. When this possibility materializes, the distinction between performance and legitimacy will take a unique form—namely, as the distinction between *freestanding performance* (that is, performance whose meaning for citizens differs from its official meaning in the regime's legitimation discourse and that is hence uncoupled from legitimacy) and *inclusive legitimacy* (that is, legitimacy understood as inclusive of whatever performance is internal to it).

This new distinction enables me to make a further, rather different point about the contribution of the CCP's performative success to its legitimacy from my earlier one. Implicit in my earlier point, with its distinct scenario, is the notion of inclusive legitimacy such that good performance makes an internal, organic contribution to legitimacy by being embedded in the same master narrative of which legitimacy itself is an integral part. A different scenario is suggested by the notion of freestanding performance. By definition, freestanding performance is performance external to or uncoupled from legitimacy, but this does not mean that it cannot impinge on legitimacy in some other way. When freestanding performance impinges on legitimacy, then, what happens is not that performative success contributes strictly to legitimacy but rather that such success helps ameliorate a lack of legitimacy, with the result that although legitimacy itself is not enhanced, its lack is nevertheless made to matter somewhat less, other things being equal. We approach here a situation in which a political order is "adhered to from motives of *pure expediency*," as distinct from the more reliable motive of conformity based on legitimacy.[10] There are thus two ways in which a regime's performative success can make a positive difference with regard to legitimacy—through enhancement in one case and mere amelioration (pure expediency) in the other. We only have to make this distinction to realize what a huge difference there must be between enhancement of legitimacy through internally related good performance, on the one hand, and amelioration of a lack of legitimacy through externally related, freestanding good performance, on the other. What may appear to be the same performative success in fact stands in two radically different relations to legitimacy—an internal relation to legitimacy or an external one to a lack of legitimacy—and the mechanisms involved, as well as their effects, are correspondingly divergent.

The commonsense understanding of the matter is rather confused because it does not draw this much-needed distinction. By *performance legitimacy* it seems to mean amelioration, in that it takes compensation to be the chief mechanism mediating positive performance and not-so-positive legitimacy. Yet the very notion of performance *legitimacy*, if taken at face value, pushes one toward the other interpretation. Despite this confusion, a more charitable reading may suggest that what is usually meant is amelioration of a *lack* of legitimacy rather than enhancement of legitimacy.

I mention this confusion not only because it is worth clearing up but also for a much more important purpose, and that is to suggest that precisely this confusion is (understandably) caused by the complex and evolving reality on the ground. First, though, some recapitulation is in order. When I say, as I did earlier, that the current CCP leadership is still largely enjoying the right to rule, I mean to emphasize that this is a matter of legitimacy strictly construed rather than of performance as in so-called performance legitimacy. I also wish to recall that the performative success of the party can contribute to legitimacy enhancement only if the party is able to hitch such success to what remains of its legitimacy, and this requires that what is left of its legitimacy must be substantial enough to begin with. What we find here is, in a nutshell, legitimacy enhancement through performative success. Now, it is possible to doubt that there is much lingering legitimacy to begin with and hence to doubt that there can be much performative enhancement of legitimacy. In other words, in appraising the role of the CCP's performative success in relation to its legitimacy, it is possible, indeed perfectly reasonable, to question how much of what we are witnessing is enhancement and how much is mere amelioration. While I would still insist, for reasons already given, that the current CCP leadership still enjoys the right to rule to a substantial degree, I am equally strongly inclined to add that this mandate is rather shaky and incapable of transforming all performative success into legitimacy. Thus, all one can cautiously and plausibly say is that we are witnessing both enhancement of legitimacy and amelioration of a lack of legitimacy, in ever-evolving proportions.

For my purposes it is quite unnecessary to make a more precise or definitive assessment than this. What is important, rather, is to recognize a broad trend. Having noted that both enhancement and amelioration through performative success have been at work under the current leadership and before, I think it safe to suggest that the future will see an ever-dwindling proportion of enhancement in favor of mere amelioration. This is for the simple reason, more on which in a moment, that there will be less and less legitimacy for performative success to be hitched to and thereby enhance.

It is not difficult to see where this process of waning legitimacy and the shrinking possibility of legitimacy enhancement through good performance will lead us. For sooner or later an inflexion point will be reached at which a critical mass of legitimacy can no longer be maintained, with two devastating consequences. In the first place, without a sufficiently large mass of legitimacy to soak up performative success, the very possibility of legitimacy enhancement through performative success will be lost. One shudders at this prospect—the prospect that performative success, however otherwise impressive, will one day no longer be capable of enhancing the CCP's distinctive legitimacy. What about amelioration of the lack of legitimacy, then? The problem is that with legitimacy enhancement now out of the equation, there must be an irredeemable lack of legitimacy to compensate for, which is indeed what it takes to render legitimacy enhancement no longer possible. This leads, then, to the second devastating consequence, and that is the radically reduced efficacy of amelioration when there is simply too much of a lack of legitimacy to ameliorate, even assuming what would otherwise be considered a high degree of (freestanding) performative success.

It is at this point, a true inflexion point, that the unprecedented legitimation crisis I spoke of earlier will stare China in the face. If this is the case, the implication is profound: what is truly necessary to maintain the political status quo in its essentials is not so much the near certainty of unceasing performative success as the indefinite continuation of the CCP's current and only legitimacy as rooted in the vitality of its communist teleological-revolutionary past. What is most to be feared, accordingly, is not the party's alleged overdependence on performance but rather its reliance on a terminally implausible revolutionary legitimacy both in its own right and as a condition for appropriating performative success.

Excursus on Daniel Bell and Political Meritocracy

It is worth making a digression to show, in terms of the distinction just established, why Daniel Bell's defense of what he calls the China model is mistaken insofar as it is based on the notion of performance legitimacy. Bell says, in the introduction to his 2015 book, that he is arguing for *political* meritocracy as distinct from what may be called administrative meritocracy.[11] I do not see anything really or sufficiently political about such a meritocracy. This is because, first, Bell passes over the fact that the legitimacy of the CCP is bound up with the communist revolution stretching back to the two crucial years of 1921 and 1949. No matter how much things have changed since the start of the reform four decades ago, the CCP itself has not given up its communist revolutionary legacy. This fact alone means that Bell's argument for political meritocracy solely in terms of performance legitimacy is seriously skewed by removing the CCP's self-professed foundational element of its legitimacy from the equation.

The second reason why Bell's argument is insufficiently political is that he proceeds on the openly stated assumption that China's one-party political system is, in his words, "not about to collapse." Bell says that one can simply make this assumption and "argue for improvements on that basis."[12] I think this is less prudent than a political argument should be. If (a big "if") this assumption is correct, Bell's entire argument becomes quite plausible and persuasive, at least to some—which makes this a crucial assumption. I have my own reasons for questioning this assumption, as presented elsewhere in this chapter and in Chapter 2. But here it suffices to defer to the CCP itself, which is obviously conducting its business on an assumption very different from Bell's, and this fact deserves to be taken seriously. The party's own assumption is seldom named but is implicit in the scale and intensity of its current measures to strengthen its "political security" *(zhengzhi anquan)*, from which it is not difficult to glimpse a corresponding lack of certainty regarding regime perpetuation.

It is necessary therefore to bring politics—or more politics—into Bell's argument and see what results from this change. To this end, one must first try to pin down what it is that we, including Bell, must be talking about when we speak of meritocracy in the current Chinese context. The CCP was not set up, in 1921, as a meritocratic organization in the sense in which we are using the term *meritocracy* today. Nor even did it come to power, as the founder of the People's Republic of China in 1949, as a meritocratic organization. It was a Leninist vanguard party, but that is totally different from what Bell means by *meritocracy*. According to his understanding of meritocracy, the party mutated into a meritocracy only in the reform era, especially after the reform got its second lease on life in 1992. For, from that point on, it started to pursue economic growth with grim determination and, initially and for quite some time thereafter, at all cost. The result was not only stunningly rapid and sustained economic growth but also, more important for our purposes, a renewed legitimacy for the CCP. Since this revived legitimacy clearly bears some important causal relation to good economic and other performance, it has come to be called performance legitimacy. Bell's name for it is "political meritocracy."

The problem with political meritocracy as explained by Bell is that it is too vague a concept in its semantic relation to legitimacy. Some clarification is needed and can be facilitated by my distinction between *enhancement of legitimacy* through good performance and *amelioration of a lack of legitimacy* through good performance, as drawn earlier in this chapter. I think what Bell means when he talks about CCP-style meritocracy is best understood as what I am calling legitimacy enhancement through good performance. The matter becomes clearer still if we make a slight terminological adjustment and call it legitimacy enhancement *through meritocracy,* meritocracy being a matter of good performance.

The point of translating Bell's notion of meritocracy is to show that meritocracy cannot stand alone—that is, cannot serve as its own source of legitimacy. Rather, meritocracy finds its precondition in some already more or less legitimate political arrangement, and it finds an important element of its usefulness in contributing to the enhancement of the legitimacy in question. We misunderstand meritocracy, as meant by Bell, if we think that it is self-sufficient or that it *is* legitimacy itself. Meritocracy is nothing but a way of doing things—involving institutions and personnel—that reliably produces good performance, however good performance is understood in a legitimate political order in the first place. As such, meritocracy is only of secondary importance—because it is parasitic on legitimacy.

By the same token, meritocracy is also not on the same level as democracy and is thus, strictly speaking, not fit to be pitted against democracy, or mixed with it. After all, democracy is first and foremost a principle of government—a way of conferring legitimacy on government, not merely a method of producing the personnel to administer a political unit at whatever level. The village-level elections that Bell talks about have little to do with legitimacy: they are a procedure for producing officials at the grassroots level and derive their seeming legitimacy-engendering function from endorsement higher up the chain of command, ultimately from the CCP's authorization. Bell is definitely not talking about a mixed regime on the model of Aristotle or Polybius.

This, then, is what I think Bell means—or must mean if his overall argument is to make clear sense: namely, that the real alternatives, in the Chinese context, are not democracy versus meritocracy but democracy (as a basis of legitimacy) versus communist one-party rule (as a basis of legitimacy). When Bell argues for meritocracy in China, therefore, he is actually pitting communist one-party rule against democracy and favoring the former. This does not make him an "apologist" for the CCP, however, but instead the defender of a kind of meritocracy that is made possible by the party. For Bell favors communist one-party rule for a particular reason, and that reason is only that it delivers better performance—of a generically modern and therefore essentially bourgeois kind—than democracy would, at least in the Chinese context. (This is why Bell is indifferent regarding the choice between the current CCP and another CCP, with the second C in the latter standing for Confucian, as the guarantor of meritocracy and would probably favor the latter, other things being equal.) Bell's reasoning may be spelled out thus: in the current Chinese arrangement, meritocracy (performance) helps enhance communist one-party rule (legitimacy), and the latter, in turn, is good at producing and maintaining a meritocracy—in a virtuous circle. It is this combination of two elements that Bell is actually pitting against its alternative, which also consists of two elements—namely, democracy (legitimacy) and the (supposed) relative absence of meritocracy and hence a lower level of performance. One upshot, among others, is that it would not pay to initiate democratic change in China to fix a system that not only isn't broken but is in fact working reasonably well, though not perfectly.

This seems the most plausible way of making sense of Bell's argument for political meritocracy. Thus understood, the argument is vitiated by two assumptions. The first, already noted, is that the CCP is not going to face a potentially fatal legitimation crisis. The second assumption, an unspoken one, is that performance matters more than anything else, which forgets that performance is not legitimacy and that legitimacy matters even more, both in its own right and as a precondition of performance.

Recall my point that China's current meritocracy is parasitic on legitimate communist rule. I earlier first translated Bell's notion of meritocracy as meaning legitimacy enhancement through meritocracy and then showed the enhancement to be reciprocal, in that communist one-party rule also enhances meritocracy. Now, it may be that Bell does not care that much about legitimacy enhancement through meritocracy. For he seems to care rather more about meritocracy enhancement through communist one-party rule. Whatever the case may be, it remains true that meritocracy is parasitic on legitimacy—that is, on the legitimacy of communist one-party rule. Given this dependence, and given that it would not be prudent to rule out the possibility of a legitimation crisis, we must be cognizant of a possible scenario in which the legitimacy of communist one-party rule will drastically weaken or even disappear, leaving meritocracy with little or nothing to be parasitic on.

What then? Bell, in the second appendix to his book, presents a dialogue concerning meritocracy in both a communist form and a Confucian form, which end up being indistinguishable. In so doing, Bell is betraying, ever so subtly, a lack of confidence in his assumption that China's communist one-party rule is rock-solid. Whether the hidden substitute combination—Confucianism as a new basis of legitimacy plus meritocracy—will work is a matter I will take up briefly in Chapter 3.

Good Performance Is Almost as Essential as Legitimacy

Distinguishing between enhancement of legitimacy and amelioration of a lack of legitimacy is a crucial conceptual step in our attempt to pinpoint the crux of the CCP's future legitimation crisis. The most important upshot of this distinction, as we have seen, is the absolute indispensability of a substantial amount of legitimacy in order for good performance to play the highly important role of an additional boost. It follows from this relation between legitimacy and performance that, for the purpose of assessing the likelihood of a serious legitimation crisis in the foreseeable future, it makes the most sense to concentrate on legitimacy, although the impact of performance is by no means negligible. This is what I shall do, but first there is one further step to take in clarifying the relation between legitimacy and performance.

This step involves showing that legitimacy and performance are even more internally related, and hence even more closely related, than I have been able to demonstrate through the notion of inclusive legitimacy—so called, as the reader will recall, because it is natural to think of legitimacy as including some kind of performance that is internally related to it. In other words, every type of legitimacy requires as a basic condition of its fulfillment a certain degree of good performance as defined by the legitimacy in question. What this means is that the performance in question, the performance covered by inclusive legitimacy, has no political meaning or significance apart from the legitimacy to which it organically contributes. For performance is essentially a matter of competence in realizing the shared ends of a society, no matter what these ends happen to be and how they have come to be formed. Since shared ends reflect and are supported by shared values, competence regarding the former also involves, at a deeper level, a reasonable degree of fidelity to the latter. It is only against this background of shared ends and values that there can be such a thing as good performance by a ruler, and, if so, all good performance must be legitimacy enhancing.[13] Incidentally, if this is the case, then the notion of amelioration of a *lack* of legitimacy through *good* performance appears to be a contradiction in terms, and it is therefore necessary to revisit the notion in order to be more exact about what it means and is meant to be used for. This I will do in due course. For now, I want to emphasize that just as with shared ends, so with the shared values underlying them, performance is normally measured with reference to them as they are (more or less) given, or as if they were given. Moreover, because, and to the degree that, they are given and taken for granted, they recede into the background. That is to say, these shared ends and values, which do the work of legitimation, can disappear so much from view as to create the illusion that performance alone is what matters. When we speak of the good performance of the CCP in recent decades, for example, the shared ends and values all revolve around economic growth, rising living standards, and national rejuvenation, against the carefully engineered backdrop of a not-so-distant past of national weakness, individual poverty, and disruptive class struggle. The party has played a leading role, of course, in creating the shared ends and values in the first place, but it is only after a consensus has emerged that we have sufficiently unproblematic and objective-looking standards by which to measure its performance. And it is only competent performance *based on publicly embraced standards* that can serve as a boost to legitimacy. Such legitimacy is made all the more secure if and when those in power are able to effectively articulate the shared ends and values and thereby put their stamp on the legitimacy-giving source, as the CCP seems to be doing in terms of the Chinese Dream.

It is not at all surprising that the legitimacy generated in this way has been considerable. After all, insofar as the CCP is given credit for good performance, this must mean that it has well served the needs, interests, and values of Chinese society as these have evolved in the reform era. It is another matter, a debatable matter, exactly how well it has done so, by public standards, in view of the corruption, inequality, and environmental degradation that have caused so much resentment or dissatisfaction, for these things too have come to belong to the performance dimension of legitimacy in a way not always amenable to the CCP's control. What is clear, and only natural, given the thoroughly *internal* relation between a ruler's good performance and society's values, is that the better the CCP's performance is regarded, the greater its legitimacy will be. Indeed, because of this internal relation, good performance is always required for legitimacy and bad performance is always detrimental to legitimacy. This internal relation between legitimacy and performance, which cuts both ways, makes the uninterrupted maintenance of legitimacy a very tall order indeed. In good times it is possible for the party's performance to be so dazzling that it seems to render the very question of legitimacy superfluous and even invisible, not least given the further fact that the party is already in power and has all the coercive and ideological instruments of state power at its disposal. But it is possible for this to happen, or to imagine it happening, *only for a time,* because maintaining good performance according to existing standards is difficult enough, maintaining consensus about the ends and values by which performance will be judged on an ever-evolving basis can be very tricky in its own way, and maintaining both simultaneously over time is next to impossible under the modern conditions of life. We do not yet know how successful the Chinese Dream will be—as performance, as consensus about ends and values, and as calibration between the two—and it would be premature to count on its unhampered success.

Just remember how Mao's earnestly pursued communist project came to grief. Unlike the goals and aspirations of the reform initiated by Deng, communism did not emerge with much (credible appearance of) spontaneity from within Chinese society. Instead, for better or worse, it was overtly imposed on Chinese society as a goal toward which, upon the CCP's seizure of power in 1949, the entire people had henceforth to move whether they liked it or not. As such, communism was no ordinary end and value but a *telos,* an overarching goal with Reason and Science and History on its side. It thus provided not merely a mundane and contingent standard for what was to count as competent performance but, well beyond this, something so unimpeachably grounded and so ultimately important as to give meaning and purpose to everything else—including political power. It was the CCP's resounding answer to the question of why it, the *Communist* Party, was alone fit to wield political power. One of the most striking features of a teleological notion of legitimacy is that good performance is so closely bound up with it as to be hardly distinct, and this means that bad performance will sooner or later bring down the telos itself and all the legitimacy based on it. This, indeed, has been the fate of the teleological legitimacy that the CCP was able to construct for itself at a time when it believed in communism and, naming itself accordingly, believed in its ability to deliver the goods. The result was a distinctive legitimation crisis, a crisis of perceived *bad performance* as measured by the communist telos. In the end, it was disappointing performance, not so much the cognitive discrediting of the telos itself, that brought the Mao era to an end, rendering a major new departure necessary and forming the basis of the consensus around which Deng's reform was launched.[14]

This is where we are today. Mao's communism may have been discontinued, revolution may have been given up as a means of accomplishing society's ends and values, and the teleological conception of legitimacy may have been filled with new content, such as the Chinese Dream, that is massively depoliticized compared with the old communist telos. But today's CCP still rules by a logic that makes legitimacy and performance so mutually dependent that the party-state is simultaneously and equally vulnerable to legitimation problems and performance problems. Indeed, serious performance problems cannot but be legitimation problems, and vice versa. And, as I have already suggested, such problems can occur not only in the form of inadequate performance with reference to taken-for-granted ends and values but also at the level where ends and values are determined and calibrated with performance. It is only in this comprehensive light that we can properly appreciate the double shortfall, mentioned at the start of this chapter, in all its gravity.

The Paradox of Legitimacy

I must now make a digression in order to prevent a possible misunderstanding—and also to further bring out, by means of a contrast, the special character of the CCP's systemic vulnerability to legitimation crises. Nothing in the previous section must be taken to imply that legitimacy and performance are *necessarily* so tightly joined together that they must stand or fall together. All I was claiming is that this extremely close relationship is true of the CCP—the CCP of today no less than the CCP under Mao—and that this makes the one-party rule in China extremely fragile and costly to maintain. The crux of the matter, as we have seen, is too close a connection between legitimacy and performance. It is, paradoxically, precisely for this reason that an inclusive legitimacy like China's must learn how to rely for its durability on a normative source—legitimacy in a strict, narrower sense— that is to a significant degree independent of contingent performance. This paradox gives the tall order confronting the Chinese political system a twist that the CCP has so far shown little willingness to face up to.

I have noted that the CCP still enjoys a substantial level of legitimacy amounting to the right to rule. This right is one that the party has been able to maintain without interruption since 1949, and it should come as no surprise that the party is so used to ruling, and the country is so used to being ruled by it, that political power in communist China has acquired a nearly de facto—that is, objective and unquestioned—character. It is simply a fact of life. The leading position of the CCP is so much taken for granted— positively endorsed or grudgingly conceded or numbly treated as close to a natural phenomenon—that, except for brief periods such as those in 1957 and 1989, there has been a nearly universal lack of motivation, belief, and agency when it comes to challenging the CCP's hold on state power. Small wonder, then, that maintaining the party's legitimacy has come to seem entirely a matter of performance. The extremely close relation between legitimacy and performance is understood—misunderstood—through the eclipse of the more important part of the equation. The prior question of the right to rule has simply been preempted or bracketed, almost in the manner of conservation of energy, including intellectual energy.

The problem is that this cannot last forever, if only because of the enormous difficulty of meeting all the requirements for maintaining the CCP's kind of inclusive legitimacy—and because the only effective way of responding to this difficulty is the paradoxical move of developing an alternative, narrower source of legitimacy more or less uncoupled from performance. The need for such a source is already evident in the CCP's proneness to legitimation crises. As the CCP's inclusive legitimacy continues to decline, this need will only grow stronger.

The alternative source is required not to show how well those *already authorized* (or, more strongly put, justified) *to be in power* are using that power to serve public ends but rather to make clear why they are authorized to be in power in the first place. In other words, it speaks to legitimacy *ex ante* rather than performance *ex post*—to the normative origin or basis of political power regardless of performance as long as the latter is lawful. Legitimacy in this sense is whatever is *"ex ante* effective in legitimating decisions."[15] Since decisions are a matter of performance, legitimacy is whatever is *ex ante* effective in legitimating performance and is, ipso facto, independent of performance. I am tempted to describe this as *exclusive legitimacy* (exclusive of performance) in contrast with inclusive legitimacy, provided that we bear in mind that performance does not thereby cease to impinge on legitimacy in important ways short of undermining it altogether.

I hasten to note that I am simplifying the matter, for now, by understanding legitimacy in terms of the *normative* origin or foundation of political power. As a matter of fact, this origin or foundation could also be cosmological or sacred and in either way would go beyond what is usually regarded as normative. I am leaving aside the cosmological or sacred for my present purposes because I take it, pending further argument, that under modern conditions, and hence under the conditions of Chinese society today, legitimacy is a matter solely of the normative basis of political power.

The notion of exclusive legitimacy just introduced leads to a new distinction between legitimacy and performance that is very different from the one drawn earlier. The earlier distinction, as the reader will recall, is between inclusive legitimacy (inclusive of performance internally related to legitimacy) and freestanding performance (performance without internal relation to legitimacy). By contrast with this earlier distinction, the present one involves a strict, narrower notion of legitimacy whose unique feature is its relative independence from performance, and, correlatively, a notion of performance that is relatively loosely related to legitimacy (although it need not be freestanding). It may have already occurred to the reader that this is the kind of relation between legitimacy and performance that is characteristic of a democratic regime. We know this to be the case because it is possible for a government that enjoys democratic legitimacy (conferred, say, by so-called free and fair elections) to perform badly with regard to what happen to be the main goals of society and still maintain a working minimum of legitimacy and hence stability.

As we also know from the experience of democracies, the notion of inclusive legitimacy is applicable to a democratic regime as well. For a democratic regime, in addition to relying on a strict basis of legitimacy that answers to the need for authorization of state power, can hope to work well only when it is able to back up this legitimacy with a good enough level of performance and, especially, to refrain from acting in ways, even if lawful, that are perceived to undermine society's important ends and values. In this sense, a democratic regime too is under great pressure to secure a reasonable level of performance legitimacy in the form, above all, of publicly acknowledged success in "the purposeful struggle to improve the practical circumstances of life."[16] This combination of strict, exclusive legitimacy and positive performance gives rise to a distinct kind of inclusive legitimacy. We may call it *democratic* inclusive legitimacy in that while the good performance in question is internally, organically related to the legitimacy (hence inclusive legitimacy), its relative shortage will not undermine legitimacy in the way typical of a nondemocratic arrangement (hence democratic legitimacy). Thanks to *this* inclusive legitimacy, then, we have a political regime that is supported on two legs—legitimacy and performance—that are mutually reinforcing when things go well but that do not so easily collapse together when performance happens to be weak. This is the unique strength of democratic inclusive legitimacy, a strength that lies, above all, in the presence within it of a strict, exclusive legitimacy that is relatively self-sufficient and independent and is relatively loosely connected to performance even when the latter organically contributes to it. And this is what China will need if it is to achieve what has so far been the elusive goal of enduring legitimacy and stability.

Performance Legitimacy versus Ideological Legitimacy

Lest we entertain too rosy and unsophisticated a view of the strict, exclusive legitimacy that is part of democratic inclusive legitimacy, I want to propose a further distinction, based on Louis Althusser's account of ideology, between performance legitimacy and *ideological* legitimacy, and place democratic exclusive legitimacy in the latter category. In spelling out this distinction, I also intend to shed further light on the nature and limitations of performance legitimacy.

Althusser, as we have seen, distinguishes between the Repressive State Apparatus (RSA) and the Ideological State Apparatuses (ISAs). It should be easy to see that what we normally call legitimacy—that is, legitimacy proper—is actually ideological legitimacy, in the straightforward sense that it is produced by the ISAs. This notion of ideological legitimacy can of course be used pejoratively and critically by drawing attention to what is false (the preeminence of the dominant class's interest masquerading as the equal interest of all) and functionally reprehensible (the maintenance of class domination) in a claim to legitimacy, however well-grounded the claim may appear to be (thanks to compromises with the less well served classes, backed up with ideological rationalization). Since I am conducting a prudential argument, however, I shall use this notion with a largely descriptive intent, only hinting at its potential for the purpose of ideology critique.

Descriptively, ideological legitimacy entails the existence of ISAs. This simple idea has profound implications. If we recall that the ISAs are largely nonexistent in China, we will immediately realize, in the present context, that the party-state does not, indeed cannot possibly, enjoy ideological legitimacy—what we normally simply call legitimacy. It is for this reason, and because the RSA does not serve as a source of legitimacy as distinct from coercion, that the party-state must rely instead on the so-called performance legitimacy, as a substitute for the unavailable ideological legitimacy. The effectual distinction, then, is that between performance legitimacy and ideological legitimacy. But what exactly is performance legitimacy when viewed in contrast with ideological legitimacy?

Performance legitimacy is definitely not legitimacy produced by the RSA, for that would be a contradiction in terms. Yet it also is not legitimacy engendered by the ISAs, for the latter are nonexistent in China, as already noted. Thus, if performance legitimacy is to make any sense, it must be located in a space where positive affects—pleasure, approval, or at least more or less willing acquiescence—are produced without either repression or ideology (in Althusser's strict sense) playing a direct role. There is indeed a space of such affects, and it is characterized, in the advanced global bourgeois civilization of which China has decidedly become a part, by the twin pleasures of possessive individualism and consumerism. Such affects are called, in the CCP's own latest terminology (as briefly discussed in the Introduction), *huodegan,* the sense of acquisitive success, and *xingfugan,* the sense of satisfaction derived from it and from such other sources as ever-expanding opportunities for pleasurable and empowering consumption. In its ability to produce such affects for the swelling ranks of the middle classes, and to use such affects to channel attention and energy away from political concerns, China is second to none. Here then is the basic formula for performance legitimacy: *performance* consists in the steadily rising production of commodities whose acquisition and enjoyment help create positive affects in a population imbued with bourgeois values and aspirations, along with the provision of gainful employment and opportunities for upward social mobility, while *legitimacy* stems from the attribution of such affects and their material condition of possibility to the party-state as leader of prosperity and reeducator of affects.

Thus, the absence of the ISAs need not mean that the party-state maintains its rule by means of the RSA alone. Far from it, for there is little doubt that the bourgeois lifestyle, as distinct from satisfaction of the bourgeois demand for some say in political matters, is itself a powerful instrument of co-optation—even at the hands of the CCP. Indeed, a nominally communist party-state presiding over a largely capitalist economy and an essentially bourgeois society has a special need precisely for this kind of co-optation, which is none other than the so-called performance legitimacy. A liberal democratic capitalist state stands to benefit from such performance legitimacy, too, but it also has at its disposal the ISAs, which are useful for times good and bad, but especially for bad times. The CCP, by contrast, has cornered itself into a position of having to do without the ISAs, and that is why performance legitimacy is so indispensable and why good economic performance in particular looms so extraordinarily large in its political calculations. This is a fact rich in ironies, for performance legitimacy in today's world is essentially bourgeois legitimacy and, as it happens, the CCP relies on it to a degree far surpassing the degree to which the traditional capitalist states do. Because the latter's capitalism differs from China's so-called state capitalism by virtue of their liberal democracy, they feature an abundant array of ISAs and can therefore afford to have less, or less desperate, recourse to the purely bourgeois performance legitimacy that has come to underpin China's self-professed communist rule.

To think of performance legitimacy in this way—as purely bourgeois—is to locate it squarely in society—that is, in bourgeois society—in the capitalist mode of production. Viewed thus, performance legitimacy, while accruing to those who govern, does not reside in the state, for it is produced by neither the RSA nor the ISAs, the latter nonexistent in China in any case. If there is any sense at all in treating performance legitimacy as a species of legitimacy, it has to be because, while only ideological legitimacy is legitimacy proper, performance legitimacy has something in common with it that is far from negligible. That is, while such things as lifestyle and fashion, real estate ownership and stock market speculation, entertainment and tourism, and the rest of consumerism do not exactly win hearts and minds in the absence of the appropriate, voluntarily embraced interpretations typically produced by the ISAs, and for this reason are not themselves ideological, they nevertheless perform a function of pacification that is to some degree (but only to some degree) shared by ideology. This is what performance legitimacy is all about: pacification through the material production of positive affects, including pleasure and visceral approval, rather than the discursive production of consensus and consent, the latter being the mode of operation specific to ideological legitimacy.

The nature and effects, on the one hand, and the limitations, on the other, of performance legitimacy derive from, respectively, its overlap in function with and its difference in mode of operation from ideological legitimacy. Such limitations need not preclude the sublimation of performance legitimacy into some semblance of ideological legitimacy, as can happen, for example, through the reconceptualization of individual prosperity and pleasure in terms of national wealth and glory. But such sublimation is hamstrung by the absence of the ISAs.

This is not just a matter of sublimation—say, into love of country—necessarily failing to rest on a communicatively secured basis of shared reasons and thereby to both temper and solidify affect with cognition. For what performance legitimacy is also incapable of producing in terms of positive affects is the all-important sense of civic agency, as distinct from the truncated, atomistic sense of agency accessible to the consumer of commodities or the possessor of property. In a broadly capitalist order such as China shares with the so-called free world, only ideological legitimacy is able to accommodate a sense of civic agency, and, when it does that, it has to rely not only on the ISAs, as strictly construed by Althusser, but also on democratic institutions. In this connection, one may choose to follow Antonio Gramsci in employing the distinction between the state and civil society, thereby at least implicitly allowing for a greater potential autonomy of civil society from the state than is granted by Althusser. Alternatively, one may prefer to use Althusser's distinction between the RSA and the ISAs, thereby viewing the relationship between bourgeois civil society and the capitalist state as ultimately one of subordination. As far as my present purposes are concerned, there is no need to choose between Gramsci and Althusser, for what would remain unaffected is the need to appreciate the decisive role of democratic institutions in creating and sustaining a sense of civic agency. There is also no doubt that a plausible and widespread sense of civic agency is part and parcel of ideological legitimacy. Even if we opt for Gramsci's distinction and locate this part of ideological legitimacy on the side of the state rather than civil society, the latter roughly corresponding to Althusser's ISAs, there need be no inconsistency in attributing to the state, as conceived by Gramsci in contradistinction to civil society, a decisive role in the creation of ideological legitimacy. What matters, for our purposes, is just that a sense of civic agency is an indispensable element of ideological legitimacy under modern conditions, and that democracy is a necessary condition for giving plausibility to civic agency and therefore for supporting a sense of civic agency.

More generally, to use Althusser's terms, ideological legitimacy depends on a ratio of power and visibility between the RSA and the ISAs that leaves ample room for the latter: other things being equal, the more the ratio favors the ISAs (without of course ever outweighing the RSA), the greater will be the strength of sheer ideological legitimacy. What is important to add is that the existence of political institutions of democracy, however they fit into Gramsci's and Althusser's different conceptual schemes, will tilt the balance further still in favor of ideology as distinct from repression.

It is of course not difficult to imagine that, even in the absence of civic agency, the spread of individual prosperity and enjoyment can help feed a collective sense of strength and approbation bordering on a conscious love of country that typically could only be produced with the aid of the ISAs. But inasmuch as a sense of *civic* agency is missing, there can be little truly *agential* appropriation of whatever is positive about one's nation. This means that the resulting love of country will be disproportionately dependent on perceived benefits and, in this sense, essentially opportunistic. It is surely improbable that such fair-weather patriotism, as it were, would be sufficiently deep and durable to serve as an effective replacement for the absence of ideological legitimacy.

Indeed, what is true of an opportunistic love of country is true of performance legitimacy in general, sublimated or not. That is why the CCP's current formula for regime stability and perpetuation cannot be counted on to work indefinitely—and why the lasting solution is not to maintain performance legitimacy alone as much as possible, important as this is, but to add ideological legitimacy to the state's repertoire. It bears repeating that ideological legitimacy, as distinct from the crude propaganda effects achievable by the RSA, presupposes the existence and proper functioning of the ISAs in general, and that the civic component of such legitimacy requires credible democratic institutions in particular.

CHAPTER TWO

The Question of Regime Perpetuation

WE ARE NOW IN A POSITION to look more closely at the substance of the legitimation crisis soon to be faced by the Chinese Communist Party (CCP). One idea previously explored has crucially prepared the ground: the hypothesis that the future of the party-state's legitimacy and the shape and timing of any legitimation crisis will be determined chiefly by the trajectory of the CCP's communist revolutionary legacy rather than by contingencies of its performance. So it is on the growing weakness of this legacy that I shall focus, by examining the various crisis tendencies in which it is already manifesting itself. These tendencies are especially worth investigating because they have the distinct potential to escalate into a full-blown legitimation crisis, not least for posing an unprecedented challenge to regime continuation at or near the next leadership succession.

Since my aim is to assess the likelihood of a potentially fatal legitimation crisis in the foreseeable future, it is advisable to exercise due caution by proceeding on two assumptions: first, that the CCP still enjoys a substantial amount of its old communist revolutionary legitimacy; second, that the party will be more or less able to maintain its current level of economic performance (with, say, only gradually and moderately decreasing growth, compensated by higher-quality growth), although in reality it may not. The second assumption, holding the CCP's performance roughly constant at its current level, will help concentrate the mind on the implications of waning revolutionary legitimacy. It will also provide a suitably tough test for the prognosis that a terminal crisis affecting this legitimacy will be enough by itself to cause a comprehensive legitimation crisis of unprecedented magnitude.

A natural way to begin unpacking this looming crisis is to revisit the notion of amelioration of a lack of legitimacy through good performance, a notion that at this point needs further clarification. As we have seen, given the extremely close relation between good performance and a society's shared ends and values, good performance is invariably legitimacy enhancing. It seems to follow that the very notion of amelioration of a *lack* of legitimacy through *good* performance is a contradiction in terms. If we nevertheless have reason to retain this notion, as I think we do, it is necessary to spell out exactly what it means and is useful for. I have already given a hint of its usefulness, and that is the rather uncertain character of such legitimacy as the CCP still seems to enjoy. It is next to impossible to ascertain what proportion of what we are observing in China at this moment is legitimacy enhancement and what proportion is mere amelioration. Indeed, this has been the case for a long time, probably stretching all the way back, to one degree or another, to the time of Deng Xiaoping.

We do not have to look far to find the reason, residing as it does in a fundamental and obvious series of facts about the reform first launched by Deng and still in progress: that the CCP has initiated and carried out the reform; that the reform has taken the country a very long way from its communist revolutionary origins, whatever the exact degree to which China has ended up capitalist today; and that the party has nevertheless been determined to maintain its public, official identity as a communist party and the public, official identity of China as a socialist country. Given the undeniable, at least partially (say, partially capitalist, partially not; partially state capitalist, partially otherwise capitalist) capitalist reality on the ground, the CCP's ideological interpretation of the reform and its stubborn self-description in socialist terms were already stretching credulity to the breaking point at least as far back as Jiang Zemin's reign. What we have been witnessing for quite some time is the decisive breach of any credible link between reality and official description. Since the description in question has to do with the nature of China's political and social identity, and, by the same token, of the CCP's own identity, this breach cannot but be a momentous disruption of public belief in what the party stands for—indeed possibly in the party in its entirety. However great its achievements in the reform era, and however much credit it has received from the populace as a result, there can be little doubt that the CCP has lost itself in the process. It has lost its old self and not yet found a new self. And it is difficult to imagine it fashioning a credible new identity for itself that remains unambiguously socialist or communist without reversing the broad sweep of what the reform has been about. As things stand, we have to say that the CCP no longer has a publicly understood and accepted identity; what it says about its identity—about this identity in its double relation to Marxism, on the one hand, and to the reality on the ground, on the other—is simply not plausible. The master narrative it has cobbled together, from one leadership to the next, does not command much credence. Given what is at stake, this is nothing less than a crisis—a *plausibility crisis*.

The Plausibility Crisis

What is at stake is the CCP's legitimacy. True, the party has been able to keep up an incredible level of performance in the reform era. True, this must mean, given the nature of the link between good performance and society's ends and values, that the party has massively contributed to the realization of Chinese society's ends and values—in addition to helping create those ends and values in the first place. True, given the inseparability of realizing society's ends and values, on the one hand, and boosting the ruler's legitimacy, on the other, all of this must have translated into genuine legitimacy for the CCP. This is one reason why I am prepared to attribute a substantial amount of lingering legitimacy, of the right to rule, even to the CCP of today. Despite all this, there are nagging doubts about the exact relation in which the party stands to Chinese society's ends and values. For all that the party has itself helped give shape to these ends and values, it is highly implausible that they are communist, or even socialist, ones.

Under Mao Zedong, revolutionary legitimacy drew its meaning and power from a mixture of many elements. Mao's rule was both *charismatic* and *traditional* (to use Max Weber's terms), with a revolutionary leader supported by an openly Leninist vanguard and a hidden (because superficially rejected) Confucian paternalism. Substantively, it was *eschatological* (a particular instantiation of the teleological, with communism all but envisioned as paradise on earth, achievable in real time rather than in the fictitious space of heaven), *proletarian centered* (dictatorship of the proletariat), *scientific/rationalistic* and hence *performance oriented* (scientific socialism, modernization, catching up with the West, and so on), and *nationalist* (anti-imperialism and—setting the Chinese revolution apart from its Russian forerunner—national independence, or *minzu duli,* as well as a cleansing of the shame of humiliation suffered since the Opium War). Of these elements, the charismatic, the eschatological, and the proletarian are, with the death of Mao and of communism and the rise of capitalism, completely gone—the equivalent of removing Christ and paradise from Christianity. Still intact and indeed accentuated are the scientific / rationalistic and performance-oriented features, as well as the nationalist, while the traditional is partly making something of a comeback and partly just becoming more explicit. So the CCP now has a legitimation formula, as it were, that essentially comprises only the scientific / rationalistic, performance-oriented, and nationalist—with the traditional playing a secondary, somewhat ambivalent role, and with the charismatic and the eschatological figuring only as mnemonic and rhetorical remnants. Missing too is the moral ethos of liberation—liberation *of* the proletariat, above all, and *from,* among other things, an emergent *guanliao zibenzhuyi* (comprador-bureaucratic capitalism, the pre-1949 counterpart of today's crony capitalism) and remnants of a supposed *fengjianzhuyi* (feudalism), of which Confucianism was considered a part—that used to pervade the CCP's old legitimation discourse. The result is not merely a truncation of the old communist revolutionary legitimacy but its positive evisceration. For the scientific / rationalistic, performance-oriented, and nationalist features used to find their meaning in the eschatological—and in revolution (including the charismatic revolutionary leader) as the pathway to it—and now, with the eschatological and the revolutionary effectively abandoned, they cease to be what they once were. We are left, without fanfare or even acknowledgment, with a new legitimation formula—the combination of economic success and national rejuvenation—that bears little relation to the CCP's old communist teleological-revolutionary identity.

The CCP knows this full well. All it takes to square the circle is to decide whether it *is* a square or a circle—to adjust its identity to the new ends and values of Chinese society (and own up to the resultant identity change) or else to attempt to transform those ends and values into greater consistency with its self-professed identity. Neither option is viable, however, because the second option is ruled out by the very nature and direction of the reform, which has itself reached a point of no return, and because the first option would amount to political suicide, at least at this point in time. With so much of its being and fortune inextricably tied to its communist revolutionary origins, the CCP cannot simply walk away from its no longer coherent public self-understanding as a *communist* party. It would be sheer folly and recklessness to do so simply because this self-understanding has become incoherent and implausible.

Yet the CCP cannot avoid paying a heavy price for this incoherence and implausibility, which is why the price deserves to be called a plausibility crisis. The price is an ineradicable uncertainty over the party's legitimacy—over how much legitimacy it enjoys, indeed whether it really does enjoy much legitimacy in the first place. This is, above all, because there is no clear, unmistakable political agent—that is, one with a clear, unmistakable identity—to whom legitimacy can be attributed. While helping realize society's ends and values is undoubtedly productive of legitimacy, it is by no means a simple and straightforward matter, given the peculiarities of the Chinese situation, how the party can reap full benefit from this fact. This means that the CCP's good performance may not be as legitimacy enhancing as it appears at first sight. By the same token, we cannot be entirely certain that what appears to be legitimacy enhancement is not in fact mere amelioration of a lack of legitimacy. The line is not so clear because the CCP's identity as the performer of positive deeds is not so clear.

I noted in the discussion of legitimacy enhancement versus mere amelioration that we must be witnessing both in ever-evolving proportions; it is thus a matter of determining what the reality on the ground happens to be at any given time. Which of these two scenarios we are inclined to see at any given moment is dependent not only on the reality on the ground but also on how we are disposed to view that reality. Since, in a case of clearly identifiable good performance, neither the good performance itself nor its contribution to society's ends and values is in doubt, and only the exact identity of the CCP is, it must largely be a matter of interpretation whether we are witnessing enhancement of legitimacy or mere amelioration of a lack of legitimacy. It is, to a significant degree, a matter of what we think of the CCP, especially how closely we are inclined to tie its identity to its legitimacy.

There is little doubt that it matters a great deal how good the performance happens to be when we make the judgment. The more impressive the CCP's performance, it seems, the less rigorous or squeamish we tend to be in our instinctive demand for plausibility when it comes to the tension between the CCP's public self-understanding and the reality on the ground, especially if we are clear beneficiaries of the good performance in question. This could be a matter of the relative flexibility of our demand for plausibility or perhaps of fluctuation in how greatly plausibility matters to us. Whichever is the case, and the two actually shade into each other, there can be little doubt that the CCP's ambiguous and elusive identity makes any judgment about its legitimacy both difficult and unstable.

But such judgment we must make, and this task is made easier if we maintain a conceptually clear distinction between enhancement of legitimacy through good performance and amelioration of a lack of legitimacy through good performance, for all the reasons adduced in Chapter 1. Those reasons still stand; what has changed is only the realization, which is only to be expected, that interpretation, not just the reality being judged, is an important factor affecting our judgment. As a matter of fact, interpretation always plays a role in judgments of legitimacy, so, to be more precise, what is special about the case at hand is that, given the exceptional amorphousness or ambiguity of the CCP's identity, interpretation plays an even larger role than usual. This makes whatever legitimacy the party may still enjoy shakier and more uncertain than it would otherwise be. Also left standing is my judgment that the party still enjoys a considerable degree of legitimacy, making it possible that much of what good performance is doing is still legitimacy enhancement as distinct from mere amelioration. I hold this judgment because there are independent reasons, as already noted, for considering the CCP still to command the right to rule. It is no accident that this mandate is closely related to what remains of the CCP's identity as rooted in its communist revolutionary past.

The Crisis of "Revolutionary Spirit"

Rooted in its communist revolutionary past? After all, communism—the striving for communism—is a crucial part of that revolutionary past and, as such, has completely lost its plausibility as the CCP's public self-description. This is part of the plausibility crisis. So how can the revolutionary past still retain any resonance and potency when it is hollowed out with the cessation of the communist project?

An important part of the answer is that the CCP's revolutionary past has three dimensions: its form is teleological; its (teleological) content is communism; and its means of execution, including the mentality of its participants, is revolution. What is most important for this discussion is that these dimensions, while inextricably linked under Mao's leadership, are distinct and can be separated. Thus it is that, although communism as the (teleological) content of the revolutionary past is dead, the revolution itself, as a way of acting and feeling, still retains part of its old aura. Traits fostered by revolutionary war and its aftermath include strength of will, willfulness, toughness, discipline, harsh instincts, grim determination, habituation to primitive relations of authority, the readiness to resort to violence, a callousness regarding means and human cost in general, and an apparent loftiness of spirit as manifest in courage and self-sacrifice. All of these were motivated by or channeled through ostensible belief in the great cause of communism, which provided reasons both for brutality against enemies (and one's own comrades) and for self-sacrifice. Those who participated in the revolution, including its more peaceful post-1949 phase still under the leadership of Mao, were shaped as much by the sheer experiential aspect of the revolution as by its ostensible communist content—indeed much more so.

The era of reform has seen the parting of these two dimensions of the CCP's revolutionary past. With the communist content gradually but decisively left behind, successive leaderships of the party since Deng have nevertheless managed to retain something of the old "revolutionary spirit" *(geming jingshen)*—pure or disembodied revolutionary spirit, one might say, because its erstwhile substance is completely taken out. This remnant of the pure revolutionary spirit is the necessary psychological-characterological accompaniment to the CCP's right to rule today. Not that this lingering revolutionary spirit is without substance—the Chinese Dream, for example, is part of its new substance—but what gives the current leadership the strength of will and toughness of mind absolutely necessary for asserting the exclusive right to rule is what remains of the revolutionary spirit itself.

Only those who still abundantly partake of this spirit have any chance of success in acquiring and maintaining enough intraparty legitimacy to contain internecine factionalism, the Achilles heel of a Leninist party, as the CCP has been able to do since 1949. And only they will have the toughness and audacity to suppress another June 4. These manifestations of the right to rule, indeed the *will* to rule, come, above all, from the substantial remnant of the revolutionary spirit. Of course, the CCP's impressive record of economic performance in the reform era must have lent extra strength to its will to rule, as has its new agenda, "the great rejuvenation of the Chinese nation," which has replaced the old communist one. But no amount of good performance by itself will do the trick, keeping intraparty factionalism under control and creating the credible appearance of the will to prevent or, if necessary, put down a rebellion like June 4.

Where, then, is the crisis of the revolutionary spirit? The answer: in the foreseeable future. For the material and political conditions of life that had created and sustained the revolutionary spirit essentially came to an end with the passing of Mao, and it did not take long thereafter for what had remained of such conditions to dissipate almost completely. From then on, the days of the revolutionary spirit were numbered. It was largely a function of experience and memory how long the revolutionary spirit's new, dematerialized lease on life beyond Mao would last. Now, with the almost complete passing of leaders tested by revolutionary war and ennobled by communist victory, we are seeing the dematerialization of the revolutionary spirit in a further sense and truly its last gasp.

Bluntly put, as far as its impact on Chinese politics is concerned, the revolutionary spirit will come to an end with Xi. This is not merely because he possesses a unique combination of personal attributes but, far more important, because he belongs to a generation of leaders whose exit from the political stage will mark a true inflexion point in the CCP's collective experience and memory. This generation—those now in their sixties—is the last still able to help themselves substantially to the revolutionary spirit for purposes of legitimacy. It is the last generation still in remotely plausible contact with the CCP's "original aspiration" *(chuxin),* as referred to in the party's most prominent current maxim, "Stay true to the original aspiration" *(Buwang chuxin).* If the exact substance of "the original aspiration" (communism) has surely lost its resonance, the revolutionary spirit that constitutes its affective and characterological dimension is something else. The latter retains some of its potency if we understand it not so much in political and ideological terms as in the form of a certain toughness of mind and nerve when it comes to defending the CCP's right to rule at all cost. This toughness has a great deal to do with the organic link that Xi's generation has to the revolutionary violence that brought the party to power in 1949—a link made possible by substantial direct exposure to the first-generation revolutionaries, especially on the part of the sons and daughters of these revolutionaries *(hong erdai)*. The fact that Xi is among those sons and daughters, backed and emboldened by many just like him, makes a huge difference, not least in terms of self-confidence and sense of entitlement, stakes and resolve, and habits of struggle and leadership still substantially rooted in the past.

Indeed, this lineage is in turn supported by the culturally ingrained, and not particularly Marxist, belief that those who have seized power through the barrel of a gun have a prima facie title to rule it (until their Mandate of Heaven runs out). In this sense the revolutionary spirit is, in its last gasp today, none other than a lingering ethos in which the scions of the People's Republic of China's founders are still able to maintain a reasonably strong right to rule. It is an open secret that this bloodline is the principal repository of the revolutionary spirit, such as it is. If the right to rule based on an unspoken revolutionary bloodline obviously still commands substantial deference, it is no less obvious how grudging that deference has become. All signs indicate that this right will not extend, even to the slightest degree, to the grandchildren of the country's founders, not least because the latter have grown up in a reform era that has seen revolution make way for capitalism. One of the most predictable yet fatal by-products of the reform is that the revolutionary spirit no longer has a movement or project as its body. Its only remaining host is the experience and memory of Xi's generation. What reason is there to doubt that the CCP's right to rule, based in large part on the politico-cultural capital of violent seizure of power, and most immediately reflected in the very will to rule, will end with Xi and his generation?

With the revolutionary spirit and the concomitant confidence and strength of will gone, the nature and ethos of Chinese politics will have changed beyond recognition when the time comes for the next batch of leaders to take over. They will be a different breed of leaders who, without the intangible benefit of the revolutionary spirit, will find it much more challenging to maintain intraparty legitimacy and legitimacy in the country at large. They will lack strong political authority of the kind now possessed by Xi and, especially, lack the will to act decisively in a possible repeat of the Bo Xilai challenge or, especially, of June 4. It is at such junctures that the crisis of the revolutionary spirit will make its formidable impact felt.

Two Crisis Scenarios Due to the Waning of Revolutionary Spirit

One must not make the naïve mistake, however, of assuming that ordinary Chinese people care much about such things, indeed about the legitimacy of the political power ruling them. All Chinese cannot but be concerned with how their lives are affected by the exercise of political power, and hence they are not indifferent to the performative success or failure of their government. But they take more than a passing interest in the legitimacy of their government only under extraordinary circumstances. They do so, that is, only when their daily lives come under exceptional strain or threat and when, moreover, a heightened level of fear or resentment is mobilized through effective articulation and organization by some of the more morally sensitive or politically resourceful members of their society. It is unlikely, however, that, when the occasion presents itself, the latter will step forward mainly from outside the ranks of the CCP itself, or that, if they do, they will have much of an impact by themselves. No popular uprising will succeed without the acquiescence of, or significant internal division among, powerful elements within the party itself.

In order to maintain the legitimacy of its rule over the country, then, the CCP must first continue to enjoy legitimacy within its own ranks, especially at the higher echelons. The legitimacy that matters most is intraparty legitimacy, and hence the most dangerous decline is that of intraparty legitimacy. Herein lies the CCP's most daunting challenge, one that has become public knowledge since Bo's dramatic downfall. With the partial exception of this publicly aired intraparty conflict, it is next to impossible to get an accurate and intimate sense of how this challenge is working itself out at the higher levels of the party, given the closely guarded inner workings of political power in China. But what we do know is ominous enough. First, there can be little doubt that intraparty legitimacy will be increasingly difficult to maintain—in all probability dramatically so after the current leadership steps down. When we speak of the CCP's declining legitimacy, we will fully appreciate the seriousness of the situation only if we bear in mind that the chief and most consequential manifestation of this decline is within the party itself. In this regard, the apparent success of Xi's attempts to impose party discipline and cohesion, to extract intraparty loyalty, and thereby to halt the slide in intraparty legitimacy gives little ground for hope on behalf of the CCP if one takes into account the extraordinary measures, not least the awesome anti-corruption campaign, needed for such success—and the extraordinarily powerful leader, Xi, needed to force such measures through. Second, it is reasonable to think that intraparty legitimacy will be even harder to keep intact than legitimacy in the country at large, if only because those within the party tend to be much better informed about the party's vulnerabilities and the precariousness of its seeming cohesion. This awareness increases the higher up one is in the party hierarchy, with those at or near the top having access to information that affords them a holistic appreciation of the major crisis tendencies, along with the personal risks they face as leading members of the ruling elite. It is difficult to imagine the party leadership after Xi being able to confidently maintain intraparty legitimacy once the revolutionary spirit and the aura of revolutionary violence have ceased to play any role in the collective psychology of the CCP.

This predictable dip in intraparty legitimacy upon Xi's retirement will make the party ever more vulnerable in the face of two potential scenarios. In the first scenario, we see the all too familiar undoing of a strongman's work after his demise or departure, letting loose the factionalism and disunity hitherto contained with an iron fist. We then see this more or less spontaneous implosion turn into a self-conscious legitimation crisis within the CCP's own ranks, reflecting as it must the resurfacing of the party members' awareness, up to this point repressed or otherwise denied expression, of the CCP's critical lack of legitimacy in the country at large. The rest is also easy to imagine: an intraparty legitimation crisis creates the occasion for the release of a hitherto suppressed and pent-up sense of legitimation crisis enveloping the entire society, followed by all manner of outward manifestations, including possible protests and demonstrations of a kind that most have been too afraid even to publicly contemplate since 1989. What it is reasonable to imagine happening next will depend largely on how a post-Xi CCP openly caught up in crisis is disposed to react.

This brings me to the second scenario, which in a way carries over from the first but can also be approached independently. From among the possible protests and demonstrations in the first scenario, or, alternatively, the numerous "incidents of mass unrest" happening in China every year, one could escalate into a major rallying point for a public outpouring of accumulated grievances that would be difficult to put down without visible blood-shed. If things were to get to this stage, the CCP's will to take decisive action would be severely tested, and one should not be surprised if the prospect of a bloody suppression were to trigger a crisis of intraparty disunity with rather different consequences from those of the events in 1989. Such an unsettling chain of events is unlikely to occur in the near future, for the present leader-ship still obviously has the will to suppress social protests at very consider-able cost. The visibility of this will is itself a powerful deterrent, and it be-speaks a corresponding degree of confidence that the current leadership has in its intraparty legitimacy, as well as in its legitimacy in the country at large. In this context, the will to put down all opposition is part and parcel of the will to rule, which, in turn, is the psychological dimension of the right to rule. But this level of confidence and this level of deterrence cannot continue in-definitely, indeed cannot survive much beyond the next leadership succes-sion. Ever since 1989, the CCP has been rightly fearful of social unrest and acted resolutely on the hard-earned lesson that it cannot afford a repeat of June 4.[1] The present leadership is no exception. The next leadership, however, will inherit the fear but not the resoluteness. There is simply no escaping the fact that a sharp decline in political authority increases the likelihood of so-cial unrest and political agitation and at the same time weakens a regime's will to use violent means to crush a rebellion even when such means are necessary.

The Identity Crisis

First the plausibility crisis involving the original teleological substance of the CCP, then the crisis of the revolutionary spirit—the combined upshot is ominous. In response to this twofold crisis, the party has spared no effort in fashioning for itself a new identity more in tune with the new social and po-litical reality and new popular aspirations. But this cannot be easy. Given the fundamental split between China's new reality and the CCP's historically determined self-description, the party cannot but feel pulled in two directions at the same time. It must, on the one hand, be seen to be sticking steadfastly to its historically given communist identity, this being the only identity it has ever had and can ever have as long as it remains a *communist* party, if only a largely nominal one. The unavoidable result, thanks to the ever-widening gap between this identity and the CCP's at least partially capitalist deeds, is the plausibility crisis already discussed. Thus it is easy to understand why the party must, on the other hand, move obliquely and subtly, yet still visibly, away from its old communist identity in favor of a new identity less jarringly at odds with China's new capitalist reality.

The principal means of this strategic move is the CCP's depoliticization of its teleological form: retaining the teleological form itself but pouring into it a new, less politically specific or distinct substance. Hence, the crucial importance of something like the Chinese Dream. There is no mention of communism in the Chinese Dream, nor even of communism *after* the realization of the Chinese Dream. After all, a Chinese *communist* dream—that is, a communist dream for China alone—would be a contradiction in terms, while a Chinese dream of communism *for the entire world*, admittedly free of self-contradiction, would be tantamount to declaring war on the globalist capitalist order if it is taken seriously. But more importantly, the conspicuous absence of the CCP's foremost defining feature (communism) from its new mission statement ("the great rejuvenation of the Chinese nation") is clearly motivated by the need to overcome the plausibility crisis. The Chinese Dream, covering as it does individual prosperity and happiness (as *huodegan* and *xingfugan* continue to be touted by no less an authority than Xi Jinping), as well as national rejuvenation, is conveniently generic and responsive to the increasingly generic values and aspirations of today's Chinese. This in fact is the source of its appeal. It is a *Chinese* dream and, as such, could be every Chinese man's and woman's dream, not exactly a *communist* party's dream, and definitely not a dream *of communism*. It could just as easily be every Chinese *capitalist's* dream: official propaganda makes no more mention of capitalism's (eventual) demise and replacement—just imagine the shock waves such talk would create in the domestic and global stock markets! Yet this cannot be the be-all and end-all of the Chinese Dream. For the party must have an essential place in this dream, and that is why, despite steering clear, for the most part, of any open invocation of communism, the CCP never tires of linking the Chinese Dream to the crucial year of 1921, the year that saw its founding as an unambiguously communist party. The very mention of the CCP and 1921 in the same breath is a reminder of the original communist identity of what has now morphed into a less politically distinct and more functional organization. If it is imperative for today's CCP to create for itself a new, more flexible identity, it is no less imperative to make sure that this new identity's strong and uninterrupted link to 1921 is not forgotten. The party simply has no other way of renewing an identity that is intimately connected with its unique history and its historically given self-understanding. To be sure, the party has chosen to accentuate the appeal to nationalism in the Chinese Dream at the expense of communism, but this very appeal must be at least implicitly predicated on the incorporation of national rejuvenation into the communist revolutionary master narrative. Otherwise the CCP would in principle be dispensable to the *meaning* of the Chinese Dream and only instrumentally and hence contingently essential for its *realization*. For the CCP, this is definitely not good enough.

Thus it is that the CCP is constantly pulled in two directions—both away from its communist identity and toward it. It cannot maintain a resolute, unambiguous identity that is at once organically linked to its communist past and coherently related to its quasi-capitalist present. Getting too close to its communist past will reinforce the plausibility crisis. On the other hand, moving too far away from this past in the interest of increased coherence with the present will cause the CCP to lose itself, the only self that is compatible with its very name. In this latter case, the implausibility of the party's self-description will undoubtedly be reduced, but only at the cost of a different crisis that is no less serious and debilitating: a *crisis of identity*. Caught between its history and its name, on the one hand, and its new ends and deeds, on the other, the CCP of today knows not what its own identity is, and, in this very important sense, it cannot be said to be doing well *as a regime*. The party cannot decide which crisis is worse—the plausibility crisis or the identity crisis—for each is devastating in its own way and neither can be mitigated without aggravating the other.

Further light can be shed on this dilemma by clarifying the relation between political power and ideological power.[2] Over many decades, the CCP has developed an inflexible, even fixed relation between its political power (as the only organization with the right to rule China) and its ideological power, because the latter is defined and severely limited by the very name and idea of the Chinese *Communist* Party. The CCP can get away with exercising its political (and economic) power in noncommunist ways, but only for so long. It cannot do that indefinitely without undermining the credibility of its ideological power and thereby weakening its position of leadership, which is based on its distinctive combination of political and ideological power. It cannot do so, that is, without causing or worsening a plausibility crisis. What is even more certain is that the party cannot simply dispense with this ideological power—its name and all—for all its inflexibility. For without this unique ideological power, the CCP would stand to lose both its identity and its exclusive claim to political power based on this identity, and for this double loss—an identity crisis and political crisis in one—no gain in ideological flexibility would be able to compensate. Yet a very heavy price will be paid if the CCP, precisely for this reason, sticks to this ideological power, inviting unanswerable criticisms of its uses of political (and economic) power and giving bite to charges, say, of false pretense and hypocrisy regarding what China fundamentally is and is doing. Between the rock (plausibility crisis) and the hard place (identity crisis) there is nowhere to hide, and only constant ducking can delay the shipwreck—but for how long? When all is said and done, the party will have to live or die by the special relation between political and ideological power by which it is defined and empowered and yet in which, to the same degree, it is trapped. The dilemma is now made almost unbearably intense by the certainty that the ideological power associated with the CCP's name will suffer a steady and irreversible decline.

What has prevented this dilemma from getting even worse for the current CCP leadership, as for its three predecessors to one degree or another, is the lingering vitality of the revolutionary spirit. When this spirit is gone, the plausibility crisis and the identity crisis will only grow in intensity and lead to far more serious consequences. Xi Jinping alone stands between today's relative calm and tomorrow's storm.

Xi's Anticorruption Campaign and Its Dilemma

The current leadership took over at a special moment in the progressive deterioration of the moral-political condition of the party and, by natural influence, of the country at large. By 2012, after more than ten years of moral anarchy and reckless self-aggrandizement under Jiang Zemin, followed by another ten years of impotence (including, presumably, impotent good intentions) and inaction under Hu Jintao, the CCP had become truly rotten to the core. Nothing better epitomizes the near-terminal character of the rot than the dramatic fall from grace of Zhou Yongkang, General Guo Boxiong, General Xu Caihou, and Ling Jihua, four truly impactful movers and shakers in Hu's reign who between them had controlled the security apparatus, the military, and the day-to-day running of the party. What was this rot, as evidenced in the shocking malfeasance of these powerful members of the party, but the moral and behavioral manifestation of a near-terminal legitimation crisis? What was the urgency of stopping the rot but the desperate need to prevent it from making a mockery of all of the present-day CCP's claims to the communist revolutionary legacy?

When Xi came on the scene, he was faced with a fundamental choice: allow the rot to continue unto death by following largely in Jiang's and Hu's footsteps or try to stop it, in which case he would have to take a leaf from Mao's book, at least initially.[3] This was the first fork in the road that Xi confronted on his assumption of power. He made the right and harder choice, or so it seems, and he did so, presumably, because he cared in a way that Jiang had not, if only given the different circumstances, and because he was able to amass a degree of power that Hu had sorely lacked. However complex and mixed Xi's motives may have been, there is no denying the singularly momentous significance of his assumption of the party's leadership. For he is the only top CCP leader since Mao—that is to say, the only CCP leader in the entire reform era—who has had both the occasion and the apparent motivation to tackle the party's legitimation crisis as seriously as it deserves and who, in addition, has acquired sufficient power to act on his apparent sense of crisis. It is only in this light that we can adequately grasp (which is not to endorse) the meaning and significance of the anticorruption campaign, the crackdown on dissent, the tightened control over the media, and the intensification of propaganda, all of which add up to a perceived sharp turn to (methodological) Maoism.

What is unique about corruption is that it affects both legitimacy and performance and does so in complex and subtle ways. Whatever one may think of the present leadership and its anticorruption campaign, one has to give it credit for making the only serious and determined attempt to fix the problems of rampant official corruption that have piled up over two decades or longer. These problems require urgent fixing because they are fast destroying the CCP's claim to power and even its sheer power. It is difficult to say how successful the campaign has been, or could realistically be, if only because the amount of corruption that needs fixing is immense. Given the way corruption has operated by creating networks of protective complicity, it is almost inconceivable that significant pockets of integrity and cleanliness exist anywhere at the higher levels of the CCP. This applies not the least to Xi's political enemies, with the result that from its very outset the anticorruption campaign cannot but have been an exercise in killing two birds with one stone—and choosing the right birds, not necessarily (all) the worst birds, to kill. Only a reckless leader with misguided righteousness would target his allies and in the process risk undermining himself and dooming the very fight against corruption. Yet to act otherwise would be arbitrary and be seen as arbitrary, thereby compromising the legitimacy gains of the campaign. And there is nothing like arbitrariness to create an atmosphere of fear in which cadres no longer dare to throw caution to the wind in promoting local economic growth, thereby drawing positive attention to themselves and maximizing their chances of promotion. Whatever may have been the *positive* effects of corruption on economic growth given the alleged absurdity of the state regulatory apparatus and other factors, such effects are now largely gone. This very phenomenon will have a negative impact on the legitimacy of the CCP, depriving it of what has been an effective tool of legitimacy enhancement or amelioration through performative success even while improving its image on the issue of corruption. It is as yet unclear whether the latest strategic shift in emphasis from sheer growth to greener, more balanced, and higher value-added growth will be successful enough to compensate for slower growth.

With all these complications, and there are more, it is both rash to fault the anticorruption campaign and premature to celebrate it. The only thing we know for sure is that China is stuck with it, for better or worse, or perhaps for both better and worse. For once the campaign began, it could not be stopped without encouraging corruption to return with a vengeance, unless it was credibly shown that corruption had been largely rooted out and most of those guilty caught and adequately punished—but everyone knows this to be a near impossibility. Until such evidence is available, the anticorruption drive has to go on for yet another reason: any perceived wavering in determination would betray weakness on the part of the leadership and invite all-around pushback. And as long as the fight against graft continues, so must the purge of enemies and saboteurs that is an integral part of it. Under China's current circumstances, an ongoing anticorruption campaign has to be an ongoing purge, and such a high-stakes combination requires, objectively, an exceptional concentration of power, both for effectiveness and for sheer self-preservation. If the antigraft component of the campaign is commendable and indicative of strength, the element of purge is a clear sign of regime weakness and even danger. Both are uncannily reminiscent of Mao's situation during the Cultural Revolution and the fate of his legacy thereafter.

For now, we can count on Xi to continue this campaign and to maintain the appearance of determination and effectiveness in bringing it to fruition. But there is no telling what is going to happen with the next batch of leaders. To the degree that the present leadership deserves credit (or blame), it is precisely because it is special, because it has gone beyond the call of duty, as it were, and surpassed conventional expectations (unsurprisingly, both for good and for ill). In the authority it has created for itself on the basis of its institutional power and in the way it has used that authority, it has definitely exceeded what could be expected as a matter of course from the political system itself, and exceeded what most observers did expect. The immediately preceding leadership—of Hu Jintao—provides ample proof, and it, rather than the present one, exercised a degree of political authority closer to what one has reason to expect in the age of postcommunist political cynicism and irreverence. But, after Xi, even Hu would be an impossible act to follow, given the progressive worsening of the plausibility and identity crises and especially the fast-receding revolutionary spirit. No one in their right mind would bet on the respectable clout of Hu, let alone the unexpectedly high authoritativeness of Xi, being passed on to the CCP's future leadership.

Against this background, that future leadership will find it next to impossible to carry on the anticorruption campaign and yet, equally, it will not be able to afford to drop it. The present leadership is stuck with the campaign, but so far it has shown itself to be up to the challenge. The problem for the next leadership is that it will be stuck with it but will not be up to the challenge. Xi's launch of the anticorruption campaign was a truly fateful move, necessary as it was, and it has no chance of coming to a good end unless the present leadership or its successor finds a new basis for its political authority and, with it, a new way of conceiving and handling corruption.

The Strengths and Liabilities of Xi as the New "Core"

We have been assuming an unproblematic leadership succession when Xi's time is up, but this is an increasingly questionable assumption. To appreciate what is at stake, we must take care to distinguish between two problems: leadership succession and regime perpetuation. The first problem may appear to have been largely resolved since Deng stepped down from (the direct exercise of) power. But it is manageable only on the assumption that regime perpetuation or at least indefinite continuation does not itself become a problem. With each change in leadership, however, this is an assumption that has looked ever more extravagant to make. This is the context in which the next leadership succession—from Xi to his successor—will take on an unprecedented level of importance, for it is bound to be overshadowed by the larger question of regime perpetuation. Indeed, the dramatically higher stakes are already prefigured in the widely mooted possibility—some would even say necessity—of postponing the next leadership succession.

Looking at the matter with detachment, one must first of all try to understand what it would mean for the leadership succession to be delayed—against what has come to be perceived as a hard-won norm essential for the CCP's stability and public relations. It would be trivializing the extraordinary stakes of the matter to attribute the delay, should it come to pass, entirely or even primarily to personal ambition, important as it undoubtedly is. For it is not implausible to think that, next time around, what has previously only been a matter of leadership succession will have an unprecedented impact on regime perpetuation. If this is true, the objective and deeper meaning of postponing the leadership succession—the message, as it were—can hardly be denied: regime perpetuation must trump leadership succession, and Xi is (regarded as) indispensable for regime perpetuation.

Whence the (perceived) indispensability? Well, the writing has been on the wall for some time, and perhaps the best way to read it is to use the Aristotelian categories of the One and the Few (that of the Many not needed in the present context). In the history of the CCP, Mao was the paradigmatic case of elite rule dominated by the One. Deng continued this tradition while whittling it down somewhat, both by necessity (he had considerably less authority than Mao) and by design (in order to create a stabilizing precedent), and giving noticeably more say to the Few. Crucially, in a formally instituted and acknowledged way, Deng remained the "core" *(hexin)* of the leadership. When Jiang Zemin took over, he inherited the all-important core status, and this meant keeping largely the same balance between the One and the Few, despite many differences. For this reason, Jiang could be said to be personally responsible for what happened under his watch, for good (the very considerable loosening of political repression and the corresponding expansion of civil society, among other things) and ill (not least crony capitalism and official corruption), to an extraordinarily high degree befitting the rule of the One. The decisive change came with Hu Jintao, Jiang's successor, for he was never able to acquire the core status and had to share power with the Few to a degree unprecedented in the history of communist China. By then *the Few* had come to mean essentially other members of the CCP's politburo, especially its standing committee. But, far more significantly, Hu had to contend with Jiang, who in one way or another almost managed to hang on to his former core status, behind the scenes, and to exert greater influence on the Few surrounding Hu than Hu himself could. The result was a greatly altered balance of power between the One and the Few, and, for the first time in communist China, we had a regime closer to oligarchy than to one-man rule. Significantly, it was during this rule of the Few that the crony capitalism and official corruption first unleashed by Jiang became truly rampant, eventually endangering the very survival of the CCP. What may have been perceived in the first six years or so of Hu's rule as continued liberalization—from Jiang's reign—seems in retrospect to have been largely an epiphenomenon.

It should thus come as no surprise, especially with hindsight, that the attempt to put official corruption under control and save the CCP was to coincide with the shift of power from the Few to the One. It appears that Xi was expected to more or less continue the oligarchic pattern, as the first among equals in the manner of Hu. After all, he too was handed the reins of power without the core status. But Xi himself, as it turned out, had other ideas, setting in motion an unprecedentedly resolute and systematic anticorruption campaign and in the process emerging decisively as a new One above the Few and having the core status conferred on him in due course. To be sure, the anticorruption campaign has also been a purge of the Few (and their most important supporters), and vice versa. Viewed from a detached perspective, however, this coincidence is simply a function of the causal relation between rampant official corruption and the rule of the Few, although this is far from being the only thing it is. Among other things, it is also a Legalist masterstroke, meting out reward and especially punishment, and creating loyalty and especially fear, at a time of loose party discipline and cohesion—balanced and tempered by the Confucian-like recourse to high-minded moral exhortation. And, of course, anyone with the most rudimentary knowledge of Chinese history will recognize in the new One-Few configuration the paradigmatic subordination of vassals (*chen*) to ruler (*jun*)—almost all the way from the First Emperor to Chairman Mao.

Whether one applauds the new rule of the One (as one has to, at least conditionally, if one approves of the anticorruption campaign) or condemns it (as one must, in response to the escalation of political repression), the toughest question confronting the CCP down the road will be how to shift once again from rule of the One to rule of the Few. For China's social circumstances today will not permit any rule of the One to last. They will not allow an irrevocably broken politico-cultural paradigm to be restored except under a state of emergency—and even then with extraordinary difficulty. It is quite extraordinary that Xi has been able to establish himself as the One atop the Few when the difference in talent and virtue within the top layer of the CCP's elite is generally regarded today as not so great as to warrant anything approaching kingship. Against this patent lack of marked superiority, the revived personality cult surrounding Xi is serving as an indispensable counter, almost predictable within the tradition of a Leninist party. Using this and other means, Xi has succeeded against the odds, arguably in response to objective needs of the CCP, but there is little reason to expect his successor to beat the odds again. For better or worse, Xi's will be the last rule of the One, and therefore the next leadership succession will at the same time be a reversion from rule of the One to rule of the Few. Could this unavoidable move be a recipe also for a reversion to the rampant official corruption that had required rule of the One to fix in the first place? Could this be an unwitting recipe for even worse things now that the fragile new politico-cultural paradigm established by Deng is further weakened by discontinuation? Or is there reason to hope for orderly political liberalization, for a change—as distinct from the disorderly (corruption-ridden) liberalization of the past on the one hand and the orderly (corruption-curbing) retrenchment of the present on the other? The answer will depend crucially on what Xi does while he still wields power as the One.

Xi's Enhanced Power, the Country's Increased Dependency

It is now clear that Xi has no formal, including constitutional, obstacles to staying in power as the One indefinitely, even for life—subject only to the irremovable contingencies of personal health and political power struggle. Nevertheless, the historic lifting of term limits on the presidency is more symbolic and symptomatic than substantively important in itself, given that (as commentators have never tired of noting) the presidency is less powerful than the positions of party general secretary and chairman of the party's central military commission, both already free of term restrictions. There is no denying the symbolic significance of this constitutional amendment—namely, that the One is absolutely indispensable for all that truly matters to the CCP and, in its view, to the Chinese nation. The One is indispensable not only in the sense that Xi is indispensable for filling the position of the One but also in the potentially further-reaching if less definite sense that the One, no matter who occupies the position, is henceforth required for leading the party and governing the country with the requisite authority. The latter sense, understandably unacknowledged, is nevertheless one that cannot be denied without making the constitutional amendment appear ad hoc and creating other undesirable impressions. How seriously this at least rhetorically unavoidable implication is actually intended will become known for sure only in the fullness of time, but not without major consequences—not least if term limits have to be reintroduced in the absence of a successor strong enough to step into Xi's shoes.

For now, Xi is the indispensable One—the Indispensable One. The constitutional amendment provides the most incontrovertible proof possible that this is what the CCP publicly thinks. This is the symptomatic significance of the scrapping of presidential term limits, revealing a stunning belief—and readiness of belief—in the dependency of the entire party and country on the leadership of one man, in the person of Xi. The constitutional amendment is indeed the enactment of this belief, the transformation of a passing intraparty consensus, in all likelihood a forced one, into an enduring national, public fact. Whatever opposition may have been over-come in the process only goes to show how weak, wavering, and pathetic that opposition was, if indeed it existed sufficiently to warrant the name. It does not matter either that the belief in Xi's indispensability may not be sincerely held even within the ranks of the party, for this (if true) has patently not been enough to stand in the way of the constitutional creation of Xi's indispensability as an overwhelmingly important *public* fact. In this sense, the very fact that the CCP has supported or acquiesced in Xi's symbolic indispensability and the nation's symbolic dependency is enough to show that what is symbolized is, in all probability, true. The apparently unobstructed collective investment in the symbol is itself symptomatic. Now Xi *is* indispensable, or has become so, and one should not be surprised if indispensability generates yet more indispensability—to the point where the stability and well-being of China are indissolubly linked to the political and personal fortunes of one leader. We may have already come to this point; one arguably has more to fear for China's future from Xi's leaving the political stage than one did even from Mao's, with no other political figure sufficiently tried and tested to take over from Xi, reassuringly for party and country, as Deng was known to be able to do (after a brief interval) from Mao. This is yet another aspect of the return to more unpredictable times.

No one can, or should, rule out the possibility of a fierce power struggle at the very top of the CCP, even of a coup at Xi's expense. The degree of such a possibility is contingent on Xi's perceived strength, the latter in turn subject to how successfully Xi steers China's economy and negotiates its increasingly complex role and standing in the world. It will also be contingent on how collectively desperate and resourceful Xi's enemies—all actual and potential victims of Xi's anticorruption drive and purge—are. But make no mistake: any successful attempt to unseat a leader whose eponymous thought has been written into the party and state constitutions so recently and with such seeming unanimity would be tantamount to collective suicide, spelling the beginning of the end of the CCP itself by broadcasting the emperor's nakedness to the whole world. Indeed, it would not be farfetched to hypothesize that this very logic was among the most decisive considerations motivating the constitutional amendments in the first place.

Xi's position is truly historic. For our present purposes, how he will acquit himself in this historic position is, above all, a matter of whether he will use his now de facto and constitutionally sanctioned indispensability to increase this indispensability, and hence the country's dependency on him, even more; or to achieve the opposite, to gradually and prudently wean the country from the ultimately undependable dependency on one leader, however wise and capable—in other words, whether he maintains and strengthens the rule of the One, or paves the way for the eventual introduction of the (mixed) rule of the Few and the Many (which is what democracy can realistically aspire to in the real world), thereby empowering the Many as a way of averting the instability of the rule of the One and checking the corruptibility of the rule of the Few.

Time to Prepare for Stormy Weather

All signs *so far* indicate that Xi is pursuing the first option rather than the second, and the signs are observable in how he has gone about setting the CCP on the right course. For, once Xi had decided to stop the rot of the party and to stem its near-terminal legitimation crisis, as discussed earlier, another fork awaited him down the road, where he would have to turn in one of two directions in search of a long-term cure for the legitimation crisis. One option was seeking to revive the CCP's old communist revolutionary legitimacy, while the other would involve a departure from the party's beaten track, an attempt to fill the political void with some kind of democratic legitimacy. After several years of waiting filled with hesitation and second-guessing and some wishful thinking, on the part of all manner of observers, it has now become clear that Xi has, at least for the time being, rejected a new, avowedly democratic beginning with Chinese characteristics in favor of an unflinching affirmation of the CCP's habitual recourse to political and ideological retrenchment in the face of danger. This is his preferred battle plan for saving the CCP. Unlike at the first fork, however, he has made not the harder but the easier choice—and yet what may well turn out to be the less effective one in the long run.

This is not a normative judgment but a prudential appraisal. I have already noted Xi's unique combination of attributes: his seemingly exceptionally keen concern for the fate of the CCP, his correspondingly acute sense of the party's legitimation crisis, the apparent strength of character he has displayed in acting on this sense of crisis, and his apparently instinctive knowledge and deployment of the party's Confucian-Legalist and Leninist legacies. That Xi is unique among the party's top leaders in the reform era in these regards shows him to be truly special, at the very least a hard act to follow. But timing matters, too. Xi witnessed the near-terminal condition of the patient, which must have triggered his physician's calling, not to mention his survival instinct as a member of the collective patient. Much more importantly, he happens to belong to the last generation of Chinese who were toughened by the harsh and sometimes brutal conditions of the new, communist China created by Mao and his comrades, and who had beaten into them at least second-hand memories of the blood-soaked and sacrifice-laden communist revolution, not to mention the ruthless persecutions the party all too readily inflicted on its own, including Xi's father. In this Xi is not unique, admittedly, for it is a matter of generational experience. But if we put this together with his unique combination of attributes, which shape his sense of and response to the CCP's legitimation crisis—and do not forget, of course, his huge political capital and sense of entitlement based on a revolutionary bloodline with an inexorable expiry date—we immediately realize that he is not a hard act to follow but an impossible one. What next? What will happen when his time is up—if only for reasons of health or sheer human mortality now that presidential term limits have been removed?[4]

Up to now, Xi has succeeded in resetting important rules of the political game, such as with respect to official corruption and party discipline; in enforcing the new rules with an authority almost unique in the reform era; and thereby in altering and improving conduct and appearances and even, among many ordinary citizens, the CCP's image as it relates strictly to behavior. But these and many other successes have not led to changed hearts and minds that could form the basis of a durable transformation in moral, political, and institutional culture capable of lasting beyond his tenure. Indeed, by scaling back to the point of nonexistence the Ideological State Apparatuses that were already extremely weak and limited even under his predecessors, he has ruled out that very possibility. The result is even greater reliance on the Repressive State Apparatus and, in terms of elite and mass psychology alike, on the role of fear. This means that the current political effectiveness of the CCP, such as it is, will last only as long as the exceptionally high level of fear lasts, and that fear will endure only as long as its source—a greatly feared leader—is around. It would not be at all implausible to see here one of the deeper reasons for the removal of presidential term limits. The problem with this constitutional measure, however, and, at a deeper level, with the role of fear in politics, is that fear works by appealing to incentives rather than beliefs and therefore is ill suited to addressing the CCP's legitimacy deficit. Indeed, however signally the recourse to fear may have succeeded in arresting the surface consequences of this deficit, such as official corruption and the executive weakness of the central leadership, it has also inadvertently highlighted the legitimation crisis and, indeed, revealed, via a very simple political inference, how serious the CCP itself thinks this crisis is.

Unless Xi believes he is able to fix the legitimation crisis once and for all while he holds the reins of power and thus to leave his successor with a CCP in rude political health and no legitimation crisis to reckon with, he should be worried. He may, on account of this very worry (and for other reasons), see fit to prolong his tenure as paramount leader beyond the ten-year span that had come to be taken for granted until the 2018 constitutional change, perhaps even to maintain his grip on power for life if necessary. But this does not solve the problem beyond delaying the inevitable. It is in this sense that I have said that Xi alone stands between the present and the inflexion point in the CCP's legitimation crisis. If for this reason the inflexion point is not exactly staring China in the face today, we know that it *will* within a more or less fixed time span in the foreseeable future. This makes for a looming legitimation crisis in a truly ominous sense—a clear and present danger lodged in a definite future.

When the time comes, Xi will no longer be around, politically speaking, to shield China from danger but, even more consequentially, all the conditions for keeping the communist revolutionary legacy plausible and vital will be gone as well. In a matter of years, by the time the present leadership leaves the political stage or soon thereafter, the communist revolutionary legacy will have suffered an irreparable double loss—the loss of almost all living memory of the revolution, even at second hand, and the total loss of the revolution's contemporary relevance as a worldview or way of life. This double loss, involving as it does inexorable interactions between evolving reality and changing collective psyche, is fast progressing before our eyes, and its completion in the near future is unstoppable. When this inflexion point arrives, the communist revolutionary legacy will have lost all vitality, all life to give new life. And this means that there will no longer be *any* living, throbbing communist revolutionary material to work with in order to creatively renew the only legitimation discourse the CCP has ever known how to use. With the fountainhead dried up, all ideological extensions or accretions, nationalistic or Confucian or any other, will lose their vitality as well, or else they will have to come into their own and gain a new, independent lease on life, which is a very tall order indeed and unlikely to happen soon, if at all.

One must not be deceived, therefore, by the appearance that the current leadership of the CCP is more confident, more assertive, and more in control than its predecessors. This appearance, even if largely reflective of reality, is precisely the problem. Not only is the present leadership the exception that proves the rule, but the present time is the last opportunity for such an exception to appear. If one thing about the next leadership succession can be known with almost total certainty, it is that the new leadership will be much weaker than the present one. Indeed, even for the present leadership, it is not all fair weather, with challenges to its political authority reflected in repressive measures that have delegitimating consequences no less than deterrence effects, and reportedly taking the oblique form of a new type of self-preserving inertia and passiveness on the part of fear-ridden cadres. So one can imagine how impossibly daunting it will be for a much weaker future leadership to cope with the twin challenges of legitimacy and performance. One can count on the coming of rainy days, definitely rainier days.

Let corruption then stand as one example of how implausible it would be to expect the indefinite continuation of the status quo—and of the urgent need to prepare for the coming of stormy weather while the sun still shines, if none too brightly. Even if the present leadership is not the only one capable of such preparation, it is without doubt the one in the best position to undertake it. There is no better, and timelier, use to which the present leadership could put its unrepeatable authority. If truth be told, it is difficult to imagine China remaining credibly "red" after Xi. As a matter of fact, through no fault of Xi's, China has already changed its "color," as part of the larger metamorphosis set in motion by Deng; what it has not yet done is only to own up to this fact. The resulting mismatch of reality and name, rather than the scheming of domestic turncoats or foreign instigators, has set the stage for a so-called color revolution. The challenge, however embarrassing and difficult to manage, is for the CCP to acknowledge this mismatch and organize a planned and gradual, if initially unannounced, color reform, as it were, instead of one day falling victim to a less orderly and less benign color revolution. Such a course of action would be no more than a belated political reform aimed at squaring name with reality—*a reality created by the CCP itself*; the resulting rise in consistency would, in turn, bring changes to the perception of the reality and thus also to the reality itself. This is the only way to resolve, once and for all, the plausibility crisis, the identity crisis, and the crisis of "revolutionary spirit," which together have conspired to drive the party to progressively more desperate and unsustainable measures in the interest of survival. If Xi has the wisdom and courage to accomplish this feat, he will have put his indispensability—his unchallenged power made possible by the 2018 constitutional amendments—to good and indeed historic use, and he will be justly remembered as the most admirable One in CCP history.

PART TWO

The Democratic Challenge

CHAPTER THREE

The Case for Democracy

WE ARE IN THE MIDDLE of making an essentially prudential case for democracy in China. This case falls naturally into two stages. The first stage, just presented, was intended to show that China's current political arrangement is on the brink of a potentially fatal legitimation crisis and therefore needs major change in order to avert the crisis. The second stage now takes the further step of demonstrating that democracy alone can provide an appropriate answer to the legitimation crisis and serve as a new and better basis for legitimacy and hence stability. It is not by accident that these two stages of the argument have a common thread, in that the crucial factor in determining whether a political regime is in crisis and whether a different one is the answer to the crisis is the presence or the lack of fit between a political regime and the nature of the society it rules.

It will have emerged that the current political regime in China has lost its fit with the social reality on the ground—as will have a thinly veiled hint that democracy is likely to have a much better fit with it. Viewed in this way, the legitimation crisis of the Chinese Communist Party (CCP) is, at its heart, the process whereby this lack of fit is becoming ever more serious and apparent. The lack of fit, in turn, has resulted from the fact that the party itself has initiated a quasi-capitalist (that is, in part state capitalist) reform while, by necessity, holding fast to the communist revolutionary legacy as the continuing basis of its legitimacy, its right to rule. It is not surprising that the CCP has had great difficulty imposing its tattered revolutionary legitimation discourse on the brand-new, distinctly nonrevolutionary social reality that the reform has brought into being. What is to be marveled at, rather, is how much success the CCP has had in hitching its impressive performative success, all of it part of the new social reality, to its increasingly antiquated species of legitimacy. No one would have dared to predict four decades ago, when the reform had just gotten under way, that a party still calling itself communist would be able, for so long and with such effectiveness, to maintain its right to rule in a society whose lived, everyday reality was to become no longer remotely communist. It is all the more remarkable that this incredible run is being stretched even longer by the current CCP leadership, with their exceptional crisis consciousness and equally exceptional determination. For all this quite extraordinary resourcefulness, however, they will not be able to delay the inflexion point indefinitely. For when the lack of fit between political regime (meaning especially its mode of legitimation) and social reality becomes irreparable and patently so, the political regime must make way, or else it will sooner or later descend into a paralyzing legitimation crisis.

What the no longer-fitting political regime must make way for is, naturally, whatever regime will better fit the new social reality. Given this social reality, and as long as it remains largely of the same kind, the latter regime will be the only prudent and hence sustainably viable option—whether or not it deserves to be deemed a better regime in abstraction from the nature of the social reality. The new regime need not be better; it only must be better fitting. This, then, is the prudential reason for a new regime. Since in the present context the new regime must, as it happens, be a democratic one, what I have been moving toward turns out to be a prudential case for *democracy*. However, to be more precise, the case must be made, first, for the need for a new, better-fitting regime (that is, for the old regime's loss of fittingness) and, only then, for democracy as the fitting candidate to meet this need.

I can think of no better way to spell out this prudential case for democracy than by returning to the very origins of democracy—to the first debate over democracy.

If ancient Athens was the world's first democracy, the Sophists may be regarded as democracy's first philosophical teachers and defenders. Democratic *politics* was the soil from which the Sophists arose, answering the need for effective speakers in the council, the assembly, and the law courts, and the call, which fell on the Sophists, to instruct citizens in Athens, Syracuse, and other democracies in the Aegean world in the art of persuasion. But even more important was their role in articulating a conception of democratic *society,* which rested, in turn, on a conception of knowledge and virtue diametrically opposed to that of the philosophical partisans of aristocracy such as Socrates and especially Plato.

In this Protagoras has come down to us as the greatest Sophist, in the form of the few surviving fragments of his writings and, of course, of Plato's reconstruction, in the dialogue *Protagoras,* of his confrontation with Socrates. In this dialogue and elsewhere (especially *The Republic* and *The Statesman*), where Socrates and Plato argue for the equation of virtue with knowledge, for knowledge as solely concerning the highest and absolute good and hence as the preserve of the best and brightest, for such an exalted conception of the good as being the purpose of political life, and for an equally exalted conception of knowledge-virtue as the basis of rule (the potential philosopher-king's reluctance notwithstanding), Protagoras differs radically on every count. An unabashed agnostic, he derives from his skepticism about the existence of the gods his famous conclusion that "man is the measure of everything," meaning (presumably) that there is no other, higher court of appeal when it comes to knowledge, virtue, or the purpose of human life, including that of political life.[1] Given this mundane, which is to say purely human, standard, knowledge is no longer qualitatively different from opinion, virtue comes within the reach of every citizen (with its acquisition both requiring education and being consistent with its universal accessibility), and life in the polis can have no higher purposes than those of the human beings who take part in it. Thus, neither knowledge nor virtue nor political life has any reason to be the privilege of the highborn or the best endowed.

After all, "man is the measure of everything"—with "man" understood in all the mundane contingency and diversity observable at any given time. It so happens that the Sophists both sprang from democracies and, as teachers of democratic practice, were the best and most widely traveled. Thus they saw firsthand the different mores and customs in many places and, on this basis, came up with the sharp distinction between nature and human convention. As far as the latter was concerned, they evinced a philosophical and practical open-mindedness that bears comparison with what today we sometimes call pluralism and relativism. Small wonder that they could readily see both sides of an issue and founded their pedagogy in teaching pupils how to argue both sides of a case. This is more like, say, Habermasian communicative action (or, more precisely, practical discourse) than sophistry in its frequently intended pejorative sense. Hence it is closer to the mark when the intellectual bent of the Sophists is compared to that of the eighteenth-century Enlightenment in Europe. But a perhaps more exact counterpart in modern times is American pragmatism, so much so that to read Protagoras's speech in Plato's dialogue and the surviving fragments of his writings is to be constantly reminded of John Dewey and perhaps even Richard Rorty, among others.[2]

What is distinctive in Dewey's pragmatism and even more so in Rorty's neopragmatism is, above all, the all-encompassing character of their pragmatic-democratic thinking, which cuts across knowledge and action, facts and norms, politics and society, and, in so doing, brings Protagoras's idea of man being the measure of everything to its logical conclusion.[3] Just as Protagoras may be considered the theorist of democracy for the ancient Greek world, so the likes of Dewey and Rorty are intellectual spokesmen for our modern democratic age. Except for its exclusion of slaves and women, which in any case Protagoras's philosophy does nothing to justify, and for its preoccupation with war, the world of Greek democracy is remarkably similar, in the relevant respects bearing on our present discussion, to our modern democratic age.

In this similarity, what stands out above all else is a democratic conception of human beings as *social* (as distinct from Aristotelian, strictly political) animals, coupled with a democratic conception of knowledge and virtue. Democratic politics is of course important—understandably more so in the ancient Greek world than in ours because ours is incomparably richer in the possibilities of social life—but it is necessary and fitting only in the context of a democratic conception or, better still, a democratic reality of social life, as well as a democratic epistemology. In other words, a democratic regime needs to rest on the basis of a democratic society, which it can help reinforce and enlarge but can seldom conjure out of thin air. It is not without significance that Protagoras, in responding to Socrates's challenge to the democratic conception of virtue and politics, employs an allegory in which Prometheus first bestows on human beings the gifts of fire and skill in the arts only to have these incomplete gifts rendered truly beneficial by Zeus through the further gift of universal civic virtue.[4] This suggests that the polis, as seen by

Protagoras in contradistinction to Socrates, Plato, and Aristotle, has no higher purpose than to enable human beings to take full advantage of their ordinary abilities and talents in a shared social life of peace and enjoyment. The epoch-making significance of Protagoras's philosophical argument for democracy lies in its plausible account of democratic social, epistemological, and moral relations in the light of which a democratic regime is left as the only fitting political arrangement.[5]

Some clarification is in order. As a matter of empirical, historical reality, it is true that there was not, and could not have been, nearly as much social or private life in the ancient Greek world as we have today. The energy that is nowadays devoted to life in society or the private realm, to the exercise of the so-called liberties of the moderns, was channeled overwhelmingly into life in the polis, consisting as it did in the liberty of the ancients. Almost the only meaningful way to be a social animal was to be a political animal. To understand the raison d'être of democracy, however, we must take a conceptual step back from the historical, material contingency of the Greek world and see behind or beneath this contingency the fact that a political regime always stands in some relation—of more or less fittingness or lack of fittingness—to the society with which it is conjoined. This is the case even when social life happens to be less, even much less (as in the ancient Greek world), prominent than political life. And this is entirely consistent with the fact that there are times when it is possible for politics, including democratic politics, to remake society, and with the fact that all social relations are politically constituted to one degree or another. But no matter how a set of social relations, a form of social life, or a kind of society may have come about, once it has become entrenched and is no longer amenable to a political regime's efforts to remake it, it is the political regime that must make itself fit the state of society.

In treating Protagoras as the originator of this line of argument, then, I am understanding "society" in the sense of the socioeconomic condition and structure of a place or community, not (anachronistically) as a somewhat independent domain distinguished from the "state" in our modern way. It was only with Alexis de Tocqueville that this *type* of argument for democracy—the argument from the nature of society—came to be expressed in its distinctively modern form. While mindful of this undoubtedly significant development, I shall nevertheless treat it, for my purposes, as an internal variation within a larger species of argument. This means that the society / regime distinction as used in my discussion is a general one that is meant to cut across the rise of (bourgeois) society as a distinctively modern phenomenon variously remarked on by Jean-Jacques Rousseau, Benjamin Constant, François Guizot, Tocqueville, Karl Marx, and Hannah Arendt, among others. This general society / regime distinction is larger than the specifically modern distinction between a Hobbesian "state" and a commercial "society" à la Montesquieu, thought of as a distinct order in its own right. Thus, while I will draw on Tocqueville, in particular, for his insights into the connection between society and regime, I see his insights as belonging, in the first instance, to the same kind as can be found in Niccolò Machiavelli, whom I shall invoke briefly, and even Protagoras. This does not mean that modern society, predominantly bourgeois and set apart from a uniquely centralized state, does not have its special implications with regard to political regime. My point is simply that the close relation between society and regime is a general fact not confined to the modern world. Yet it is equally important to note that the general argument for a democratic regime from the nature of society takes on particular pertinence and force in the modern setting.

To return to Protagoras's argument for democracy, my basic point is that his most powerful and ingenious contribution is to have sketched a highly plausible conception of human nature in democratic terms. This conception involves, above all, a more or less egalitarian mode of human sociability, entailing and in turn being supported by a more or less egalitarian epistemology. Once this democratic theory of human nature is accepted in principle and, better still, has substantially infiltrated social reality, it is but a short step, both conceptual and practical (which is not to say practically easy), to political democracy.

By this point, Protagoras's case for democracy may begin to look uncannily familiar. This is because almost exactly the same type of argument was to be made famous for our time by Tocqueville in *Democracy in America,* in which he attempts to show that once equality of conditions *(l'égalité des conditions)* has come to prevail in a society, it will lead naturally, if not necessarily immediately, to the adoption of a democratic political regime.

But it is worth bringing up another important figure who anticipated Tocqueville's argument. I am referring to Machiavelli, in whose *Discourses* we find the most succinct expression of a similar argument: "Let, then, a republic be constituted where there exists, or can be brought into being, notable equality; and a regime of the opposite type, i.e. a principality, where there is notable inequality." Why? Because "otherwise what is done will lack proportion and will be of but short duration."[6] In speaking of notable equality or notable inequality, Machiavelli, like Tocqueville, is referring not to the character of a political regime but to the shape of social circumstances, especially the proportion of the wealthy to the (more or less internally equal) middle class and the balance of power between town and country. Thus what we have here is an exemplary case of forming one's realistic or effective normative political preferences in the light of the social circumstances that happen to prevail and are likely to endure. In the case of "notable equality," here understood strictly as characterizing the social circumstances of a polity, Machiavelli is saying there is no reasonable chance of anything other than a republican government enduring for long, although he rightly gives equal emphasis to the prevalence of civic virtue as a condition for a republic to survive and flourish. This argument from *social* circumstances to *political* regime is the essence of Machiavelli's reasoning, which we find also in Protagoras before him and in Tocqueville after him. To be sure, a republic as Machiavelli understands it is not exactly what Tocqueville means by democracy or what we mean by it today. It is instead a mixed regime in the Roman mode, more concerned with expansion and self-defense than with commerce, and especially in greater need of civic virtues of a more martial and communitarian kind, than is true of the democracies of today. But the underlying thought is much the same in relevant respects.

Since I am making what is essentially a prudential case for democracy, I do not want exactly to take the side of Protagoras, Machiavelli, or Tocqueville insofar as any of them expresses a strong normative preference for democracy (or republicanism) that is *independent of* consideration of social circumstances. I leave open the question of whether, and to what extent, they express such a preference. What is important and decisive for my purposes is (only) that Protagoras (even as he exists mostly in the pages of Plato), as the first theorist of democracy, has carried the day in our time while Socrates and Plato, for all their incomparable intellectual influence, have lost their battle on behalf of aristocracy.[7] Whatever their respective philosophical merits, history has won the argument for Protagoras against Socrates, at least for now and as far as we can see into the future.

Imagine now, in the shadow of Protagoras's historic victory, a democratic society coupled with a democratic epistemology, but one that operates without a democratic political regime. We would say that its current regime, not being democratic, is not fitting. We would say that the life and spirit of the country is split against itself and that an already democratic society is in need of a democratic political regime. This is exactly the situation we find in China today. Only China has gone much further in its evolution as a democratic society with a democratic conception of knowledge and civic virtue than Protagoras's Greek world ever did or could.

This new democratic reality and social imaginary can find no more definitive expression than in Xi Jinping's first public speech on November 15, 2012, as general secretary of the CCP: "Our people have an ardent love for life. They wish to have better education, more stable jobs, more income, greater social security, better medical and health care, improved housing conditions, and a better environment. They want their children to have sound growth, have good jobs and lead a more enjoyable life. To meet their desire for a happy life is our mission."[8] The worldliness of Protagoras is written all over this conception of the good life and of the role of the CCP as devoted entirely to furthering it. Man is the measure of everything, says Protagoras. Take human beings—human beings as we find them—as the point of reference (yiren weiben), proclaims the party's new philosophy as reflected in Xi's speech. Gone is the elevated telos of an "intelligible" communist future that must be superimposed on mundane, merely "sensible" goals in the here and now. Gone with it is the need for a self-styled vanguard whose privileged members alone are supposed to possess the elevated Marxian knowledge and noble revolutionary virtues required to lead the masses out of the cave on their way to earthly paradise, as in the depiction of the Greater Leader (Mao Zedong) as the (red) sun. The leaders of the party today are no longer looked up to as if they formed a species apart, as Mao and Zhou Enlai once undoubtedly were by generations of Chinese who instinctively shunned all thought even of their mortality. Philosophically and ideologically, if not quite politically and institutionally, today's CCP has been cleansed of all traces of Platonism.[9] All but in name, Marx—the Leninist, Platonic Marx—has been replaced by Protagoras. Which means that, all but in name, democracy's time has come. It is time to rectify names.[10]

Systemic, Objective Pressures for Democracy

What I have just set out is the plain truth of the matter. This does not mean that the plain truth will be plain for everyone to see, especially for those who have long been in power and in the habit of exercising power in a certain way. For them, this plain truth about the necessity of democracy for China can easily be blocked by two convenient illusions: first, that performative success can permanently serve as a boost to or even substitute for legitimacy (that is, as legitimacy enhancement or amelioration); and, second, that the old communist revolutionary source of legitimacy can be revived.

It is important to dispel these illusions, for otherwise they serve as a mistaken and irrational basis for action and this is dangerous. I am not sure how difficult it will be to show these to be illusions, but there is at least one good reason to be hopeful: both the plain truth about the necessity of democracy and the correlative fact that these are illusions are due to circumstances actively brought about by the CCP itself. And it takes only brief reflection to see that these circumstances of the CCP's own making amount to nothing less than systemic and objective pressures toward democracy.

As far as *economic conditions* are concerned, there has occurred, thanks to the reform, a much greater division in function between the political and economic domains, the latter including state-owned enterprises, especially those categorized as "for profit" as distinct from "welfare or public service" firms. Although the CCP is still firmly in charge of both domains, it is increasingly dealing with them as involving two distinct kinds of activity, with the market granted for the first time its own relatively independent logic and imperative, and with private enterprises taking up a huge chunk of the economy in terms of both gross domestic product and especially employment. We might say that the economy, even as it remains firmly under the control of the party-state, has become radically more important and more independent in relation to political power. Even if this does not weaken the power of the party-state, it certainly reduces the sheer political part of its power in favor of the economic. And this cannot but have a profound impact on the nature and extent of political power and thereby on the CCP as a political institution, making it more functional and less ideological. I would not argue that this in itself makes Chinese society more democratic, if only because I have my doubts about the effects of unchecked economic power on the nature of social relations. But there is little doubt that here we have one important instance in which the CCP has learned to manage China through the essentially Western practice of separations. And we know, of course, that the formal separation of the political and economic domains is a crucial feature of capitalist liberal democracy. While the degree of this separation in China is nowhere near its Western counterpart's and, generally speaking, the separation itself neither means nor entails democracy and may even curtail democracy, as it does to one degree or another in Western countries, such separation clearly reduces both the need and the justification for a nondemocratic form of government. It is definitely the case that the more strongly a society is marked by such a separation, the less its government requires or even permits a leadership with a teleological vision, such as that of the CCP. Thus we have here a gradual and unobtrusive yet very consequential development for China. No less consequential are two sociological by-products of the growing importance of the economic domain, much of it privatized: first, an increasingly sizable middle class naturally, if not always uninhibitedly and consciously, drawn to broadly liberal and (bourgeois) egalitarian values, and, second, a growing entrepreneurial class with an even greater, if as yet understandably unarticulated, reluctance to defer to unelected political power. These and other offshoots of China's economic transformation merge into the more general condition of social equality that I will come to shortly.

Ideologically, the four-decade-old reform has turned China into a very strange animal. This animal walks like a duck (though not completely) but does not quack like a duck, and therefore it is both a duck and not a duck. China is, in very important respects, including both values (for example, rationally pursued greed) and institutions (for example, the stock market), a capitalist society.[11] But it still calls itself communist, and as long as it does so and is strongly motivated to do so, it will not quite be a capitalist society. The motivation for maintaining a communist identity may remain for quite some time, boiling down to the determination of the CCP to prolong its exclusive leadership, including over an economy that will therefore not be allowed to become quite as autonomous as in Western capitalist democracies. Hence the state-owned enterprises, even the "for-profit" ones that strictly make up state capitalism, have as their first imperative the perpetuation of CCP rule. But this is now. It is difficult to believe that, say, ten to twenty years from now China will still be able to call itself communist. And it is even harder to believe that ten to twenty years from now this appellation, even if still in use, will continue to serve as a remotely plausible justification of the CCP's exclusive hold on state power. Cognitively, communism is already a thing of the past, despite its remaining part of the name of the party that still rules in China. Nevertheless, the political capital of the name is not yet exhausted, thanks both to awe-inspiring memories of the more positive achievements of the party in its conquest and building up of China and to lingering fears evoked by the more brutal part of the Maoist legacy. Most of this will be gone in the foreseeable future. Links to the revolutionary past, cognitive and affective, positive and negative, will be greatly attenuated in ten to twenty years, if not sooner, to the point where the name "communism" will no longer produce even a faint echo in collective memory or the national political psyche. The so-called historical nihilism *(lishi xuwu zhuyi)* whose spread the CCP is trying so hard to stop will, well within a couple of decades, have few mnemonic and affective remnants of the revolutionary past even to annihilate. The fear of historical nihilism is the fear of a CCP leadership that is destined to be the last generation still able to avail itself of the political capital of the revolutionary legacy. Although members of the current leadership do not thereby become larger than life—as Mao once was and Deng Xiaoping was, too, if to a noticeably lesser degree—they, especially Xi, nevertheless still manage to create some kind of aura around themselves, whether this aura provokes love or hate. Their appeal to the revolutionary legacy handed down from their fathers' generation does not come across as entirely a joke, and their ideological invocation of whatever is contained in that legacy is likewise not to be dismissed at the level of political gesture and deterrent. They are plainly still imbued with a lingering "revolutionary spirit." Yet even they use the remnants of the communist revolutionary legacy sparingly and mostly on special, strategic occasions. For these are veritably no more than the last remnants and, as such, are increasingly also a liability, serving as a reminder of what the CCP has ceased to be and of a gaping void of legitimation that it is incapable of filling. It is easy to imagine, then, what challenge will befall the next generation of leaders, and the generation after that. One thing is for sure: they will have to manage without the political capital of the communist revolution, and they thus will be a different breed of leaders ("public officials" will be a more suitable name), having had scant experience of the formerly communist China and never been much exposed to the revolutionary past even at second hand. In the absence of all this help, it is almost unthinkable that they would have the audacity and the ability to maintain their leadership and their claim to leadership without a plausible measure of freely expressed popular consent. No longer inflatable by credible connections with the revolutionary past, the prestige of future leaders will inevitably shrink, and they will require a direct, minimally believable mandate from the people as their newfound equals.

The provision for this popular mandate, if and when it happens, will be the culmination of a process of change whose interim stage, having to do with the nature of *social conditions,* is already too far gone to be reversed. What we find at this interim stage is what I have elsewhere called a substantive populism.[12] By this I mean the fact that the CCP now sees its official business as that of furthering the popular, essentially apolitical goals of prosperity and happiness. The subjects of these goals are ordinary Chinese, and the goals are as ordinary Chinese themselves see and value them. This is true also of the sublimated, and more nationalist, form in which these goals have been presented, as the Rise of China and, latterly, the Chinese Dream. As far as mainstream goals and values are concerned, the CCP does not claim to know better than ordinary Chinese do and does not openly presume to second-guess the people it otherwise still leads. This is a profound change: the party no longer sees itself as pursuing the lofty goal of a far-off communism and leading the populace in this pursuit, whether or not the latter is willing to go along, but instead finds its new mission, along with its new claim to power, entirely in its ability to further the widely shared goals, whether at the individual or the national level, of ordinary Chinese.[13] This is a thoroughgoing populism, except that it is not subject to any credible formal procedure for registering and affirming popular preferences, such as democratic elections, and that is why I call it *substantive* populism. Even without the much-needed introduction of proper democratic procedures, however, this substantive populism already bespeaks what Tocqueville calls a democratic state of society or equality of (social) conditions.

In view of these profound changes in economic, ideological, and especially social conditions, it is difficult to believe that things can simply go on as they are without gradually adding up to an irresistible pressure for corresponding political change. Compared with 1978, the year known for the

Xidan Democracy Wall, and 1989, the year of the aborted democracy movement, China today may be, or may appear to be, subjectively further removed from democracy. Yet objectively, with the remarkable advance in equality of conditions since the early 1990s, the country is much closer to democracy than ever before. Nay, objectively, it is already on the verge of democracy—and that is why strong countermeasures are needed and everywhere in evidence. And this fact, the objective advance of democracy, cannot but also be registered, however subtly and obliquely, in mass consciousness, including political consciousness.

As China continues its current economic and social transformation, the equality of conditions will only be enhanced and reinforced. It will not be very long before an even greater equality of conditions, accompanied by an even stronger and more entrenched sociopolitical psychology nourished by such equality, makes it much harder to justify and maintain a completely vertical political structure devoid of credible popular consent, other things being equal. And other things will not be equal, because future leaders of the CCP, progressively distanced from the legitimating origins of the revolution, will not be able to command nearly as much authority, and provoke nearly as much fear, as the present leadership does. Thus, barring unforeseen successes or catastrophes of an extraordinary magnitude, the pressure for an alternative basis of legitimacy will inexorably grow. China will have to adopt democracy in one way or another, or else it will incur more and more unbearable financial and political costs for the maintenance of stability until the proverbial last straw breaks the camel's back.

From Social Equality to Political Democracy

In the brief sketch just given of the economic, ideological, and especially social factors favorable to democracy, I have highlighted a strong trend toward equality as the most crucial factor in the unique suitability of democracy for modern conditions. This is not just any equality and must therefore be carefully defined. It so happens that there is no better way of pinning down this equality than in terms of what Tocqueville calls the democratic social state *(l'état social démocratique)*, characterized by a general and pervasive equality of conditions.[14] Although Tocqueville's notion of equality of conditions is a familiar one, two brief observations will not come amiss.[15]

First, it cannot be emphasized enough that the democratic *social* state is distinct from *political* democracy.[16] For Tocqueville, democracy is first and foremost a type of *society* that contrasts in its entirety with all other types of society inasmuch as they are marked by a general inequality of conditions. Indeed, this contrast is so fundamental that all societies that derive their character from an inequality of conditions in one way or another can be lumped together under "aristocracy" in the exceptionally broad sense Tocqueville gives the term. This is a momentous enough transformation in the eyes of Tocqueville to warrant his description of democracy and aristocracy as marking not so much different political regimes as "two distinct kinds of humanity."[17] In our modern kind of humanity, what is no longer acceptable is the hierarchical organization of presumed human differences, conceived in terms of intrinsic superiority and inferiority, into a rigid aristocratic order based on rank and status. The advent of this new kind of humanity has required nothing less than a revolution, as exemplified by the American Revolution and the French Revolution, whose goal, especially when viewed in the light of their long-term consequences, was the permanent eradication of fixed vertical differences within human society.

Second, it is worth noting that the so-called equality *of conditions* does not mean economic equality or any other kind of quantitative equality, or equality of outcome in general.[18] Rather, the equality in question is essentially a matter of equality of membership in a largely inclusive society. This, in turn, gives rise to a notion of equality as a threshold qualification for participation in a largely inclusive social life: the qualification to join a mobile, competitive form of life that is open to all and whose outcomes for each and all, including possibly highly unequal quantitative ones, are not known in advance and can never be fixed once and for all. The basic qualification itself, as distinct from what one makes of it, and perhaps ideally protected against excessive advantages of family background, is the same for everyone. This sameness, in turn, bespeaks and embodies the sameness *of* everyone, a kind of *qualitative* likeness much commented on by Tocqueville and others after him.[19]

As a well-defined notion, then, Tocqueville's "equality of conditions" means the removal of any politically or coercively maintained fixed hierarchies, as in an aristocratic order, and the resultant, highly consequential leveling of all to a basic human sameness that is variously captured in such notions as universal human rights, careers open to talents, and equality of opportunity. In other words, this is social equality in a special sense— *social* as distinct from political, and *equality* in the sense of a basic human sameness rather than quantitative equality or equality of outcome.[20] If to speak of basic human sameness sounds slightly overstated, one can make essentially the same point in terms of the dramatic reduction of power differentials in society, which Norbert Elias places under the very helpful concept of "functional democratization." Writing in the same spirit as Tocqueville did but with less (indeed seemingly no) normative involvement, Elias says that functional democratization "is not identical with the trend towards the development of 'institutional democracy'" but rather represents "a shift in the *social* distribution of power"[21]—in other words, a growing equality of (social) conditions.

The reason why the notion of equality of (social) conditions, or social equality for short, is so important is that, while it is not itself democracy in the political sense, it produces a momentum in its direction that is well-nigh irresistible. That Tocqueville also calls it the *democratic* social (as distinct from political) state is telling. Since I rest my case for democracy so heavily on this notion and its implications, it is worth spelling out the inner connection between social equality and political democracy further than in my earlier discussion of Protagoras and Machiavelli. This will allow me, having just described the domains (economic, ideological, and social) in which this equality has found expression in China, to return to a higher level of abstraction and, more than in my treatment of Protagoras and Machiavelli, proceed in the form of explicit arguments. My aim is to drive home the point that just as advancing equality of conditions rules out the revival of the CCP's old revolutionary legitimacy, so it points to only one appropriate way to make up for the latter's demise. And that is political democracy broadly construed as a regime compatible with equality of conditions.

Following the spirit though not entirely the letter of Tocqueville, I would like to treat equality of conditions in the social state as the first and most important *condition for democracy*. This makes sense if we distinguish, as Tocqueville does, between the general conditions of a society and the political system of that society. As is well known, however, Tocqueville regards social equality not as a condition for democracy but as the most important part of it. His point, semantic and terminological, is well taken, for he is largely correct in claiming that so closely related are equality of conditions as a fea-ture of the social state and democracy as a property of the political system that both must be seen as constitutive of democracy. But Tocqueville is more subtle than this claim gives one to understand, in that he does not say that equality of conditions will automatically and immediately lead to a demo-cratic political system. What he suggests instead is more open and flexible yet by no means ambiguous. "One has to understand," he writes, "that equality ends up by infiltrating the world of politics as it does everywhere else. It would be impossible to imagine men forever unequal in one respect, yet equal in others; they must, in the end, come to be equal in all."[22] In other words, once equality of conditions has become a fact of life in a society, there comes about a natural and powerful momentum toward a democratic po-litical system, a momentum that will not cease until the goal is reached, al-though it is impossible to say how long it will take to reach the goal and what exact form its arrival will take. A crucial part of this momentum, one might add, comes from the fact that equality of conditions, as understood by Tocqueville, is not merely an empirical fact. Over time, through being af-firmed and valorized by those fighting to gain or entrench this condition, it becomes also a moral fact, as it were, inspiring its own expansion into all relevant aspects of human life. Democracy—that is, political democracy—is an all too natural step of this expansion.

I see no reason to depart from the core of Tocqueville's insights in this regard. It is nevertheless necessary to make ampler allowances than he seems to have done for the length and difficulty of the progress from social equality to political democracy. And it is for this reason that I have chosen to treat social equality as a *condition* for democracy rather than *part* of it in order to give extra emphasis to the point—Tocqueville's point—that equality of conditions is not yet political democracy and need not immediately give rise to it. This extra emphasis is especially called for in the Chinese context, where the road leading from social equality to political democracy is likely to be much more tortuous than was true of the early American experience that Tocqueville commented on. Despite this, Tocqueville's basic thought is left intact—namely, that social equality stands in an extremely close and powerful causal relation to political democracy.

Implicit in this thought is a distinctive argument for a democratic po-litical system. Given equality of conditions in a society, so the argument goes, it is fitting that a democratic political system should be established in that society. Let us call this the *argument from fittingness,* where the fittingness is a matter of ensuring that equals act consistently as equals across all relevant domains of life. Although this argument is based on a causal—that is, social and psychological—understanding of human society, its normative implications are clear and its normative force undeniable: as equality of conditions makes a democratic political system fitting and yet does not produce an automatic and immediate shift to such a system, it is morally desirable to act in such a way as to bring about that shift whenever possible and to do so sooner rather than later. Until this happens, the political system will lack (moral) fittingness and (social-psychological) stability.

So far I have been speaking of political democracy's fittingness under equality of conditions from the third-person perspective, which is largely what Tocqueville does. I should think that this fittingness is obvious even from this third-person perspective. If this is the case, the same fittingness becomes all the more undeniable from the first-person perspective, which itself cannot be denied to anyone under equality of conditions. For, under equality of conditions, how can anyone sensibly and persuasively tell citizens to their face, *in a first-person context of action rather than observation,* that they are not free and equal enough to have democracy or not reasonable and rational enough to make democracy work for the benefit and dignity of the imperfect beings that all humans happen to be? When we move from the third-person to the first-person perspective, we are making natural progress from Tocqueville to Jürgen Habermas—from a sociological to a discourse argument for democracy.[23] There is a sense in which Tocqueville made the first move, and Habermas's theory of communicative action, including his discourse argument for democracy, is but the impressive upshot of shifting—democratically, as it were—from the third- to the first-person perspective, and of deriving what Habermas calls rationalization of the lifeworld (as if it were an independent phenomenon) from the more fundamental process of equalization of conditions. But thanks to Habermas, among others, Tocqueville's case for democracy in terms of fittingness acquires a natural extension that makes it well-nigh unarguable (from the first-person perspective).[24]

The argument from fittingness can be made stronger still, for reasons that will lead to a further, somewhat different argument, which I will call the *argument from governability.* Tocqueville does not mention these reasons, at least not explicitly, but they can be naturally added to his line of thought. Indeed, this further argument can be treated as an extension of the argument from fittingness, stating the consequences of a regime's lack of fittingness (which the argument from fittingness itself does not do) and showing the consequences to be dire. As I have noted, equality of conditions as understood by Tocqueville boils down to a qualitative sameness of all members of society. And this, in turn, means that no one can have the title to rule. For, strictly speaking, the title to rule is predicated on inequality of conditions, such that those who are naturally and qualitatively superior in one relevant respect or another have the title to rule over their inferiors. Democracy at its core is nothing but the disavowal of such inequality and hence of the superiority that creates the title to rule. Insofar as democracy is nevertheless regarded as compatible with the practice of ruling, it exists to make acceptable the periodic suspension of the absence of a title to rule by creating, as it were, temporary licenses for public office through such means as so-called free and fair elections. It creates a government under a qualitative equality of conditions that would otherwise give no one even the temporary legitimacy to exercise political power. Strictly speaking, the result is not quite what is usually called the democratic form of government, if only because a democratically elected government is far from self-government and, for the most part (that is, with the partial exception of the legislative branch), does not exercise the enormous power at its disposal in a remotely democratic manner.[25] If this method of selection nevertheless has something commendably democratic about it, it is only because it is made necessary by the equality of conditions that prevails in the social state. It is, in principle, the least objectionable response to such social conditions and provides the closest (which is not to say truly close) approximation to the political principle of sovereignty of the people that most naturally follows from such conditions. Thus it is that any political power that behaves as if it had some title to rule that could bypass some credible expression of popular consent (a deliberately vague and flexible formulation to which I shall return) would come across as an affront to the modern moral and political sensibility.[26] The greater the equality of conditions, the more egregious the affront, and there comes a point in the progress of equality of conditions where a society becomes positively ungovernable in the total absence of popular consent. Elias captures this point with his characteristic de-

tachment and clarity when he writes, referring to the historical experience
of modern Europe, "Except where the institutionalized balance of domination corresponded to the actual power differentials of the mass, the increase
[in the power of the mass] showed itself in the diffuse manifestations of discontent and apathy, and in looming rebellion and violence."[27] There is no
reason to think that any modern society, including China, will be immune
to this law once equality of conditions becomes firmly established in it as a
fact of life and as common sense. Equality of conditions is well on its way to
becoming just those things—a fact of life and common sense—in China. As
this happens, a crucial normative fault line—the general demand to be per-
suaded rather than compelled on important matters of public interest[28]—
will appear in China for the first time. Because this normative fault line will
occur as a real and objective event in China's political culture and collective
moral psychology, one may expect the governability of the country to depend
more and more on reasonably open and democratic channels for the expression of public opinion and popular consent. Thus, the argument from governability, far from possessing only normative force, is supported by the incorporation of this force into the causal nexus of political life.

To those who point to the apparent stability of China today in empirical
refutation of this argument, I will simply add that there is no better proof of
the potential for ungovernability than the gargantuan cost of shoring up this
stability. And let us not forget that the measurable material cost of budget
and manpower is compounded by an incalculable psychological cost in the
form of resentment and fear and the sense of impotence cumulatively burned
into the national psyche.

It is a separate, and prior, question whether there is an argument of comparable clarity and force for equality of conditions itself, for acting in such a way
as to bring about equality of conditions in the first place, or at least for preferring equality to inequality of conditions. Tocqueville takes up this question, and
his approach to it is instructive. He treats as his point of reference (human)
nature as opposed to convention and asks whether equality of conditions (democracy in the broad sense) or inequality of conditions (aristocracy in the
broad sense) is closer to human nature, such that the convention based on it
does less violence to human nature. His answer is somewhat ambiguous, or
one might say dialectical, in that he believes that equality of conditions is, on
balance, closer to human nature, especially on account of the tendency of the

human affections (say, in the family setting), and yet he also thinks that there are certain good things in human nature, such as the love of higher things and the quest for nobler accomplishments, that the convention based on inequality is better suited to bringing out. In the end, however, Tocqueville takes the plunge (undialectically, as it were) in favor of equality of conditions, in the (pious?) hope that the manner of realizing it will leave at least some room for the good things that inequality of conditions used to make possible but only at the cost of great distortions of other aspects of human nature. What we find, then, is an argument for equality of conditions from human nature. I suspect that Tocqueville was influenced in making this argument by the reality that he saw in America and foresaw as the destiny of Europe. As we know, he went so far as to treat the onward march of equality as providential. Providential or not, the reality of equality of conditions that Tocqueville identified as the hallmark of democracy was and is here to stay, and, given his dialectical view of the pros and cons of equality and inequality, one could reasonably suggest that Tocqueville's argument from human nature is supported and in part motivated by an implicit argument from reality based on the sheer recognition that equality has already become a fact of life. The latter argument makes a virtue of necessity, to be sure, but does so not only because the necessity is simply there but also because the necessity itself contains important virtues despite leaving out other virtues. It may therefore be more precise to think of the overall argument as an *argument from (largely benign) necessity.* Whether or not this reading of Tocqueville is correct, the argument from necessity as I have just explained it is one to which I myself subscribe.

I have teased out, then, three arguments for democracy from Tocqueville's account of equality of conditions. What is remarkable about these arguments is their special, conditional kind of normative force, which is at the same time a species of prudence. The argument from necessity, which applies to equality of conditions itself, derives its normative force from confronting equality of conditions as already largely a fact of life and finding both sufficient strength and, on balance, sufficient virtue in it to conclude that it is neither possible nor desirable to return to inequality of conditions. On this basis, the argument from fittingness proceeds to make the obvious point that, *given* equality of social conditions, democracy is the most morally appropriate and, implicitly and as a matter of prudence, the most stable regime type. The argument from governability then brings out this prudential implication by attending to the consequences of an inappropriate regime and reasoning from a regime's lack of fit-tingness to a country's lack of governability. What makes the combined case of these latter two arguments compelling is that it is at once normative (showing democracy to have the best moral fit with equality of conditions) and prudential (showing democracy to be the most conducive to stability under equality of conditions), and inseparably so (in that what is prudential here rests on perception of the normative and is hence itself normative).

While separate and distinct, then, the three arguments are marked by their *unity of operation*. For once the argument from necessity is triggered by social reality, as it were, as it must be to one degree or another in any modern society, the arguments from fittingness and from governability will automati-cally come into play, although it may take time, even a difficult process, for them to translate into reality. In this way, the three arguments add up to an integral case for democracy that is far from being purely or merely normative. They also derive their force from the *fact* of equality of conditions and find their causal potency in the *laws* of social and political psychology under equality of conditions. For this reason, once equality of conditions has be-come a fact of life in a society, as it clearly has in China today, the combined force of these arguments becomes inescapable. With their moral and pruden-tial appeal resting on undeniable factual and causal premises, these argu-ments are compelling to an exceptional degree. They may even be thought of as laws of society that any government presiding over a country marked by equality of conditions ignores at its peril and at the cost of the country it rules.

A View from Marx and Historical Materialism

It should not be difficult to see a close affinity between Tocqueville's causal view of historical change and Marx's. What Tocqueville and Marx have in common in this regard is traceable all the way back to Aristotle (and indeed Protagoras, if more speculatively) and is more directly attributable to the fact that François Guizot was a significant influence on both, Marx's class and personal antagonism to Guizot notwithstanding. This is not to suggest anything like total resemblance in terms of approach to historical explana-tion between Marx and Tocqueville. For Marx is the originator of historical materialism, and what sets historical materialism apart from Tocqueville's view, as it does all other views before Marx, is—to simplify for our present purposes—the way Marx goes one step beyond identifying the decisive influence of the social on the political. Marx does so by positing, behind this influence, the prior and deeper determining influence of the economic on the social itself. Think of the political in terms of legal relations and forms of state, think of the social as civil society, then think of civil society itself as being internally divided between social structure and political economy, and we see how Marx traces the causal relation among these elements from one to the next: "My investigation led to the result that *legal relations as well as forms of state* are to be grasped neither from themselves nor from the so-called general development of the human mind, but rather have their roots in the material conditions of life, the sum total of which Hegel, following the example of the Englishmen and Frenchmen of the eighteenth century, combines under the name of 'civil society,' that, however, the anatomy of *civil society* is to be sought in *political economy*."[29] Exactly the same layered explanation is found in Friedrich Engels's 1883 preface to *The Communist Manifesto* such that "*economic production* and the *structure of society* of every historical epoch necessarily arising therefrom constitute the foundation for the *political and intellectual history* of that epoch."[30]

In neither text is democracy mentioned, to be sure, and, in any case, Marx means by *democracy* what is tantamount to human (as distinct from merely political) emancipation, not bourgeois democracy, reserving the term *republic* for the latter. But the main point is not affected—namely, that social structure determines the political system, and that economic production, in turn, determines social structure—and we can easily fit Tocqueville's insight regarding the relation between democratic society and democratic political regime into the first half of Marx's proposition. I for one would be perfectly happy to have Tocqueville's insight augmented by the second half of Marx's proposition, although—and this is beyond the scope of our present discussion—the relation between "base" and "superstructure," indeed the very formulation of the distinction itself, needs to be understood with greater precision and sophistication than Marx himself was able to provide.[31]

The important point is that, whatever adjustments may need to be made with regard to the second half of Marx's proposition, Marx is almost at one with Tocqueville with regard to the first half. In other words, Marx and Engels would make the same kind of arguments I have been making (with the help of Tocqueville)—and would indeed do so even more forcefully, treating China's need for political democracy as a need arising from the increasingly democratic character of Chinese society *independently of anyone's will*, a need (to use Engels's phrase) not "engendered in the minds of man." And they would see my prudential argument for democracy in China as—again to borrow a phrase from Engels—"nothing but the reflex, in thought, of [a need] in fact."[32] I myself would not go that far. But their (hypothetical) claim is, at its core, a perfectly reasonable one: that, considering its social structure (and economic development) today, China is ripe, or will soon be ripe, for a bourgeois democratic revolution. If one does not like the phrase "*bourgeois* democratic *revolution*," containing as it does two potentially offensive terms, let it simply be said that China's increasingly democratic society is creating an objective and irresistible need for transition to a democratic political regime.

That no paralyzing crisis has yet occurred on account of the mismatch between social structure and political regime is, on a broadly Marxist view, due to the fact that there is no comparable mismatch further up the chain of determination—that is, between economic production and social structure. In other words, the relations of production have not yet turned into the proverbial fetters of productive forces, because the mismatch between social structure and political regime—with the social structure itself being still largely consistent with economic life—is at one remove from the deeper and more fundamental mismatch that, according to Marx, would cause a social revolution and end a mode of production and life to make way for a new one.

That said, there is no sound reason, even from a Marxist standpoint, to dismiss the admittedly less important mismatch between social structure and political regime as being incapable of producing highly debilitating effects of its own. This is true especially when such effects, in turn, produce side effects on the relation between social structure and economic production, and even more so in view of the largely independent momentum of the looming legitimation crisis.

Democratic Pride Strengthens the Desire for Democracy

It will have emerged from my discussion of the fittingness of democracy under equality of conditions—only reinforced by the considerable if partial affinity between Tocqueville and Marx—that the sense of fittingness is both normative and psychological. Being psychological, it is subject to causal forces. In particular, there seem to be causal forces at work that bear on the dynamics of the relation between democratic society and democratic political regime.

These causal forces are well captured by Jon Elster in terms of what he calls mechanisms—a mechanism being "a specific causal pattern that can be recognized after the event but rarely foreseen."[33] One mechanism identified by Elster is the *spillover effect:* "The spillover effect says that if a person follows a certain pattern of behavior P in one sphere of his life, $X,$ he will also follow P in Y."[34] Now recall what Tocqueville has to say about the relation between democratic society and democratic political regime (in a passage cited earlier): "One has to understand that equality ends up by infiltrating the world of politics as it does everywhere else. It would be impossible to imagine men forever unequal in one respect, yet equal in others; they must, in the end, come to be equal in all."[35] This is, of course, the inspiration behind my argument for democracy from fittingness. Insofar as this argument is psychological (in addition to being normative), its basis lies in the spillover effect—in the idea that the sense of fittingness will not cease to agitate for change until the effect is achieved.

It is worth noting, however, that the spillover effect does not seem to preclude the influence of a different, indeed diametrically opposed, mechanism. The latter is what Elster calls the *compensation effect:* "The compensation effect says that if [a person] does not follow P in X, he will, if he can, do so in Y."[36] If it is true that members of a democratic *society* will not rest satisfied until they also become citizens of a democratic *polity* (spillover effect), it seems no less true that their desire for a democratic polity need not be very intense and that one cause of this lack of intensity (as distinct from a lack of desire) is precisely that they already enjoy to a considerable degree the benefits of a democratic society (compensation effect). There is yet one further complication in that the compensation effect can work in conjunction with the *crowding-out effect.* "The crowding-out effect says that if he does follow P in X, he will not do so in Y."[37] Where the compensation effect works by providing alternative *benefits,* the crowding-out effect does so through powerful *distractions.* These, both benefits and distractions, make up the psychological dimension of so-called performance legitimacy and explain why performance legitimacy can help create the appearance of legitimacy proper and, by the same token, why a substantial drop in performance legitimacy can be politically dangerous.

What are we to make of these complications? The correct approach is not to deny or make light of the compensation effect or the crowding-out effect but instead to give due weight to another important causal factor, pride, and to determine what outcome the new balance of factors is likely to produce.

Thomas Hobbes famously speaks of pride as a potent force in human nature. As such, pride gives rise both to the need for the Leviathan and to the Leviathan's limits. Now, under equality of conditions, the Hobbesian generic pride becomes *democratic* pride, whatever else it may also be. Nothing is more natural than for pride to be shaped by the condition of social relations and to learn gradually to assert itself as such relations become more equal. There thus comes a point in the growth of equality of conditions where the Leviathan will have to adjust its sovereign might—and its form—to democratic pride. This, of course, is only part of the causal trajectory of democracy, but its potency must not be underestimated. And the power of democratic pride is such that members of a society marked by equality of conditions cannot, sooner or later, help but think of themselves as worthy of being recognized and treated as political equals, at which point they will expect their government to bear some credible resemblance to the ideal of popular sovereignty. It is not plausible to believe that democratic pride will cause their desire for a democratic polity to be unbearably intense, under normal circumstances (defined in terms of the normal presence of the compensation effect and the crowding-out effect).[38] Nor, on the other hand, is it plausible, or prudent, to believe that democratic pride will not, under normal circumstances, even be sufficient to create a reasonably strong and sustained desire for a moderate degree of political participation (such as is available in the so-called mature democracies today). This is why I have described the object of democratic pride as a regime that bears some credible resemblance to the notion of popular sovereignty—no more, no less.

This is another way of saying that our sense of democracy's fittingness under equality of conditions, itself both cognitive and normative, is reinforced by democratic pride and that this should make the desire for democracy based on fittingness that much stronger. To be sure, democratic pride is one causal factor among others and its object is one good among others. Yet, being a species of pride, and one that is bound to be widely shared under equality of conditions, it surely must be strong enough not to easily give way in the face of the compensation effect and the crowding-out effect. In other words, democratic pride must surely be able to assert itself with reasonable (that is, neither overwhelming nor negligible) force despite such benefits or distractions as prosperity, opportunities for pleasure, or even individual liberty. Even when such benefits or distractions abound, democratic pride must be reckoned with. When they dwindle or disappear, it will be a force to be marveled at or feared.

Equality of Conditions and Its Effects

There can be little doubt that social equality as described has arrived in China. We can therefore no longer pretend that democracy is not an option, or not a good option, for China. We cannot even plausibly claim that whether democracy is a good option in principle is open to reasonable normative disagreement, nor even that democracy, while normatively appealing, is an option that had better be taken but *need not* be taken precisely because its appeal is (merely) normative. The decisive factor that has emerged from our reconstruction of Tocqueville's arguments for democracy is what Chinese *society* has come to be like and what *political* arrangement best fits such a society. On this basis, I would like to suggest again, this time in more concise terms, that the CCP has itself helped create in China a very considerable degree of equality of *social* conditions and that the *political* implications of such conditions simply cannot be ignored any longer. To put it bluntly, the party will soon have no choice but to compensate for its fast-receding links with the original, revolutionary foundation of its legitimacy with a plausible new rationale based on democracy. All it takes to appreciate this coming necessity is to observe and reflect on the broad trajectory of equality of conditions in communist China so far and its already profound effects on social and political relations and, somewhat more slowly but no less surely, on collective political psychology.

I have already given a rough sketch of the progress of equality of conditions in its economic, ideological, and social manifestations. Switching now to a bird's-eye view, one can see the appearance and expansion of this equality in communist China as the upshot of two momentous processes. The first is a *quasi-democratic* leveling that happened under Mao's leadership, whereby people were made politically and legally equal in principle, but subject to the exclusion of so-called class enemies (lots of them, and their ranks could swell whenever the need arose), and in a manner compromised by the politically enforced urban-rural divide. In the era of reform, this divide has completely lost its moral and political legitimacy, although it is yet to be administratively dismantled. At the same time, the category of class enemies that underlay and compromised Mao-style egalitarianism has been abolished so that political and legal equality now extends in principle to all. These changes, especially the latter, constitute the second momentous process that has propelled equality of conditions forward, this time courtesy of the temper and exigencies of the reform era. Since one mechanism at work in this second process is the discursive cessation of class conflict and its inherently conflict-promoting goals, the process may be thought of as a *quasi-liberal* neutralization (that is, a moderation or deintensification) of values in Chinese society, somewhat comparable to the shift from the passions to the interests and the rise of liberal toleration that happened in early modern Europe.

The discursive removal of the category of class enemies along with their so-called reactionary values entails also the discursive evaporation of the proletariat and especially of those proletarian values that used to be pitted against so-called bourgeois ones. The result is a quasi-bourgeois, humanistic universalism that was anathema in Mao's time. Today, all people supposedly want essentially the same things and hold essentially the same values, at least in the sense that where differences in aspirations and values still exist, they are no longer conceived in terms of good and bad, still less in terms of good and evil, and even less in terms of *political* good and evil. One world, one dream, we are told (as by the Chinese motto for the 2008 Beijing Olympics), with the Chinese Dream continuous (according to Xi Jinping) with the American Dream, among the dreams of other nations. Likewise, the happy and prosperous life of all Chinese, regardless of class (hence class is not even mentioned), and as the people themselves understand it, has become the express goal of the CCP. Furthermore, the achievement of this goal by China, says Xi, will contribute also to the realization of similar goals by other members of the now harmoniously conceived family of nations—that is, a community of the shared future of humankind *(renlei mingyun gongtongti)*.[39] According to new Chinese official doctrine, then, what amounts to an all-encompassing equality of conditions, with no one (either individual or nation) deserving to be left behind, has descended not only on China but on the entire world.

Almost as noteworthy is another consequence of the two waves of equalization in CCP-led China, and that is the transformation of the family as a
site of authority. The traditional patriarchal system started to crumble, in
Mao's China, thanks especially to a sustained effort to equalize relations between men and women, both within and outside the family.[40] Then, in the
decades of reform initiated by Deng, the relation between parents and children
has undergone an equalization that is no less profound in its impact on the
family and beyond. The combined result of these two changes is the decisive
erosion of the subordination of mother and children to the father, indeed of
children to parents, and hence the comprehensive weakening of familial authority. This becomes especially obvious when we observe, say, the difference
in filial disposition between the generation born in the 1950s and the so-
called post-1980s or post-1990s cohort. Thus, in today's China, it can no
longer be said of the family, as it always could within the Confucian tradition, that it is the training ground for obedience to authority—a flexible virtue
that is easily transferable from the family (filial piety) to the state (loyalty).
Although Chinese parents by and large still have a considerable say in their
children's lives (especially concerning marriage and property), the deference
shown them is based more on emotional and financial solidarity between the
generations than on sheer patriarchal or parental authority, of which remarkably little is left after Mao's egalitarianism and Deng's pragmatism. Almost
to the same degree that they have trouble accepting the familial authority of
their parents qua authority, young Chinese today, especially the urban and
the better educated, evince a nonchalance toward political authority that was
unheard-of in the entire Chinese past, including the communist episode.
True, these young people may belong to the fan club of this or that star or
celebrity, but only because they choose to do so, under such influence as they
are willing to accept. In the final analysis, they defer only to themselves, like
latter-day believers who decide for themselves what to believe, how they believe, and whether they believe at all. Whatever views these young Chinese
consciously hold of democracy, there can be little doubt that theirs is a thoroughly democratic mentality, in a broad sense. The political implications of
these changes—the collapse of familial authority and its gradual yet inexorable extension to the political domain—are already profound and will become increasingly so. Equality of conditions erodes and finally destroys not

only parental authority and that of elders but also the deification of rulers that once seemed natural under inequality of conditions.

It is much to the CCP's credit, from today's vantage point, that it has helped bring about equality of conditions in one way under Mao and in another under Deng and his successors. The combined upshot of these two egalitarian waves has changed China beyond recognition. Whatever the material achievements of the economic reform, its greatest social and political consequence undoubtedly has been the broad kind of equality of conditions that Tocqueville thought he observed in America nearly two centuries ago. Aside from the presence of the CCP and some of its consequences, I daresay that the equality of conditions found in China today compares very favorably indeed with its American counterpart back at the time of Tocqueville's journey through eastern America. For we see in China today the public recognition, without exceptions (such as slavery), of exactly what Tocqueville had in mind as equality of conditions—the qualitative sameness of people as distinct from the quantitative difference between, say, rich and poor. And we see the implications of this newfound equality behind everything that is happening in China—the throb and restlessness of a new, pervasively competitive life; the desperate worship of money, success, and celebrity as the only markers of an ever-mobile, insecure superiority; the unstoppable rise in economic and other quantitative inequality; the seething resentment and protest against it, stemming directly from a passion for equality and informed by the demand for equality of opportunity (a derivative of equality of conditions, just as economic inequality and other inequalities of outcome are a natural consequence of the same equality of conditions); and, in art, culture, and taste, the disappearance of everything that used to be considered high or noble or simply qualitatively different.

There is every reason to believe that this unprecedented equality, incomplete and sometimes inconsistent as it may be, is here to stay and needs only time to run its natural course, bringing with it an ethos of individualism and a passion for stability (conducive to rather than incompatible with capitalist competitiveness, including "creative destruction"), prosperity, and hedonism. It is none other than this product of the CCP itself, whether intended or not (one cannot say it was unintended entirely and all along), that has stripped the old revolutionary legitimacy of its aura and indeed emptied the past as such of the power to confer legitimacy on any regime seeking to govern here and now. By the same token, advancing social equality leaves political democracy as the only appropriate alternative to make up for the shortfall caused by the demise of revolutionary legitimacy.

It is worth emphasizing that this is not because—and definitely does not have to be because—equality of conditions is bound sooner or later to produce an overwhelming subjective preference for democracy. It is one thing to suggest that democracy may well come knocking on the door before we know it so we had better be prepared for this eventuality and start thinking about it now, and something else to believe that this will happen because, or chiefly because, democracy will definitely one day become the conscious popular political preference in China. There is no axiom of political life that dictates that democracy must under all circumstances come about democratically, and no reason to believe that a more democratic regime will become an urgent and worthy cause in China only when democracy has turned into an indubitable object of popular desire.

Thanks to the compensation and crowding-out effects, such desire is unlikely to possess sufficient vigor or foresight as long as the CCP manages to do a reasonably good job of maintaining economic growth, rising living standards, and social order—thereby creating the very reasonable apprehension that all of these good things could be jeopardized if China were to gratuitously or for other dubious reasons switch to a politically different and untested (in China) way of doing things. There is also the fact that democracy is the so-called liberty of the ancients and, as such, is in modern society naturally outweighed in importance and salience by the so-called liberties of the moderns, those liberties that people have occasion to use in their everyday, nonpolitical lives. These modern liberties exist plentifully in China today as a result of the economic reform, although they are de facto freedoms that have yet to be publicly affirmed and protected as such. I will discuss later this ambiguous status of individual freedoms in China. For now, suffice it to say that, whatever one's views on democracy may be, in general or with particular reference to China, one should not be surprised by a lack of popular desire for democracy in China, if this indeed turns out to be the case, and need not hastily attribute such lack *entirely* to conscious fear of offending the current political and ideological orthodoxy.

Far stronger is the likelihood that the apparent dearth of popular desire for democracy in China, if true, is due largely to what is known as adaptive preference formation, the adjustment of desires to opportunities—that is, the formation of preferences through subconscious adjustment to forcibly imposed social or, as in the present case, political conditions. One should therefore not be surprised, either, if the lifting of such conditions one day is followed by the sudden eruption of a pervasive unwillingness to accept any but a democratic regime. Indeed I very much suspect that something like this will happen, just as I expect an outpouring of passion for democracy from those who already have this passion but feel too inhibited to give open expression to it in the repressive atmosphere prevailing today.

Whatever the case may be, consciously held and openly expressed political preferences should not be treated as decisive, especially given the serious absence of freedom of conscience and expression in China today. All too often we simply cannot know with confidence what people's preferences are. To the degree that more or less reliable information is available, we have reason to doubt whether even truthfully expressed preferences are *true* preferences—true in the sense of being largely free from distortion by excessive adaptation. Perhaps most important of all, if there is any increased preference for democracy, it may well be expressed—indeed known to the citizens involved themselves—only obliquely in the form of a correspondingly decreased willingness to follow and obey the still-undemocratic political authority of the CCP, at various levels, except under strong pressure or inducement. Compared with this highly consequential (potential) change in political *attitude,* what people's political views happen to be, and what they say those views are, is of decidedly secondary importance.

Thus, when I speak of democracy being the only appropriate response to the demise of revolutionary legitimacy, I do not mean this in a purely (and superficially) subjective sense—in the sense that democracy will be openly, knowingly, and strongly desired by so many that it cannot be resisted any longer. Rather, the steadily increasing appropriateness of democracy I have in mind is, first and foremost, systemic and objective. Continuing changes in economic, ideological, and especially social conditions are bound sooner or later to produce an incapacitating deficit in political authority, regardless of the citizens' political cognition as distinct from their effectual political attitudes. And such a deficit will have to be compensated for in one major way or another.

This is not to imply that what is happening objectively today lacks a subjective dimension or that such a dimension is unimportant—far from it. The subjective dimension comes into the picture to the degree that the deficit in political authority has a strong adverse impact on the deference of citizens toward political authority, irrespective of their views on democracy. Moreover, this deficit has no chance of being effectively addressed unless the remedy has an enduring fit with the deeper political psychology of a modern citizenry that is shaped, above all, by equality of conditions, again irrespective of what people actually take to be their own political preferences. In these ways, the subjective dimension is of crucial importance, and yet it works at a level that is deeper than what citizens happen to think at a given time. It is at this level that two of the arguments I earlier advanced for democracy—the argument from fittingness and the argument from governability—have their true and strongest force. Against the objective backdrop of equality of conditions, it stands to reason that democracy alone is capable of being judged fitting—enduringly and nonopportunistically—in the eyes of citizens and thereby making them stably governable. The longer this objective backdrop lasts and the stronger the equality involved, the closer citizens' subjective preferences will be to the natural affinity between social equality and political democracy. But there is no reason to think that a decisive, conscious shift in subjective preferences will happen overnight or to insist that it must happen before a country, such as China, finds it necessary to start earnest preparation for the passage from social equality to political democracy.

In China especially, waiting would be an unaffordable luxury. As we have seen, the impending double shortfall in legitimacy and performance will create a dangerous weakening of authority whose very unprecedentedness calls for unprecedented measures. In this context, equality of conditions both contributes to the weakening of political authority and limits the range of fitting responses to it. Given the natural affinity between social equality and political democracy, it makes democracy the only fitting response to the looming legitimation crisis and hence the only response that has the potential to work not merely as a stopgap but enduringly. It is the only response that is both prudent—going after stability via legitimacy—and realistic—working with a notion of legitimacy that is in keeping with the most important circumstances—that is, equality of conditions—on the ground.

This means that democracy is at once sorely needed and possible. What a cruel challenge it would be if things were otherwise! As it is, the challenge is daunting but not impossible. This view of the need for democracy and of its possibility is realistic, not romantic, just as the view of equality of conditions on which it rests is. And, much as waiting is a luxury that China can ill afford, so starry-eyed democratic idealism can only be a recipe for quick disappointment and equally quick disaster. This is not to deny the normative case for democracy—the normative part of the larger, prudential case for democracy—but one must be careful not to take it further than has a reasonable chance to come true in the real world. For democracy is no panacea and does not offer any remotely reliable formula for making a modern society prosperous and just, or not too quantitatively unequal. It does not even contain anything like a foolproof formula for stability—the kind of stability we value democracy for—and may even turn stability into a challenge of its own. All the same, under entrenched equality of conditions, democracy alone has the *built-in potential* to produce a stable political order, and this is because it has by far the greatest fit with a society marked by equality of conditions and, indeed, also with the long-term sociopolitical psychology of members of such a society.

In keeping with this normative modesty, the CCP need not adopt any particular model of democracy, Western or otherwise, nor should it approach democracy in a dogmatic fashion focused narrowly on elections. The task it has unwittingly fashioned for itself by creating a society of equality of conditions is broader and more flexible: to devise a type of regime that is most consistent or at least reasonably consistent with equality of conditions. It will be an inestimable boon for China if the party is able to rise to the challenge by choosing democracy in this broad yet definite sense.

Completing a Process Already Under Way

The most important lesson to take away from our brief encounter with Tocqueville is that to appreciate the deeper need, and case, for democracy, we must not think of democracy as a narrowly political question. This lesson is generally ignored in commonsense approaches to the question of democracy, including democracy for China. I believe it would not be a caricature to suggest that such approaches incline us to treat the question of democracy for

China as, at least conceptually, a fairly simple and straightforward one. Ac-cording to the conventional wisdom in these approaches, (a) democracy is a matter of political regime rather than of society; (b) as a political matter, de-mocracy has to do chiefly with the form of government rather than, say, the ends of government (beyond the nearly automatic invocation of "for the people"); (c) as a form of government, democracy is essentially majority rule based on the free and fair election of the most important public officials by universal suffrage; (d) thus conceived, democracy is nowhere to be found in China and, for those who take democracy to be the only legitimate form of government, the task is to set out the normative case for democracy and to devise the political means to establish democracy in a country where none exists today—hence to bring about *wholesale* change *from scratch*.

What is missing from such a picture is any inkling that profound changes are already afoot in China that may in the foreseeable future make democ-racy more or less unavoidable, not merely desirable. There is little doubt that such changes are taking place in the economic, ideological, and especially social conditions of China. And it is not difficult to foresee, given the intrinsic connection between social equality and political democracy as already spelled out, that they will make any regime other than a democratic one harder and harder to justify and maintain. Indeed, earlier changes along the same lines have already done so to a degree that would have been hard to imagine only four decades ago. If such changes continue, as they almost certainly will because no political forces exist that are strong enough to arrest them for long, it will only be a matter of time before democracy comes knocking on the door and the call must be answered in one way or another.

This is how the question of democracy will present itself in China in the near future: not on the strength of subjective, normative inclination but under the pressure of systemic, objective circumstances. To the degree that it is already clear—from the combination of fast-disappearing revolutionary legitimacy, the insufficiency of economic performance as enhancement or amelioration, and unstoppable progress in equality of conditions—how the foreseeable future is likely to unfold in this regard, this is indeed how the question is already presenting itself in China today. The circumstances that will one day thrust the question onto center stage are ones to which one must respond while taking into account a mixture of normative and other con-siderations, of course, but they will confront normative agents and normative deliberators with an objective fact not of their own conscious, normative making. The question is only how well China is prepared for the unavoidable and, given the unavoidable, what it will take for the country to make the best, in both normative and prudential senses, of a type of government it will have no choice but to adopt under social circumstances that are here to stay.

To speak of democracy becoming unavoidable in the foreseeable future is to suggest that democracy is *already* a partial reality in China and that this partial reality will only become more complete with time. Therefore, to be more precise, the question is not whether China will be ready for democracy, as if democracy were something totally new and alien, but whether China will be able to complete a process that is already well under way—a comprehensive transformation for which only the last, political steps are yet to be taken. In this light, the circumstances that will one day make these last steps difficult to resist, though they offer no guarantee that the steps will be taken well, are themselves nothing but components of a partially democratic reality with its own powerful momentum. More simply put, China is already, today, a partially democratic country.

It is largely thanks to Tocqueville—and to predecessors such as Protagoras and Machiavelli—that we are able to see things in this deeper perspective, one that affords the prescience much needed as a guide for timely political action. Once we think of democracy as a matter not only of regime type but also, more profoundly, of the nature and dynamic of a society, we see right past the shortsightedness of conventional wisdom. This, in turn, allows us to raise the question not only of future democracy for China but also of already existing democracy *in* China. The latter question, that of democracy *in* China, has the advantage of being a suitably complex one: complex because China is democratic in some respects but not others, democratic to some degree but not entirely. By examining this question, we will be able to see different aspects of China, different interests and powers, and, above all, contradictions that derive from such differences. It is these contradictions that we will need to grasp if we are to get the facts of the matter right and, on this basis, draw accurate conclusions both about the powerful dynamic at play in the completion of such democracy as is already present in Chinese reality and about the enormous difficulty of bringing about this completion in an orderly and positive fashion.

Consent, Representation, and Democratic
Credibility

What is it, exactly, that might be accomplished when the partial democratic reality in China is brought to a proper completion? What will count as proper completion? Why will that constitute a more dependable answer to the quest for legitimacy and stability that has so far eluded China? These questions demand answers, especially because there are so many examples of democracy without stability. This fact raises a further set of questions, having to do with the exact relation between stability and democracy: What is it about democracy that, when it works reasonably well, makes for stability? And how is stability possible despite so much disagreement and discontent, indeed regarding the practice of democracy itself? More modestly put, for the last question may seem to call for an overly ambitious causal answer, what is it that is constitutive of what we may call democratic stability—the kind of stability that democracy is uniquely capable of providing under modern conditions when it works reasonably well in this regard, even when it is not working well otherwise? Whatever it is, that is what China needs to have in its quest for legitimacy and stability and what it must learn from so-called advanced or mature democracies, despite all the problems they have. Indeed, at least for our present purposes, the presence of democratic stability is chiefly what makes a democracy advanced or mature. What is this democratic stability? What is, as it were, the democratic formula for regime perpetuation?

For all its problems, democracy—or constitutional democracy, to be precise—must be granted one unique advantage, and that is its proven capability to serve as a basis for a relatively stable political order, for regime perpetuation. This advantage is neither arbitrary nor ahistorical (or "universal" in a corresponding sense), for it rests, above all, on the equality of social conditions that characterizes the modern world.

In making this particular kind of case for democracy in China, it is important to avoid any hint of romanticism about how well democracy is doing, say, in Europe or the United States. To this end, as well as to clarify the notion of consent used earlier without explanation, I would like to invoke a distinction that Jean Hampton draws between what she calls convention consent and endorsement consent.[41] Convention consent is the somewhat grudging consent, or acquiescence, that can reasonably be assumed to be (implicitly) granted to a political regime thought of as the outcome of some (hypothetical) constitutional convention. The consent is grudging in that it signals not moral approval of the regime but only that the regime is considered preferable to anarchy or the ending of anarchy by means of sheer domination. This is the degree of consent that must be (hypothetically) attributed to any convention that is capable of establishing a minimally legitimate government; hence convention consent. By contrast, endorsement consent is more or less wholehearted consent, by virtue of having exactly what convention consent lacks—namely, moral approval of a regime—and it offers this approval on the basis of considering the regime to be at least reasonably just. For my purposes, I would gloss "reasonably just" as falling between what Antonio Gramsci calls domination (as distinct from hegemony) and what Marx calls human emancipation (as distinct from political emancipation), for this is the intermediate normative space, as it were, in which democracy, as a legitimate regime, can realistically be expected to operate.

Given the strict meanings of convention consent and endorsement consent as defined by Hampton, it seems quite clear that European and American democracy today enjoys much more than mere convention consent and yet considerably less than remotely universal endorsement consent. If judgment of a society as reasonably just is a necessary condition of endorsement consent, as Hampton stipulates, we have reason to doubt that endorsement consent would be readily forthcoming in the United States or Europe today. There is simply too much public resentment against the growing distributive injustice in favor of the "1 percent" and against the all but irredeemable complicity of the political establishment in this travesty of democratic equality.

This does not mean, however, that democracy enjoys only convention consent in the United States and Europe. Indeed, it seems that moral approval is still generally granted to *something* about the political arrangement, but what? It is fairly obvious that the way democratic government happens to be working, with its enactment of laws and adoption of policies and the effects thereof, does not receive anything like pervasive endorsement consent. Instead we see widespread discontent with democratic government at this *primary* level. This discontent also seems to extend to the *secondary* level, which consists of the rules defining how democratic government is to operate, as well as how it is to be selected and periodically replaced through an electoral system. This can be seen in the political apathy and sense of disenfranchisement that increasingly afflict democracies in Europe, as well as the United States, where, for example, in the eyes of a very large number of people, *Citizens United* and *McCutcheon* have made a bad situation even worse. It is very doubtful that the electoral system itself, the system that is responsible for producing a democratic government, is now able to command broad and unqualified endorsement consent, for so many citizens feel more impotent and frustrated than empowered in the political process.

One is indeed tempted to push further and ask whether the discontent, and the lack of endorsement consent implied by it, does not sometimes go all the way to the *tertiary* level, to the highest-order rules that set the parameters for secondary rules and define how they, including those of the electoral system, are to be revised if necessary. The answer to this kind of question at the tertiary level—that which involves nothing less than the constitution—is harder to determine. But the important thing is that even if the answer turns out to be discouraging, there still seems a further level, a *quaternary* level, to which endorsement consent may retreat. For, despite all the lack of unqualified endorsement consent, most people in advanced democracies do not seem to want *extralegal* revolution, or to abandon democracy in any other way. They may withhold endorsement consent from the way government actually performs, even from the way government is selected and replaced, and, for some, possibly even from the constitutionally stipulated way of changing how government is to operate and how it is to be selected and replaced. If this is so, then almost the entire practice of electoral democracy seems to be in trouble and there looms the specter of a widespread sense of permanent disenfranchisement. However, as long as most people oppose extralegal revolution and do so as a matter of settled preference, despite *Citizens United* and *McCutcheon* and worse, there must be presumed to be some quaternary institution that still commands their full endorsement consent.

There is indeed such an institution, and it is the rule of law—the rule of law in a deeper and more abstract sense than the constitution. To be more precise, it is *democracy as the rule of law* or *democratic rule of law*. This is exactly the meaning of democracy that Hampton seems to have in mind and, in any case, needs to postulate. But when Hampton says that her "analysis presents modern democracies as committed, above all, to *the rule of law,* a phrase that on this analysis means government established by rules that define not only

structure, scope of authority, and officeholder selection but also how the preceding rules can be changed,"[42] she seems to be situating the rule of law at a
level no deeper than the tertiary one. This is not good enough, for it does not
allow for any fallback in the event that endorsement consent is lacking even at
the tertiary, constitutional level. To provide for such an eventuality—that is,
to create a locus for endorsement consent when all three concrete, tangible
levels have failed or do not suffice—a fourth, truly foundational level is required, however amorphous and ineffable. This level must be deeper and
more abstract than what Hampton in the foregoing quote makes it out to be,
deeper and more abstract even than the constitution. It is the level not of the
constitution per se but of the spirit of the constitution, and, by the same token,
not of the rule of law in its existing form but of the spirit of the rule of law—in
a word: constitutionalism. As such, it must be the repository, in terms of
public political culture, of the very rationale for having a democratic constitution in the first place: to settle differences, however great, through peaceful
and relatively civilized contestation according to open and revisable rules,
however flawed, instead of lapsing into the proverbial state of nature or re-
sorting to revolution as its real-life equivalent. This is how Elias sees the deeper
workings of democracy or the democratic rule of law, which exists to stabilize
"bloodless trials of strength" or "bloodless compromises" under modern conditions of functional differentiation, interdependence, and corresponding
self-constraint.[43] To borrow the language (not the view) of Jürgen Habermas
while cleaving to the more realistic picture of Elias, this may be tantamount, if
need be, to preferring even distorted communication, which democracy has
so much trouble regularly rising above, to naked or violent strategic action,
which it has found a reasonably (though not entirely) successful way to avoid.
When such a preference establishes itself as the instinct and ethos of a people,
backed up with constitutionally enshrined basic rights, as it seems to have
done in the countries of Western Europe and North America, aided no doubt
by relatively favorable circumstances (and, in our time, also by the defeat of
communism as a viable fundamental alternative), something takes shape at
the quaternary level that seems capable of absorbing endorsement consent as
a last resort and thereby keeping at bay regime-threatening conflict and disorder despite a less than perfect constitution.

Once we have a clear view of this four-level structure, there seems little
doubt that the great resilience of a mature democracy principally resides in

the way it provides multiple, progressively deeper and firmer loci of endorsement consent. If endorsement consent is insufficiently strong at the primary
level, it can find considerable compensation, as it were, at the secondary level,
and both of these levels can rely, in case of slack, on the powerfully centripetal
tertiary, constitutional level, which, in turn, has underlying it an even more
seemingly indestructible quaternary level. The advantage afforded by such
depth of structure becomes very striking indeed if we compare this model with
its Chinese counterpart. Although it is difficult to render a precise comparison
briefly, one can nevertheless say without great distortion that in the Chinese
case the main and, given the fast-disappearing revolutionary legitimacy, potentially sole locus for endorsement consent (or lack thereof) is available at the
primary level, that of the making of laws and policies and their implementation. That is why performance legitimacy is such a life-and-death matter.

Unsurprisingly, there is something Hobbesian about this distinctively
modern Western accomplishment. Thus what seems to be at work at the quaternary level is, as it were, *negative democracy*—a set of rules and institutions chiefly designed to secure the *absence* of violence or revolution in the
selection and replacement of government rather than any reasonably assured
and just delivery of more positive goods. While negative democracy by its
very nature cannot provide performance legitimacy, which is available chiefly
at the primary level, its very negativity—its catering to the extremely strong
fear of political evil in the shape of violence and tyranny—is precisely what
makes it so powerful. The current situation in the United States, for example,
seems to require some such understanding if we are to be able to explain why,
despite the alleged unconstitutional system of "double government" and the
alleged reality or prospect of "the fall of the constitution and the rise of a
shadow government," endorsement consent still seems to be widely granted
to *something* about the political arrangement taken as a whole.[44] This object
of *endorsement* consent can be none other than the democratic rule of law
construed in the deepest sense. Even if what thus retains endorsement consent does not quite qualify as *reasonably just,* as Hampton requires of endorsement consent, there is little doubt that moral approval is still amply
present in it,[45] enabling democratic rule of law to serve as a legitimate basis
of reasonably stable government.

It is necessary at this point to bring in a notion that Hampton does not
invoke and that I have so far studiously avoided: representation. It is a truism

of modern democracy that democracy is a matter of representation, of the state representing society—that is, the interests of or in society. According to this truism, those represented are not only interest-bearers or passive beneficiaries in society but also citizen-agents who, through political participation, help reproduce the representative organs of the democratic state and maintain the health of such organs. It was once thought to be a unique advantage of modern democracy that the system of free and fair elections based on universal suffrage, aided by a reasonably well-informed public sphere, is able to take care of both the material and the agential interests of the represented—to make the state truly representative (of society) and the representation itself truly democratic (by giving citizens real political powers). Such a scenario, if made good, would lend real credibility, beyond mere empirical credence, to the fundamental animating idea of democracy—namely, sovereignty of the people.

Alas, this scenario is not much found in reality, and therefore what I have referred to as the truism of modern democracy is actually only a commonplace that is far from true. We know this from the fact that too much of what happens at the primary level (what democratic government daily does and is able to deliver for society), and at the secondary level (how the representative organs of the democratic state are reproduced) as well, is not credibly the object of endorsement consent. In plainer language, there is woefully insufficient endorsement consent at the more tangible levels of democratic politics. As I have noted, we have to retreat to the tertiary level (of allegiance to the constitution), or even all the way to the quaternary level (of politico-cultural faith in democratic rule of law as an alternative to violent conflict), in order to locate a reasonably secure object of endorsement consent. In other words, endorsement consent still exists, but it has become abstract.

What this retreat signifies is that representation—the state representing society by reasonably justly and effectively serving the interests in society and by providing citizens with real opportunities for political participation—has become, or turned out to be, largely a fiction. Many undoubtedly still believe the fiction, but a dangerously large number are having second thoughts. It follows, especially for the more skeptical, that the function of the electoral system has undergone a fundamental change. In the real world it no longer serves to make real and credible the representative function of democratic government but instead only to make visible and plausible a new kind of consent. What characterizes this new consent is that it has parted company with representation and therefore is an endorsement only of the democratic rules of contestation—that is, democratic rule of law—without much solid hope for such contestation to produce representativeness in terms of desired outcome. If we are not to shy away from the truth of the matter, we may have to admit that this is more or less the only purpose left that is still reasonably well served by free and fair elections. Of course, as long as elections continue to be held, they may be counted on to help shore up the fiction of representation for the more credulous, unless or until democratic politics becomes even less representative than it is today. It is essentially this combination—of abstract endorsement consent and a fiction of representation kept half-alive by an electoral system that is no longer representative despite being (formally) free and fair—that is keeping the democratic system afloat.

Keeping the democratic system afloat, I may add, in the all-important sense of serving as a reasonably effective mechanism for (peaceful) regime perpetuation. I will say, without the slightest irony, that this is no mean achievement. And I say this because, for all the problems now besetting European and American democracy, it is alive and well in a limited sense— namely, democratic rule of law—and for a limited yet extremely basic and important purpose—namely, the provision of a reasonably stable and enduring political order. It is alive and well because at the quaternary level, as democratic rule of law, democracy still commands widespread moral approval. This moral approval, in turn, allows otherwise unrepresentative free and fair elections to serve their (ideological) function of helping create a not insubstantial semblance and sense of political agency—something no nondemocratic system is remotely capable of doing to the same degree! These two factors combined—general moral approval of democratic rule of law and a modest sense of political agency made plausible by free and fair elections—give democracy a unique appeal (despite its element of make-believe) and resilience (despite its vulnerability to disagreement and discontent). As the only political form compatible with modern equality of conditions, democracy faces no truly formidable threat from any nondemocratic alternative under circumstances of reasonable peace and prosperity. Such achievement of Hobbesian peace, and much more, by apparently democratic means that effectively hide the unpalatable absoluteness of sovereignty is a truly astounding political invention.[46] For this reason alone, China has extremely important lessons to learn from European and American constitutional democracy.

We are now in a position to spell out what it would mean for China to become a wholly democratic country, complementing its already largely democratic society with a democratic political regime. To this end, I want to make sharper and more explicit a distinction toward which I have been working so far. This is the distinction between representation, (endorsement) consent, and the credibility of claims to representation or consent. Using this distinction, and mindful of the messiness of the real world, one could with reasonable realism define democracy in terms of more or less credible representation and consent, with the degree of credibility depending crucially on the relevant institutional mechanism (with its attendant ideology). Complications immediately arise, and one of these is caused by the possible divergence between representation and consent. These may be said to converge when endorsement consent is present at all levels, not just at the highly abstract levels of allegiance to the constitution and faith in democratic rule of law. Accordingly, the existence of abstract endorsement consent alone—implying as it does strong disapproval of what happens at the more concrete levels of political outcomes and processes—is distinct from representation and signals its relative absence. A further complication exists in the shape of the difference between two capacities of the represented—as passive interest-bearers (with the interests located in *society*) and as active citizen-agents (with the agency pertaining to and manifest in the *political* sphere). It is here that the mechanism for making representation and consent credible plays an essential but rather complicated role.

Representation can be real or unreal—that is, nonexistent—despite claims or beliefs to the contrary. Consent, on the other hand, is either actual—that is, actually given or withheld (without duress)—or hypothetical—that is, not actually expressed but such as can be reasonably inferred. There is a sense, of course, in which hypothetical consent may be said to be real or unreal, too, depending on the reasonableness of the inference, just as actual consent can be regarded as more or less real according to its degree of freedom from self-misunderstanding and misinformation, but this can be mostly set aside for our purposes. For what is important is that there is nothing as effective as *actual* consent, or more precisely the opportunity to give or withhold actual consent, for lending credibility not only to the alleged existence of (real) consent but also to claims to (real) representation. The opportunity to actually give and especially withhold consent serves to make government democratic not in the sense of self-government—it is the consent to *be governed* and *be represented*—but in the more modest sense of government having to depend *openly* and *verifiably* on the citizenry for legitimacy.[47] That is why free and fair elections, however open to partisanship and manipulation and otherwise flawed, are so difficult, indeed well-nigh impossible, to get rid of once they have become part of a mature democratic political regime. A well-functioning free and fair electoral system serves to translate *actual* consent smoothly and unobtrusively into what is *believed to be real* consent and, potentially, credible (believed to be real) representation. Even when otherwise lacking in substance, elections stage highly visible and powerfully charged ritual enactments and affirmations of endorsement consent to the political system at regular intervals. A large part of their credibility comes, no doubt, from the perception that the opportunity to give or withhold consent, as made available by a free and fair electoral system, allows significant scope for citizens' political agency, an important (objective and subjective) good in its own right in addition to its supposed instrumental role in securing tangible benefits.[48]

Given this conceptual scheme, we can say that American democracy today, for example, has evolved a reasonably effective mechanism for making abstract endorsement consent credible. A crucial element of this mechanism is the opportunity for actual consent as made available by the system of free and fair elections, although it is worth emphasizing that what this helps make credible is not so much representation as abstract endorsement consent. We may add, and this is a subtler point, that where American democracy is not doing well in terms of the representation of interests (and, by the same token, is thwarting political agency with regard to interests),[49] it is compensating, as it were, by still providing relatively plentiful scope for political contestation and, in this way, for citizens' political agency and sense of agency (as distinct from favorable outcomes). Thus we are witnessing not only the coming apart of representation and consent but also the divergence within political agency between activity and sense of participation, on the one hand, and efficacy regarding interests and outcomes, on the other. At one time or another in its history, American democracy may have succeeded much better in securing endorsement consent at concrete levels, in giving more efficacy to political agency, and hence in making credible not only abstract endorsement consent but also representation. But it is not doing even reasonably well now in terms of representation or effectual political agency, and the prospects of improvement are not bright. Roughly the same assessment can be made of Europe.

There is no reason for China not to aim for a higher degree of representation than is being achieved today in the Western democracies.[50] Indeed this is what the CCP is already doing in those various ways that fall naturally under the rubric of performance legitimacy. There is little doubt, given its use of performance as a crucial prop for its legitimacy, that it cares very much about consent as well. The problem is that the consent being sought, however real (or unreal), is for the most part not actual consent. Therefore, even if the consent claimed cannot simply be ruled out as unreal for being hypothetical, it lacks the credibility that is indispensable to legitimacy. What the CCP badly needs is an institutional mechanism for making credible its claimed success at representation, as well as the popular consent or support it claims to enjoy as a natural consequence. Given the less than shining record of *electoral* democracy, one has every reason not to make a fetish of elections. There is nothing intrinsically amiss with the CCP's apparent desire to achieve representation while bypassing "Western-style" free and fair elections. The name of the democratic game is credibility—credible representation and credible consent—not elections as such. But credibility, in turn, requires (a regime's) claims to representation or consent to be falsifiable to a reasonable degree. Certainly, free and fair elections are a blunt instrument for enabling falsification, but they have earned their far from negligible status as a minimally trustworthy method in the absence of better ones. If the CCP is unhappy with this method, for one reason or another, it must find a better one.[51] Any mechanism that can produce the needed credibility (of representation or consent) is democratic in the requisite sense.[52]

In this, the CCP definitely has its work cut out for it. In seeking a better method than elections, it must meet two other conditions. Whatever mechanism is used to make representation and consent credible must also, first, be (at least minimally) responsive to the desire of many citizens for political agency. If a proposed mechanism lacks such responsiveness, it is unlikely that it will do much to make representation or consent credible. In this regard, performance legitimacy clearly falls short, for it lacks an agential dimension, taking care of interests only but not participation. Then, second, the mechanism must be capable of supporting, by helping create the necessary credibility, an abstract endorsement consent just in case representation fails or is ineffective and only the recourse to something much deeper—say, allegiance to the constitution or faith in democratic rule of law—can save the day.

All of this makes China's achievement, or completion, of democracy a very tall order. One has no reason to make the task even harder, and unnecessarily so, by being dogmatic either about what democracy is or about how it can best be achieved. Only the bare essentials must be insisted on. Representation is extremely important, but it is also extremely difficult to achieve. Failing a reasonable degree of representation—always a distinct possibility—we need to rely on abstract endorsement consent. Both representation and consent must be made credible, if not by free and fair elections, then by some other equally or, one hopes, more effective mechanism, and either method must leave reasonable scope for political agency, as an instrument and for its own sake. In a nutshell, democracy is a matter of credible representation and/or credible consent—"and/or" because representation and consent may diverge, in which case credible abstract endorsement consent may have to suffice. Within these parameters, China has a good deal of room to maneuver, drawing on its possible strengths in representation (of interests) and overcoming its clear weaknesses with regard to actual consent and political agency. In addition, it needs to make up for its lack of some political deep structure, as it were, that is worthy of abstract endorsement consent—that is, something capable of commanding endorsement consent at a sufficiently deep, abstract, and enduring level. This does not have to be exactly like the democratic rule of law in its English, French, American, or any other historical versions. Even here, there should be scope for experimentation and invention rather than mere imitation. The only thing that would be hard to imagine is how any political arrangement could be stable in China that is not democratic in the general, relatively flexible senses just sketched or, in other words, that defies the modern equality of conditions that China shares with Europe and North America and much of the rest of the world.

Tian, Hence Confucianism, Is Not a
Viable Alternative

It should come as no surprise that there used to be a Chinese functional equivalent of the democratic rule of law. How else could the Chinese empire, universal and all-encompassing in its conception, have lasted for more than two thousand years despite all the upheavals of dynastic change? I am referring to *tian*—that is, Heaven as a cosmological being sharply distinguished from ancestral spirits, moralized, and accorded the highest authority, and, as such, conferring only a conditional, nonpermanent mandate on rulers and thereby allowing them to be held to account in terms of such a mandate. This *tian* did for the entire duration of Chinese imperial rule what democratic rule of law (or constitutionalism more generally, depending on how far back we go in history) has been doing for modern European and American societies, especially as we now find them. It served as a foundation for, and gave ultimate legitimacy to, one dynasty after another that each saw its fair share of strife and discord at all levels below *tian.* It provided a potent source of continuity through all the violent dynastic successions. It underlay the dominant Confucian normative order centered on *ren* (humaneness) and embodied in *li* (rituals), thereby raising human normative conventions to the level of Heaven-ordained justice and at the same time subjecting such conventions to a higher authority. And it lent its name, and all the unarguable legitimacy implicit in the name, to the ruler (*tianzi,* son of heaven), his rule (*tianchao,* heavenly reign), and his domain (*tianxia,* all under heaven). It gave the emperor his unique role as the indispensable link, dramatized through ritual observances, between cosmic processes and human fortune—with the successful performance of this role, as manifest in the relative absence of natural catastrophe and famine, confirming the presence of *tianming* (mandate of heaven). And, in a master stroke as full of tension as it was ingeniously stabilizing, it set itself, in the shape of *tiandao* (the way of heaven) and *tianli* (the principle of heaven), apart from and above the ruler, thereby constituting a source of legitimacy immune to the unworthy behavior of rulers and turning the Confucian scholar-official class into something of an independent countervailing moral force within an otherwise undivided imperial sovereignty.

When the last imperial dynasty, the Qing, fell in 1911, it was nothing less than *tian* as the deepest foundation for imperial rule that came to an end—what turned out to be an irreversible end. Because the Qing was thus the last dynasty, its fall meant the end not only of a dynasty but also of the entire species of rule grounded in *tian*—the demise not merely of a particular dynasty but of the Heavenly Reign as such.

What followed was the inauguration of a republic, the first in China, much like what happened after the French Revolution, at least in the generic sense of creating an altogether new basis for political rule. And just as the dust took a long time to settle in the wake of the revolution in 1789, so after 1911 one quest after another for legitimate and stable constitutional, republican rule ended in failure until the CCP seized power on a basis that neither relied on *tian* nor was exactly republican. For the basis of the brand-new political order established by the party was thoroughly teleological, as opposed to either cosmological or constitutional. The telos was communism, of course, a worldly goal that under Mao was meant to be realized according to a more or less definite schedule. As long as this supposedly scientifically grounded teleology was credible, aided immeasurably by an aura of ruthless invincibility due to successful revolutionary violence, it looked as if a worthy substitute for *tian* had been found, a new basis for legitimate rule no less solid and enduring.

This has turned out to be an illusion, and that is why we are back to square one—why, as I intimated earlier, China is today no closer to accomplishing the task of replacing *tian* than it has been since 1911 or 1949. To be sure, China is incomparably more stable and cohesive today, as well as stronger and more prosperous, than it was at either of those earlier times. But this has been due to a teleological warrant of legitimacy that is now well on its way to losing all its credibility and efficacy, and due to a complementary or compensatory performative success that is not guaranteed to continue indefinitely. The gaping void that opened up with the fall of *tian* is as unfilled as ever. The rule of the CCP as a bona fide *communist* party—that is, until the launch of the proto-capitalist reform in the late 1970s—has turned out to be no more than an interregnum. But what will this interregnum lead to?

At the fundamental level, the highest meaningful level of abstraction for the matter at hand, the choice is between *tian* and democracy, between the reinvention of *tian* and the inauguration of democracy (up to the quaternary level, as democratic rule of law). This choice is comparable to the one posed, in the European context, by Tocqueville in terms of democracy versus aristocracy, with the latter covering all regime types or bases of rule that do not belong under democracy. In the case of China, given its long and unique tradition, the fundamental choice is between democracy and *tian* as the foundation of a legitimate political order. So which should be chosen? The one to be *reinvented* or the one to be *inaugurated*?

Taiwan has already opted for democracy. For all the problems with its democratic practice (and one should expect no less), it has taken a giant leap toward dispensing with *tian* as the basis of a legitimate and stable political order. Time will tell how definitively successful this leap was. So far, however, most signs have been encouraging if we take care to disentangle the performative success of democratic governments from the different kind, and different order, of success involved in establishing the basis of government in the first place.

I am bringing up the case of Taiwan not only as a positive example in the Chinese quest for legitimacy and stability after the demise of *tian* but for another important reason as well. This has to do with the place of the Confucian tradition in the newfound democratic political order. It is safe to say that the Confucian tradition was much better preserved under the Kuomintang in Taiwan than under Mao on the mainland—with the result that cultural Confucianism is arguably still more alive in Taiwan than in mainland China, notwithstanding the entrenched Japanese influence, as well as more recent complications caused by the sharp rise in separatist tendencies that have not spared cultural identity. Yet it is no less safe to say that Confucianism is not part of the foundation of Taiwan's new democratic political order. This is true at least in the sense that, as far as the basis of legitimacy is concerned, Confucianism is not in competition with democracy in Taiwan, and that, if it were, its defeat or marginalization would be predictable. Thus, in whatever form or to whatever degree that remnants of the Confucian tradition are continuing to play a role (I am not implying that the form is important and the degree large, or otherwise), it remains the case that the fundamental choice is between inaugurating democracy and reinventing *tian* and that Taiwan has taken the plunge for the former. It has emerged from its Kuomintang-led interregnum as a polity founded on what seems to be an enduring democratic basis.

Indeed, the same can be said, in spirit if not detail, of a country such as South Korea, which, unlike Taiwan, can be described as a (partly, but only partly) Confucian democracy.[53] There is nothing incoherent about what is called Confucian democracy, but only provided that the role of Confucianism is not to rival or dilute democracy but only to help shape the political preferences of the demos, both substantive and procedural.[54] This proviso gives us, as it were, unalloyed democracy, one whose democratic core is left intact. If one insists on thinking of it, in a case such as South Korea, as alloyed with Confucianism, it is so alloyed only in the same sense in which democracy in Europe and North America is alloyed with Christianity (in one form or another, and often coexisting with other, lesser religious influences and with consciously secular values once derived from religious traditions). All democracies are alloyed in this way, in that they all have as their sovereign a people who, in turn, must have some self-understandings that make their influence felt in political life and yet stem from sources other than democracy itself. Thus Confucian democracy makes perfect sense, subject to this proviso, and it makes sense in a way that "Confucian liberalism" or "Confucian *liberal* democracy" would not, liberalism being a species of universalism or universalistic humanism that essentially, in its constitutive intent, transcends culturally peculiar identities.

There is an extremely important sense, however, in which whatever Confucian values and practices are able to figure in a Confucian democracy will no longer be what Confucianism fundamentally was and is. This is because Confucianism, as the Chinese tradition's foundational, comprehensive discourse, is at the deepest level a cosmology. It is this cosmology that underlies the moral Confucianism that, in turn, informs political Confucianism (which, it should be added, in turn always in practice worked in tandem with Legalism). Without this cosmology, a ruler could still be a sage (*shengren*) but no longer a Son of Heaven, and a dynasty could at best only be sagely rule short of Heavenly Reign, and this simply is not good enough. What is merely moral, Confucian or otherwise, cannot be beyond debate or dispute, so it, in turn, requires a kind of grounding or naturalization that in the Chinese tradition only *tian* is capable of providing. Also, of course, what is merely moral is, paradoxically, something that rulers could more easily and certainly more visibly fall short of, leading to potentially delegitimating consequences. Without *tian,* too, the ruler's domain, conceived as All under Heaven, would be devoid of ultimate justification, which no amount of merely normative discourse could adequately furnish.

Even if one were to think of *tian* as a noble lie à la Plato, one would have to concede that it has been so woven into the fabric of Confucianism as to be indistinguishable from a truly held article of faith. For Confucianism, from its very inception, took itself to be following the only correct way, and this had to be conceived as the Way of Heaven. Thus knowledge regarding the disposition of Heaven rather than only of mere humans was required of the ruler in his capacity as the Son of Heaven and as the arch-mediator between Heaven and human affairs. To give up the notion of *tian* would be to give up the notion of *tiandao,* which, in turn, would be not only to jettison the now embarrassing idea of *tianzi* but also, more generally, to open the way to conventionalism without foundation, to mere human normativity, to pluralism, relativism, or perspectivism—in a word, to democracy! And this is exactly what has befallen Confucianism in our day now that it has been divested of *tian* and *tiandao* at the hands of its more liberal interpreters. Whether or not this was a good move in itself, this plainly could not have been what Confucius and his followers believed in their own day, and *tian* could not have been merely a noble lie invented to serve some pressing purpose and dispensable when no longer needed.

What is of paramount significance, then, is not whether Confucianism, considered (in the spirit of a thought experiment) as a "philosophical" scheme independent of time and place, has to rest on a cosmology revolving around *tian* but whether, considered as a historical discourse legitimating a particular kind of rule, however flexibly or broadly conceived, it is capable of coherently dispensing with such a cosmology. The plain fact is that since the Western Zhou's decisive invention of the Mandate of Heaven, especially since the establishment of the Confucian-Legalist state in the Han dynasty, no imperial rulers with the least concern for what we would today think of as legitimacy as distinct from sheer domination have chosen to dispense with the Mandate of Heaven and no Confucian scholars have remotely advised them to do so. The extraordinary weight of this historical fact places the burden of proof squarely on those who argue otherwise today while maintaining that what is left after the removal of *tian* is still political Confucianism.

For all the reasons just adduced, *tian* is an essential part, indeed the deepest part, of Confucianism, although it has seldom been the part most talked about. It indeed makes good sense that it does not attract as much discursive attention as normative Confucianism does, notwithstanding the latter's basis in the former. Given its nature and its role, *tian*, once known to be there (that is, everywhere), is best invoked ritually or as necessary but otherwise, for the most part, left in the background, securely taken for granted.

When many varieties of contemporary Confucianism make light of cosmology or even remove it altogether, then, the result is not just Confucianism revised and updated but, well and truly, Confucianism dismembered and eviscerated. With the all-important *tian* taken out, what remains of Confucianism is ripe for incorporation into a modern, essentially non-Confucian worldview. There Confucianism gains a new lease on life but only as a supplement. However substantial this new role may be, it is defined and delimited by something more basic that is not supplied by Confucianism itself. This is manifestly true of Confucian democracy, where an attenuated, purely normative and cultural Confucianism plays second fiddle in a political regime that is founded on a different, democratic basis. In other words, democracy is *ti* (essence), and Confucianism only or largely *yong* (instrumentality). Cosmology alone, its distinctive cosmology, gives Confucianism its foundation and life source and guarantees its integrity and self-sameness. It is thus only after its dismemberment or evisceration that Confucianism is fit to enter into combinations, as it were, such as Confucian democracy, whose center of gravity lies elsewhere than in Confucianism. The vacuum left by the abandonment of cosmology in general and of *tian* in particular is filled with democracy. Democratic rule of law has taken over the foundational role that *tian* used to play but is no longer able to play.

This is not to take issue with Confucian democracy, or similar uses of Confucianism, but only to suggest that no such appropriation of Confucianism can change the fundamental choice facing China after the passing of the revolutionary teleological interlude: *Tian* or democracy? Without explicit invocation of the Mandate of Heaven, there can be no truly Confucian approach to political legitimacy. Inasmuch as Confucian democracy and moderate Confucian political perfectionism in their different ways have opted for democracy, they are Confucian only in a secondary sense.[55] Neither of these is Confucian in the deep, foundational sense of a self-sufficing paradigm independent of and fit to be pitted against the modern Western paradigm of democracy—democracy in Tocqueville's broad sense as defined in contrast with aristocracy. When all is said and done, all such Confucianism must be taken to (implicitly) subscribe to democracy in the broad sense and, by the same token, to democracy as an essential modern political concept in terms of which Confucianism must reorient and remake itself.

Confucianism does not, that is, serve as a *grounding* for democracy, still less for a nondemocratic order, but only serves to give an already (self-)grounded democracy a certain culturally distinctive *form*. The latter role, while consequential in many ways, is not of the first importance, for it does not make Confucianism a fundamental *alternative* to democracy and is not intended to do so.

The alternative, the only alternative, is the reinvention of *tian,* the revival of Confucianism with a cosmology, or, simply, cosmological Confucianism.[56] This is the radical mission of Confucianism conceived as *ti* rather than merely *yong,* Confucianism not as a supplement to democracy but, with the help of *tian,* as an alternative to democracy. Whether this is desirable is another matter, and there is no need to take it up for our purposes, although my view is easily inferable from the discussion. In comparison with it, however, all other versions of Confucianism pale in ambition (as distinct from normative appeal), useful as they are at lower levels of meaning and consequence—that is, useful only in the form of variations on the dominant theme of democracy.

The same is true of what is called political meritocracy, Confucian or otherwise, for it, too, is not foundational but must be attached to something that is. As it happens, the meritocracy (of sorts) we see in China today finds its place and meaning in the CCP's current agenda and is parasitic on whatever legitimacy underlies this agenda. As such, this meritocracy is more a matter of the efficient execution of shared, taken-for-granted ends,[57] such as economic (first high-speed, then high-quality) growth and the Chinese Dream as its ideological form, than of the disclosure and imposition of ends—say, communism—in the manner of prophets like Mao (albeit a somewhat derivative prophet given his debts to Marx). Thanks to its already entrenched equality of conditions, China today simply has no room for new prophets, for any ends-regarding meritocracy. Thus political meritocracy today has to appropriate an existing ends-regarding mandate, such as derived from what I earlier called substantive populism, rather than truly define ends for itself and hence what counts as merit in the meritocracy, as Maoist communist meritocracy once was able to do in its capacity as the self-proclaimed vanguard. In the final analysis, then, political meritocracy today is only an administrative meritocracy, for it is essentially a matter of performance with respect to largely given or taken-for-granted ends, and of leadership only in this largely instrumental sense, and this means that its source of legitimacy must be found elsewhere.

Although otherwise not directly comparable, nationalism too fails to be a fundamental option, for the same reason. Like Confucian democracy or political meritocracy, and unlike *tian,* it is no substitute for democracy; it does not qualify for such a role even in principle, devoid as it is of its own raison d'être and hence parasitic on some independent source of legitimacy such as communism (source of revolutionary patriotism), democracy (source of constitutional patriotism), or *tian* (basis for a paradoxical patriotism devoted to one part of *tianxia* and presupposing divisions thereof).

We are thus left, after the communist revolutionary interlude, with *tian* as the only fundamental alternative to democracy. Only a Confucianism that embraces this alternative is a radical, truly distinctive Confucianism, Confucianism as *ti,* as a paradigm in its own right, rather than as a cultural remnant finding a new lease on life in a modern, democratic paradigm.

The question is whether such Confucianism has any reasonable chance of reinventing a lost *tian* as the Chinese alternative to democratic rule of law for the purpose of securing legitimacy and stability in today's China. Certainly, radical Confucians with this sense of mission exist. The most sophisticated among them are conscious of the need for nothing less than the reinvention of *tian,* conscious of the deep reasons underlying this need, and conscious of the difficulty of accomplishing such an audacious task. Intellectually, at least, they must be credited with knowing what they are doing and what it takes to succeed. One sign that they are aware of the enormous odds against their project is that even they are not above making compromises with the reality and sensibilities of the modern world. Jiang Qing, an ultraconservative Confucian, for example, while attempting to reinvent a comprehensive political Confucianism equipped with a full-blown cosmology, nevertheless is prepared to settle for a mixed regime with a popular component, in a manner somewhat reminiscent of Machiavelli (of the *Discourses*) or even of the eighteenth-century British constitution.[58]

There is a sense in which Confucian cosmology has died twice: first, as part of the modern process of enlightenment or nihilism (depending on one's perspective) that has caused the proverbial death of God, and, second, as a result of the relentless uprooting in Mao's China of what had remained of the Confucian legacy, especially during the Cultural Revolution. After this double death, it is extremely doubtful, to put it mildly, that Confucianism can be brought back to life, root and branch. From a purely political point of view, any revival or reinvention of a *comprehensive* Confucianism, one with an all-encompassing worldview, would leave no room for Marxism, the CCP's official doctrine, and hence no room for the CCP itself as a nominally Marxist party. Small wonder, then, that the CCP, despite its eagerness to tap the legitimation potential of Confucianism, has stopped well short of embracing anything remotely resembling a Confucian cosmology. It is revealing, in this connection, that the Confucian-sounding suggestion, made by some astute scholar-ideologues, that the party is now entrusted by the Mandate of Heaven with the sacred mission of restoring China's former glory has so far not been taken up by the party itself.[59]

And one must not forget that this temptation is being resisted by a CCP whose original wellspring of revolutionary legitimacy is running dry. With this source of legitimacy turning out to mark only an interlude, albeit an extremely consequential one, we are left only with *tian* versus democracy. If not *tian,* then democracy, for there is nothing else that could impart legitimacy beyond the contingent, short-lived effects of mere performative success. Throughout Chinese history rulers have never seen fit to dispense with legitimacy proper and settle for mere performance legitimacy. In traditional China, legitimacy proper resided in the Mandate of Heaven, with performance legitimacy subordinate to and reflective of it. In CCP-led China, legitimacy proper resided in a communist teleology, again with performance legitimacy subordinate to and reflective of it. To suggest that performance legitimacy by itself will suffice today is tantamount to admitting that the category of legitimacy proper is being left empty *and* claiming that political authority and social stability can be maintained over time without filling it in one way or another. This is surely the most audacious claim in the entire history of Chinese political thought! At least the CCP has not made this claim; nor, of course, the admission.[60] And it speaks volumes, in this context, that the CCP has unabashedly assigned a place to democracy on its list of socialist core values.[61] Whatever the party may mean by democracy, it unmistakably, by virtue of the sheer fact of having democracy appear on that hallowed list, acknowledges democracy at least as an essentially contested concept—that is, as a concept that the party knows it cannot bypass in its self-legitimation and hence a concept it has no choice but to contest and appropriate to its own advantage. This is extremely important, for the door to democracy is thrown open, discursively open, by the CCP itself.

CHAPTER FOUR

Democracy and the Self-Protection of Society

IN MAKING MY PARTIALLY Tocqueville-inspired case for democracy in terms of equality of conditions, I have had to leave out something of crucial importance—the connection between equality of conditions and capitalism. I did so to better concentrate on the connection between equality of conditions and democracy, in turn largely because Tocqueville himself did the same, seeing almost no link between equality of conditions and capitalism. Because of this omission, my account of equality of conditions is incomplete, my account of democracy in terms of equality of conditions incomplete to the same degree. Correcting this omission is much more than a merely academic exercise, for this brings a key term into our discussion, *democratic capitalism,* and, parallel to it, a key function of democracy, the *self-protection of society.*

While these are the most direct and obvious consequences of the omission and its correction, they are not the only important ones. For the economic performance that either enhances legitimacy or ameliorates its lack is largely the performance of a capitalist or proto-capitalist economy, and therefore it is impossible to get an adequate picture of China's current legitimation crisis without taking a careful look at what its capitalism is like. Furthermore, we will find, as an important by-product, that the effects of unsatisfactory economic performance on legitimacy confirm, from a new and distinct angle, the extreme closeness of legitimacy and performance we have already observed.

There are two other, more general gains to be made from thus resituating democracy and the legitimation crisis in the context of capitalism. One is an understanding of Western democracy that is two-dimensional, involving democracy's relation both to the state (constitutional democracy) and to capitalism (democratic capitalism), hence of democracy as an (effective or failed) antidote both to imperium, state power, and to dominium, the power of private property. The other, drawing on the first, is the possibility of a more accurate comparison of China's current legitimation crisis with that of Western democratic capitalism. The combined result promises an appraisal of China's democratic challenge, as well as the democratic challenge in the world at large, that is more accurate and more sober than it would otherwise be. Such an appraisal, taken together with the lessons of democratic stability, will counsel Chinese to exercise modesty and vigilance in equal measure when deciphering the experience of European and American constitutional democracy and democratic capitalism.

Democracy and Capitalism

Suppose that I have made a plausible enough case for democracy—one that rests crucially on the political implications of equality of social conditions. Such a case, however plausible, remains an overly general, because truncated, one. For it neglects, albeit in the present case purposely, to specify the nature of the society in which equality of conditions happens to exist, that gives rise to the need for and the momentum toward democracy, and that helps determine the kind of democracy needed and possible. Equality of conditions in what kind of society, then, or, in other words, what kind of equality of conditions? By equality of conditions, Tocqueville obviously has in mind early nineteenth-century America, and he gives us to understand that such equality was not much compromised by what he calls industrial or manufacturing aristocracy (the corporate elite, as it is sometimes called today) and that therefore democracy did not have much to fear from this (in his view) rather superficial departure from social equality.[1] Either Tocqueville was mistaken about America, at least partially, and about the relation between democracy and capitalism in general, or times have changed. Or both, as I think is actually the case.[2] In the world today and as it has been for quite a long time, democracy is part of a larger politico-economic order best described as democratic capitalism. As such, democracy finds both its raison d'être and its limitations in a somewhat subsidiary and largely reactive role in relation to capitalism. Thus, equality of conditions as it exists today is equality of conditions as defined and shaped by capitalism, with its inherently *unequal* relationship between capital and labor, and by democracy reacting to it. In our time, therefore, the question of democracy is the question of democratic capitalism, and, as part of this question, the legitimation crisis of democracy is the crisis of democratic capitalism.

To get a fuller picture of democratic capitalism, it is helpful to distinguish three ideal-typical relations in which democracy can stand to capitalism. Corresponding to these three relations, we can also speak of three meanings of democracy. The simplest way to spell out these ideal-typical relations is by attending to the interplay between the (capitalist) economic sphere and the (democratic) political sphere. Three broad models or possibilities immediately present themselves. In the first, the political sphere is dominated by the economic sphere, with *democracy serving capitalism.* In the second model, the political sphere is balanced against the economic sphere, with *democracy counteracting capitalism,* in the form of the social democratic welfare state. The third model differs from the first two in being more imaginary than real, although what is imagined is a rational response to the real. What this model imagines, as Karl Marx does in "On the Jewish Question" among other works, is a scenario in which the very distinction between the two spheres is overcome, with *democracy transcending capitalism* in the direction of socialism and beyond. Thus it is not inaccurate to describe the project to bring about such a scenario as "democracy against capitalism."[3]

In the first model, democracy serving capitalism, it is obvious that democracy is little more than a contingent derivative of capitalism: it serves the needs of capitalism under conditions created by capitalism. The classic statement of this situation comes from Joseph Schumpeter: "Historically, the modern democracy rose along with capitalism, and in causal connection with it. But the same holds true for democratic practice: democracy in the sense of our theory of competitive leadership presided over the process of political and institutional change by which the bourgeoisie reshaped, and from its own point of view rationalized, the social and political structure that preceded its ascendancy: the democratic method was the political tool of that reconstruction. . . . Modern democracy is a product of the capitalist process."[4] Schumpeter immediately goes on to ask, with refreshing candor and bluntness, the question of "how well or ill capitalist society qualifies for the task of working the democratic method it evolved." His answer is equally candid and blunt: "Capitalist society qualifies well. The bourgeoisie has a solution that is peculiar to it for the problem of how the sphere of political decision can be reduced to those proportions which are manageable by means of the method of competitive leadership. The bourgeois scheme of things limits the sphere of politics by limiting the sphere of public authority; its solution is in the ideal of the parsimonious state that exists primarily in order to guarantee bourgeois legality and to provide a firm frame for autonomous individual endeavor in all fields."[5]

In the second model we find a more equal relation, so to speak, between democracy and capitalism than is envisioned by Schumpeter. But make no mistake: here democracy is allowed to serve as a counterweight against capitalism only *within* a capitalist order, and, as long as this is the case, there is no guarantee that democracy will continue to be allowed to do so.

As long as democracy is allowed to counteract capitalism, however, we have what deserves to be called *democratic capitalism*[6]—democratic not in the sense of capitalism itself having become democratic but in the nevertheless significant sense of capitalism being substantially affected by the democratic process. A key ingredient of this democratic capitalist order is the taming of the working class as a precondition for the capitalist class to concede universal suffrage. Another key ingredient is the constitutional separation of the economic and political spheres such that the rights of property and capital in the former are effectively protected from the democratic operations of the latter. In this regard, what Karl Polanyi says of the United States—"The American Constitution . . . isolated the economic sphere entirely from the jurisdiction of the Constitution, put private property thereby under the highest conceivable protection, and created the only legally grounded market society in the world. *In spite of universal suffrage, American voters were powerless against owners*"—is true of democratic capitalism in general.[7] Thus when universal suffrage finally arrived, it did so with crucial features that made it largely compatible with capitalism.

While Polanyi is largely correct about voters in a capitalist democracy being powerless against owners of capital, he fails to emphasize something very important—namely, that it is possible even for a tamed working class and a subordinated political sphere to obtain very considerable concessions from the capitalist class. Such concessions take the form, essentially, of nearly full employment, relatively decent working hours and conditions and wages, and a reasonable level of social provisions for such things as education, health care, and retirement—in other words, a capitalist welfare state. And these concessions are made possible, above all, by organized labor with the bargaining power and ideological resources, combined with the ballot box, to alter the balance of power among capital, the working class, and the state. This happens without fundamentally challenging the capitalist system. Nevertheless, the social democratic welfare state deserves to be considered an impressive moral and political achievement *within* capitalism, replacing the hard domination of the capitalist class with a softer, more consensual, and, one might even say, more "humane" hegemony.

The problem with social democratic capitalism, even within its own terms of reference, is that this distinctive arrangement may well not last, because the balance of power needed to make it work is a modus vivendi liable to be upset in the course of class struggles. In other words, within the second model, democracy counteracting capitalism, always lurks the danger of its regressing to the first model, democracy serving capitalism. For this reason, the reliable humanization of capitalism, as it were—or, in the words of Polanyi, the "endeavor to make society a distinctively human relationship of persons"[8]— requires none other than the overcoming of capitalism by undoing the subordination of the (democratic) political sphere to the (capitalist) economic sphere. This very necessity makes the third model—democracy transcending capitalism, or socialism understood as "the tendency inherent in an industrial civilization to transcend the self-regulating market by consciously subordinating it to a democratic society"[9]—intelligible and attractive; hence the permanent residual appeal of Marxism even after it has ceased to be a main source of inspiration for political movements. Yet viewed from within capitalism, this model will naturally look utopian, and, because capitalism has so far won in the real world, as signaled by a lack of progress beyond merely political and hence partial emancipation, it *is* utopian.[10]

I have brought up this third, largely utopian model because it best brings out the rationale for democracy in the context of capitalism. It is a rationale that is largely shared by the second, social democratic model, but is not pursued by it with sufficient rigor and soberness. For our purposes, what is important is just this shared rationale, and perhaps no one has spelled it out with greater clarity than Polanyi, whose classic statement on this subject retains its full relevance today.

The Rationale for Democracy in the Context of Capitalism

According to Polanyi, there is something deeply problematic with the application of the market mechanism, or unimpeded commodification, to land, money, and, for our purposes, especially labor. This is because

> to allow the market mechanism to be the sole director of the fate of human beings and their natural environment indeed, even of the amount and use of purchasing power, would result in the demolition of society. For the alleged commodity "labor power" cannot be shoved about, used indiscriminately, or even left unused, without affecting also the human individual who happens to be the bearer of this peculiar commodity. In disposing of a man's labor power the system would, incidentally, dispose of the physical, psychological, and moral entity "man" attached to that tag. Robbed of the protective covering of cultural institutions, human beings would perish from the effects of social exposure; they would die as the victims of acute social dislocation through vice, perversion, crime, and starvation. Nature would be reduced to its elements, neighborhoods and landscapes defiled, rivers polluted, military safety jeopardized, the power to produce food and raw materials destroyed.... Undoubtedly, labor, land, and money markets *are* essential to a market economy. But no society could stand the effects of such a system of crude fictions even for the shortest stretch of time unless its human and natural substance ... was protected against the ravages of this satanic mill.[11]

Polanyi is saying (and he is not mincing words) that, left to itself, capitalism can be counted on to cause both suffering and alienation through the forced commodification of things that are not commodities. In the face of the satanic mill of a "pure" market, nothing is more needful than the "self-protection of society." Democracy, though explicitly mentioned not in the quoted passage but only later in his account, exists to provide such protection. Refreshingly,

Polanyi sees democracy not narrowly as only an antidote to imperium (that is, political domination) but instead as a reaction to the distinctive combination of dominium (that is, social domination) and imperium that is capitalism. This is what democracy is *for* under an equality of conditions that renders otherwise equal citizens and equal bearers of human rights vulnerable to the dehumanizing ravages of the capitalist market left to itself.

We do not have to look far to find the reason why democracy can serve the self-protection of society against capitalism, at least in theory. After all, the capitalist class makes up only a small minority in a capitalist society. Thus, in a capitalist society that happens also to be a democracy with universal suffrage, it stands to reason, apparently, that the majority, by exercising their political rights, will see to it that their most important interests will be protected against the capitalist class. It was just this simple reasoning that made the capitalist class in the nineteenth century and even the early twentieth so fearful of the working class and the poor in general that they found nothing more important than keeping universal suffrage at bay. "But the more the labor market contorted the lives of the workers, the more insistently they clamoured for the vote,"[12] and thus exactly the same reasoning in reverse motivated the struggles of the working class for universal (manhood) suffrage, culminating in the Chartist movement of 1838–1848, which ended in bloodshed and failure:

> In England it became the unwritten law of the Constitution that the working class must be denied the vote. The Chartist leaders were jailed; their adherents, numbered in millions, were derided by a legislature representing a bare fraction of the population, and the mere demand for the ballot was often treated as a criminal act by the authorities. Of the spirit of compromise allegedly characteristic of the British system—a later invention—there was no sign. Not before the working class had passed through the Hungry Forties and a docile generation had emerged to reap the benefits of the Golden Age of capitalism; not before an upper layer of skilled workers had developed their unions and parted company with the dark mass of poverty-stricken laborers; not before the workers had acquiesced in the system which the New Poor Law was meant to enforce upon them was their better-paid stratum allowed to participate in the nation's councils.[13]

Meanwhile, a parallel development took place in the United States whereby the taming of the working class was supplemented by a constitutional separation of the economic and political spheres that effectively protected economic power from political equality.

Fast-forward to the twenty-first century. What Polanyi (following a famous poem by William Blake) calls the satanic mill of capitalism is no longer so satanic, and for this reason no longer so desperately resisted, at least in developed capitalist societies. In the meantime, all the advanced capitalist democracies have instituted universal suffrage, not just the universal manhood suffrage that was one of the goals of the failed Chartist movement. Yet at the same time the satanic mill has moved to the so-called emerging markets, including China, whose laborers, often working under alienating conditions not so dissimilar to those of the nineteenth century, alone make possible the mass consumerism in the apparently more humane developed economies, as well as for the growing middle class in their own. In this way the organic bond between capitalism and the satanic mill—*somewhere* in the commodity chains—remains uncut. Also intact is capitalism's preferred way of taming, and best utilizing, the working class, by pitting its members against one another, within the same country and, now, in our age of globalization and with unprecedented effectiveness, across national boundaries. Small wonder, therefore, that the relocation of the satanic mill to developing economies has coincided with the progressive worsening of the plight of the working class in the developed democratic capitalist countries. If, as Polanyi emphasized, the working class got the vote only after it had been tamed sufficiently to no longer pose a deadly threat to the capitalist class, it is no less true, as Polanyi also noted, that the working class had allowed itself to be tamed in large part because, as in the economic boom after the Chartist movement, the capitalist class was able and willing to make significant concessions. Indeed, progressive concessions and the particular impact of World War II led to the great invention known as the capitalist welfare state.

Today, however, what was once taken for granted in the heyday of the welfare state when it came to the self-protection of society already seems to belong to the irreversibly lost good old days. Instead of the working class uniting for the self-protection of society (if not for communism), it is the capitalist class around the world that is more united and more powerful than ever before. And this is because it has captured—appropriated as an indispensable part of its global hegemony (hegemony in Antonio Gramsci's precise sense)—the only thing that can offer ordinary people a modicum of protection in a capitalist society: democracy. Thus, Polanyi's understanding of the raison d'être of democracy in terms of society's self-protection is anything but outmoded. As a matter of fact, in the face of the unprecedented cohesion and power of the global capitalist class, democracy is more necessary than ever before.[14]

It is only in this light that we can adequately grasp the nature of legitimation crises in democratic capitalism. A legitimation crisis occurs when democracy seriously fails to achieve the self-protection of society against the dehumanizing (and denaturing) effects of unregulated or ill-regulated capitalism and when such effects undermine the values in terms of which people understand themselves and their society (such as solidarity, shared prosperity, and progress in terms of intergenerational upward mobility). But, as Wolfgang Streeck tells us, a legitimation crisis can also happen when the self-protection of society is considered by the owners and managers of capital to have gone too far, by the standards of market justice as distinct from social justice, and when the capitalist class reacts to diminishing profit margins by holding back from the investments society badly needs.[15] Thus, a legitimation crisis signals the failure of democracy from one point of view and the (excessive) success of democracy from another. In this light, democracy permanently seesaws between the dominance of capitalism and the self-protection of society—as long as we live with the capitalist organization of the economy. Democracy exists to see to it that the seesawing motion does not come to a stop on the side of capitalism.

Polanyi's understanding of democracy in terms of society's self-protection against the satanic mill of capitalism also furnishes a common denominator for assessing the relative merits of different political systems, or different configurations of the same political system. It may indeed be regarded as the most important common denominator for the comparative evaluation of modern political arrangements. It applies to all modern societies, not just democratic ones, as long as they have a more or less capitalist market economy.

There is little doubt that China lends itself to this kind of comparative evaluation vis-à-vis democratic capitalism. This in itself marks the extent to which China is already a capitalist society: the satanic mill of capitalism already represents the greatest danger to Chinese society and protection against this danger its chief challenge. We must not forget the already partially capitalist character of its economy and of its equality of conditions when we consider what China has to gain from becoming a democracy and what form such a democracy is likely to take and should best take. By the same token, we cannot rule out the possibility that, in becoming more formally democratic, China may do worse, not better, with regard to the self-protection of society against capitalism, even considering that it is not doing particularly well right now. China does not yet properly have its own Wall Street, Silicon Valley, and military-industrial complex to contend with—one of the mixed blessings of the strict monopoly of political power held by the Chinese Communist Party (CCP).[16] Its billionaire class, though already mighty and growing, is not yet calling the shots. If economic freedom for Jack Ma and people of ambition and energy like him is part of the CCP's formula for stability, this same formula gives the party itself no uncertain control over the ground rules of the game and a huge chunk of the game itself in the shape of state-owned enterprises. But things can change quickly with the advent of a formal, constitutional democracy that, as it happens, does not see the protection of society against capitalism as one of its chief missions. Thus, for all who value democracy especially (though by no means exclusively) for Polanyi's reasons, it is necessary to place at the top of the democratic agenda the imperative to prevent such a scenario from materializing. To this end, it is worth taking a brief look at how democratic capitalism is faring in Western Europe and North America with regard to the self-protection of society against capitalism.

Lessons from the Crisis of Democratic Capitalism

This takes us back to the model of democratic capitalism erected in Western Europe and North America in the wake of World War II. That model has since largely served as the point of reference for appraising the good and ill of democracy.[17] Known as social democracy in Europe and the New Deal in America, this model featured, above all, a relatively evenly balanced compromise between capitalism and democracy, with the state performing a difficult but largely successful balancing act between the demands of capital and the claims of the rest of society, between market justice and social justice.[18] That the state was able to do so, and for so long, is, in retrospect, quite an extraordinary achievement.

This combination of *democratic capitalism*—of capital's preeminence in the economic sphere, on the one hand, and (formally) equal citizenship in a democratic political sphere, on the other—is inherently, and hence normally, tilted in favor of the former. This uneven balance resides in a defining feature of capitalism that democracy can do little to change: "Capitalist society is distinguished by the fact that its collective productive capital is accumulated in the hands of a minority of its members who enjoy the legal privilege, in the form of rights of private property, to dispose of such capital in any way they see fit, including letting it sit idle or transferring it abroad."[19] It follows that "economic crises in capitalism result from crises of confidence on the part of capital; they are not technical disturbances but *legitimation crises of a special kind.* Low growth and unemployment are results of 'investment strikes' on the part of owners who could invest their capital but refuse to do so because they lack the necessary confidence."[20] There is obviously only one way to avoid "investment strikes," and that is to make the profit-dependent owners and managers of capital reasonably happy by satisfying their expectations, which for this reason alone are "more important for [the capitalist system's] stability than those of the *capital-dependent* population; only if the former are satisfied can the latter too be satisfied, while the reverse is not necessarily true."[21] If this need not mean that the capitalist class has an invariably overwhelming threat advantage, it does nevertheless mean that the default situation is one in which this class calls the shots. As Streeck puts it, "The fact that the *'psychological'* trust of capital in political conditions is the main *technical* prerequisite for the functioning of a capitalist economy sets narrow limits to the correction of market justice by democratically empowered social justice. A basic asymmetry of a capitalist political economy consists in the fact that the demands of 'capital' for an adequate return operate in effect as empirical preconditions for the functioning of the whole system, whereas the corresponding demands of 'labor' count as disruptive."[22]

In this light, one should not be surprised that the golden era of democratic capitalism—social democracy in Western Europe and the New Deal in America—gradually unraveled after nearly three decades of remarkable success (the *trente glorieuses*) following the war. This is an extraordinary case of the exception proving the rule. And when theorists such as Streeck seek to explain the fortunes of democratic capitalism in this way, their point is not merely experiential and inductive but finds its basis in the nature of capitalism itself—in the idea that this nature of capitalism is not changed, and cannot be changed, when capitalism is yoked with democracy. This means that the fruitful coming together of capitalism and democracy we are talking about is only an apparent success, because it is an exception incapable of outlasting the rule. It is in this sense that Streeck speaks of postwar democratic capitalism in Western Europe and North America in terms of a "forced marriage" or "shotgun marriage."[23] "In reality, the history of capitalism after the 1970s, including the subsequent economic crises, is a history of capital's escape from the system of social regulation imposed on it *against its will* after 1945. . . . These promises capitalism was neither able nor willing to fulfil *forever*."[24] Thus, strange as this may sound, the default position is separation or divorce; what must be deemed a departure from the norm and calls for explanation is the marriage itself: how it happened by force and what the force was. If this is the case, what I earlier identified as one of the ideal-typical relations between democracy and capitalism—democracy effectively countering capitalism—turns out to be the product of extraordinary circumstances rather than a stable model.

The extraordinary circumstances that "forced" the seemingly successful marriage between democracy and capitalism were World War II and its aftermath, which brought a dramatic change in material conditions and in ethos, not least in public expectations regarding social justice and democratic participation, and a shift in the balance of power between capital and the citizenry sufficient to push the state to cater to the interests of the latter as never before. The result was the modern welfare state as a unique compromise between the capitalist class and the rest of society, between the former's demand for market justice and the latter's claim to social justice. What makes this compromise unique is that the combination of historical circumstances favorable to it was exogenous and highly contingent, and, as it turned out, unrepeatable and incapable of indefinite extension. It is not preordained that the second model in the ideal-typical relations between democracy and capitalism, having once carried the day against the first, will continue to do so indefinitely. It was rather only a matter of time before the positive effects of the war on social justice wore off and the exception revealed itself as such—thanks, as far as timing was concerned, to a combination of accumulation and legitimation problems in the 1970s and after. If we want a general causal explanation, therefore, no better one can be found than along the lines suggested by Streeck, to the effect that, "looked at with hindsight and in the light of the turbulences that followed, the quarter century immediately after the war should without difficulty be recognized as truly exceptional." And this is because the *normal* condition of democratic capitalism is "ruled by an endemic and essentially irreconcilable conflict between capitalist markets and democratic politics that, having been temporarily suspended for the historically short period immediately following the war, forcefully reasserted itself when high economic growth came to an end in the 1970s."[25]

What has happened since is a series of politico-economic balancing acts increasingly shaped by an ever more powerful—or, to be more precise, ever more *normally* powerful—capitalist class. If the global inflation of the 1970s and the explosion of public debt in the 1980s reflected in large part desperate attempts by the democratic state to prolong the gains of social justice under more challenging circumstances, their replacement by rising private indebtedness in the 1990s and beyond, followed by the sovereign debt crisis and redoubled fiscal austerity since 2008, marks the definitive triumph of neoliberalism on behalf of capitalism.[26] What this triumph represents, above all, is a profound shift in the balance of power between democracy and capitalism, in favor of the latter. To use Polanyi's terminology, the democratic measures for the "self-protection of society" have been significantly rolled back and the "satanic mill" of capitalism—predominantly financial and digital capitalism today—has regained much of its profit-maximizing freedom from the goals and constraints of the wider society.

Profound and momentous as this change has been, what is most characteristic of it is that it has brought us back to the *normal* state of affairs for democratic capitalism. That this is the case finds additional support in Walter Scheidel's demonstration that whatever equalizing effect on the distribution of material resources may be attributable to the rise of postwar social democracy "would at least in part have been driven by the pressures of war."[27] Now that the pressures of war and their lingering effects on ethos, values, and especially balance of power have worn off, capitalism has quite naturally regained its edge in its relation with democracy. To the degree that the democratization of capitalism after 1945 was due to the pressures and effects of war, one should expect nothing less than "a process of de-democratization of capitalism through the de-economization of democracy."[28] By the same token, the so-called oligarchic shift in democratic capitalism in recent decades is nothing out of the ordinary: a shift back to normal, not away from it, and therefore something that was just waiting to happen.

For this reason, the suggestion that the oligarchic shift is a phenomenon largely peculiar to American democratic capitalism, as made by Jacob Hacker and Paul Pierson, misses the deeper, structural balance of power favoring capitalism that is inherent in democratic capitalism as such.[29] Insofar as the United States does differ from (especially continental) Europe, it is a matter of degree rather than kind. The cautious optimism that the pendulum will almost inevitably swing back to democracy (presumably short of a helping hand from what Scheidel calls the "Four Horsemen" of leveling: mass-mobilization warfare, transformative revolutions, state collapse, and catastrophic plagues), again as evinced by Hacker and Pierson, among many others, is more an article of faith than a belief grounded in the *normal* power of democracy in democratic capitalism.

It may well be that the normal power of democracy is not strong enough to sustain a marriage of equal partners with capitalism. If we combine the insights of Streeck and Scheidel, then this does seem to be the case. And thus it is in the era of neoliberalism rather than in close temporal proximity to the equalizing and democratizing effects of the war (that is, during the heyday of European social democracy and the American New Deal) that we see the true—that is, the normal—face of democratic capitalism, the greater ease with which democracy serves capitalism (by legitimating it as compatible with democracy) than counteracts it (by effectively pitting social justice against market justice).[30] If so, Polanyi's call for the self-protection of society against capitalism cannot simply and safely be left to the normal workings of democratic capitalism. It will always remain an extremely tall order, an uphill struggle, as long as we stay within the parameters of capitalism, democratic or otherwise.

While Polanyi's line of thinking still stands, we would do well, for both diagnostic and prognostic purposes, to make certain empirical adjustments in his description of capitalism's destructive impact on human life, which fits the nineteenth and early twentieth centuries better than the late twentieth and early twenty-first. For the capitalism that has won out in today's Western Europe and North America is no longer exactly that of the "satanic mill" Polanyi speaks of, and the "self-protection of society" that has been weakened by the neoliberal onslaught is far from completely dismantled, thanks to the residual power of democracy. The troubles of Western democracy, however serious, are those marked by the erosion of exceptionally effective measures for the self-protection of society rather than by their nonexistence or disappearance. A welfare state diminished by fiscal austerity and mocked by runaway inequality and the power of private-sector creditors still stands as a bulwark against the mass immiseration of the not so distant past. So in the wake of the drastic rollback of democracy and the welfare state at the hands of neoliberal capitalism, there is a sense in which life proverbially goes on in Europe and North America, almost as usual. As long as the condition of the vast majority does not come once again to resemble the "satanic mill," the oligarchic shift that is in fact the normal state of democratic capitalism may simply continue without major challenge.[31] When all is said and done, Ernst Bloch's insight into the desire for "the transformation of the totality" is unlikely to find the necessary material conditions in twenty-first-century Europe or America.[32]

This is not to deny that democratic capitalism is in the firm grip of a legitimation crisis. To have a clear understanding of the nature of this crisis, however, it is necessary to remember that it is democracy that has been put on the defensive in what was once—in a departure from the norm—a more evenly balanced tug-of-war with capitalism. In this important sense, the current legitimation crisis is a crisis of democracy (within democratic capitalism) rather than of capitalism—and of the welfare state as democracy's historically most important by-product. Despite sluggish growth, the capitalist class is not exactly reeling from accumulation problems, for it has found a way of mitigating the impact of such problems through a new pattern of production and distribution in its favor made possible by deregulation, mobility of capital, and other measures that comprise today's finance- and IT-dominated capitalism.[33] Until accumulation problems really hurt the capitalist class or the method of shifting the burden of such problems onto the rest of society provokes uncontrollable social rebellion, it may be somewhat misleading to describe the legitimation crisis of democratic capitalism as chiefly a crisis of capitalism. It is rather a crisis of democracy vis-à-vis capitalism: a situation in which the expectations of the capital-dependent population rather than those of the profit-dependent owners and managers of capital go unsatisfied, and in which social justice rather than market justice is losing its sway.

What are we to make of this undeniable decline of democracy in the West? How are we to rethink the relation between democracy and capitalism in the light of this decline? I have already provided part of the answer by showing that, given the very nature of capitalism, the oligarchic shift must be seen as marking a return to the normal condition of democratic capitalism. To this it is necessary to add another part of the answer, one responsive to the timing of the onset of the crisis. Since we are talking in particular about the failure of *social* democracy—that is, of democracy counteracting capitalism—we need to figure out the crucial factors that, beginning in the late 1960s and early 1970s, made it more difficult for democracy to counteract capitalism in the interest of social justice.

I have already noted the revolt of the capitalist class against the social democratic welfare state. While this revolt was directed against the entire social democratic distribution of power and profits, its victory came as a result, above all, of defeating organized labor.[34] But most important of all is that these developments took place under the circumstances of an intensified class struggle that had itself been caused by a prolonged downturn in the capitalist economy. For our purposes, what matters is not why this happened but *that* it happened—and its effects. As growth stalled, so did progress in social justice, because the comfortable profit margins once required and indeed presupposed by the political efficacy and material benefits of the democratic welfare state had simply disappeared.[35] Bluntly put, it was a matter of which class was to bear the brunt of the crisis of capitalist economic growth. Neoliberalism was the capitalist class's economic and ideological means— under what had become normal circumstances well over two decades after the war—to shield itself from the effects of the profit squeeze and shift them onto the rest of society. Organized labor used all the means afforded it by the democratic system to fight back, but to no avail, thanks to the new balance of power and of opinion in the neoliberal state. In the process, democratic participation lost much of its meaning for ordinary people, as it ceased to work as a reasonably effective means of bringing about the redistribution of wealth in favor of the working masses. Austerity severed the once taken-for-granted link between democracy and social justice, and for a growing number of citizens this meant in effect the loss of democracy's substance and raison d'être: the self-protection of society against capitalism (in Polanyi's formulation). This was not exactly a cause for celebration by the rich and powerful, however, in that democracy's sinking fortunes soon started to drag down the legitimacy of the capitalist game itself, as evident in the ominous spread of antiglobalist sentiment.

In this light, the crisis of democracy reveals itself as part of a much larger crisis, one that also implicates and hurts capitalism. I see this larger crisis as a fourfold one: stagnant economic growth, the demise of social justice, the hollowing-out of democracy, and the delegitimation of capitalism. That these four components of the larger crisis hang together as one integral crisis is due to the mutual dependence among economic growth, social justice, democracy, and capitalism's legitimacy. Growth creates the material conditions not only for relatively full employment but also for social justice—for the relatively amicable redistribution of wealth downward. "Since profit is everywhere, the concept of allocating it rationally between players becomes popular, as does the possibility of redistributing wealth downwards. The era feels like one of 'collaborative competition' and social peace."[36] It would definitely be naïve to think of growth as a sufficient condition for social justice under democratic capitalism, but, just as definitely, growth seems to be a necessary condition, at least in the absence of Scheidel's "Four Horsemen" of leveling. Social justice, in turn, is, for ordinary citizens who securely enjoy liberties of the moderns and seek the socioeconomic means of taking advantage of such liberties, the main substance of democracy and the core of its appeal. Given this, whoever is opposed to social justice cannot (coherently) be well disposed toward democracy, either.[37] Capitalism for its part is dependent on the positive link between social justice and democracy for its moral image, its public relations. The idea that capitalism can have democratic legitimation on the cheap—on the basis of a formal democracy largely devoid of social justice—may well be an illusion. In this context, "No bourgeois, no democracy,"[38] Barrington Moore Jr.'s way of summarizing a Marxist thesis, acquires a new meaning in our age of mass democracy—namely, no reasonably prosperous and happy middle class, no *legitimate* capitalism. Thus, when things go well, they go well together, with economic growth giving democracy room for maneuver and allowing capitalism to appear compatible with social justice, while making it possible for social justice to lend substance and purpose to democracy and for the positive link between democracy and social justice to impart moral standing to capitalism. This is the benign circle of social democracy, or social democratic capitalism, for which growth serves as a necessary (though not a sufficient) condition. By the same token, a prolonged crisis of economic growth may be counted on to trigger a comprehensive crisis of democratic capitalism. How, within the confines of a capitalist system in which society depends on capital, and capital on profits, can a prolonged recession not bring in its train a retrogression in social justice and the hollowing-out of democracy, and how can those outcomes not lead to the erosion of legitimacy for capitalism? No (substantial) economic growth, no progress in social justice; no progress in social justice, no well-functioning democracy for the "organized extraction of mass loyalty";[39] no robust social justice and democracy, no solid legitimacy for capitalism. In a nutshell, democracy will be in trouble when it is no longer able to feed on high growth as its indispensable room for maneuvering under democratic capitalism.[40]

When this happens, the intrinsically problematic nature of the relation between democracy and capitalism, softened and even hidden in good times, comes to the fore. Interestingly, we find Polanyi pitting democracy (the self-protection of society) against capitalism from the Left and Friedrich von Hayek pitting capitalism against democracy (social justice) from the Right. Thus we have two exceptionally serious thinkers converging on what to both of them is a fundamentally conflictual relation between democracy and capitalism while perceiving and fearing the threat from exactly opposite directions. It would be hard to think of a more striking intellectual confirmation of the deep-seated tension between democracy and capitalism, just as there could be no sharper reminder than the recent experience of Western democracy—the most successful in modern times—that this tension does not favor democracy.

Insofar as it is helpful for China to look to Europe and North America (among other places) for inspiration and lessons regarding democracy, it is a democracy in defeat and in crisis that presents itself. It is anything but a pretty picture:

Trade union membership fell ... throughout the world of democratic capitalism, and often enough as a result of successful efforts at
union-breaking by governments and employers. Collective bargaining
declined as a consequence, and with it the wages at the lower end of
the labour market, while the earnings of shareholders and, even more
so, managers improved dramatically, making for a stunning and sustained rise in inequality inside democratic-capitalist societies. Needs
for "restructuring" under alleged pressures of "globalization" were
and continue to be invoked to justify retreat by governments from politically guaranteed full employment, the growing individualization of
the employment contract, increasingly precarious employment, the
renewal of managerial prerogative, the privatization of government
services, and "reformed"—i.e., recommodifying—social policy—all
of which can be observed almost everywhere in rich democracies. . . .
Capitalism withdrew from the commitments extracted from and entered into by it at the end of the Second World War. However this process may be interpreted or explained, it cannot possibly be conceived
as having been driven by a rising influence over policy by democratically organized citizens.[41]

Such negative fortunes of democracy in the West are of considerable relevance for pondering the prospects of democracy in China—all the more so
if we take into account the latest mutation in capitalism in the shape of surveillance capitalism.[42] How long will high economic growth last in China?
Will China take advantage of such growth to develop democracy while the
sun shines? Or will it use the performance legitimacy gained through growth
to delay democracy until democracy becomes unavoidable and yet the sun
no longer shines so brightly? How well, in the event of democratic change,
will China be able to foster a positive link between democracy and social justice? How well will the CCP be able thereby to reclaim its socialist credentials and do so in a new—that is, democratic—setting? More generally, when
democracy is in retreat vis-à-vis capitalism in Europe and America, what can
democracy mean and do in China, a country adopting more and more capitalist ways and values? Must democracy mean in China what it has meant
in the West—namely, "the political anonymization of class rule" (more on
this later) and the resultant autonomy of the market from a constitutionally

circumscribed state—a political formula that has done more to facilitate capitalism than to protect society? And with what likely consequences, in a country where the nature and composition of the capitalist class, the level of economic and legal development, and the moral and cultural tradition are all very different from their Western counterparts? How well prepared will a newly democratizing China be to counter the unprecedented challenges to democracy posed by surveillance capitalism, when the so-called mature democracies of the West are already being thrown off balance? Last but not least, must China not pay some heed, out of prudential and moral concern for itself and the world as a whole, to the far from improbable end of capitalism in the not too distant future and prepare itself accordingly, with regard to democracy and otherwise?[43]

Why Neoliberalism Has Not Entirely Conquered China

What has weakened democracy in Europe and America is, of course, the antidemocratic capitalism that has come to be known as neoliberalism—in the plain words of Colin Crouch, "that fundamental preference for the [capitalist] market over the [democratic] state as a means of resolving problems and achieving human ends."[44] It would not be incorrect to think of neoliberalism as the softer, less satanic version of the satanic mill in our time—softened and made more palatable by the partly constraining and partly propagandist discourse of human rights and corporate social responsibility. Although there are as yet no democratic institutions in China for neoliberalism to conquer, this has not prevented neoliberalism from finding a far from negligible foothold there. It has been noted that Deng Xiaoping, credited as the chief architect of China's reform, was something of a believer in neoliberal doctrine, if not under this name. This view is given considerable plausibility by the exceptionally high tolerance for inequality and environmental degradation that has marked China's reform almost from the beginning—something that cannot in the late twentieth and early twenty-first centuries and in a supposedly socialist country be explained away in terms of the unavoidable crudeness and ruthlessness of primitive accumulation—and by the large-scale, Chinese-style privatization and deregulation that have characterized the economy.

There is ready proof of a different kind as well, in that some important items on neoliberalism's agenda happened to be part of China's old socialist way of doing things—such as the weakness of trade unions—now adapted to capitalist ends. As Paul Mason writes, "The destruction of labour's bargaining power . . . was the essence of the entire [neoliberal] project: it was a means to all the other ends. Neoliberalism's guiding principle is not free markets, nor fiscal discipline, nor sound money, nor privatization and offshoring—not even globalization. All these things were byproducts or weapons of its main endeavour: to remove organized labour from the equation."[45] It makes one shudder to think how this most central of neoliberal objectives was achieved in reform-era China with little effort and no fanfare, for prevention sufficed and no dismantling was necessary.

It is also worth remembering that the start of China's reform coincided almost exactly with the onset and early spread of neoliberalism in the heartland of European and US democratic capitalism. There has never been any doubt that the capitalist market economy China was so eager to learn from the West was the one newly reshaped in the image of neoliberalism. This is especially true of the swelling ranks of economists, from whom have been drawn many of China's most important officials presiding over the economy. Margaret Thatcher and Ronald Reagan are generally well thought of among them and by the Chinese public at large. Hayek and Milton Friedman (and the Chicago school in general) are the economics profession's intellectual heroes, and, through their Chinese disciples' tireless propaganda, even heroes, or at least influential in terms of their ideas, among a significant part of the educated population. It is a remarkable feature of China's ideological landscape that almost everyone who has a serious grudge against the past and present misdeeds of the supposedly communist party-state is reacting, or overreacting, to these misdeeds by converting to neoliberal beliefs about the virtues of the market and the vices of the state. For such people—and they are legion—progress means shrinking the state (state-owned enterprises) in favor of the market (the private sector)—that is, promoting *guotui minjin* against *guojin mintui,* where *min* refers to *Marktvolk* as if they were equivalent to "the people."[46]

Despite all this, neoliberalism has *not* conquered China the way it has done Europe and the United States. True, neoliberalism is very strong in China *as ideology,* which arguably has infected the CCP itself, especially its higher echelons, even more than ordinary people. True, many practices have been adopted in China that were inspired by neoliberal ideas in one way or another. True, and most importantly, the present leadership of the CCP has gone so far as to publicly assign a predominant role to the market in re- source allocation and in the operation of the economy as a whole. But when all is said and done, the party has not seen fit to inaugurate a sufficiently autonomous system of economic exchange to relieve itself of its preeminent, political responsibility for a well-functioning economy—and thereby of the need for nonstop, counterproductively obtrusive political legitimation of its authority. And it will not be able to do so as long as it is in charge. It is exactly for this reason that neoliberalism cannot go very far—not nearly as far as it has in Western democratic capitalism—before it runs up against insurmountable obstacles posed by the very presence of the CCP and the consequent lack of an autonomous market.[47]

It is widely thought that its four-decade-old reform has turned China into what in certain key respects is a capitalist economy and society. There is no better argument for this view than the fact, noted earlier, that the para- mount challenge faced by Western democracies—namely, the protection of society and nature against the satanic mill of a dominant market—is now also one of the main challenges confronted by China today. It has not quite become as singularly overwhelming a challenge in China yet, however, because the country has not developed "the political anonymization of class rule" that, as Jürgen Habermas shows with admirable percipience, strictly characterizes the political organization of capitalist societies and the dis- tinctive crisis tendencies to which it gives rise. Thanks to the supposedly autonomous character of economic exchange under capitalism, the political order is freed from the burden of direct, openly political legitimation. What happens instead is that "the property order has shed its political form and been converted into a relation of production that, it seems, can legitimate itself. The institution of the market can be founded on the justice inherent in the exchange of equivalents; and, for this reason, the bourgeois constitu- tional state finds its justification in the legitimate relations of production."[48]

It is easy to see that if this is what capitalism is like in its political and, by the same token, its economic organization, then China is not yet entirely the capitalist entity it is so often taken to be. However significant the extent to which China has become capitalist, it has definitely not developed a sufficiently autonomous system of economic exchange to make the rule of the CCP politically anonymous and to shift the burden of legitimation to the independently grounded relations of production. In this particular regard, China is not *able* to quack like a capitalist duck, and, because of this, it cannot quite walk like a capitalist duck, either. It must rely instead on a different kind of legitimation, a more or less teleological legitimation (in the form, say, of communism in the past and of the "great rejuvenation of the Chinese nation" now), and it must allow its policies and actions to be informed and constrained by this legitimation to a substantial degree if it is to make such legitimation even minimally plausible.

What Is Special about China's Legitimation Crises

As a result, the pressure points inherent in China's political order and the locus of the attendant legitimation crises are rather different from those found in Western democratic capitalism. Not handicapped by the Western-style separation between an autonomous market and a liberal constitutional state, the Chinese party-state has more room for maneuver, more power over the economy and hence over all the things affected by the economy. This may partly account for its economic successes in recent decades, although these achievements have exacted a huge human and environmental cost for which the party-state must be held responsible to the same degree. On the other hand, not being handicapped by the Western-style separation between an autonomous market and a constitutional state must also mean not being shielded by such a separation, either, when the latter would come in handy.

Under democratic capitalism, as long as the ideology of separation is credible and effective, there is a mutually protective relationship between the economic system (free exchange) and the political system (constitutional democracy). The economic system, supposedly autonomous, shields the political order and those running it from bearing the brunt of the blame for socalled economic crises, notwithstanding the fact that the electoral system encourages politicians to exaggerate their role and make undeliverable promises with regard to the economy, thereby eroding popular belief in a constitutive fiction of the democratic capitalist order. The political system, also supposedly autonomous, in turn shields the economic system through its commitment to free exchange and through the legitimation of this commit-ment by means of constitutional democracy.

Thus the way to overcome performance problems under democratic capi-talism is almost invariably thought to lie mainly in fixing the economy rather than correcting what has gone wrong with democracy, unless it is believed (as it seldom is) that improved democracy would bring greater economic growth. The occasional outburst of social anger can make it fleetingly look as if a legitimation crisis triggered by performance problems has become a fully conscious crisis of social integration and hence a crisis directly of the democratic component of democratic capitalism. But public attention always seems to have a way of returning to economic measures—now especially monetary measures adopted by the nondemocratic institution of the central bank—giving one reason to think that the public secretly or not so secretly knows and accepts the irrelevance and impotence of democracy in relation to the autonomous market.

Without the benefit of some such ingenious compartmentalization, the Chinese party-state is more vulnerable than its Western democratic coun-terpart, having to take the lion's share of responsibility for economic failures no less than successes. This is the main reason why a high level of economic growth is so important, and a lack of it so politically delegitimating. Another reason, incidentally, is that, much as a capitalist democracy must somehow keep its capitalists happy in order to foster investment and growth, so the Chinese party-state must channel disproportionate gains to its own class of cadres in return for their loyalty and economic initiatives, and thus high growth rates are necessary for Chinese-style trickle-down economics to work. Neither of these reasons, however, is merely a matter of purchasing legiti-macy.[49] In the first, in particular, it is a matter of discharging a political re-sponsibility, and lessening a political vulnerability, that comes with a system of political leadership that has chosen not to divest itself of the great power over, and with it a corresponding level of responsibility for, the economy and all that goes with it. Under this system, there is simply nowhere for the CCP to hide when the economy is not doing well or doing less well than before.

This means that the Chinese party-state cannot speak of economic crises in the same way Western democratic governments can. In their strict sense, economic crises are serious disturbances of a market economy conceived of as an autonomous system and, as such, presuppose a degree of separation between system integration and sociopolitical integration that is simply absent in China. For this reason, every crisis in China that otherwise resembles an economic crisis is directly a political crisis. The CCP's role is so defined that it cannot convince anyone that "it no longer rules"[50]—including over the economy. Not that it even wants to! And this is what chiefly holds China back from becoming fully capitalist.

This has not prevented the party-state, however, from making various attempts at self-exoneration. Such attempts run a built-in risk of incoherence, for reasons already hinted at, and yet they are not completely incoherent. To begin with, the party-state's direct control of the economy is nowhere near total. As is well known, the economic reform initiated by Deng has privatized great swaths of the Chinese economy and, as part of this process, brought about a degree of denationalization and decollectivization of the means of production that is seen, with good reason, to have diluted the formerly socialist character of the Chinese economy. Thanks to this profound transformation of the economy and of the CCP's relation to it, we now have an intermediate situation in which the party-state still presides over a nonautonomous, so-called socialist (whose most precise meaning is none other than "nonautonomous") market economy and yet is no longer in direct control over the entire economy. It directly controls only state-owned enterprises, which, although extremely important and powerful, yield pride of place to the private sector in terms of share of both gross domestic product and (urban) employment.

This new, intermediate role of the party-state in relation to the economy is entirely in keeping with the massive depoliticization of the party since the start of the reform four decades ago. Depoliticization does not mean, of course, the political anonymization of the CCP's rule. Far from it, as is evident from the party-state's unwillingness and inability to hand the economy over to an autonomous market and thereby shield itself from the delegitimating consequences of economic failures. What depoliticization means, instead, is that the CCP has made the successful running of the economy its main task and the chief means of enhancing its legitimacy—along with the maintenance of social stability essential to this task. In other words, the principal function of the CCP is to preside with efficiency and stability over a nonautonomous (yet to a large degree private, capitalist) economy. Depoliti-

cization refers, then, to the reinvention of the CCP as a functional organization devoted single-mindedly to economic development, while the limits
to this depoliticization reside in the need to keep the economy nonautonomous and to give it some semblance of a *partly* correctly so-called socialist
market economy.

Thanks to this makeover, the CCP has understandably found it necessary
to allow the market to play as large a role in the economy as is consistent with
its not being a fully autonomous market—that is, consistent with the CCP
having a kind and degree of authority over it that is not possible in a constitutional democracy. This is a further sense in which we can speak of the depoliticization of the party: depoliticization means giving the market *as
much say as possible,* subject to what is left of the party's prerogative. It is only
in this sense that we can reasonably understand what the present leadership
means when it says it will allow the market to play a decisive role in resource
allocation. The parameters within which this is applicable are taken to go
without saying, or else China would cease to be a so-called socialist market
economy. To take the CCP to task for not being as good as its word is to (deliberately, ideologically) misunderstand what is involved and to call on the
party to give up the raison d'être of its existence. Considering how China has
gotten to this point, and understanding that going beyond it may amount to
political suicide, the role the CCP has been willing and able to assign to the
market is very considerable indeed.

Much of the CCP's willingness and ability to go this far was the result of
overcoming strong domestic political, ideological, and indeed economic resistance on China's way to joining the World Trade Organization in 2001.
Since then, China has become the world's second-largest economy, gradu-
ating from being a peripheral part of the global capitalist order to its current
status as a key player. In both capacities, China has transformed itself to the
very limits of its CCP-defined identity, having had to play by the rules of a
game set by powerful capitalist democracies, with their ideology of an autonomous market and a noninterfering state. This means that China has become as capitalist as it can be, short of relinquishing its self-understanding
as a socialist market economy.

The upshot of these developments is that, on the one hand, the CCP remains in charge of the economy, which means that the economy is not treated
as autonomous. Yet, on the other hand, the economy has acquired many key

institutional and ideological characteristics of capitalism, which means China now faces largely the same challenge of protecting society from the ravages of capitalism as democratic capitalism does. Meanwhile, the CCP has evolved into a largely functional organization with a predominantly economic agenda, and this means that it is both less able and less motivated to carry out the self-protection of society—a brand-new task thrust in front of it by the economic reform. This, then, is the hybrid China that is our subject when we talk about making it democratic or more democratic.

Like democratic capitalist states, China, with its own distinctive market-state relation, is liable to suffer both problems with the economy and failures in the self-protection of society. Unlike them, however, the Chinese state is not systemically shielded by the separation of the economy and the political order as supposedly autonomous arrangements, and thus it is more liable to experience both economic and social problems as direct, inescapable threats to its legitimacy. When such problems become serious and intractable, they take on the character of legitimation crises. These crises are what they are because they raise questions about whether the CCP is capable of developing both the motivation and the ability to solve them. They raise questions, that is, about the normative raison d'être of the party. And because this raison d'être has hitherto had its source in the identity of China's political system, such questions strike at the very roots or normative underpinnings of this system. Although, as we have seen, the Western constitutional state is by no means immune to the adverse impact of disruptions that occur in the supposedly autonomous economic system, the legitimation crisis to which the constitutional state is subject is of a lesser order of magnitude compared with what can befall the Chinese party-state. In the event of major performance disruptions, the Chinese party-state is fully without ideological protection from either the democratic character of the state or the autonomous character of the economy.

In this light, the close internal connection we saw between the CCP's legitimacy and performance turns out to be even closer. Or, to be more precise, we could say that we have just uncovered yet another dimension of that internal connection. What defines this further dimension is that, lacking the buffer provided by the separation between constitutional state and autonomous market, the CCP is directly exposed to the possibility that serious performance problems, whether regarding economic growth or the self-protection of society, will immediately translate into legitimation problems that cast doubt on its very fitness to rule. Hence it would be closer to the truth, in the case of the Chinese party-state, to see the line between legitimacy and performance as essentially blurred and even to suggest a causal account in which serious performance disruptions tend logically (that is, in the absence of the buffer) to prompt questions regarding legitimacy.

How Legitimation Crises Translate into Pressures for Democracy

The most important upshot of such questioning is a larger-looming specter of democracy, somewhere in the popular imagination and potential agitation, as an alternative to what China is now. In the case of European and American capitalism, which is already democratic, no such upshot follows from even a serious legitimation crisis, which for this reason alone must be taken to carry an altogether different meaning and level of threat. On the one hand, as already noted, the political order has its rear covered by the supposed autonomy of market exchange and by the correlative constitutional limits on state action and, by implication, on state efficacy. On the other hand, with regard to the self-protection of society, even when democracy is viewed as ineffective, nothing is left but to hold out the hope of electing a more competent or well-meaning government next time or strengthening the existing democratic system. Barring truly catastrophic breakdowns (which, incidentally, the 2008 financial crisis turned out not to have qualified as), democratic capitalism is able to keep at bay all desperate outcries for an alternative to itself—for there does seem no alternative![51]

Not so in China, lacking as it does also the second buffer enjoyed by democratic capitalism—that is, the absence of any plausible alternative to democracy (in addition to the first—that is, the supposedly autonomous character of the capitalist economy). In an age when democracy is almost universally embraced as the only fully legitimate basis of government, any regime not performing satisfactorily is likely to add fuel to calls for democracy if it is not already regarded by its own people as democratic. China is not yet so regarded, and thus, whenever its government is found seriously wanting in its performance, democracy naturally springs forth, in consciousness if not in action (depending on the room for dissent), as an alternative and, over time, as one that is long overdue. This is where legitimation crises in China have a political significance and effect that are very different from those in European and American capitalist democracies. In China such crises have a built-in potential to mutate into the pressure for democracy, as they did in 1989 and could do anytime now. That the CCP is making such mutation more difficult and costlier than ever shows that it is acutely aware of exactly such a possibility and of the logic behind it.

Without the dual buffer of constitutional state and autonomous market economy, the Chinese party-state lives in constant fear that major performance problems—regarding growth, welfare, and social stability—will give rise to questions about its legitimacy and pressures for democratic change. Such questions come up in times good and bad but are all but irresistible in not so good times. Why are *they* in power? Why *only* they, and *always?* Why must their view on this or that matter—on any public matter—be the last word, and even when they are not doing that good a job? In good times, the party-state is able to deflect or even preempt such questions by encouraging citizens to assess how competently the rulers, *once in power,* are exercising that power and to forget the distinct, prior question of how they have come by the title to that power in the first place. But this subterfuge depends for its success, in present-day China, on a level of performative success that is simply unsustainable. What is thus to be feared is not only bad times but the very possibility of bad times. And surely no one in one's right mind would want, for purposes of legitimacy, to count on China, whatever its absolute level of performance, comparing favorably with arguably relevant other countries (whether some large developing economy in terms of per capita gross domestic product, or a failed state in terms of order). Neither this kind of comparative solace nor the stratagem of deflection can be a recipe for enduring legitimacy, and, by the same token, neither can long stave off the pressure for democracy as exactly such a recipe.

It is another matter, an equally important matter, what form such pressure will take. In China today, it is essential to distinguish two kinds of pressure, based on whether it stems from concerns about the state's excessive power over the economy and the market's consequent lack of autonomy, or from demands for the better self-protection of society. In terms of class interests, one would generally expect the first kind of pressure to come from the capitalist class and the second from the grass roots of society. The actual picture is made a lot more complicated, however, by the successful propagation of neoliberal doctrine in recent decades among the general population and by the widespread and indiscriminate resentment of state power as such—the latter made somewhat understandable by, among other things, the state's massively preferential treatment of state-owned enterprises, in glaring contrast with the unapologetically shabby treatment by state-owned banks of relatively small private enterprises. What is nevertheless clearly discernible in Chinese society, among rich and poor, officials (temporarily in the closet) and ordinary citizens, is a one-sided understanding of democracy that largely identifies it with a constitutionalism granting autonomy to the market and limiting the power of the state. Almost completely lacking is a conception of democracy aimed at containing or counteracting capitalism for the sake of the self-protection of society. This is unfortunate, even though calls for the protection of society are by no means absent and can take *other* forms, such as the commonsense demand on government, democratic or not, to make better and more equitable provisions for education, health care, and so on. For the raison d'être of democracy is misguidedly narrowed and the appeal of democracy correspondingly weakened. At the same time, the enormous moral capital of democracy is all too easily delivered to capital's project of state capture, depriving the cause of social justice of this moral capital and leaving democracy free of the need to be even reasonably just. Last but not least, the very framing of the demand for social justice in isolation from democracy tends to translate sooner or later, and all too one-sidedly, into a pressure for economic growth, which may not be conducive to greater social justice and can be used as a reason precisely to weaken its appeal.

To the pressures just described—whether directly for constitutional democracy or indirectly via social justice—the CCP must respond in one way or another. These are pressures with Chinese characteristics, springing as they do from legitimation crises in a society that is substantially but not fully capitalist and not constitutionally democratic. Hence they are pressures of a kind to which, as I have noted, Euro-American democratic capitalism is largely immune when faced with otherwise similar legitimation crises. As part of the same package, however, the Chinese state does not have to contend with an extremely powerful and cohesive capitalist class the likes of which have brought democracy to heel in Euro-American democratic capitalism and have indeed largely captured the state in the age of neoliberalism.

This too is an extremely important factor to take into account if we are to appreciate the complexities involved in China's progress toward democracy.

There is a sense in which the Chinese state is more advantageously situated than its European or American counterpart vis-à-vis the capitalist class. It is true that, given its huge dependence on economic growth—whether high speed or high quality—to ward off major legitimation crises, and given the already enormous size of the private sector in the Chinese economy, the Chinese state finds it imperative to secure the cooperation of the capitalist class. Despite this new relation in which the CCP stands to the capitalist class, it remains somewhat less true of China than it is of European or American democratic capitalism that "the demands of 'capital' for an adequate return operate in effect as empirical preconditions for the functioning of *the whole system*."[52]

What is particularly thought provoking, indeed chillingly so, is that it is democracy itself that has allowed the state to be so beholden to the capitalist class. Or, to be more precise, it is only when there is a combination of constitutional democracy and autonomous market economy—that is, only in democratic capitalism—that the capitalist class can acquire this degree of power. For this outcome is possible only through two conjoined processes—namely, constitutional democracy's effective delimitation of the state followed by the capitalist class's successful revolt against an already vulnerable democracy.[53] And, as the still-ongoing ascendancy of neoliberalism has shown, this is a degree of power that seems increasingly capable of neutralizing the very purpose of democracy as the self-protection of society.

It is a chilling thought that, if and when China is able to make big strides in the direction of constitutional democracy, it may well find itself increasingly confronting a powerful and cohesive capitalist class poised to defeat the purpose of democracy just as its Western counterpart has done. By the same token, it will have contributed to an unprecedented expansion of neoliberalism's dominance and a corresponding, globally consequential setback in the self-protection of society against capitalism. Lest we rush to a conclusion in favor of the status quo in China, however, a different chilling thought must be introduced.

This further thought arises from a scenario—some would say an amply realized scenario, despite all the successes of the anticorruption campaign—in which the Chinese state, freer though it is from an overwhelmingly powerful capitalist class, is letting loose on society a class of people who may be no less predatory than the capitalist class in Europe and America. And what is especially detrimental to democracy in this scenario is that this class of people comes overwhelmingly from within the ranks of the CCP itself. Herein lies the true meaning of official corruption in China in the reform era: not the self-enrichment perpetrated by so many cadres at various levels of the party and government—however illegal and rapacious—so much as the creation of an entire crony capitalist class. The existence of this class is enough to turn countless citizens against the state in favor of the market, the supposedly autonomous market that is the more easily believed in because it is an untried fiction in China. Small wonder that neoliberalism has had so little trouble conquering so much of China's ideological space. More seriously, the fact that Chinese-style crony capitalism has grown from within the ranks of the CCP itself has eroded and undermined the party's legitimacy as nothing else could. We have well reached the point where, if the party does not soon put a definitive stop to crony capitalism, it will cease to be distinct from the crony capitalist class and will be nothing but its creator and spokesperson. It is not at all obvious that this state of affairs poses a lesser threat to the self-protection of society than the capitalist class does under democratic capitalism. How different are the lawless crony capitalist predators aided and abetted by the CCP in China from the legal or semilegal but not much less crony capitalist predators unleashed by neoliberalism in Europe and America?[54]

Faced with these options, I believe that one can confidently prefer one to the other only out of self-interest or intellectual laziness or by entertaining massive illusions about either one and about the differences between them. A lot rides on this judgment. If it is largely correct, not forgetting the near inevitability that a neoliberal order implanted in China will be many times worse than its original model in the West, then this is what follows: for those who care about democracy in China and do so with the self-protection of society as part of their agenda, democracy must mean a politico-economic arrangement that effectively protects society *both* from the legally permissible predators of neoliberal advanced capitalism *and* from the lawless predators of Chinese-style crony capitalism. This is a tall order, of course, but any democratic future that falls well short of this twofold objective simply leaves so much to be desired as to raise the question why a democratic future is worth trying to bring about in the first place.

The point I am making is not meant to contribute to an abstract normative argument for a particular way of approaching democracy; for my purposes such an argument is well supplied by Polanyi. Rather it is intended to
address, especially, a distinctive pressure for democracy noticeable in a
country fast becoming capitalist in important respects while remaining a
one-party state. On the one hand, this pressure can be most accurately articulated as a call for the protection of society against capitalism as the principal form of dominium in our time. On the other hand, the fact that China
is still a one-party state serves as a constant reminder that society also needs
protection from imperium. Indeed, it is clear from the very phenomenon of
Chinese-style crony capitalism that imperium and dominium can work together in a way that imperils society more than either alone is capable of
doing. Meanwhile, Western democracies have shown themselves to be vulnerable to a different kind of combination of imperium and dominium,
thanks to the unprecedented capture of the state by the capitalist class in the
age of neoliberalism.[55] Thus, if we care about containing both imperium and
dominium and especially preventing their collusion, whether in China or in
the West, we must (in the case of China) not only contend with the imperium of the party-state but also guard against, and (in the case of the West)
pause to rethink, any constitutionalism that protects capitalism more than
it does society.

Tocqueville and Marx, or a Dual Perspective on Democracy

If the reader has sensed a certain tension in my account of democracy, this
perception is entirely accurate, the tension itself reflecting a profound contradiction between democracy and capitalism. Raised to a higher level of abstraction, this contradiction is one that exists between (civil) society and the
(political) state. In a capitalist democracy, the only kind of democracy yet
known in the modern world, civil society is marked, above all, by the capitalist relations of production, while the political state features a democratic
arrangement both partly made possible by these relations and compromised
by them. Yet it would be inaccurate to see bourgeois civil society only in terms
of the inequality that is at odds with the equality supposedly underlying the
political state. For bourgeois civil society, unlike, say, European feudal so-

ciety in one way and the imagined communist society in another, is both equal and unequal. It is Tocqueville's great insight, though by no means his alone, that such equality as characterizes bourgeois civil society, which he terms equality of conditions, makes democracy in the political state not only possible but also, over time, necessary. If we think of equality of conditions in civil society as *societal* democracy, as Tocqueville does, then we are led to see, first, that societal democracy is more basic than *political* democracy and, second, that democracy is indivisible in that the former, once it has arisen, will unleash a powerful dynamic leading toward the latter.

Neither of these propositions—the determinative role of civil society in relation to the political state, in general and with respect to democracy in particular, and the unity or indivisibility of sociopolitical progress—would have been alien to Marx, except for the fact that Tocqueville fails to see, or at least to attach sufficient importance to, the other side of bourgeois civil society—namely, its intrinsically unequal or undemocratic character. It is here that Marx better captures the more complex and fraught relation between civil society and the political state. For Marx, political democracy would be a contradiction in terms, in that the state itself, and ipso facto democracy as a feature of the political state, is rendered necessary precisely by the undemocratic (or insufficiently democratic) character of civil society, and because civil society determines the character of the political state more than the other way around. That is why Marx refuses even to attach the name "democracy" to the bourgeois state, calling it instead a "republic."[56] The point here is not terminological nicety but Marx's claim that bourgeois democracy is not true democracy, for its formal principle is not its material principle,[57] yet it is nevertheless a democracy of sorts—that is, "a state may be a *free state* without man himself being a *free man*"[58]—thanks to its formal principle. In other words, it falls well short of full, "human emancipation" while deserving nevertheless to be regarded as the outcome of a partial, "political emancipation."[59] "*Political* emancipation certainly represents a great progress. It is not, indeed, the final form of human emancipation, but it is the final form of human emancipation *within* the framework of the prevailing social order."[60] Such is the bourgeois "republic" that Tocqueville unequivocally calls democracy. It would be hard to deny the essentials of Marx's claim even if we take into account the very considerable improvements that bourgeois democracy has wrought since his time, such as universal suffrage and the welfare state. Yet, at the same time, even Marx, rigorously interpreted, would not negate the truth enunciated by Tocqueville, provided it is seen as the partial truth that it is. Because Tocqueville's truth is no more than partially true, it is only reasonable that we should add to it the corrective, albeit differently partial, truth uncovered by Marx. More importantly, as long as we are stuck in a capitalist world, as long as the transcendence of capitalism is not on the horizon, there is something to be said for both valuing bourgeois democracy and recognizing its limitations—that is, for adopting both Tocqueville's perspective and Marx's, and therefore neither entirely on its own.

Thus combining Tocqueville and Marx, we are able to see that bourgeois civil society is both equal, in Tocqueville's sense, and unequal, in Marx's, neither canceling out the other—precisely with the result we are witnessing today. For isn't it the case that societal democracy in Tocqueville's sense must lead sooner or later to political democracy, or else the political state will be unable to ensure regime stability and perpetuation? Yet isn't it also the case that political democracy by itself cannot remotely live up to the full potential of democracy until or unless society can move beyond the capitalist and other intrinsically unequal relations of production and thereby become democratic in Marx's sense?[61] Short of the materialization of this potential, capitalist democracy is a compromise formation reflecting the equality (in Tocqueville's sense) and the inequality (in Marx's sense) that coexist in our form of sociopolitical life. Within this formation, a state form is democratic to the degree that it allows the struggle for greater equality (in Marx's sense as well as in Tocqueville's, for even the equality dear to Tocqueville is seldom fully assured) to take place, and in the measure of success that it permits such struggle to achieve.[62] And it is, at the same time, undemocratic in that both the room for such struggle and the possibility of its success are limited by the role of this state form—capitalist democracy—in maintaining the dominance of the capitalist class in society and hence inequality in Marx's sense.[63]

For analytical purposes, then, Tocqueville and Marx are each important in his own way. Tocqueville helps us see the political implications of societal democracy and the sheer necessity of political democracy for regime stability and perpetuation under modern conditions. Marx, showing that political democracy, along with the very separation of political state and civil society, is precisely symptomatic of the lack of full societal democracy, sheds complementary light on the inevitable contradictions and frustrations of political democracy once it is achieved.

By taking note simultaneously of Tocqueville's and Marx's insights, we put ourselves in the best position to see the same fundamental challenge that confronts China and the West (and all modern societies, for that matter) and, at the same time, the different contradictions that characterize their respective conditions. In China and the West alike, the fundamental challenge is that of advancing societal democracy, for in a modern setting nothing is more determinative of the quality of political life than the degree of democracy present in civil society. If we are being honest, we have to say that even in terms of *societal* democracy alone, regardless of political democracy, the Western countries are today, by and large, more advanced than China. This may not be as radical a difference as appears at first sight, however, in that it is quite possible that the degree of democracy present in a society is, in our capitalist world order, in turn largely a function of that society's place in the global value chain. The higher a society is situated in the economic value chain, it seems, the more elevated its standing in the moral value chain, as it were, the latter including such things as human rights and political democracy. If this is true, then the moral appraisal of societal democracy becomes a far more complicated matter than we normally take it for, and, as far as the coexistence of equality and inequality is concerned, all modern societies to date are equally in the systemic grip of the contradictions of capitalism.

Be that as it may, China today, on top of sharing this fundamental Marxian challenge with the Western and other democracies, faces the additional problem best identified by Tocqueville—namely, that of moving from societal democracy, limited as it is, to a corresponding degree of political democracy. Until China accomplishes this move, it will be at the mercy of a contradiction from which all political democracies, Western and otherwise, are free. This may not be a philosophically very exciting contradiction, but it is one that bears on nothing less than regime stability and perpetuation under modern conditions, hence posing an enormously consequential question of political prudence. True, the political democracies in the world today are all capitalist democracies, and, as such, they necessarily fall well short of societal democracy in Marx's sense and are therefore full of the unresolvable contradictions and unappeasable disappointments symptomatic of a compromise formation. But to take proper note of this fact is not to dismiss another fact of a different, far from insignificant order. For it is no mean achievement that the advanced political democracies in the world today have managed to accomplish the mundane but all-important passage from societal democracy to political democracy. They have thereby removed a contradiction whose presence unfailingly prevents the establishment, under modern conditions, of a relatively stable political order based on relatively credible ideological legitimacy. This is something that China has yet to accomplish, and it would be an extraordinary non sequitur to dismiss this Tocquevillian challenge for China by pointing to the failure of actually existing political democracies to rise to the other, Marxian challenge.

Nor does such failure amount to a general argument against democracy. For the failure, rather than *of* democracy, is precisely perpetrated *against* democracy. In strictly Marxian terms, it is a matter of so-called democracy being confined to the political state and kept largely out of civil society, thereby giving rise to the very dualism of political state (idealism) and civil society (materialism). Less strictly speaking, it might be treated as a matter of societal democracy being insufficiently strong to render political democracy more truly representative. In either case, the cause of the problem is not democracy but rather its confinement or evisceration by relations of domination in bourgeois civil society. Even political democracy as critiqued by Marx is not the cause of the problem but merely its symptom. One can see, in this light, what an utterly confused and self-defeating move it is for those in the West who otherwise think of themselves as supporters of democracy to blame it for their countries' problems and to look to so-called meritocratic systems for a better political alternative. One can see, too, why the Chinese Left, if it is serious, should have no business echoing and even encouraging this development.

It is even more important to see, especially in the case of China, that democracy presents two distinct sets of problems, the Marxian and the Tocquevillian. There is little doubt that the latter is the more urgently pertinent for China today. This urgency is dictated by a basic feature of present-day Chinese reality—namely, that societal democracy in Tocqueville's sense, already undeniably present and daily advancing, has yet to lead to political democracy, and until it does, regime stability and perpetuation will remain the CCP's paramount challenge. Only when this long-delayed move is attempted or at least seriously contemplated can—and must—the even more challenging set of problems raised by Marx be brought properly and with full relevance into the foreground. Despite its own official self-understanding, China is largely at a stage whose political predicament is especially well captured by Tocqueville. Nevertheless it should take no more than a reasonably serious effort at democratic extrication from this predicament for China, already substantially characterized by the capitalist mode of production, to be ripe for the Marxian critique of bourgeois democracy— indeed also for the less uncompromising and more realistic social democratic warnings against the corrosive powers of capitalism. There is reason, then, to place Tocqueville in the foreground for now, with Marx, and social democracy, kept ready as a necessary dialectical counterforce whose insights and admonitions of a different order we would do well to bear in mind even as we contemplate the Tocquevillian passage from a limited societal democracy to some form of political democracy. Here lies the vital relevance to China's democratic reform of a thinker such as Polanyi who combines the intellectual perspicacity of a Marx with the sober realism of social democracy at its best.

It is a great illusion held by segments of the Left in China, new and old, that China today remains a largely socialist country despite its profoundly transformative economic reform and, as such, is axiomatically superior to liberal democratic capitalism—based on the kind of logic Georg Lukács once stubbornly held with regard to the Soviet Union under Stalin. But this illusion is hard to sustain in the face of undeniable consequences of the reform— among these, a level of economic inequality worthy of the most unflattering picture of capitalism, despite China's justifiably lauded success in its campaign against grinding poverty; the unmistakably bourgeois aspirations, as well as commodity fetishism, now informing the CCP and ordinary people alike; the introduction of capitalist relations of production and private property rights, along with the successful reshaping of the economy on the basis largely of capitalist market principles and incentives; and the very fact of China's spectacular rise within a global capitalist order aided and abetted by the greatest capitalist powers. The Left is not alone, however, in misreading the exact nature and full magnitude of China's democratic challenge. For more than a few Chinese liberals subscribe to the serious misjudgment that democracy as actually practiced in the West and especially in America—

that is, liberal democratic capitalism—has largely delivered on the promise of democracy and thereby attained a status and success close to moral finality. This is part of the "end of history" thesis of which all too many well-meaning Chinese citizens remain to be fully disabused—no less than some of their opponents need to part with the poorly examined belief in actually existing socialism's superiority to democratic capitalism.

If we are free from the illusion and the misjudgment just noted, we should have little hesitation in treating the question of democracy for China at the present stage as, first and foremost, a prudential matter of regime stability and perpetuation. Thus the only compelling presentation today of democracy's claim to the urgent attention of the Chinese leadership and citizenry alike, given actually existing democracy's many serious flaws and given China's rising fortunes under an alternative political system, is by asking, insistently and rigorously, whether prudent democratic reform or resolute continuation of the status quo is more conducive to the country's social and political stability, all things considered. For this reason, the kind of case I am making for democracy in China has perforce to be more Tocquevillian than Marxian, or, what amounts to largely the same thing, more Machiavellian or Hobbesian than Aristotelian. If my discussion of Marx, Polanyi, and other thinkers of the Left seems in places a departure from this prudential conception of the argument, it is worth emphasizing that the seeming departure is actually meant to strengthen the prudential argument. For, without developing a sufficiently strong antidote in political institutions and political culture, particularly in society itself, against the evisceration of democracy by capitalism—one of the chief lessons being daily taught by actually existing democracies—a superficial, formal completion of the Tocquevillian move from societal to political democracy will not well serve the purpose even of regime stability and perpetuation.

CHAPTER FIVE

Contradictions and Arrested Transitions

THE TWO OUTSTANDING FEATURES of China that have emerged so far are that it is not a democracy in one sense but very much one in another and that it is capitalist and yet not quite capitalist. While it would be simplistic to think of such a contradictory state of affairs as suggesting a transitional stage leading to a known destination, there is clearly something fundamentally unsettled about China's present condition. After four decades of unceasing reform, producing as many unintended as intended consequences, and driven as much by unintended consequences as by deliberate initiatives, China is still very much a work in progress in key aspects of its politics, economy, and much else. This is not because China is yet to become like, say, the United States as a capitalist economy or a democratic polity, as it must or is destined to be, but rather because its own reform has unleashed dynamics that have not run their full course and contradictions that have not worked themselves through. These are motions and fault lines in China's own moral and political condition.

It is essential to understand these factors if we are to form ideas about China's democratic challenge that do justice to the complexity of the reality on the ground. I have already argued that it will soon be necessary for China to replace its defunct, revolutionary legitimacy with a new, democratic one. But necessity is one thing and the difficulty involved quite another. In the case of China today, the necessity and the difficulty are bound together: China's path to democracy will be as difficult as it is necessary, best seen especially in the contradictions to which I have referred. These contradictions, in turn, can be usefully captured and assessed as they unfold at the level of moral and political culture.

In this chapter I want to give a glimpse of China's moral and political culture on the move—those elements of it that have been part of China's recent evolution as an incompletely democratic country and partially capitalist society. This is all the more necessary in that even Chinese citizens themselves and foreign observers who know the country well often fail to fully appreciate how far, since the start of the reform, China's moral and political culture has evolved, propelled by changes in its social and economic conditions. And it is precisely because China has gone this far that it has great difficulty going even further and yet does not have the live option of standing still. Given the powerful dynamic set in motion by its own reform, China has no choice but to go much further.

But where? Surely not just toward *more* democracy in some generic sense, for the substance, temper, and internal balance of a democracy are shaped to a significant degree by culture, including especially moral and political culture. Part of the answer, then, must lie in those elements of China's moral and political tradition that still speak to the unique reality and needs of the Chinese condition. Thus I want to spare some attention, toward the end, for two such elements as they intervene in the contradictions within China's current moral and political culture and make their influence felt on the further evolution of what is now only a partially democratic and partially capitalist China.

Since the very idea of a partially democratic and partially capitalist country implies as its point of reference a more fully democratic and capitalist one, there is perhaps no better way to present my account of China than through comparison, where appropriate, with the United States. And it so happens that there is a common denominator for such a comparison. If I were to single out one thing as the most profound outcome—and dynamic—of China's reform in the past few decades, I would without hesitation point to the rise of the so-called liberties of the moderns. It is for the first time under Chinese communist rule that a vast domain of private life has emerged, making available an unprecedented range of liberties for the pursuit of wealth, pleasure, consumption, lifestyle, and so on. Since my focus is on China, I will bring in the United States, or sometimes the West more generally, for comparison only where it helps throw a characteristic of China or a problem of democracy into sharper relief as an object of understanding or appraisal. My aim is to use comparison to bring out pertinent questions or initiate much-needed reflection, not to suggest or imply that China must follow the United States or the West in general, unless that is where it ought to be heading given its own, internal dynamic and the state of its current contradictions.

Whether it is a good thing to head there is another question. Good or bad, it is the fate of modern societies, under the pressure of equality of conditions, to *have to* move in the direction of political democracy, or else they will sooner or later suffer an inescapable, dangerously debilitating and destabilizing legitimacy deficit. Likewise, it is the fate of modern individuals, because of a psychic economy and moral psychology fostered by equality of conditions, to *have to* enjoy freedom in order to be moral agents, or else they will end up with an equally incapacitating agency or subjectivity deficit. The fate of modern societies and that of modern individuals come together in that only political democracy can give individual liberty the range and protection that moral subjectivity requires.

But neither democracy nor liberty, fated as we are to embrace them, is an entirely unambiguous good, a good that especially in practice is without questionable consequences. Some of these consequences are questionable precisely because they undermine the most important reasons for valuing what democracy and liberty supposedly represent in the first place. And yet there seems no plausible and better alternative to democracy, not only in the political sphere but, as I will attempt to show, even for the purpose of moral life under modern conditions. We have no choice but to confront complexities such as these if we want to take democracy with the seriousness it deserves and with a (relative) freedom from illusions that alone can make it work. Accordingly, my reflections will take me further afield than the more mundane aspects of moral and political culture and will be more speculative, and perhaps more theoretically ambitious, than in any other part of the book. An important advantage of such reflections is that they will allow me to piece together a fuller and more nuanced picture of democracy than elsewhere in the book—so as to affirm democracy with the necessary sobriety and with an openness to new, different ways of making it work for China.

For Chinese democracy—that is, any but the most superficial and predictably counterproductive attempt at exogenous transplantation—will have to grow out of China's own, internal dynamic and its own, internal contradictions.

While some of these contradictions can and simply must be overcome, such as the contradiction between the existence of essential de facto freedoms and their lack of valorization and legal protection, other contradictions may well be of a different, deeper kind. I believe we are dealing with contradictions of the latter category when we consider China's twin needs for democratic legitimacy and a manner of political integration of sufficient centripetal force to hold the vast and complex country together. The same is true when we ask how we can reconcile the importance of liberty in a modern society, which China already is, with the still-powerful pull in today's China of the so-called priority of the good (a term to be explained in due course). Such contradictions are different and deeper because we cannot overcome them. We can only work through them in one way or another, and having to do so is the unique fate of being Chinese in the modern world.

A Most Important Common Denominator with the United States

Four decades ago, before the era of reform had started, one could certainly undertake to compare the moral and political cultures of China and the United States and gain much illumination, as some scholars must have done. I daresay, however, that whatever would have served as a suitable common denominator for getting the comparison off the ground back then would surely have given the comparison the predominant character of a contrast, the bringing to light of big and profound differences.

Back then, an American visiting China would have found the experience out of the ordinary, whether in a positive or negative sense. None of the modern liberties really existed in China in those days and, indeed, few of the pleasures and opportunities of modern life were available that would have made such liberties necessary and their absence a source of frustration. Americans in China would have felt like the proverbial fish out of water, gasping for air and desperate to get back to where they belonged, unless they were of that rare breed of foreigners who identified so much with the Chinese revolution as to be able to make light of everything else. Similarly, a mainland Chinese who set foot in the United States for the first time would have suffered a veritable culture shock—a term that was indeed much used back then to describe just such an experience. A Chinese in America in those days would no less have been a fish out of water, or perhaps a fish finding it-self in waters initially too choppy for comfort, surrounded (to break off the metaphor) by a dazzling array of consumer goods and a tempting yet discon-certing absence of inhibitions about pleasures and enterprises.

Today, many an American or other Westerner would feel quite at home in China, as legions in fact do, in metropolises such as Beijing or Shanghai. True, they complain about air pollution, control of the internet, and, espe-cially if they are in business, a lack of the rule of law (although a so-called authoritarian state takes in the slack and provides plenty of stability and predictability for commerce and investment). But such complaints are clearly meant to be directed at a twenty-first century society in which the liberties, conveniences, and opportunities of the moderns have come to be taken for granted. A lingering, nominal communism has not stood in the way of stock markets and golf courses and billionaires. Meanwhile the better off among the mainland Chinese have left their erstwhile culture shock entirely behind, many of them seeking wealth and happiness and security across the Pacific with little sense of their foreignness in a land that until recently had served as the quintessential bourgeois other. They even have come to share the griev-ances against China typically aired by Americans and Europeans, and many of them have settled in America as their new home, or second home, precisely for this reason, among others. Those who have thought better of emigration find the opportunities for career advancement, comfortable private life, or, in the case of the more ambitious, aggrandizement available in Beijing or Shanghai or Shenzhen too attractive to give up. One hears some of them speak, not without condescension, of American cities other than New York, San Francisco, and Los Angeles as "second-tier cities" (a term for ranking the clout and glamour of Chinese cities) or complain that too much of the US infrastructure is decrepit. Some even have among their negative perceptions of a city like Los Angeles the fact that there are simply too many Chinese wan-dering around as tourists or living there already—presumably mostly main-land Chinese, not a few of whom are thought to be corrupt former officials or their family members.

How times have changed, how China has changed, in barely four decades! As if the changes themselves were not breathtaking enough, they even find official expression in the recently invented idea of the Chinese Dream. It is a distinctively modern dream, supposedly cherished by all moderns today, of the kind of prosperous, comfortable, secure, and peaceful life known only to the moderns and uniquely prized by them, and, by extension and as a necessary means, of a motherland rich and strong enough to make all this possible. Thus, even in its nation-centered version, the Chinese Dream bespeaks a massive democratization and bourgeois westernization compared with the erstwhile vanguard-imposed and class-based project of communism.

Thus it is that today we have between China and the United States a common denominator for the purpose of comparison that did not exist at all in, say, 1977. This common denominator—liberties of the moderns—now looms large, and it promises to shed much light on China's moral and political culture if we examine China's way of organizing modern liberties in comparison with the American way. Today, liberties of the moderns rank especially high among the things China has in common with the United States, and the two countries may be said to be more alike than they are different. They are both quintessentially modern societies, given the preeminence of modern liberties in them. Their differences, great as they are, lie only in the way such liberties are organized.

China Abounds in De Facto Freedoms without Affirming Freedom as a Value

Some of you must be taking exception to my characterization of China in terms of liberties of the moderns and hence also to my adoption of such liberties as the common denominator for comparing the moral and political cultures of China and the United States. Modern liberties *in their typical or in any reasonably strict sense,*[1] you may say, do not yet exist in China despite its admittedly profound transformation in recent decades; some of you may even suggest that modern liberties, *even as construed without the foregoing qualification,* are nowhere to be found in China. I would say that you are right in the first case but seriously mistaken in the second. In fact, I can think of no better way of starting my comparative exercise than by showing why this is so. To this end, I want to identify, at the level of ideal types, three reasons for, and three corresponding narratives of, freedom.

The first is of a kind that reflects the importance that a certain type of freedom has for members of modern societies given the very nature of modern life. Benjamin Constant famously distinguishes between the liberty of the ancients and that of the moderns. The liberty of the ancients is so called because it is constitutive of a domain of life—the public or political—that was especially important for the privileged equals, the citizens, among ancient Athenians. The liberty of the moderns, in contrast, derives its name from its usefulness in a domain of life—the private—that is especially useful for participants in modern bourgeois or petty-bourgeois life. As is well known, Constant gives pride of place to the private domain and hence to the kind of liberty required in it, because it is there that members of modern societies happen to find the most extensive scope for pleasurable and self-constituting activities, thanks to the fact that "the progress of civilization, the commercial tendency of the age, the communication amongst peoples, have infinitely multiplied and varied the means of personal happiness."[2]

I have already described the appearance of liberties of the moderns as the single most profound outcome of China's economic and social reform. Some clarifications and qualifications are now in order. There is no denying that modern liberties abound in China today. If one spends some time in Shanghai, for example, one will soon discover that few individuals whose sole passion is the enjoyment of success and happiness in the private realm, including foreigners accustomed to all the nice things that advanced capitalism has to offer, have reason to feel deprived of liberties. It is arguable that these liberties fall short of what Constant calls liberties of the moderns. "The aim of the moderns is the enjoyment of *security* in private pleasures," writes Constant, "and they call liberty the *guarantees* accorded by institutions to these pleasures."[3] Constant also insists, in a well-known statement, that "political liberty is [individual liberty's] guarantee, consequently political liberty is indispensable."[4] It is true, in this light, that such individual liberties as one can find in China today are without guarantees in the form of either the rule of law or political liberty and are therefore—especially in the case of the freedoms of speech and publication that matter so much to intellectuals and social activists—subject to constant reversal and even repression, as we have seen in the past few years. Yet it is hardly less obvious that they are of sufficiently secure availability to most people for most purposes as the typical modern individual in China today goes about what Constant calls his or her speculations, enterprises, and pleasures.

It is another measure of how much China and the United States have in common in terms of modern liberties that Jean-Jacques Rousseau's distinction between the bourgeois and the citizen and his strictures against modern society based on this distinction are almost equally applicable to both—except that the Chinese are less citizens than Americans are (much as the French were back in the eighteenth century, compared with the English) and, in this sense, even more purely bourgeois.

The upshot is that in China today, modern individual liberties are available, for the most part, only in a de facto sense, and yet they largely suffice for the mundane uses to which such liberties are typically put. I characterize these liberties as only de facto in the sense that they are not articulated and valorized as liberties and are not legally guaranteed and culturally supported through such articulation and valorization. Thus, while they serve the practical purposes of everyday life, they are not raised to the level of a moral *value*, a socially affirmed and individually embraced value. Despite their lack of valorization, however, these liberties do exist, and they seem to serve the purposes of most members of Chinese society well enough. In this way, China today largely lives up to a very plausible formula of modern liberty—namely, that of people "living as they please, within the bounds of the law and their own incomes."[5] Thus, if the typical uses of modern individual liberties are all we care about, then we have to say that in China today the de facto freedoms do not strictly require moralization and institutionalization into positively affirmed and legally and politically protected liberties.

It is obvious, however, that de facto liberties are far from sufficient for some purposes and therefore are insufficient for those people who find such purposes important. Among such purposes are those of religious freedom, for example, and undeniably there is a sizable portion of the Chinese populace for whom the existing de facto liberties do not provide nearly enough room for practicing their religion, as a matter of private life, openly and without fear.[6] Such people and such purposes, the religious being only one example, require for their satisfaction a second, different kind of freedom and a different narrative of the rationale for freedom. They require the higher liberty, if you will, to conduct the spiritual and moral part of their lives in a way that nonviolently departs from that of others and from the mainstream. The liberty in question, often known as liberty of conscience and freedom of thought, is at bottom the liberty to *be,* and this, in turn, means the second-order liberty, as it were, to be free—reflectively and consciously free. What we find here are a distinct need for freedom and a distinct kind of freedom often traced to the existential challenge posed by the religious wars of sixteenth-century Europe and to the gradually evolved liberal solution to challenges of this broad category, culminating in what John Rawls calls reasonable pluralism. What is most important in providing a narrative for this kind of freedom is that, given the very nature of this need for freedom, de facto liberties simply will not suffice, even if they exist to an extent that would otherwise cover the need. For those who have this need and who prize freedom out of this need, the freedom cannot but present itself as *consciously* affirmed—as mattering, for this reason, on the second-order (reflective) level as much as on the first-order (de facto) level. For them, it is as if freedom is always already valorized, always already a value, and this value only comes to be more firmly held and more intensely striven for in the face of what is perceived as unreasonable interference or repression.

It may appear, however, that this need and this freedom, accompanied as they are by an act of valorization and by the resulting concept of freedom as a value, are present—or at least happen to be present—in China only for a minority of the citizenry. In a way this is indeed the case, as can be seen in the fact that practitioners of religions are among the most insistent in their pursuit of freedoms and among the most explicit in going about their pursuit under the very description of freedom. Yet what they are pressing for is not so different from the freedom that is required to be moral agents or moral subjects. It is true that their quest for freedom takes a more conscious and more combative form, but this is only because theirs is a kind of subjectivity that happens to have more obstacles placed in its path in China today than is usually the case. The desire to be moral subjects, to have a significant measure of agency in one's moral life, however, is a generic desire and, as such, is no less keenly felt by the seemingly more silent majority who happen not to encounter so seriously or so frequently the problems that afflict the more religiously inclined.

This brings to the fore, then, a third reason for freedom, as distinct from the religious one per se, and that is the need for freedom as a condition of moral subjectivity. This is the kind of freedom I discuss in my earlier book, *Moral China in the Age of Reform*. The relatively secure presence of this freedom is one of the great strengths of American moral culture, despite all the criticisms that can fairly be made of its uses and of the unequal relations of power to which it is often subject. If I were to associate this notion of freedom with an influential figure in modern thought, it would be Immanuel Kant. In his short essay "An Answer to the Question: 'What Is Enlightenment?,'" Kant recommends a certain intellectual and moral maturity in the name of enlightenment and identifies a certain freedom as a condition of this maturity. This is a distinctively nonpolitical liberty and is meant to be exercised in the public as distinct from the private use of reason. To make intellectual and moral maturity possible is the be-all and end-all of this freedom. As is well known, freedom is, for Kant, a regulative idea; the same I take to apply to maturity as Kant speaks of it. In this regard, I both draw on Kant and depart from him. By *moral subject,* I mean someone who is willing and able to act with maturity, to take responsibility for himself or herself as an individual and as a member of society—doing so, I might add, in such things as securing a living, finding happiness and meaning in life, and cooperating with others. In fact, this is the kind of responsibility every member of a modern society has no choice but to carry insofar as he or she is successfully socialized as what is called an individual. Thus, while Kant's notion of freedom, and by the same token his notion of maturity, may be metaphysical, my notions of freedom and subjectivity are sociohistorical, intended as they are only for members of a distinctively modern society.

In my account, intellectual subjectivity is the minimal ability and willingness needed in one's relation to the objective or factual dimension of the world, and moral subjectivity is the minimal ability and willingness needed in one's relation to other subjects qua subjects—in both cases, but especially the latter, with the minimum defined by the requirements of human life in a modern setting. This minimum, varyingly met in empirical cases, is a presupposition of all that is due to an equal citizen and legal subject in the modern sense. Subjectivity, as I use this notion, does not require more than this minimum and therefore the way people make choices and take responsibility, either as individuals or as citizens acting together, need not show perspicacity, wisdom, thoughtfulness, or any other such quality. Subjectivity, in my sense, while a condition of such positive qualities, does not requires or guarantee any of them.

If to this understanding of subjectivity we add the post-Kantian (say, Louis Althusser's) insight that a moral subject is always a subject in the double sense of *subjection* ("subjected to") and *subjectivity* ("subject of"), then moral subjectivity is anything but simple, and a moral subject is seldom as good or wise, indeed never as much an agent in the first place, as we may hope it is. Freedom likewise. Yet, contradiction ridden as it is, moral subjectivity is something one cannot do without, and, given the nature of modern life, this subjectivity, in turn, cannot do without freedom, conditioned and compromised as the latter is. Freedom is not a bed of roses but rather a field of political contestation and ideological engineering. Still, there is no bypassing freedom as a condition of moral subjectivity in the modern world.

How the Absence of Freedom as a Value Has Led to a Moral Crisis

When we try to understand China's moral culture today, the first thing worth noting is the absence of freedom as a (moral) value amid plentiful de facto freedoms. This lack, however, does not warrant the view, still widespread, of China as an unfree society. If it were unfree, how would one describe and understand the hugely enlarged space for action—for what Constant calls the modern individual's speculations, enterprises, and pleasures—compared with Mao Zedong's time or even with the earlier years of reform? Nor would it be accurate to say that what I am calling de facto freedoms boil down to economic freedom, although it is true that, among all the de facto freedoms now visible everywhere in China, economic freedom comes closest to enjoying the moral and political status of a value. For these de facto freedoms cover all areas of life other than political dissent and participation. Thus it is not true that freedoms do not exist in China, or that they are confined to economic activity.

The problem instead is that despite their range and abundance, de facto liberties do not add up to a publicly recognized value and cannot draw moral significance and political and legal protection from the presence of such a value. This is a fact of the utmost consequence precisely because China is already, in many areas of everyday life, a free society in a de facto yet still very important sense. In a radical departure from the first three decades of communist rule, the better part of them characterized by the collectivization or nationalization of virtually all the means of production, the party-state of today no longer sees it as its prerogative and responsibility to provide every citizen with a livelihood and a worldview through what used to be the nearly total political control and supervision of every aspect of life. Although the state still looms large in their lives, sometimes oppressively so, there can be no doubt that today's Chinese find themselves having to exercise choice and discretion as they have never done before under communist rule. In things large and small, they have to fend for themselves, without anything remotely resembling the state's past guidance or help, in an ever-expanding private sphere. This new necessity—with new, de facto freedoms as the other side of the same coin—applies to the economic aspect of a Chinese person's life much as it does that of his or her counterpart in the United States. At the same time, the new combination of necessity and de facto freedom extends to everything that belongs to one's moral and spiritual life (if, or especially if, one is not a member of the Chinese Communist Party [CCP]). This has an importance that is hard to exaggerate, for it introduces a problem, a contradiction, at the heart of moral life in China.

Everywhere one looks in China, one sees that moral life has been left untouched in any positive way by all the official propaganda: individuals receive little plausible, credible, internalizable, and hence effective moral guidance from the state. Despite this universally known fact, members of Chinese society are unable to turn to other sources of moral guidance, for these are simply not allowed to exist and compete with the CCP. But above all, they are not permitted to fend for themselves *as far as their moral life is concerned*, for a very simple reason: they are not permitted to think of themselves as free moral agents, because freedom itself is not allowed to serve as a moral value in society—a moral resource that helps people give existential meaning to their de facto freedoms and impart moral-volitional unity to their actions. They may have their de facto freedoms intact, since the state has kept a low profile in this regard and, for all intents and purposes, stayed out of their moral lives. Moreover, they are not prevented from choosing different ways of (private) life for themselves, provided they do so strictly *as individuals*. Yet something crucial is missing—freedom as a moral value, which alone can give public expression to their actual self-reliance, place it under a properly moral light, and thereby enable the merely de facto free individuals to come into their own as moral subjects. Short of this step forward in China's moral culture, the new conditions of life and the new de facto freedoms will continue to call for a new moral subject that cannot come into being. The merely de facto free individuals will remain as they are, with plenty of scope for action and yet no claim to their moral lives and moral selves amid all their de facto freedoms. The result is a prolonged moral crisis—a crisis of moral subjectivity caused by the *lack of freedom as a value* amid the rise of de facto freedoms—that has shadowed China's economic and social reform.

The Communist Moral Culture Dead and beyond Resuscitation

The crisis of moral subjectivity is symptomatic, therefore, of a fatal deficiency within China's existing moral culture. It has grown out of that very deficiency and represents a challenge to which China's existing moral culture is totally unequipped to respond. For the plain fact is that this moral culture still pretends to be an essentially communist one—a continuation, if a somewhat embarrassed one, of its Maoist predecessor. It does so, has to do so, for exactly the same reasons that the CCP retains its name and public self-understanding despite the profound change in its nature. But these reasons, though themselves an important part of present-day Chinese reality, cannot make that reality other than it is and therefore cannot prevent the collapse of all three pillars of the old communist morality—communism, asceticism, and altruism. Communism, the teleological underpinning of all things moral in the Mao era, is no longer a plausible, still less an actually pursued, goal of the CCP or the populace. Asceticism, a matter of necessity in Mao's time and the sociopsychological basis of self-denying morality, has been swept aside by rising prosperity and a new, proto-capitalist economy that relies on hedonism and consumerism. And altruism, in the sense of readiness to make sacrifices not only for individual others but also and especially for the collective and the country, has lost its object and rationale in a radically transformed society where it no longer makes sense to give up one's own so-called selfish interests in order to "follow the party" and "serve the people." For all intents and purposes, the brave new China we see today is a bona fide capitalist society in the most vital goals and values that make up its dynamic, economic and otherwise (except for the CCP's imperative to keep itself in power), and inform the everyday aspirations and pursuits of ordinary people. For such a society, the old communist morality is almost entirely obsolete and useless, and this means, above all, that the old communist moral subject—

with its belief in communism, its ascetic libidinal organization, and its daily practice of altruism—is also obsolete and useless. A capitalist society has no need and no place for a communist moral subject.

What is needed instead—objectively rather than as a matter of optional preference—is a bourgeois moral subject. This is indeed all but openly acknowledged in the CCP's own understanding of the goals and aspirations that are high on China's agenda, both official and popular. What is the much-touted Chinese Dream, for example, but a variation on the prototypically bourgeois American Dream, with a collectivist or nationalist dimension thrown in for good measure? In fact, as already noted, Xi Jinping implied almost as much in his conversation with Barack Obama at the former Annenberg Estate in California. And who is the agent and beneficiary of the moderately prosperous society *(xiaokang shehui)* China is at present striving to establish but a bourgeois subject or, somewhat less jarringly to the lingering communist sensibility, a middle-class subject? If such visions as the Chinese Dream and a moderately prosperous society appear bland and nondescript, this impression is made possible by, and therefore is symptomatic of, a transformation in values that is anything but bland and nondescript. Underlying the substantive and rhetorical neutrality of the Chinese Dream and a moderately prosperous society is the disappearance of class and class struggle from the theory and discourse of the CCP. Gone is the entire category of class enemies against whom the proletariat used to be defined, and gone with it, therefore, is the working class as a class for itself. Gone also are all values and aspirations defined in class terms, as either proletarian or bourgeois, and as being locked in deadly conflict. The result is a universalism that used to be absolutely anathema to the party, and there can be no doubt that this newfound universalism is a bourgeois one, reinterpellating the formerly privileged proletariat as no more than aspirants to membership in the bourgeois or middle class. In a radical departure from its own past conception and rhetoric, the CCP now treats the human being, both qua individual and qua species, as the preeminent standard *(yiren weiben)* and unabashedly takes up a worldview that smacks of the humanism of the bourgeois Enlightenment. All people supposedly want essentially the same things and hold essentially the same values, with all but the sharpest of conflicts (those involving terrorists and dissidents) now belonging under what used to be called "contradictions among the people" and thus having the character of what is treated as reasonable pluralism in the United States. The happy and prosperous life of ordinary Chinese, as they themselves understand such a life, has become the goal of the party and the very raison d'être of national rejuvenation. The principal contradiction of the new era (the Xi era) is thought to exist between the ever-rising aspirations of the people, no longer divided by class, on the one hand, and the insufficiency and unevenness of socioeconomic development, on the other. The apparent blandness and neutrality of the CCP's latest vision are nothing but a reflection of the profound change just briefly summarized. However muted and laconic the presentation of this change may have been in official pronouncements, make no mistake: this is a sea change, a paradigm shift in values and therefore also in the CCP's self-understanding, in its own conception of its nature and mission.

It is easy to understand, then, why the old communist moral subject is no longer serviceable and why a new moral subject—an essentially bourgeois one—is needed in its place. It is indeed from this fact, more than from any other, that we know for sure that China is no longer a communist society, a society on its way to communism, and that what is still called the Chinese Communist Party is no longer a communist party.

Yet the pretense continues that things have not fundamentally changed. The official agents of propaganda are still in business and are indeed still operating in their exhortative mode. The CCP still sees itself as the moral guide of the entire population, which it still treats as in need of moral tutelage, although it can do little to positively fulfill this self-appointed role and is aware of this ineffectiveness as fully as anyone else. The culture industry, when co-opted by the official propaganda machine as it has to be from time to time, still churns out films and television dramas celebrating the heroic personalities and deeds of the revolutionary decades as if monumentalizing the past could still effectively lend legitimacy to the present and serve to teach moral lessons to those living today. And the official propaganda machine itself, through its television programs and newspapers among other media, has never stopped putting on public display contemporary role models with supposedly exceptional loyalty to the party and love of the people. All of these productions bear only the most tenuous connection to the present in terms of the morality needed and possible today, and all of these agents speak with a voice that cannot but fall on deaf ears.

Thus it is that times have radically changed, thanks to the economic and social reform initiated by the CCP itself, and yet the only morality currently on offer is all but entirely lifted from an era predating the reform and therefore does not speak to the new reality and the new needs and problems of today. There can be only one outcome—a moral vacuum, a moral no-man's-land.[7] The so-called proletarian virtues (in the shape of communist-inspired asceticism and altruism) have evaporated, along with the proletariat as a class for itself or even labeled as such. Bourgeois goals and aspirations have staged a triumphant comeback, not least among the ranks of the CCP, but without the accompaniment of a bourgeois morality or even the official permission for such a morality to emerge. What is the rampant official corruption openly acknowledged by the party itself but, in large part, the taking of illegal shortcuts to achieve bourgeois goals? What could better explain the prevalence of such corruption than the absence of a morality, along with its necessary legal support, that is suited to the new capitalist or quasi-capitalist society? And what is China's moral crisis but the effects of the lack of such a morality on an entire society?

This is not to say that the morality needed in China today will come into being simply on the strength of the need itself if only the political obstacles to its emergence are removed. Nor is it to pretend that bourgeois morality itself, even in the best-ordered capitalist societies, does not have its own serious problems today, not least with the paradigm shift from a society of producers to a society of consumers.[8] What are, or can be, today's bourgeois virtues anyway, other than those left over from the society of producers and from a past able to draw on the ideological resources of the Protestant ethic, among other things? How much room is there, with capitalism itself increasingly divested of its earlier ideological interpretations, even for virtues as such, given how capitalism by nature, left to its own devices, is disposed to organize human life around external rather than internal goods and over time to erode practices as distinct from institutions?[9] Insofar as such virtues still exist, how long can they last when the needs and imperatives of the society of consumers seem to corrode them further with each passing year? These are real and very serious problems, but they are, as it were, other societies' problems—the kind of problems confronting, say, American society in its moral and political organization of liberties whose possibilities and constraints are made more complex by the ever-faster and more intractable evolution of an endlessly resourceful digital capitalism. They are not yet the problems that China has the luxury to face as its foremost moral challenges, although it behooves its citizens to spare some thought for such problems, which have definitely hit the country in a big way as well.

The problem that stares China in the face is this: the morality of an earlier, communist China is entirely obsolete, and a morality capable of creating new moral subjects and supporting a new moral order is yet to be born—yet to be *allowed* to be conceived. The proletarian virtues have disappeared for good, and no new virtues have been established in their place. In the meantime, China is a society without a relevant and effectual morality. This means, to put it bluntly, that China is a society without a morality—a morality "fit for purpose." It does not have virtues to go with its newfound liberties of the moderns. This is yet another sense in which these liberties are only de facto liberties.

It would nevertheless be incorrect to say that moral subjectivity is simply missing. What is lacking, rather, to use Althusser's helpful terminology, is a set of Ideological State Apparatuses (ISAs) working relatively independently from and yet broadly in support of the Repressive State Apparatus—and hence also any moral subjectivity properly informed by the avowed precepts and values of the supposedly communist state. What moral subjectivity there actually is has thus been formed by default rather than design—that is, under influences other than those ostensibly exerted by the propaganda and cultural organs of the party-state. Not the least of such influences are those originating from the ISAs of liberal democratic capitalist states, especially America. For all the growing national pride and political anti-Americanism evident in China today, the general population has lost little interest in things American and Western, not least when it comes, for rich party members and affluent ordinary citizens alike, to the dead serious business of their children's education. The conclusion is inescapable: all too many Chinese are still powerfully drawn to the values propagated by the American and Western ISAs. Much as they are partial to their own country in one way or another, their hearts and minds are often engaged elsewhere. After all, who can deny that they inhabit a capitalist society and embrace a bourgeois way of life? And yet the state of which they are citizens is unable to develop plausible values catering to their need for subjectivity and indeed does not even have the ISAs to produce such values in the first place.

Whatever the precise degree of American and Western influence, it by no means amounts to a complete ideological takeover. The CCP sees to it that this does not happen, most conspicuously with regard to religion, yet it has not been able to create its own moral culture. The result is a combination of partial ideological colonization and near moral anarchy contained largely by the Repressive State Apparatus. Such a condition does not mean, of course, that there are no moral subjects to be found in China today; far from it. But the fact is that such moral subjects as we can all readily bear witness to in China—disproportionately among the younger members of the middle class, or so it seems—do not owe their moral subjectivity and their corresponding moral conduct to the prevailing moral culture, for what we find is a prevailing *lack* of moral culture. Thus, with their moral subjectivity nourished largely by external bourgeois ISAs that are nevertheless not allowed to completely colonize China's ideological space—what a morally ambiguous situation!—these Chinese moral subjects, whatever their age and number, cannot but be exceptions. They are indeed the proverbial exceptions that prove the rule, and the sad rule is that China is now suffering from the profound lack of a functioning moral culture of its own, with the result that most of its members are left floundering in a moral wasteland. The de facto freedoms that now abound make it possible for people to act. Until such freedoms are raised to the level of a value, however, they will not enable people to act with an affirmed sense of self and meaning and a reasonable level of considerateness for others.

China Needs a New Moral Culture

I am inclined to think that the moral crisis confronting China exists at an altogether deeper and hence more potently dangerous level than all other problems. It is, as I have noted, a crisis of moral subjectivity—that is to say, of the demise of an old moral subject and of the absence of a new moral subject, and hence of the absence in Chinese society today of *any* moral subject constituted endogenously and by design. It is, one might say, a problem at the meta-moral level, at a level that concerns the preconditions or presuppositions of any reasonably well-functioning morality, whether we like the tenor and substance of that morality or not.

Nothing is more important for a moral culture than the distinct moral subject that is created by it and that, in turn, gives life to it by acting in accordance with it and adapting and even changing it while doing so. The moral subject is the bearer of a moral culture and, as such, a microcosm of that moral culture and its best mirror. The most important fact about China's moral culture right now is that it is not functioning as a moral culture should; it is a moral culture in crisis. It is also, if we are reasonably optimistic about its ability to change or evolve positively, a moral culture in transition. Therefore, to understand China's moral culture, its living moral culture, we must understand its crisis, especially the moral subject, or the absence thereof, that lies at the heart of this crisis. To this end, I will spell out more systematically the nature and structure of a moral subject itself.

What is a moral subject, and what does it take for the moral subject to be formed and maintained? To put it simply, one becomes a moral subject by developing a certain disposition to act morally and to do so for what one understands as moral reasons. This disposition, the state of being positively and stably disposed toward a certain way of comporting oneself in society, is nothing but *willingness*. One must *will* to act in a certain way, even when one does so for reasons that one regards as in some important sense objective rather than products of one's own will. One's reasons for so acting must be *interior* (or subjective, in one of its senses): these reasons must somehow come to exist in that inner space we call conscience or moral consciousness or moral subjectivity. They must be what Bernard Williams calls "internal reasons."[10] Thus, the creation of the moral subject is about the production of this willingness through the formation of internal reasons or, to be more precise, through the social production of moral reasons that lend themselves to acceptance and absorption by individual members of society. Put another way, becoming a moral subject is a matter of internalizing socially originated reasons that thereby become one's own and hence partly autonomous reasons, whether or not one understands one's resulting moral agency in terms of autonomy. To the degree that one succeeds in such internalization, one becomes an active and willing adherent to a morality and sees that morality as part of one's own inner nature: one becomes a moral subject. Acquiring moral subjectivity in this sense—as part of one's relation to self and society and of one's understanding thereof—is a basic need that is distinct from and irreducible to welfare or happiness. There is, especially in modern society, no better proof of the successful formation of moral subjectivity than that the willingness that is part and parcel of being moral is relatively stable under reflection—that is, the kind and amount of reflection people typically bring to bear on such matters.

A moral culture need not offer a great deal of room for such reflection, however, and such room as exists need not be conceived of in terms of autonomy. Moral subjectivity per se does not require more than a stable moral willingness rooted in reasons that are somehow internalized. This willingness can be produced, and the socially originated reasons internalized, in one of two ways distinguishable at a high level of abstraction. In the first, one acquires the requisite willingness or internalizes the given reasons by deferring to a moral leader and imitating one or more moral exemplars and, in the process, identifying with both to some degree. One engages in such deference, imitation, and identification because one sees, or is brought to see, the good as embodied in exemplary moral personalities. One thus becomes a moral subject under the description, both cultural and individual, of conforming to the good and gaining access to the good through the mediation of exemplary moral personalities. A twofold willingness is at work here: one must willingly accept the mediation involved in order to gain access to the good and then must willingly conform to it. The intersubjective relationship, the relationship between leader or exemplar and follower or imitator, is here constitutive, for the latter, of the subject-object relationship, the object being the good. What is important is not the fact of the matter so much as the descriptor—the description under which one conceives of becoming, and is enabled to actually become, a moral subject. The descriptor need not be true, still less completely true; it only has to be plausible, and plausible under the habitual degree of reflection, to those involved. On the basis of this descriptor, as distinct from whatever reality may be reflected in or distorted by it, we can give this type of moral culture the name of *morality through identification*. There is no doubt that such a moral culture, viewed as an ideal type, has historically been very important, even dominant. The moral culture of Mao's China belongs to this type, and the moral culture of China today has yet to escape its influence. If the descriptor, though it need not be true, must be plausible, it must be further noted that the plausibility of the descriptor depends on its having a reasonably good fit with *material* or *objective* conditions. For example, the once plausible descriptor of pursuing (conforming to) communism and gaining access to the true meaning of communism through the mediation of the CCP as the vanguard is no longer plausible under the real social and economic conditions that prevail in China today.

These new conditions call for a new morality, and, whatever substance the new morality may contain, it must belong to another ideal type. This other ideal type is quintessentially modern, and therefore its descriptor must be plausible under modern conditions, where a basic equality in moral agency is taken for granted and economic and cultural life is organized accordingly. This need not rule out identification with exemplary moral personalities, but such identification, even when it happens, is deemed acceptable only if it derives from and is consistent with the free exercise of one's own equal moral agency. Thus the descriptor operative in a modern morality must be drawn from that family of concepts which includes freedom, autonomy, and the like.[11] Call it, then, *morality through freedom.* When I say that the de facto liberties that abound in China today need to be sublimated into freedom as a value, what I mean, therefore, is that freedom must serve *as a descriptor* for China's new morality, as it does in modern societies such as the United States. This necessity springs not from any intrinsic superiority of American moral culture, however, but from an entirely internal Chinese consideration: the fact that the willingness that is part and parcel of moral subjectivity can no longer, after nearly four decades of economic and social reform, be produced through compulsory deference to moral authority or compulsory imitation of moral exemplars. This willingness can be produced, under today's circumstances, only by leaving people with a lot more room for choice, for reflection, for taking their own counsel, for the possibility of taking part in the evolution of their shared moral culture. As we have seen, the old, Maoist moral subject suited to the collectivistic, totally organized way of life is no longer serviceable, and the much more individuated way of life that has sprung up since the end of the Mao era requires a correspondingly more individuated moral subject. This new moral subject needs much greater room for moral initiative, which can be created and properly named only by using freedom as a descriptor. We need a new morality and a new name for it.

Can this new morality be created and a new name be given to it? I can only hope so, especially given the political complications. What I do know, or at least have reason to fear, is that if the moral crisis is not resolved, and resolved soon, it will have grave implications for China's political future, just as the political dimension of the moral crisis is already making the crisis itself much more intractable than it would otherwise be. In this we catch a glimpse of the deep continuity between China's moral culture and political culture, between its moral and its political problems, as well as their potential solutions. Nothing better demonstrates this continuity, and the danger of failing to create a virtuous circle, than a growing imbalance and tension between social equality and political inequality.

Social Equality without Political Equality

Just as it is inaccurate to say that China is not a free country, so it would be no more precise to claim that China is not an equal society.[12] Yet the opposite is not quite true, either, in one case as in the other. Once again, we find a society ridden with contradictions, one whose most powerful dynamic in moral and political culture is the very considerable equality already present and entrenched, vying with inequalities old and new and stubbornly resistant to change. Unlike freedom, however, equality has already acquired the status of a publicly affirmed value in China, well beyond official lip service, and there is no better way of capturing the spirit and meaning of this value in the Chinese context than in terms of what Alexis de Tocqueville calls equality of conditions. This is essentially, as we have seen, an equality of moral-legal status that confers the right and opportunity to take part in an inclusive yet competitive social life. What is equal, and egalitarian in spirit, is only the right of participation together with the opportunity for success, leaving it open for outcomes to be unequal, even highly so. But this is already no mean progress, amounting as it does to the egalitarian conception of all humans as minimally competent cognitive and moral agents who therefore deserve a basic level of respect and dignity. Something like this is what Tocqueville refers to as equality of conditions, which contrasts starkly with an inequality of conditions that he somewhat loosely but in this context very pertinently labels aristocracy. There is little doubt that equality of conditions thus understood has settled in China, and much of the credit must go to the CCP.

For this equality of conditions, as the reader will recall, has come about through two momentous processes, both of which have occurred under communist rule. First, Mao's China saw a massive leveling of classes whereby the majority of people were made politically and legally equal in principle.

This democratic move—democratic in the sense of removing fixed social hierarchies—was limited, however, by the fact that it was subject to the exclusion of so-called class enemies and compromised by a politically enforced urban-rural division. Notwithstanding these two major qualifications, Mao's egalitarian efforts at least deserve the name of quasi-democratic leveling. Along with a relative material equality, this leveling is China's egalitarian legacy from the first three decades of communist rule. Then came Deng Xiaoping's launching of economic and social reform. Thanks to this reform, which is still in progress, the two qualifications inherent in the Maoist conception of equality have been dropped, the first one entirely and the second at least in principle. It is worth bearing in mind that these changes have come about during a time that has also witnessed a dramatic rise in inequality—that is, material or economic inequality. There nevertheless remains a sense in which they make up a distinct egalitarian process, an epoch-making one that has advanced much further the equality of conditions first established under Mao. Insofar as this second egalitarian process features conflict reduction through the softening and universalization of values, it has a distinctly liberal, at least quasi-liberal, flavor that is reminiscent of early modern Europe's passage from war to commerce.

China now finds itself with a set of social conditions, then, that have developed out of these two momentous egalitarian processes. If Mao's China was a far cry from the so-called republican China, not to mention traditional, Confucian China, today's China is no less different from Mao's China. It is only in the new era that it makes a certain sense to say, as China's slogan for the 2008 Olympic Games did, "one world, one dream," and to have, in place of communism, a notion of the Chinese Dream that is all too obviously modeled on the American Dream. And it is only today's CCP that is able to tell the world, as Xi Jinping did in the wake of the eighteenth party congress and confirmed at the nineteenth party congress, that promoting the happy and prosperous life of ordinary Chinese, as understood by themselves, and as made possible by national rejuvenation, is the only mission of the party.

Certainly, the equality of conditions thus brought into being is far from perfect even by its own standard. I do not mean, in this context, inequality of outcomes per se, such as economic inequality, although its staggering rise in post-Mao China is a formidable problem for other reasons. This is a *quantitative* inequality that is only to be expected even from the most perfect equality of conditions. For equality of conditions is a *qualitative* equality and, as such, is entirely compatible with quantitative inequality, in principle, even if it may exist in considerable tension with exceptionally serious instances of the latter. When I say that China still falls well short of perfect equality of conditions today, I mean to suggest that this is a matter of qualitative equality.

It is true that all members of Chinese society are now taken to have the same legal status and the same rights and opportunities that come with such status. This is not just empty rhetoric, for there is simply too much reality on the ground that cannot be explained except in terms of progress in equality and of a corresponding passion for equality. Nevertheless, no one can plausibly deny that the officially and popularly affirmed equality of legal status has yet to be effectively translated into any credible semblance of equal rights and opportunities. An ugly gap is plainly visible between the concept and the practice of equality. This is because vested interests die hard, such as the de facto privileges of city dwellers vis-à-vis the claim to equal treatment by people from the countryside, and because, if truth be told, overhauling inegalitarian institutions and entitlements left over from the past is not always high on the agenda of the CCP or of the better-off members of Chinese society.

Thus, when it comes to the urban-rural divide, the undeniable progress in equality of status is as yet more a matter of public sentiment and broad policy direction than of big, concrete steps toward equal treatment—say, with respect to the extremely large number of migrant workers *(nongmingong)* in the cities. This name itself is indicative of a stubborn reality of basic inequality for whose elimination neither the CCP nor advantaged city dwellers seem remotely prepared to make the necessary "sacrifices." Likewise—and this is something that cuts across the urban-rural divide—the demand for equality of opportunity that is an intrinsic part of equality of social conditions falls victim all too often to unfair advantages enjoyed by the offspring of the rich *(fu erdai)* and the powerful *(guan erdia)*. These are just examples, albeit important and especially glaring ones, of the substantial obstacles that still stand in the way of the relatively full realization of social equality. And it is naïve to think it will be a simple and straightforward matter to clear away such obstacles or to prevent new ones from taking their place.

Despite all these challenges, the presence in China of the basic tendency toward equality of conditions is not in doubt. The egalitarian die has been cast. The good conscience that used to accompany remnants of systematic qualitative inequality has been powerfully disturbed and, for many, destroyed. All discourses in support of qualitative inequality are off-limits in public. The passion for equality is visible and growing everywhere, as is its negative expression in the form of resentment. Where remnants of old social and political habits still frustrate egalitarian moral expectations, as happens all too often even today, those expectations do not lose their collective psychological confidence and potency. Whatever else may or may not happen in China, it is almost unimaginable that the progress of social equality can be arrested for long or irreversibly rolled back.

It is doubtful, however, that this progress can ever be completed, even in principle, unless *political* inequality is removed along with what remains of social inequality. For social equality is only part of a larger egalitarian scheme of things that must also cover political equality. I believe Tocqueville is entirely correct in seeing an organic relationship between equality of (social) conditions, on the one hand, and political equality, on the other. Thus he writes, "One has to understand that equality ends up by infiltrating the world of politics as it does everywhere else. It would be impossible to imagine men forever unequal in one respect, yet equal in others; they must, in the end, come to be equal in all."[13] If this much is true, it must also be true, given the same organic relationship, that no equality is complete in any single domain of life until it is complemented by equality in all other relevant domains. Democratic social relations, holding among private persons, will not be fully equal until they are supported by democratic *political* relations, holding among *citizens*.[14]

In China today we see this integral character of equality in a certain awkwardness that marks the political sphere. In theory, political equality is now as much a part of official doctrine as social equality has been. But while social equality is, to a substantial and ever-increasing degree, a fact of life, political equality has lagged far behind. It is true that the old imperial haughtiness of political power has been much modified, and this in turn reflects an adjustment of political relations under the pressure of the profound change in social relations. After all, it makes much less sense today for officials to behave, especially to be seen to behave, as masters rather than so-called servants of the people now that the combination of quasi-democratic leveling and quasi-liberal neutralization has led the CCP to proclaim the happy and prosperous life of ordinary Chinese, and nothing but this, its only mission and raison d'être. Nonetheless, such progress in political equality has stopped well short of political *liberty,* or political democracy. Average Chinese citizens are, in truth, civic nonentities, with no credible right to fear-free participation in political life except within a range so fixed and narrow as to be meaningless, and hence their civic aspirations and capacities are systematically discouraged and stunted. This does not mean that their interests are not taken care of, to be sure, but such interests are decidedly those of private persons, not of citizens. What is sometimes called Chinese-style consultative democracy, as conducted chiefly through the Chinese People's Political Consultative Conference at the national and lower levels, is conceived accordingly and therefore is hardly more democratic than the humane society favored by Mencius, supposedly the most democratic-minded major Confucian thinker. Mencius famously says, "[In a state] the people are the most important; the spirits of the land and grain (guardians of territory) are the next; the ruler is of slight importance."[15] The kind of importance granted to the people by the CCP today is of the same kind, for the people are preeminent, now as then, only in their capacity as *min* (the masses), and their concerns are correspondingly understood in terms of *minsheng* (livelihood issues). Likewise, the aim in serving the interests of the people in their essentially creaturely and receptive capacity is, just as in Mencius's dictum (for Mencius immediately goes on to say that "to gain [the hearts of] the peasantry is the way to become an emperor"), to win their allegiance or acquiescence rather than to provide for their agential interests as citizens, as full and equal members of a republic, which China today supposedly is. For now, the idea of a republic, of the people being masters of their country, exists only on paper, and those who rule in the name of the people are yet to be subjected to a substantial and credible measure of popular consent. If political equality cannot really mean an equality of power enjoyed by all, power of the demos in the strict sense, the least it can do is allow a reasonably credible approximation to popular sovereignty by means of some degree of roughly equal political liberty, if only in the manner of a mixed regime (whether or not openly acknowledged as such).

It should come as no surprise that this gap between the substantial presence of social equality and the substantial lack of political equality, in the form of political liberty, has huge consequences for the quality and extent of social equality.[16] I have noted that, because of the organic and integral nature of equality, the equality of social conditions will always remain only partial as long as political equality is not achieved. This is especially evident at the level of political psychology. In China today the inevitable shortfall in social equality, in the equality of moral-legal status at its core, takes the form, above all, of a relationship between rulers and ruled that still bears many of the characteristic features of the creditor-debtor relationship.

As is well known, this relationship was actively promoted throughout the Mao era. For many years, all members of Chinese society were given to understand, through all kinds of political and cultural campaigns culminating in the Cultural Revolution, that they owed a profound debt to the CCP for the good fortune of living and flourishing in a new, socialist society. The debt, embodied in the peace and goodness of New China and in the incalculable loss of life and blood needed to bring them about, was so boundless it could never be fully repaid, with official propagandists going to extreme lengths, especially during the Cultural Revolution, to drive this point home. Despite the hopelessness of ever completing the payment, however, the debt was nevertheless to be acknowledged and incrementally discharged in the most concrete of currencies, through daily manifestations of loyalty, obedience, and hard work. This was the core of the political socialization all Chinese underwent in Mao's time. Everyone had to learn his or her place in relation to political power, through instruction and the experience of pain, and the place was that of a permanent debtor. Cast in this role, one became bound to the creditor and lost all good conscience in one's dealings with political power.

Even after four decades of reform devoted in part to undoing the revolutionary aspects of the revolution, the CCP has not quite stopped seeing itself as the creditor and the people as its debtors. Only the object of debt has changed, no longer a matter of being lifted from the class oppression and exploitation prevalent in the old society but instead one of enjoying ever-higher living standards and basking in the glory of China's rise as a world power. What remains unchanged is the status of the party as the leader of China, and, for all those Chinese who feel positive about the more recent record of the party, successful leader still means creditor. In the meantime, under the impact of the profound change in social relations, the creditor-debtor relationship has become more moderate and more subtle. There has even appeared a conception of government as existing to provide services to the people *(fuwuxing zhengfu)*. But this conception, partly a variation on the old theme of "serving the people," has not quite put an end to the creditor-debtor relationship; from time to time, especially on celebratory or festival occasions, the official media still unabashedly celebrate the people's gratitude to the party-state. It is rather a subtler and somewhat more modest way of prolonging the creditor-debtor relationship, with the CCP of today creating debts through what is now nicely called service, in keeping with the more equal social relations prevailing today. As part of this newly adjusted balance of power, the debtor has become more assertive but has not thereby ceased to be a debtor. As long as the CCP's leadership is still expressly or tacitly regarded as legitimate, those who live under it will remain trapped in the creditor-debtor relationship that provides the politico-psychological basis of communist rule. And with this relationship still goes the debtor's psychology of deep-seated inferiority and unworthiness vis-à-vis state power.

One fundamental change, however, has definitely occurred in what remains of the creditor-debtor relationship, and, not surprisingly, this change has its cause in the growing equality of social conditions even as that equality is thwarted by the continuing political inequality. While the debtor in the Maoist mold had a bad conscience in relation to political power, he had, as it were, a good conscience about this bad conscience. He was a debtor without internal conflict, because the condition in which he lived was not yet split between a more or less equal social state (that is, a society marked by equality of conditions) and a largely unequal political state. He was thus a single-minded and simple-minded debtor and, as such, was even, as it were, happily unhappy. Since the end of the Mao era, the debtor has progressively lost this single-mindedness and simple-mindedness. For the social and political relations that in Mao's time formed a seamless whole with no conceptual or material dividing line have to a significant degree come apart in the age of reform. The debtor now finds himself in a social state in which he has come to see himself as an equal and an individual and has gradually acquired some taste for equality and independence and a modicum of pride that goes with it. In the political state, however, he is still as far removed from any experience of political liberty or political equality as he ever was, and he has no real, material basis for seeing more worth in himself as a citizen or political agent than he ever did. Thus standing astride an equal social state and an unequal political one, he cannot but end up double-minded, unsure of his newfound equal status (in the social state) and yet increasingly resentful of his continued status as debtor (in the political state). In truth, he both is and is not a debtor, both is and is not an equal, and, in this confused condition, he is assertive and grudging but does not yet stand tall. His passion for equality is thus both stunted and heightened, and hence distorted, by his lingering debtor psychology and comportment. And the resentment that results from such distortion is directed both at the weakened creditor and at the still insufficiently strong debtor himself and is incapable of resolution or even appeasement. Observing this precarious balance, one would not be without reason in thinking that something has to give, sooner or later, and this is as true of the individual debtor as it is of the society at large that is delicately poised between a growing social equality and a stubborn political inequality.

The Advantages and Liabilities of Democratic Social Power

One of Tocqueville's insights based on observing American democracy that retains much of its truth and explanatory power today is that a pervasive equality of conditions translates into an altogether new form of power: democratic social power, or the unlimited rule of public opinion. "I observe," writes Tocqueville, "how, beneath the power of certain laws, democracy would blot out that intellectual liberty supported by the social, democratic state in such a way that, having broken the shackles formerly imposed upon it by class systems or men, the human spirit would be closely confined by the general will of the majority."[17] Democratic social power is none other than this "general will of the majority," which Tocqueville regards as an all-encompassing social phenomenon rather than a narrowly political one. As such, democratic social power is the power of *society* that springs naturally and immediately from the very fact of equality of conditions, underlying democratic political power and making it possible and palatable. It is larger and deeper and stronger than any political power, encompassing it and bending it to the rule of public opinion no less than it does actions and even thoughts in society. (This is why the US tech giants that control the digital flow of information are so incredibly powerful.) But this is the case only when a country is democratic not only in its social conditions but also in its form of government, as the United States was and is. Social power comes from equality of conditions, first and foremost, but only if it is not prevented, as it certainly is in China, from doing so by a lack of political liberty that checks the circulation of opinions in society. (This is why the Chinese counterparts of the American IT powerhouses are not nearly as powerful.) Once this obstacle is removed, social power knows no limits under equality of conditions and will end up bringing political liberty and every other liberty under its sway. Although its sway is softer and subtler, above all because it is democratic and has everyone's share in it, Tocqueville gives us reasons to worry about it because of the threat it poses to the very political liberty and other liberties whose presence makes its sway possible in the first place. This is the dilemma that Tocqueville, on his tour of America in 1831, saw at the heart of democracy, and what has happened since in the world's advanced democracies has amply confirmed his prescience. There is no more reliable indicator of the strong presence of political and other liberties than the invincibility of the social power they unleash, overrunning everything around it and not sparing the spirit of independence in the liberties themselves. And no way has been found of giving free rein to the liberties without in the very act exposing them to the omnipresent, often suffocating rule of social power. Juggling this dilemma has been an important part of the story of freedom in a democracy like the United States, and it is only appropriate both to acknowledge freedom's gains and to count its losses at the hands of social power.

For better or worse, in my personal view for *both* better and worse, China has almost never had to face this dilemma. For this is a problem that comes to the fore only when conditions of social equality are combined with those of political liberty. While China has traveled a long distance on the path toward equality of conditions, it still lives in fear or anticipation of political liberty and those in power still seem to be doing all they can to keep the spirit of equality in society from infiltrating the political sphere as Tocqueville says it must sooner or later. It is arguable, or perhaps even unarguable, that the equality of conditions in China today, viewed strictly apart from the political sphere, already far exceeds its nineteenth-century counterpart that Tocqueville observed in the United States. But as long as China does not take significant steps toward political liberty, it will not, as it were, raise itself to the level where it encounters the dilemma involving liberties and social power. For now China is largely spared the problem, but not exactly for the right reasons.

Political liberty is yet to be established. Social power, democratic social power, is yet to have the room to expand and overtake political power. In the meantime, the power that establishes rules for actions and thoughts is overwhelmingly political. Not yet in the seductive embrace of social power, China remains in the formidable clutch of political power.

This does not mean that democratic social power has not started to make itself felt in China. It is doing so, quite predictably, through the internet and social media, which equality of conditions has made available to hundreds of millions of people and which political power can do only so much to control. The network society thus spawned has, in turn, despite all the censorship, furthered and entrenched equality of conditions by "outcompeting and outperforming vertically organized corporations and centralized bureaucracies"[18] in terms of its socializing impact. The licenses that netizens are able to take are not political liberties, nor guaranteed individual liberties, but this does not necessarily make the social power they generate any less potent in areas where they have acquired a de facto permissibility if not legitimacy. When it is a matter of grievances against lower levels of government and especially against allegedly corrupt officials, or of concerns over issues deemed more social than political, such as environmental pollution or unsafe vaccines, the loosely knit community of netizens already creates a great deal of social power. If this is the chief kind of democratic social power that political power must reckon with, there is also the circulation of opinion and taste, (fake) news and gossip, taboos, and norms of social correctness that, through the power of numbers, already poses a threat to the de facto room for intellectual and moral independence currently present in Chinese society. In this we already have a foretaste of the corrosive and suffocating effect of social power on political liberty before such liberty is even allowed to exist. In the absence of political liberty, it is not surprising that the internet and social media have become the most powerful extensions of equality of social conditions. They stop short of political liberty and yet constantly take up causes that are in one way or another political. They may not be strictly political, but they are definitely democratic, and they are the closest thing in China to the infiltration of the political sphere by the spirit of equality of the social sphere. Small wonder that the more perceptive of Chinese netizens are already voicing the kind of fears and worries reminiscent of Tocqueville's warnings about democratic social power. Yet, also reminiscent of Tocqueville, they remain ambivalently supportive of the de facto liberties on the internet and the increasingly potent social power they spawn.

None of this changes the basic fact, however, that in a socially equal China political power remains dominant, having to take no more than a sideways glance at an incipient social power. In this respect China today resembles the ancien régime more than it does republican France or democratic America. China's problem is not yet the tyranny of democratic social power, one that brings the political and other liberties of individuals and the power of government alike under the sway of its irresistible, because democratic, laws. Its problem, rather, remains the overwhelmingly political form of power and the effects of this power on Chinese society and the individuals who make up this society.

It is worth spelling out why this is a problem. Surely the problem is not power itself but the nature of power—political versus social power. After all, some form of power is necessary to hold a society together and make possible the many other things that need to happen in any society. To regard political power as a problem, then, is to believe that it is less benign than democratic social power, and one thinks this way not because social power is preferable in itself but because it is a by-product of equality of conditions combined, very fittingly, with political and other liberties. Thus one accepts democratic social power as necessary, as one would political power if social power were unavailable, and furthermore one prefers social to political power in seeing the former but not the latter as the price to pay for equality and especially liberty, with an awareness that liberty is necessarily somewhat compromised by social power.

The crucial question is *how much* liberty is compromised by democratic social power. The answer turns on *how* social power compromises liberty. The answer to the latter question is that democratic social power compromises liberty, political and otherwise, in ways that are somewhat invisible, especially when compared with how political power interferes with liberty.

Social power is more or less invisible because it is more or less democratic. It is invisible to the degree that it is democratic. It is democratic in that everyone is simultaneously at its giving and receiving end, as it were, and to the degree that everyone has an equal influence on it. Exactly equal influence is impossible, of course, but provided that the inequality is not extreme and results largely from the perceived equality of opportunity to exert influence, then social power will remain more or less invisible. Democratic social power is not only the power over everyone but also supposedly the power of and from everyone. Thanks to this provenance, social power is registered somewhat like the unobstructed power of oneself; hence its invisibility.

It is through such invisibility that social power effortlessly brings about conformity to its dictates. Because conformity happens in this way, it too is invisible, not least to those who conform. To whatever degree invisible social power feels uncoercive, conformity to it is comfortable and willing. And to whatever degree a society is made up of comfortable and willing conformists following an invisible social power, that society will be reasonably stable and orderly, with its members enjoying their political and other liberties and yet doing so in such ways as to fit perfectly into grooves overwhelmingly and yet flexibly shaped by social power. Most important of all, by acting freely, feeling free, and understanding themselves as free, and yet simultaneously having their free actions and thoughts receive direction and substance from social power, members of a democratic society have little trouble becoming moral subjects and maintaining their moral subjectivity over time. Although I am presenting this picture as an ideal type applicable to a democratic society such as the United States, I do not intend it as a caricature. Some such picture worried Tocqueville mightily, as we know, as it has done some of the most perceptive thinkers since, not least members of the Frankfurt school. I will return to this worry later. For now, it is worth noting one important and positive consequence of social power—namely, that it is conducive, perhaps uniquely conducive, to the formation and maintenance of moral subjectivity. This is precisely where political power can be problematic, especially under modern conditions.

Compared with social power, political power is undemocratic in the absence of political liberty. That is to say, political power is undemocratic whenever it is not merely a mode of social power, as all political power must be in an ideally democratic society. For exactly the same reason that social power is more or less invisible, political power unassimilated by social power is highly visible, registered as being imposed from the outside and compelling the individual's unchosen obedience.

The visibility of political power unaccompanied by political liberty is one thing, however, and its coercive character another. Where willing obedience is securely and stably available, always with the help of ideology, it prevents the visibility of political power from manifesting itself as coerciveness and thereby inviting resistance. Such obedience is especially difficult to maintain, and the supporting ideology to make credible, under equality of conditions, for why should those who are accustomed to acting independently and as equals in society and thinking of themselves in this light nevertheless obey an undemocratic political power and do so willingly? No reasons for obedience are sufficiently compelling to be able to dispense with support from the manifest coerciveness of such political power, of course, and thus the resulting obedience will fall as far short of willingness as the political power is visible and visibly coercive.

This remains largely the situation in China. But a more precise understanding requires careful attention to the gap I noted earlier between the substantial presence of social equality and the substantial lack of political liberty and hence of political equality. It is not exactly that political power is running riot; it cannot easily do so in the face of an equality of conditions that is already entrenched and is steadily growing. Yet in the absence of political liberty, the equality of conditions already achieved does not translate into social power in the way it does in a comprehensively (that is, both socially and politically) democratic country, such as the United States. Where social power is lacking, political power has to do the work all by itself. This has a very important consequence regarding moral leadership. On the one hand, the presence of equality of conditions, achieved on the basis of quasi-democratic leveling (under Mao) and quasi-liberal neutralization (under Deng and thereafter), favors the weakening of all forms of moral superiority, especially if prescribed and imposed, and their eventual abandonment. It cannot but throw into sharp relief all sentiments and institutions that are at odds with the basic social fact of modern life. After all, equality of conditions means nothing but equality in legal status, including especially a basic moral status that matters far more than whatever claims, themselves disputable in principle, may be made to levels of moral attainment above it.[19] Yet, on the other hand, political inequality persists in China, albeit in a more moderate form, and, in this context, what remains of political inequality requires an ideological justification in terms of moral inequality, if only to minimize what would otherwise be an even more obtrusive coerciveness. This means that the CCP, in order to hang on with some semblance of good reason to its exclusive political leadership, must continue to claim exclusive moral leadership and to cast the otherwise equal and independent members of society as standing in unarguable need of moral tutelage.

What if most people are no more willing to accept being so cast than they are to submit to undemocratic political power and yet, in the face of overwhelming political power, become as tired and wary of asserting themselves in their moral life as in the political? The answer can only be that, just as they fail to attain agency in political life and to acquire the spirit, interest, and skills that go with such agency, so much the same thing happens to their moral life. They end up, that is, without much of a moral life because they are kept from attaining the kind and degree of agency that is necessary for moral subjectivity under the modern equality of conditions. For better or worse, and I don't think one can quite say "for better," no democratic social power is available that gives them sufficient room for initiative and participation and hence for willing and comfortable conformism. They have neither the freedom nor the freely acquired substance to become moral subjects, and in this way the moral subjectivity of an entire people, as individuals and as members of society, becomes one of the biggest casualties of undemocratic political power operating under democratic social conditions. Democratic conformism and the kind of moral subject it makes possible may be bad, but a breakdown of moral subjectivity for want of a social power that commands willing conformity is no better, and probably much worse. And yet as China gradually closes the gap between social equality and political inequality, or so one hopes, it is worth taking to heart the problems of social power that come from the moral ambiguities of democracy itself.

It is not entirely true that what is problematic with social power is its invisibility. What makes social power invisible also thereby hides its character as power and the character of power as coercive in one way or another. But why is this a problem? One problem with power, as we have seen, is the possibility that it will undermine the conditions for moral subjectivity. But this possibility materializes only when the power in question is undemocratic political power, especially when such power finds it necessary to monopolize moral leadership over society. Social power, by virtue of being democratic, does not give rise to this possibility, at least for most people. If we nevertheless find fault with social power, it is because its advantage is also its danger: what is conducive to moral subjectivity is exactly what is instrumental in creating a conformist moral subjectivity that eats away at the soul of political and other liberties. Does social power, qua social power, necessarily create this conformist danger? And when social power does turn out to be oppressive and suffocating with its ability to generate conformism and to sweep aside all resistance and even conscious awareness because of its invisibility, does its democratic character have to bear the brunt of the blame?

It is hardly deniable that power is a fact of life, social, political, and otherwise. Also undeniable is that power exists in the form of inequality and *is* inequality. Democratic power is no exception. This is especially obvious in the case of democratic political power, which is often a combination of oligarchy and popular consent.[20] But this is just as true of democratic social power. The equality of influence (or, more precisely, of the lack of influence) that Tocqueville locates at the heart of democratic equality is only relative, and even this relative equality is difficult to realize under even the most favorable circumstances.[21] Whatever equality means in a democracy, it cannot possibly mean equality of power, either political or social. But this need not be a problem. What clearly is a problem, as we have seen, is that moral subjectivity will be in jeopardy under equality of conditions if political power is too visible and too visibly coercive. This problem can be avoided, it seems, only if political power is democratic, which means only if political power becomes part of, and a mode of, social power. Thus, the rise of social power in place of, or at the expense of, political power is a great achievement of modernity, whatever its pitfalls, and the relative invisibility of power, and hence of the unavoidable inequality and coerciveness of power as power, seems the best that could be demanded of power, especially as far as moral subjectivity is concerned. What is there underlying this invisibility that can reasonably and usefully be brought to light as an object of critique and improvement? Surely not the mere fact of power itself, nor its intrinsic inequality and coerciveness.

One problem, it seems, has to do with inequality of a distinct kind or at a distinct level: not the lack of equality of power, such equality being impossible, but the lack of fair equality of opportunity that enables each and all in a democratic society to compete for relative advantage. The problem, then, is inequality as unfair advantage or in the form of monopoly even if such monopoly arises from the accumulation of advantages each of which is fair in itself. For these inequalities add up to a disproportionate influence wielded by a few, however invisibly, and thus they engender a *conformism to what is in effect a minority* and, in so doing, threaten to render null and void the political and other liberties of what in reality is a largely uninfluential majority. This problem, in both of its forms but perhaps incontrovertibly in the second (that is, monopoly), can fairly be laid at the door of capitalism. Much of the morally questionable inequality that pervades democratic social power, including democratic political power as one of its modes, is caused by capitalism's and capitalists' excessive influence on the content and dynamic of social power, which, in turn, is traceable to the rise and consolidation of monopoly over time coupled, although defenders of capitalism may dispute this, with a lack of fair equality of opportunity. Democratic social power, then, contains in its content as well as in its dynamic too much of the power of capital. And the same is true of the conformism that this social power imposes on all. This makes the conformism *more capitalist than democratic or liberal* and is the source of a distinct creditor-debtor relationship that exists not between political power and citizens, as in China, but between capital and those employed by it, as in the United States (and increasingly in China as well).[22] It could be, therefore, that political and other liberties are threatened by *capitalist social power,* not necessarily democratic social power, although liberal democracy has yet to find a way of conjoining itself to a mode of production that is not capitalist.

We must not rush, however, to condemn capitalism in this context. If we value the coexistence of social and political equality and we value democratic social power both as a by-product of this coexistence and as the only reliable way of making moral subjectivity possible under modern conditions of life, then we must appreciate the relative invisibility that both reflects social power's democratic credentials, however compromised, and allows it to serve the benign functions it does. What if the easiest, if not the only possible, form that democratic social power can take is that of the power of capital? What if, in other words, the capitalist mode of production alone has so far proved capable of providing the material basis for the diffuse, invisible social power we know today? What if the society that favors equality of conditions is itself none other than a bourgeois or middle-class society? What if it turns out that the invisible hand that drives the market is also the only invisible hand that can shape democratic social power?

Why China Needs Both Unity and Separations in a
New Balancing Act

If the hypothesized state of affairs in these questions is true, we may be reduced to throwing up our hands, on the understanding that democratic social power is inevitable under the simultaneous presence of democratic social and political conditions, that it is much to be preferred to undemocratic political power, that capitalism (liberal democratic capitalism, to be precise) is the only way of giving concrete form to this social power, and that, therefore, we must learn to live with liberal democratic capitalism as the most desirable human normative order, whatever its flaws from an "ideal" perspective divorced from the unalterable reality of human society. If things are really so, some will say, they may be a cause not for throwing up our hands but rather for sober appreciation of what we have got, of what the luckier and more sensible of modern societies have been able to achieve.

Indeed, liberal democracy is wont to claim it has achieved more than this. For it has invented a way both to replace undemocratic political power with democratic social power and at the same time to contain that social power through what Pierre Manent aptly calls the organization of separations. Manent lists six separations: separation of professions, or division of labor; separation of powers; separation of church and state; separation of civil society and the state; separation of represented and representative; and separation of facts and values, or science and life.[23] Foremost among these separations, in Manent's account, are those between represented and representative and between powers, which, along with the implicit separation (and hence opposition and contestation) among representatives, conspire to ensure that such political power as is able to escape democratic social power is largely impotent. At the same time, some of the other separations serve to bring about a like impotence, if not of social power itself, at least of citizens to interfere with one another. The result, combining these two kinds of impotence, is that the command-obedience relation that would otherwise figure between ruler and ruled and serve as a model for all other relations in society, as it tends to do in any social order devoid of these separations, is largely removed from life in a liberal democratic society. Such a "mechanism of power producing the impotence of power" is what makes for liberty, political and otherwise, and is indeed itself what is meant by liberty.[24]

This is an illuminating generalization about the raison d'être and mode of operation of liberal democracy, not least its American variety. Much of it is true, too, but the idea of power becoming impotent—rather than changing its form or location, and thereby possibly becoming more benign or more invisible—cannot but give one pause. If we believe, with Manent, that the separations add up to an insurmountable obstacle to the command-obedience relation everywhere in a liberal democracy, then it follows that members of such a society "have no other perspective for their activity and ambition than . . . to turn their desires and their efforts to domains that are foreign to power or to politics strictly speaking, to domains where properly speaking one does not exercise power over other members of society. The citizens have only to exercise their talents and to become rich or famous by exercising their talents. In a political regime ordered in this way, life consists mainly of *economics* and *culture*."[25] Economics and culture blissfully untainted by the command-obedience relation, by any power relations whatsoever! In this universal absence of power is supposed to reside the liberty that is nothing less than universal freedom from power.

Leaving aside culture with its own distinct power, we are all too familiar with the power ever present in the economic domain, the power of those preeminent in it to infiltrate politics proper and to bend it more or less invisibly to the imperatives of capital. In *this* regard, even political power is less impotent than Manent makes it out to be, and, more importantly, the economic domain is infinitely less free of power, including political power, than Manent deduces from the ideal logic of separations. It is true that liberal democratic capitalism is marked by a certain separation of the political and economic domains, which is part of the larger separation of civil society and state. Yet the separation is only formal, and what this means can only be grasped if we realize that the political and economic domains work together as one integral system of class relations while doing so, in a manner unique to democratic capitalism, through their formal separation.[26] Manent correctly identifies this formal separation but makes the common mistake of treating it as more than a formal separation—as if the economy were not a site of power, as if this power did not spill over massively into the political domain, as if the power of capital were not to a large degree social power and political power in one. Or perhaps Manent, the exceptionally astute political thinker that he is, has not really made any mistake: he may only be describing what one can *see* in a society where power is filtered through the separations, including the formal separation between the political and economic domains. For if there is one thing accomplished by such filtering, it is that power ends up being invisible or at least much less visible. As we have seen, this relative invisibility of power is a great advantage, other things being equal, and that is why, for all its flaws, democratic social power, even as made possible by capitalism, has a lot to be said for it in comparison with undemocratic political power, given modern conditions.

But this also means we are nearly back to square one, with the serious problems raised by democratic social power completely unresolved. Liberal democracy has invented a form of power whose coerciveness is more or less invisible because it is more or less hidden by its constitutive separations, not least the (formal) separation between political and economic power. This is conducive to the formation of moral subjectivity under modern conditions, whatever may be said of the character or content of the moral subjectivity thereby formed, and yet all of Tocqueville's worries about conformism and despotism over the soul are still with us, as are the concerns later raised by thinkers in the Marxist tradition about the conquest of social power by the power of capital. This balance sheet, with both the positives and the negatives on it, is worth bearing in mind as we examine the Chinese alternative to the modern Western organization of separations.

The Chinese way, both traditional and current, is not the organization of separations but the exact opposite—that is, the prevention of all separations except one. The one separation granted legitimacy is that between ruler and ruled, such that ideally all power is concentrated in the hands of the ruler and, again ideally, the ruler is perfectly good, with the result that the ruler has the ideal combination of might and right to rule over All under Heaven (*tianxia*) and to keep the entire realm in a state of wholesome unity. Formulated at this level of abstraction, the Chinese way of organizing political life belongs to a general model that is found to one degree or another in all predemocratic societies.[27] Where China is distinctive, as compared with the West, is both in the extent to which this unity is carried and in the way it is conceived and implemented.

The fundamental fact that had given shape to traditional Chinese political culture ever since the First Emperor's unification of the Warring States is the absence of competing jurisdictions, such as existed in feudal

Europe in the form of "the parcellization of sovereignty"[28] and in the modern West in the form of the separation of powers. Throughout its exceptionally long continued existence, China has, consistently and without truly subversive interruption, found it both necessary and possible to organize itself as a highly centralized bureaucratic state. The partially fraught relationship between emperor and imperial bureaucracy that came to define the Confucian-Legalist state from the Han dynasty onward does not represent even a minor departure from this pattern, being a matter not of competing jurisdictions but rather of distinct parts of the same central state authority. Nor was this pattern interrupted by periodic struggles over dynastic succession, for these were fought over the same undivided sovereignty in the person of the emperor and thus dynastic change kept constant the same appeal to the Mandate of Heaven and rested on largely the same imperial-bureaucratic institutional arrangement.

The effects of the unbroken existence of a highly centralized bureaucratic state on Chinese political culture cannot be overstated. One of these effects is the overwhelming importance of state and officialdom, both as a center of political power and as an apparatus of private appropriation—perhaps comparable in some ways to the ancien régime in France but even more unrestrained thanks to the absence of competing jurisdictions. Another effect, no less distinctive, is the ideological cohesion of the intelligentsia, especially the scholar-official class, with the state. In the absence either of horizontally competing jurisdictions, such as those presided over by the Roman emperor and the papacy, or largely even of vertically divided independent political forces, such as the estates, the traditional Chinese intelligentsia was not formed by division among and attachment to competing jurisdictions or political forces from which they could receive backing and protection; unsurprisingly, it was not known for even a moderate measure of corporate freedom and independence. These effects, or elements of traditional Chinese political culture, among others, have lasted in one way or another to this day. They thus make up the Chinese way of organizing political life, both past and, to a substantial degree, present.

The traditional name of this Chinese way is *dayitong*—the Great Unity, or, perhaps more suggestively, the Great Oneness—the oneness not only of ruler but also of his rule's moral and cosmological basis and of its mechanism of implementation, entailing as well the oneness of culture and ide-

ology, of territory, and of All under Heaven.[29] Part of this oneness is a degree
of unity of ideological power (chiefly Confucianism, as propagated by the
scholar-official class) and political power (of the emperor, following essentially Legalist principles) unheard of in the history of Europe, where, for example, the Catholic Church maintained for a very long time a far more independent ideological power.[30] Oneness need not mean a complete lack of
differences, but differences, unlike what today comes under the (liberal)
rubric of diversity or pluralism, can be organized into a benign state of harmony only when subjected to the Great Unity. Only then does it make sense
to conceive of the perfect society, as the Chinese tradition did, in terms of
the oneness of well-being called Universal Harmony *(datong),* with no one
left out of the Harmony and no one deviating from its Way. At the center of
it all is the virtuous and Heaven-appointed ruler *(tianzi,* son of heaven), who
is the perfect embodiment of the oneness of All under Heaven and its all-
powerful caretaker. With the right ruler at the center and as the rallying
point, all is well under Heaven.[31]

This conception belongs to China's checkered, (ideologically) largely Confucian past, with the ideal of unity or oneness informing all aspects of government and yet more often than not compromised and even betrayed by a
recalcitrant reality in which we repeatedly encounter rulers who are more like
tyrants than sages, conditions of apparent unity that are less harmonious than
forcibly imposed, and, unsurprisingly, regular breakdowns of order necessi-
tating renewal through dynastic change.[32] What is all the more remarkable is
that it is none other than this manifestly less than perfect Great Unity that
has helped keep China together as an empire—or what is sometimes called
a civilizational state—despite all its other failures. This paramount task of
keeping China together as an undivided jurisdiction is still with us and as
challenging as ever. It is therefore not surprising that much of the legacy of
the Great Unity is still cherished—not only on the strength of a long tradition of ideas and practices but more importantly because it answers to a
still-ongoing paramount need.

This is also why China's political system today owes a great deal to this
legacy and still needs to draw on it. With its belief in a *one-*party political
system and its claim to being the only suitable party, the CCP is carrying on
the tradition of the Great Unity. Its central role in China, if not for All under
Heaven, is to provide a new oneness. But this new oneness is new because it

has had to adapt to modern conditions and can only do so through the selective use of separations. Under social conditions that have come to mark a progressively modern China, the new oneness has to exist in tandem and tension with the irresistible need for separations. The resulting contradictions and need for reasonably stable balancing acts are unlikely ever to go away. As a matter of fact, if we look at the separations on Manent's list, we see that the separation of professions, or division of labor, and the separation of facts and values, or science and life, have already become well established in China, especially in the era of reform—notwithstanding the recent reiteration of "scientific socialism" with special reference to the CCP's new doctrine of "socialism with Chinese characteristics for a new era." At the other end of the spectrum, however, the separation of powers is still anathema, a separation that cannot be embraced without doing violence to the newly adapted oneness.

If there is any significant room for maneuver short of such violence, it is to be found with regard to the separation of civil society and state. As a matter of fact, steps have already been taken in this regard, and these involve especially the formal separation of the economic and political domains. No one can suggest that this formal separation is anywhere near complete in China or even that it can ever become complete as long as the CCP maintains its political prerogatives over the economy. Complete or not, the separation of the economic and political domains is only part of the separation of civil society and the state. For civil society cannot truly separate itself from the state until it becomes *morally* independent from the state. This means that civil society can come into its own only when it acquires all the liberties of the moderns and does so in terms of a moral value that gives protection and meaning to what are otherwise only de facto liberties. When this happens, China may also be said to have accomplished its near equivalent of the Western separation of church and state.

What is desperately needed in China today is just this separation of civil society and the state. As I have already discussed, the CCP, under circumstances of its own making, is no longer able to carry out the moral socialization of the populace by means of the old model of compulsory deference to the central authority's moral leadership. There is no better, and no more disturbing, proof of this than the fact that postcommunist China has been undergoing a profound crisis of moral subjectivity, with no end in sight.

This crisis is a compelling reason to call into question the moral subordination of civil society to the state, which in effect means that civil society can barely exist, let alone mature over time. One consequence of this subordination is that the CCP continues to place the entire burden of ensuring the moral integration of society on itself when this is neither necessary nor effective any longer, thanks to the socially decentering effects of the reform. It is high time the party allowed civil society to play a role it has itself patently failed to play all by itself. This need not mean that the CCP should completely give up its moral leadership. We know this is not going to happen, as the party's exclusive hold on political power requires its continued assertion of moral leadership—not only the rhetorical pretense to such leadership but also sufficient institutional reality of it to make one-party political leadership plausible and palatable. Why not share the role of moral socialization with civil society, then? But this would require giving civil society the moral independence and freedom it needs and, of course, allowing it to properly exist through genuine separation from the state in the first place. This is the form that the contradiction between oneness and separations takes today, and thus a successful balancing act is one that must secure the separation of civil society from the state without entailing the one separation that the CCP will decidedly not accept—that is, the separation of powers. The question is whether this is at all possible, especially as part of democratic preparation.

Priority of the Good and the Accommodation of Liberty

I see no reason why this balancing act is not possible *in principle*. There is nothing in such a possibility that exceeds the room for compromise and adjustment that are the stuff of major yet stability-preserving political change. This possibility itself has a normative dimension in that, other things being equal, its normative attractiveness would make its realization more likely, especially at the hands of a leadership with foresight, decisiveness, and prudence. It is this normative dimension we can usefully explore.

Recall that the scenario I am envisioning is that the CCP is not going to immediately take the radical step of introducing the separation of powers and thereby bringing its own monopoly of political power to an end; hence a scenario short of (political) democracy. The oneness of political powers is the only oneness left over from the tradition and from the legacy of communist rule that cannot and will not be abandoned without a radical change of heart. The possibility I am putting forward acknowledges this safeguarding of tradition and the status quo. It acknowledges therefore that the CCP's desire to maintain its monopoly of *political* power requires, as an essential condition for its plausibility and as a symbol of continuity, that it preserve also *a significant part* of its moral leadership. What I am arguing, on this premise, is that the CCP must relinquish *the rest of* its moral leadership in favor of a civil society that will thereby enjoy a moral independence backed up by morally affirmed liberties, not just the de facto liberties that are now available. This will allow civil society to come into its own for the first time under communist rule, taking over the responsibility for a major portion of moral socialization for the populace and thereby bringing to an end the crisis of moral subjectivity that the party has proved incapable of solving on its own. Given that all of this is meant to happen without incurring the separation of powers and posing a real challenge to the CCP's continued *political* leadership, the newly empowered civil society must for its part respect and be seen to respect the political leadership of the party and must therefore act with restraint not only politically but also in exercising its share of moral leadership. Its self-understanding and mode of operation must be consistent with these conditions. In return, civil society will have a significant share of moral leadership and, on the strength of this responsibility, will gradually become an independent source of moral socialization and hence of social cohesion and stability. This will be China's version, as it were, of the separation of church and state.

If something like this scenario is going to work, it must involve the real moral independence of civil society and its exercise of (partial) moral leadership. This means, in turn, that civil society must no longer be under the moral leadership of the CCP: it must be a morally independent force, for only in this capacity will it be able to play that essential role of moral socialization and social cohesion for which the systemic ineffectiveness of the party makes another player necessary. How can this be squared with the CCP's preservation of a major part of moral leadership? Remember that the need for the party to retain part of its moral leadership is political, not moral, in that this need is dictated by its continued monopoly of political leadership. It follows that what is left of the party's moral leadership must be restricted to this supporting role—perhaps a largely symbolic role—for its still-exclusive political leadership.

Given that the CCP is going to maintain its exclusive political leadership anyway, its correlative claim to a part of moral leadership will not be a bad thing. For political power needs to be held up to proper moral standards, all the more so when that power is the preserve of one political party. What better way, under the circumstances, to hold the ruling party to moral account than to do so immanently by the moral standard the CCP sets for itself in exercising what remains of its moral leadership? And what better agents to undertake such supervision than the morally (more) free and independent citizens who make up a robust civil society after first overcoming the crisis of moral subjectivity?

This is a matter, then, of the CCP shoring up its political leadership with a moral rationale and thus opening up a space for immanent public criticism. From this use of moral leadership an extremely important upshot follows, for the very fact that the moral justification is meant to impart legitimacy to a one-party political leadership is enough to determine that it is not going to be couched primarily in terms of, say, right—that is, what Kant calls "the *formal* condition of outer freedom"—"outer" in the sense of behavior affecting others.[33] After all, no doctrine of right would single out the CCP, or any other actor for that matter, in advance as being alone qualified for political leadership. One can therefore be sure instead that this justification will give pride of place to (what in philosophical parlance is called) the good, consisting of (worthy) ends and requisite virtues, such as, in China today, popular societal and national goals along with the moral, political, and administrative virtues supposedly uniquely possessed by the party for their accomplishment. To be sure, within the scenario I am talking about, liberties of the moderns will have been raised to the level of a moral value and protected as such. But freedom as a value, and right understood in terms of serving to make liberties equally accessible to all, will not be suitable for carrying the burden of moral justification needed for a one-party political leadership.

The only suitable paradigm is one that in contemporary philosophical jargon goes by the name of priority of the good. It will have become clear that such priority, in China's case, is made necessary, above all, by the *political* priority, as it were, of the CCP. I believe, however, that there is some virtue in this priority of the good that goes beyond the sheer current necessity (more fait accompli than need) of one-party leadership. As Tocqueville and many after him have reminded us, democratic social power has its own drawbacks. In the present context, these drawbacks can be partly reformulated in terms of a certain undialectical attachment to the so-called priority of the right. It will help shed light on the issue at hand if we translate "the priority of the right over the good" into "the priority of *freedom* over the good." This translation makes sense in that right exists not as an end in itself but to make possible the equal freedom of each and all to pursue their legally permissible ends as they see fit.[34] Thus, to give priority to the right over the good is to give priority to permissible individual freedom over any good, individual or especially collective, that might otherwise be used to override such freedom.

It is not my view that the priority of the good as exemplified in the (hypothetical Chinese) scenario I have just proposed is necessarily superior to the (largely Western) priority of the right. I nevertheless think there is one important thing to be said in its favor, if only because it is dialectical in a way that the priority of the right as normally construed is not. This proposal, making a virtue of Chinese political reality rather than being a mirror of it, is dialectical in the sense that, while giving a privileged status to the good, it nevertheless manages to allow the existence of liberties of the moderns, understood as resting on a morally affirmed value, and hence also the existence of a morally independent civil society. It is dialectical, especially, in that it does not reduce the liberties to the good (that is, treat the liberties as a mere function of the good—of the requirement to provide the subjective room needed to act and be in accordance with the good) or derive them from the good. The liberties retain their independent value even if the good is given even higher value and even if some tension is expected to arise as a result. In comparison, the priority of the right as typically understood, and, by implication, of freedom as well, is devoid of dialectical tension in that it tends to privilege freedom in such a way that the good ends up as little more than the pluralistic outcomes of individual free choice subject only to very permissive side constraints. After all, freedom can have priority only if it is not, in turn, determined by antecedent ends imposed by others, especially the state. The problem is that when freedom is so conceived, it becomes, in effect, freedom *from the good*—that is, from any antecedent good that is not itself the upshot of prior free choice.

It is because of this absence of dialectical tension—and, behind it, of a dialectical conception of the whole matter—that a certain species of liberal thinkers can speak of "the end of history," although they appear to have gone into hiding in the face of seeming empirical evidence to the contrary. But there is a sense in which the very doctrine of priority of the right (and, by implication, of freedom) posits the end of history—a *normative* end, and potential ending, of history conceived as a realistic utopia fully capable of coming true even if it has yet to do so. In this realistic utopia, to borrow Rawls's terminology, a permanent condition of reasonable pluralism will obtain in which reasonable comprehensive doctrines—that is, to simplify, reasonable conceptions of the good life—will coexist in peace and mutual respect on the basis of a shared commitment, made possible by an overlapping consensus, to ethically neutral principles of justice and right, which will *permanently* keep society stable for the right reasons by taking *permanent* precedence over all comprehensive doctrines.[35] Such a result, if it comes to pass, may bring passion-filled strife under control, but it risks doing so at the cost of putting an end to humanity's moral history (as distinct from its history of desire and conflict of desire), in that a permanent priority of the right and freedom will forever put the good—all the discursive and other practices informed by it, commendable or condemnable—in its place.

If one is rightly wary of talk of the end of history, there seems to me no better general reason for this wariness than the inherent dialectical tension between freedom and the good. I will go so far as to suggest that the ability to make room for such tension and thereby to rule out in principle all normative, utopian conceptions of the end of history is a necessary condition for the vitality of any moral-political order.

There is little doubt that freedom must figure prominently in such utopian conceptions, if only because human beings are irreducibly agents. What makes liberal conceptions of utopia distinctive is that freedom, justly distributed and amply aided by prosperity, alone seems truly essential in them, with the good being a function of exercises of freedom (within law). This predominance of freedom threatens, however, to undermine the very raison d'être of freedom, even as viewed from within liberalism itself. For freedom, any freedom whatsoever, makes sense only if it is understood as being directed, in one way or another and in some important sense, toward the good, and, crucially, the good that is thus necessary for freedom can, in turn, make sense only if it is not tautologically reduced to freedom by being relegated to a mere function or upshot of permissible exercises of freedom.

Conversely, the good makes sense only if it is pursued in freedom, and, crucially, the freedom thus presupposed can maintain its integrity only if it is not assimilated to the good by being treated as no more than the leeway needed to do the good or be good. There seems no better way to pin down this relation between freedom and the good than in (admittedly rather ponderous) terms of the *dialectical coprimordiality* of freedom and the good. This coprimordiality is dialectical because, and in the sense that, given the equally fundamental status of freedom and the good from the start, there exists an *irresolvable tension* at the heart of any conception of a nearly ideal human society: a constitutive antinomy within utopia, one might say, and a definitive mark of the intrinsic implausibility of all utopias and, in terms of their projected realization, of the end of history.

It is thus not difficult to appreciate the temptation in utopian, and even in merely normative, constructions to remove the irremovable antinomy that at once underlies and preempts all utopias. One way, the liberal way, to succumb to this temptation is to attenuate the good in favor of freedom. The other way, characteristic of all predemocratic and nondemocratic utopias, including classical Confucianism and Maoism, is to demote freedom in favor of the good. Not surprisingly in view of the antinomian character of utopia, both undialectical constructions make utopia ripe for dystopia—in the form of oppression (in the name of the good) in one case, and of nihilism (in the name of freedom) in the other.

One must not pretend, however, that there is no price to be paid for avoiding oppression by leaving the good completely unsupported by coercion. As Manent says of the modern liberal state, "The law permits the citizen to be indifferent to all the goods that have been the object of the human pursuit; and little by little it orders that indifference. How is it possible to believe that what the law, which is naturally awe-inspiring, allows is truly wrong?" In this way, "by subtle, indirect but infallible means, authorization comes ever more to resemble an injunction and has the same effects."[36] Yet there is nothing like unwisely applied coercion—but how impossibly difficult it is to apply coercion wisely!—to empty even what is most assuredly good of all meaning and turn it into its own mockery. And that is presumably why Iris Murdoch, one of the most trenchant modern defenders of the priority of the good, ends up treating this priority (which she calls sovereignty) as a moral doctrine rather than a political one. This leads her to support what she calls political liberalism, meaning by it a liberalism applicable to the political sphere and, to be precise, a liberalism that we should take to be neutral between its classical and Rawlsian political versions.[37] The important thing is that Murdoch, having presented a most eloquent case for the priority of the good, is prepared to confine it to the moral sphere and thereby deprive her doctrine of all (coercive) teeth. But she has a point. Yet Manent also has a point, and it would be a gross oversimplification to settle the issue completely in terms of picking the lesser of two evils. What the *combination* of Murdoch and Manent—one erring on the side of freedom despite the good and the other (in the quoted passage) gravitating in the opposite direction because of the good—shows, rather, is that it is not given to the human condition to bring freedom and the good into perfect harmony.

It is just this upshot that brings home the defining antinomy of utopia and hence the sheer impossibility of any utopia coming true and thereby marking the so-called end of history—the impossibility of a condition that we have reason to treat both as sociologically final and as ethically the last word. The closest we can hope to get to utopia is precisely by facing up to this impossibility and learning how to preserve and make the best of the tension between freedom and the good.

This tension—irresolvable tension—repels and makes futile all attempts at any reasonable equilibrium. John Skorupski, for example, presents what in some respects is a quite persuasive case against the one-sided underplaying of the good in political liberalism, but he makes a typical mistake of defenders of the good by proceeding as if there were such a thing as getting the balance right between freedom and the good. For him the correct balance is found in classical liberalism, especially that of J. S. Mill. This correct balance, being liberal, maintains permissive neutrality (the state refraining from the use of coercive means to help or hinder any reasonable comprehensive doctrine). At the same time, qua *classical* liberalism, it rejects persuasive neutrality (the state holding itself back even from the use of argument and education to further what it deems *better* comprehensive doctrines).[38] But who is to decide which comprehensive doctrines are better? What if those subscribing to the reasonable comprehensive doctrines not so favored choose to disagree and take exception to the use of public resources to promote what in their eyes are simply the preferences either of the majority or of a self-appointed elite? Isn't the very fact of reasonable pluralism—if one accepts this fact (on what grounds would one reject it?)—an ineradicable (except by illiberal means) source of embarrassment to the very notion of priority of the good, even if a moderate, classical liberal one? At the end of the day, one does not have to be a Rawlsian political liberal to have serious doubts about taking *any* dogmatic position in favor of priority of the good. There simply isn't a *correct* such position, and, thus, pitting classical liberalism against political liberalism in the one-sided way Skorupski does runs the distinct risk of getting badly out of step with the ever more permissive times we live in.

This does not mean that we can avoid taking a position, for in any political arrangement we are bound to have priority (and, as one might also say, hegemony, in a somewhat Gramscian sense) either of freedom or of the good. The only thing we can do in compensation is to see this one-sidedness, this hegemonic settlement, for what it is and seek to bring the subordinated notion, whether freedom or the good, insistently back into the moral and political culture. For, without giving the subordinate notion its due, or at least a significant measure of its due, the dominant notion itself will be on the verge of ceasing to make sense, with all of its practical consequences.

If I were to draw one general implication from this line of thinking that is especially relevant for thinking about the moral future of China, I would say that as the country learns to make its social and political life more free, it would be well advised to proceed dialectically and with as much openness as is prudent under the circumstances. It would be able, that is, to make genuine and sober moral progress only by allowing a larger place for the good than is found in liberal societies and by simultaneously developing a cognizance of the irreducibility of freedom sorely lacking in its own tradition.

In a nutshell, then, I believe that the relation of freedom and the good is essentially dialectical, that therefore neither freedom nor the good commands *intrinsic* priority, and, furthermore, that this rules out all fixing of the relation between freedom and the good in terms of some kind of reasonable equilibrium, let alone priority. The relation between freedom and the good is a riddle of the human moral and political life to which there is no right answer. Why, then, do I appear to favor the priority of the good in the context of China today? The first part of my answer is precisely that neither freedom nor the good has intrinsic reason to enjoy priority. But why give priority to the good, then, since it too does not enjoy intrinsic priority? The answer, the second part of my answer, is that this *happens to be* the way China is (and has been for a long time) and there is no realistic prospect of changing it in the near future. What I am suggesting, then, is that the question of priority regarding the relation between freedom and the good cannot be determined a priori and must therefore be treated as a matter of making the best of a cultural and political reality and guarding against suppression of the dialectical tension within whatever priority happens to obtain. I have settled for the priority of the good in the Chinese context for this reason alone. I therefore treat it as a culturally constituted, and hence a contingent, priority rather than a philosophically grounded one.

If this understanding of the matter is plausible, it may provide a way of aligning the importance of liberty and civil society in China not only with a still highly powerful moral-cultural tradition of priority of the good but also with the political leadership of the CCP. It will not resolve the contradiction, of course, because it cannot, and we have just seen that it is a good thing it cannot. What is doable and is important to do is to be cognizant of the contradiction and approach it dialectically. This means, in the Chinese context, given the culturally entrenched priority of the good (and the political primacy of the CCP), that it is freedom whose importance we must constantly be reminded of and whose place we must seek to enlarge and jealously protect, within what in a dialectical conception ought to be reasonably flexible parameters of the priority of the good.

One way to think concretely and constructively about how to achieve this objective is to take a leaf out of Skorupski's book but use it and adapt it in a dialectical spirit. I have in mind his distinction between permissive and persuasive neutrality and his characterization of classical liberalism in terms of permissive neutrality uncoupled from persuasive neutrality. The Chinese state has shown itself to be far from averse to permissive neutrality with regard to many de facto liberties. What it has yet to do is to turn this practice into *avowed* permissive neutrality. Clearly a degree of avowed permissive neutrality as extensive as that in classical liberalism would completely undermine China's culturally constituted priority of the good. But a substantial amount of avowed permissive neutrality is both necessary and possible. At the same time, one may expect the Chinese state to abjure persuasive neutrality with more confidence and vigor than can be true of classical liberalism. But, as in the case of the classical liberal state, the means of persuasion employed, to be effective, must be plausible, and, to be plausible, they must be compatible with a substantial amount of freedom—that is, they must work in conjunction with a good deal of permissive neutrality. Taken together, measures such as these will not turn the CCP into an unwitting practitioner of classical liberalism; far from it. But they will take China a long way toward creating a new moral and political culture that is more coherent and more resonant with the socioeconomic reality on the ground.

What about the fact, however, that this dialectical way of handling the contradiction between freedom and the good—by accentuating that which is not given *structural* priority—will, as long as the CCP remains in power, stop short of the separation of powers? It is certainly arguable that this separation is a necessary condition for democracy in the sense of modern representative government, although separation of powers may also serve as a way of deflecting democracy. But a more open and more basic question for China is not whether it can achieve democracy without separation of powers but rather whether democracy (with or without the separation of powers) must mean the abandonment of the Chinese moral-cultural tradition of priority of the good. There is little doubt that those who advocate Confucian liberal democracy of one kind or another have paid the price of giving up the Confucian priority of the good and subjecting whatever Confucianism remains to the liberal priority of the right. They all consider the price worth paying and, in the case of wholehearted endorsement of priority of the right, do not even think of it as price. But objectively, in the sense of a condition, it is a price. The fundamental question is whether this is a price that *has to* be paid for democracy—that is, whether what appears to be a condition, or a favorable condition, is a *necessary* condition. To be more precise, however, liberty must be considered apart from democracy in this context, for, as I have argued, liberty, not just de facto liberty but even valorized liberty, can be dialectically accommodated within a society marked by priority of the good. So the question, reformulated, is whether the Chinese moral-cultural tradition of priority of the good is a price that *has to* be paid for *democracy.*

Democracy in Society, State, and Culture: China and the West

I have now reached a point at which it seems especially appropriate to make fully explicit something that should have emerged already but has yet to be named: democratic culture. Adding this concept to my account will also make it possible for me to conclude with a schematic yet relatively comprehensive comparison of China and the West in terms of democracy.

I have, following Tocqueville, distinguished between two loci of democracy, as it were: society and the state. As far as society is concerned, it will be recalled that I have, following Karl Marx, identified a species of social inequality, in Marx's sense, that is perfectly compatible with social equality in Tocqueville's. Indeed the coexistence of Tocquevillian social equality and Marxian social inequality is the hallmark of bourgeois society and a major source of the contradictions plaguing the bourgeois democratic state.

To these loci of democracy it is necessary to add a third: culture. Thus democracy can be located in society, in the state, and in culture, and, correspondingly we can speak of *democratic society* (or societal democracy), *democratic polity or state* (or political democracy), and *democratic culture.*

Democratic culture, in turn, can be a feature of society or of the political sphere. In the former case, we have what may be called a *democratic societal culture,* and, in the latter, a *democratic political culture.* A democratic societal culture comprises the ethos, values, and habits of the heart that inform what Tocqueville calls equality of conditions in society. Obviously there cannot be a democratic society without a democratic societal culture growing from it and reinforcing it. A democratic political culture stands in the same relation to a democratic polity as a democratic societal culture does to a democratic society. Furthermore, just as one democratic society may differ from another and sometimes markedly, so the same is true of democratic state forms. But all democratic political cultures have in common the core values, beliefs, and understandings that are not only produced by but also constitutive of the democratic practices and institutions in the political domain.

Where does China stand, as compared with the West, in terms of this breakdown of the analytically distinguishable yet operationally interdependent loci of democracy?

With regard to democracy in society, I have been at pains to show that China has reached a level of equality of conditions, in Tocqueville's sense, that is essentially comparable to, if understandably somewhat less advanced than, what is generally found in modern Western countries. China has done so by undertaking truly transformative economic reform and joining the global capitalist order, especially since its induction into the World Trade Organization. By exactly the same token, China has developed a new kind of social inequality, in Marx's sense, that is specific to the capitalist mode of production. That such inequality is more pronounced in China than in developed Western societies is, to a large degree, a function of China's place in the global value chain. Thus, all things considered, as far as democracy in society is concerned, China finds itself in the same paradigmatic condition as the West and faces largely the same contradiction between Tocquevillian social equality and Marxian social inequality. In other words, it is true of both China and the West that society is democratic in one sense but undemocratic in another— a major source, in roughly equal measure, of the hopes and aspirations and of the struggles and disappointments in both places.

China differs conspicuously and profoundly from the West, however, with respect to democracy in the political state. All the Western countries have successfully made the Tocquevillian move from societal democracy to political democracy. This is one of the most important factors, though by no means the only one, that help impart an exceptionally high degree of underlying stability to their political order. China, already largely a democratic society (in Tocqueville's sense), has yet to achieve this fit between society and polity, and until it does it will continuously face—in ways, it is worth emphasizing, unique to a democratic society unmatched by a democratic political form—the specter of regime instability and even discontinuation. Thus China's political challenge is both Marxian, in terms of social inequality coexisting in tension with social equality, and Tocquevillian, with regard to the prudentially necessary extension of societal to political democracy. By contrast, the advanced political democracies of the West have largely resolved the latter challenge, especially since the end of World War II, and, in this sense, their politics is simpler, safer, and less daunting.

When it comes to democracy in culture, it is essential to bear in mind the distinction between democratic societal culture and democratic political culture. It should come as no surprise that a democratic societal culture has evolved in reform-era China in tandem with a rising democratic society. Indeed, it would be difficult to distinguish, in practice, between a democratic society and a democratic societal culture, for they evolve together as only conceptually distinct components of a phenomenologically indivisible process. One must hasten to draw a further distinction, however. For, just as social equality in Tocqueville's sense can coexist with social inequality in Marx's in a capitalist order, so in this order a democratic societal culture à la Tocqueville can be abundantly present while a democratic societal culture à la Marx is largely absent. This is exactly the case with China, its self-professed allegiance to Marx notwithstanding—and, to a lesser degree, thanks to its tradition of social democracy (in Europe) and liberalism (in the United States), with the West as well, especially since the ascendency of neoliberalism.

As far as democratic political culture is concerned, the contrast between China and the West could not be sharper. Despite the neoliberal encroachment on the Western democratic state, there is no doubting the continuing vitality of a democratic political culture in most Western states—not least as manifested in all manner of social movements, however limited their reach and enduring success. Strictly speaking, especially for the Western world as a whole, the uninterrupted existence of this democratic political culture in its present form, encompassing, among other things, both universal suffrage and the welfare state, dates back only to the end of World War II. There is a sense, however, in which this contemporary democratic political culture is continuous—in one way or another, to one degree or another, which one must take care not to exaggerate—with its predecessor political cultures, including those of classical antiquity and the Middle Ages. Many factors have contributed to these predecessors, not least the pervasive presence of multiple, competing jurisdictions, especially in the later medieval period.[39]

Such competing jurisdictions have been almost completely absent from the history of China since its unification and, unsurprisingly, so has any political culture that can remotely be regarded as democratic or republican. The not uncommon imputation of germs of democratic thought to Mencius is entirely mistaken. For what Mencius very commendably defends, as a ground even for "revolution," is, in modern language, the right to subsistence or self-preservation rather than citizenship or political agency. In this he is no more a champion of democracy or promoter of democratic political culture than is Thomas Hobbes, who too gives pride of place to ordinary people, as it were, but only in terms of their self-preservation—that is, their overwhelmingly desired protection from the fear of violent death. This is not to decry the absence of any semblance of democratic political culture in the Chinese tradition but to point up the formidable challenge to China's orderly democratic transformation in the absence of directly useful political-cultural resources. If democratic progress is a matter of positive interaction among society, polity, and culture, then there can be little doubt that China is somewhat handicapped.

I see no reason, however, why a democratic political culture cannot evolve, if gradually and relatively slowly, on the basis of contemporary social and political conditions. It definitely can, just as a democratic societal culture has thus evolved as part of an emerging democratic Chinese society. Moreover, this new democratic societal culture has gained enormously from adapting relevant influences from outside and indeed from "creatively" reinterpreting elements of China's own tradition. There is no reason why the same cannot happen for the rise of a democratic *political* culture, aided also by an already strong and vital democratic societal culture.

One condition must be satisfied, however, for a democratic political culture can evolve in China, with or without drawing on foreign and ancient sources, only if it is *allowed* to do so. This is the same condition that applies to China's much-needed passage from societal democracy to political democracy. For practical purposes, this passage, from democratic society to democratic polity, and the extension of democratic societal culture to democratic political culture are one and the same. In both cases, the necessity is strong, as is the built-in momentum, and what it takes to answer to the necessity and release the momentum is only for the CCP not to stand in the way but instead to make the bold decision to undertake prudent, gradual democratic reform. Even then, things will be anything but easy and straightforward. But at least China will have moved beyond denial and refusal and embarked on the crucial interim stage of democratic preparation.

CHAPTER SIX

Democratic Preparation

I HAVE TAKEN PAINS so far to show that, for China today, democracy is a matter of dire necessity rather than moral luxury. The need to place my entire discussion on a firm footing arises from an inescapable difficulty—that of knowing exactly, or even approximately, what to think of democracy in a situation in which democracy is presumably possible and desirable and yet not a matter of sheer necessity. The difficulty is a matter of weighing the normative and other claims of democracy against the enormous risks involved in experimenting with democracy in a country as huge and complex and, in important respects, as fragile as China if there is no urgent or desperate need to undertake such an experiment.

This difficulty melts away, however, once we come to see the dire necessity of democracy for China. For if this necessity is true, as I firmly believe it is, then thinking about democracy for China has itself become a necessity. And this intellectual necessity—or what creates it—provides a nonarbitrary and normatively nonindulgent point of departure for whatever one may go on to think and say about democracy in China. This is the case almost regardless of one's disposition toward democracy, for all that is needed is the additional assumption that democracy belongs to the range of acceptable options for China. This is a normative assumption, to be sure, but one that is weak and easy to accept. It is all one needs to be reasonably well disposed toward democracy in the present Chinese context and to be worried about its prospect. For whether one strongly likes democracy or not, and for whatever reasons, objective circumstances make democracy a necessity that is getting closer to China with each passing decade, if not quite each passing year.

Thus we have reason to think of democracy as being realistic in China—in the sense that the parties concerned have a prudential interest in making it happen. Alongside this prudential interest, the parties concerned also have, unavoidably, a normative interest in thinking about how *best* to bring about democracy and what kind of democracy is *best suited* to China's circumstances as they stand at present and as they evolve. It is natural, in this context, to put the prudential interest and the normative interest together under the integral rubric of *realistic utopia*. I borrow this term from John Rawls but use it rather differently. I mean it simply as a political vision that results from the congruence of prudential and normative interests. Here a realistic utopia gets off the ground under the impetus of a prudential interest. Subsequently it can fall short of realism by failing to attend sufficiently to the specific circumstances of Chinese society as they pertain to the orderly establishment of democracy. It can also be faulted normatively for not being a particularly attractive vision of democracy. But the normative criticism is plausible—consistent with the idea of realistic utopia in question—only to the degree that it is sensitive to the constraints that are placed on any normative conception of democracy by the existing circumstances of China. Such circumstances may be expected to evolve, not least after the successful establishment of democracy, in which case a different, more normatively attractive conception may become realistic later.

Once we are equipped with some such notion of a realistic utopia of democracy, we will be in a position to evaluate what the parties involved are doing or failing to do to bring it about. Given the special circumstances of China, the most important actor is the Chinese Communist Party (CCP), for unless it sees fit to lead China in orderly progress toward democracy, such progress will be highly unlikely in the foreseeable future and all efforts to this end made by other actors may be as costly as they are futile. But other parties, including the citizens of China and the people and governments of foreign countries, also have a stake and a more or less important role to play. Their actions and omissions too can be assessed in terms of realism and on normative grounds. Thus, to limit the discussion to domestic actors in this chapter, the CCP and the citizenry of China alike lend themselves to both prudential and normative appraisals of their actions and omissions.

I like to think, however, that, as far as the party is concerned, what is most needed is a clear awareness of its own prudential interest in putting China's gradual, orderly progress toward democracy on its political agenda. What is usually called political reform (around which a new, eerie silence has descended) would be meaningful and important only if it were part of such a visionary agenda. Thus I would be especially inclined to fault the CCP for failing to show this prudential interest and for laboring under illusions that prevent its emergence. The stakes could not be higher. Until the CCP develops this interest and does so with the requisite seriousness and determination, one would have to characterize China's prudential interest in establishing democracy as merely a theoretical one—an interest all the parties concerned ought to have in view of the reality on the ground—that has not yet evolved into a real and operative interest.

As far as Chinese citizens are concerned, the biggest danger is a lack of realism of two different kinds. Those in China who are keen to see their country become a democracy tend all too often to dream of a positive democratic future largely derived from negating what they perceive to be China's undemocratic reality. They then, as part of the same move, give their democratic dream a spatiotemporal existence by identifying it more or less with actually existing democracy in the West. By the same logic, as increasingly happens in China, those believers who later find that Western democracy does not live up to their imagination often make a U-turn, rejecting democracy as fervently as they had earlier embraced it. In so doing, they completely forget that the best case for democracy is not some exemplary practice of democracy in the West or anywhere else but China's own inescapable need for it.

If this kind of unrealism is a matter of what one can and cannot reasonably expect from democracy, there is another kind of unrealism that turns a blind eye to the political reality of China. An important aspect of this reality is the scale and complexity of China as a cultural and political entity, which poses a unique challenge for democratic government, with no suitable and worthy model or precedent to follow. Another, no less important aspect of Chinese reality is the sheer fact of the overwhelming power of the CCP, its fragility notwithstanding, along with the political necessity that this fact imposes on all other actors to work with this de facto dominant force. In my view it is foolish and foolhardy to pit democracy against the party and to make the striving for democracy simultaneously an attempt to overthrow the party. Such a strategy either would be doomed to perpetual frustration or would succeed in such a way as to court disaster by bringing down the only political force that is capable of steering China toward the orderly establishment of democracy. If the CCP is willing and able to lead China toward democracy, on its own initiative or under pressure, it deserves a chance and every support to do so. What matters is how best to ensure basic social and political stability while making democratic progress and, equally important, how best to enhance rather than sweep aside the self-protection of society in the face of capitalism while leaving behind an undemocratic one-party state. The dogmatic ruling-out of the CCP as a principal agent for achieving these goals rather than as their intransigent obstacle is a luxury China can ill afford.

In political matters we are not normally confronted with the morally simple and comfortable choice between supporting good and shunning or resisting evil. We certainly would be ill advised to think and act in such simple dichotomies in China today when considering how best to further the cause of democracy and how best to conceive of the CCP's role in it. The task of establishing democracy is a political one, first and foremost. Morality has its place in this task, and that is why we speak of a realistic *utopia*, but democracy can be successfully pursued only in the spirit of a *realistic* utopia. It must be pursued with due recognition of, if not exactly respect for, any relatively durable balance of power and with a willingness to work within parameters determined by this balance of power. Thus I suggest that the only constructive way to achieve the orderly establishment of democracy in China is to work for the maximal convergence of the citizens' normative interest in having an attractive form of democracy and the CCP's prudential interest in developing an arrangement that gives it the best possible future it could have in a democratic China. This does not mean, of course, that the CCP does not have its own normative interest, which in any case must be inextricably bound up with its prudential interest. It only means that any normative vision of democracy developed by actors other than the CCP, in their capacity as theorists or as citizens, must be carefully designed to leave sufficient room for the possibility of its convergence with the most important prudential interests of the party if it is to retain its credentials as a realistic utopia.

China's Vertical Unity

If there is one interest, at once prudential and normative, where the case for convergence is most compelling, it has to be in making sure that whatever democracy China develops is conducive to or at least compatible with holding the country together and keeping its sovereignty and stability secure. To appreciate what this entails, we need an idea of how the Middle Kingdom, past and present, has managed to hold itself together through all the vicissitudes of an exceptionally long, largely uninterrupted civilization.

Throughout China's long history, the art of ruling has involved creating and maintaining unity, preferably with harmony. Only an extremely strong central power, one with great centripetal force, is capable of holding China together and making it work in the only way it has so far known how. Thus unity is made possible *vertically,* and exclusively so, and this has been, and still is, the single most important fact of political life in China. This vertical structure of unity takes different forms in traditional and communist China, and these forms are produced and sustained differently. But the art of government required is the same in its reliance on vertically achieved unity. The art of government through separation—that is, *horizontal* separation, say, of powers, of state and society, of the political and the economic, of public and private, and, not least, of people into largely self-governing moral individuals— has been foreign to the Chinese way of making its society work and, despite profound shifts in economic, social, and psychological reality in the reform era, this has not fundamentally changed even today.

To obtain a clear, broad view of the continuity between present and past and of how communist China has adapted the time-honored formula of vertical unity to new circumstances, let us first take a brief look at the traditional, largely Confucian conception and practice of vertical unity.

It is a commonplace that the vertical structure of unity is accomplished in traditional China through a densely woven web of hierarchical relations at once political and familial.[1] Preeminent among these relations from a political point of view (a point of view that is distinct or discrete only at the second-order level, that of the observer or analyst) is the relation between ruler and minister and, by extension, between the ruler and all his subjects. But from the point of view of family and kinship (again distinct and discrete only at the second-order level), the pivotal relation is that between father and son, followed by the relations between husband and wife and between older and younger brothers. Just as the father-son relation takes pride of place among the relations, so filial piety *(xiao),* the virtue pertaining to this relation, holds the same place among the virtues. The relation between older and younger brothers may be regarded as a variation on this relation, and hence *ti,* the virtue of brotherly respect (of a younger brother for an older brother), is of a piece with the virtue of filial piety. Together, as we are told near the beginning of the *Analects,* "filial piety and brotherly respect are the root of humanity."[2] This is echoed in the *Mencius,* this time applying to all four virtues *(ren,* humanity; *yi,* righteousness; *zhi,* wisdom; and *li,* propriety): "The actuality of humanity consists in serving one's parents. The actuality of righteousness consists in obeying one's elder brother. The actuality of wisdom consists in knowing these two things and not departing from them. The actuality of propriety consists in regulating and adorning these two things."[3]

The crucial importance of the father-son relation, along with its corresponding virtue, has a lot to do with the fact that it is the strongest candidate for being a relation of *natural* hierarchy. Natural not only in an ordinary sense but also in the deeper, cosmological sense of being sanctioned by Heaven: "Heaven produces creatures in such a way as to provide them with one foundation (such as parents being the foundation of men)."[4] Once the idea of Heaven-ordained hierarchy is thus established, it can then extend to the relation between ruler and minister. If "it is the Way of Heaven that the son always serves his father," no less is it the case that "serving the ruler is like Earth showing respect to Heaven."[5] Once the ruler-minister relation too is so cast, it infuses the other relations with its more stringent command-obedience character. Affection *(qin)* and authority *(zun)* are thus perfectly joined.

With the father-son relation being paradigmatic in one realm and the ruler-minister relation in another, a homology is established between family and state, which together served as the primary survival units, to use Norbert Elias's term, and hence, unsurprisingly, also as the primary moral units. Kinship relations are political relations, and, even more important, political relations are (like) kinship relations. At the head of the state stands the ruler, who is, however, head of the state in the same way and with the same natural legitimacy as the father is head of the family. An exemplary ruler combines the roles of ruler and father and thereby unifies the family and the state. He operates along one vertical axis and at the same time serves as the linchpin of all the other vertical axes. He is at the center of a hierarchically structured totality that has never been held together in any other way.

This form of centripetal imperial rule based on the hierarchical family-state homology came under unprecedented threat from Western powers, beginning with the Opium War, and it collapsed in 1911. What followed, instead of fulfilling the promise of the newly founded republic, were nearly four decades of bloody disunity and disharmony interrupted only by the Japanese invasion and a temporarily united front against it. Thus it was that when the communists finally established the People's Republic of China in 1949, they set about restoring unity and harmony—but only among the proletariat and its allies, of course, while waging a ruthless struggle against so-called class enemies, who were seen as obstacles to the true unity and harmony that were to come with the advent of communism.[6]

Mao Zedong's China did not, however, retain most of the unequal relations that had formed the unity of traditional China. Where traditional, Confucian China had relied on the family-state homology in maintaining a comprehensively hierarchical set of relations, Mao's China adopted a communist-inspired collectivism, with command-obedience relations existing side by side with largely equal ones. For Mao removed, with impressive if incomplete success, all the rigidly unequal traditional relations except one. The result was an egalitarian society, a society in which people were equal, at least roughly so, in all respects but the political. In its new form, political inequality essentially meant two things. First, there were friends and enemies, defined in strictly class terms, and only the former, called "the people," constituted the revolutionary collective, whose members were equal. Second, the equality among members of the revolutionary collective was qualified by a rigorous chain of command within the ranks of "the people" and by the further fact that this chain of command was meant to be based on unequal levels of political consciousness (simply put, loyalty to the CCP, above all else), with those at the top forming a vanguard whose title to rule was deemed as natural, Heaven-ordained, and absolute as that of the imperial rulers of the past. From these two inequalities there emerged a new vertical structure consisting of the dictatorship of the proletariat *over* the bourgeoisie and the leadership of the CCP *over* the "people."

In its quest for unity and harmony, as well as in its almost exclusive reliance on vertical relations to that end, communist China shows a deep and broad affinity with Confucian China. Nevertheless, what we find in communist China is a much less elaborate vertical structure, in two significant respects. First, the homology between family and state has largely disappeared, so that the state must carry the burden alone and political relations must subsume or dominate familial and kinship relations. Second, inasmuch as unity is to be achieved vertically and the only vertical relation is a political one, unity can be achieved only politically. It follows from the conjunction of these two facts that the centripetal force needed to hold society together in communist China, having to do everything itself and doing it politically, must be extremely powerful, much more powerful than the ruler in traditional China.[7]

It is (as if) according to some such logic that the entire Chinese society has been refashioned under the CCP. Within the new vertical structure for achieving unity and holding the country together, there is to be only one centripetal political force and that is the party. This was a prescription, to begin with, one that had some basis not only in the Leninist precedent but also in the Chinese political tradition.[8] Over time, with the CCP's consolidation of power and penetration into the entire social body, the prescription has been turned into a fact that is hard to deny: only the party can save China, it used to be said with tireless frequency, and this remains true today. But it is a fact of the party's own making.

Everything that happens in Chinese society must revolve around this central political prescription-fact. It is part and parcel of this prescription-fact that no political force other than the CCP and those acknowledging its undisputed leadership must be allowed to exist. Consequently, the only legitimate political relations are those that exist vertically between the party-state, on the one hand, and "the people," on the other. All horizontal political relations *among* "the people" independent of the party are anathema, and thus freedom of association is permitted only within the chain of command presided over by the party. And nothing else must stand in the way of the party-state maintaining and effectively exerting its centripetal force, and that is why it makes sense that freedoms of speech and of the press must be so regulated as to prohibit the expression of any public opposition to the principles and policies of the central leadership.

To the degree that this model has worked, and the degree is high with regard to social order and economic development, China has cultivated a firm dependency on the leadership of the CCP. Because such dependency needs to be continuously reproduced, society must not be given any chance to become independent. Accordingly, the design of political institutions and the manner of political socialization, not least the inculcation of political virtues, promote dependency and discourage all forms of political agency and subjectivity other than those fit for followers. It is as if a strict moratorium has been placed on all training for capacities, virtues, and dispositions—and all experimentation with political institutions—that could one day stand Chinese society in good stead should it become necessary to adopt a democratic system of government. Thus China lacks the rudiments of a democratic or even protodemocratic political culture—a fact that exists in the most awkward and formidable tension with China's no less undeniable need for democracy in the foreseeable future.[9] In the absence of such training, experimentation, and culture, democracy, if suddenly introduced, could easily descend into chaos, and thus the frequently encountered caution regarding democracy that is based on fear of just such a scenario is by no means irrational or exaggerated. Such caution is compounded by the additional fear, also not to be dismissed, that the ensuing chaos would create the need and incentive for a new centripetal force and ideology, which could have no guarantee of being more attractive and effective than the present one.

When I alluded to the need for democratic preparation, this, then, is what I had in mind: the need arises from entrenched deficiencies, and the latter, in turn, are rooted in the time-honored Chinese practice, both Confucian and communist, of normatively ordering society through a structure of almost exclusively vertical relations. Against this background, the one thing most needed is to lift the moratorium as soon as possible, but gradually and prudently.

China Needs Both Democracy and Strong Central Authority

One of the most important reasons for proceeding gradually and prudently is that China's need for an exceptionally strong central authority—one with a strong centripetal force—is a very real one. The need goes far beyond cultural inertia or path dependency. No doubt these factors play a role: think of the administrative organization of the country in terms of prefectures and counties, the so-called *junxian zhi;* the centralized and highly rigorous ideological training and control of the bureaucracy through indoctrination based on a uniform belief and value system; and the penetration of the central authority's political will and ideological influence right down to the grassroots level in informal (Confucian) or formal (communist) ways. But they play this role in no small measure as a response to what Mark Elvin calls "the burden of size,"[10] which today takes a different yet no less challenging form. To begin with, the continental scale and complexity of a massively populated country makes a strong central authority essential if the country is to be held securely together, even with a well-designed federal system (in place of the current province-county system). This is all the more so if, as is now clearly the case, there are centrifugal forces from within— driven by ethnic or political dynamics made intractable by current as well as historical factors—that pose clear and present threats to Chinese sovereignty and territorial integrity. When these factors are considered together with the fact that the Chinese people have never had much of a chance to train and ready themselves for any type of rule other than one imposed by an exceptionally strong central authority (in its Confucian-Legalist or communist-Legalist form), the resulting "exceptionalism" is perfectly plausible, though it should not be fetishized or overly naturalized.

In this context, when I use a phrase like "an exceptionally strong central authority," I mean no more (and no less) than a central authority able to rise to the challenge of an exceptionally difficult task. The task of holding the country together in relative peace and stability used to mean, above all, the prevention of (pre-Qin-style, or, suggestively, for Western readers, medieval European-style) feudalization. It obviously has a different meaning today, but the task remains the same. Accordingly, an exceptionally strong central authority, as I use this notion, needs to be strong *only in ways required by this task,* but not (necessarily) otherwise. Thus, for example, the Confucian-Legalist state of the past was able to establish its authority through, among other things, a unique amalgamation of political and ideological power, and this took the form of a (nonhereditary) Confucianized bureaucracy that helped make the central authority exceptionally strong *in the requisite sense* while also checking the personal power of the emperor and making it *less strong* in other senses.[11] The same should apply in principle to what an exceptionally strong central authority should mean today, with its particular strengths depending on what the task requires under today's circumstances.

It is arguable, and this is my argument, that one of its required strengths is none other than democracy, while the democracy required, in turn, has its toughest test in showing precisely that not only will it not weaken the central authority of the state in relevant respects but, if implemented well, it will also significantly strengthen it, and in ways nothing else could, given the presence in China of a substantial and ever-rising equality of conditions.

Thus it is understandable that a further complication of China's situation is precisely that it is not a democracy and therefore is vulnerable to having its legitimacy challenged and, as a consequence, its sovereignty given less definitive significance than it otherwise would (or might) receive. One could not put it more bluntly yet subtly and with greater accuracy than John Dunn: "To American observers, all but inevitably, [democracy] is a category that challenges the political standing of the Chinese Communist Party and the legitimacy of all who have risen to power through it. It hovers permanently on the brink of repudiating Chinese sovereignty over Taiwan, over Tibet, over Xinjiang, and if the People's Republic ever runs into big trouble and regional warlording recommences, potentially over any substantial segment of the country."[12]

It may well be that China's not being a democracy is used, at least partly, as a pretext for some geopolitical agenda that has nothing to do intrinsically with the nature of China's political system (or human rights record, for that matter). Even so, the very invention of this pretext and not some other is itself a political reality. And the geopolitical agenda itself, supposing it exists, must have something important to do with the fact—the awkward fact—that China is simultaneously the world's second-largest economy, making it now the only credible threat to American supremacy, and yet not a democracy, like the United States. As long as this awkward fact remains, we may expect China's internal centrifugal forces to be reinforced in ways both direct and subtle by "outside forces."

When all these factors are put together, they give us reason to think that China today has an even greater need for a strong central authority than it did in imperial times. Yet, as we have just seen, China's lack of democracy weakens such an authority by rendering it vulnerable to an ideological and political pressure to which it has no adequate response except by becoming a democracy and putting itself in a position to credibly contest the meaning and form of democracy. Were this only a matter of responding to outside pressure, there could be a case for resisting the pressure and, to the same degree, strengthening the centripetal force of the leadership by putting even more power in its hands, as is happening today. But, as we have seen, the systemic, objective pressure for democracy within China itself is well-nigh irresistible, and there is no legitimate reason to resist that.

What this means is that China today stands in equally undeniable need both of democracy and of an exceptionally strong central authority. Thus, the manner in which the latter need is being met under the CCP requires major change for it to be compatible with democracy, just as democracy must be so conceived as to be compatible with the need for a central authority with the requisite centripetal force. In this regard, the fortunes of democracy in China are indissolubly bound up with a democratic or democratizing China's ability to hold the entire country securely together and safeguard its sovereignty and territorial integrity.[13] If this ability is lacking, one can be certain that the democratic project will be doomed, despite all the systemic, internal pressures for democracy, just as no future central leadership (after the present one) will be able to acquire sufficient centripetal force without the aid of democratic legitimation.[14]

Fortunately, the presence of and reliance on a strong central authority in China need not be an obstacle to democracy, and can even be an asset, for a powerful reason that resides in the very nature of the modern nation-state. No one has spelled out the affinities between the modern nation-state, centralization, and the distinctively modern democracy with greater insight than Elias:

Through centralization and monopolization, opportunities that previously had to be won by individuals through military and economic force, can now become amenable to planning. From a certain point of development on, the struggle for monopolies no longer aims at their destruction; it is a struggle for the control of their yields, for the plan according to which their burdens and benefits are to be divided up, in a word, for the keys to distribution. Distribution itself, the task of the monopoly ruler and administration, changes in this struggle from a relatively private to a public function.... Permanent institutions to control them are formed by a greater or lesser portion of the people dependent on this monopoly apparatus, and control of the monopoly, the filling of its key positions, is itself no longer decided by the vicissitudes of "free" competition, but by the regularly recurring elimination contests without force of arms, which are regulated by the monopoly apparatus, and thus by "unfree" competition. In other words, what we are accustomed to call a "democratic regime" is formed. This kind of regime is not ... incompatible with monopolies as such and dependent for its existence on the freest possible competition. On the contrary it presupposes highly organized monopolies, and it can only come into being or survive under certain conditions, in a very specific social structure at a very advanced stage of monopoly formation.[15]

In this light, there is no contradiction between centralization and democracy; instead centralization paves the way for democracy (of the modern kind we are discussing), and democracy is, in turn, all but dictated by centralization. What matters—what gives centralization and democracy their proper meaning—is above all the "public" character of the political arrangement that emerges at the stage of monopolization marked by the rise of the nation-state. Thus democratization is "the phase in which a relatively 'private' monopoly becomes a 'public' one."[16] It is no accident that the CCP presents its chosen state form as a public monopoly—as evident in its very name, the People's Republic. The important thing is that the only way to give reality to this self-presentation and make it credible is, according to Elias's logic, to match centralization with democratization. And, as he shows, it takes a strong national monopoly to create a truly public—that is, democratic—one.

In this light, too, we can pin down more precisely what it means to claim that China requires an exceptionally strong central authority. There is no mystery to such a claim, and no cause for fetishizing what is in fact an understandable need whose strength varies with circumstances. "Growth in the 'power' of the central functionaries is, in a society with a high division of functions, an expression of the fact that the dependence of other groups and classes within this society on a supreme organ of co-ordination and regulation is rising; a fall in the latter appears to us as a limitation of the former."[17] On this understanding, the exceptional concentration of power in the

Chinese state ("central functionaries") is, in principle, nothing but a reflection of the exceptionally high dependence of other groups and classes on its capacity for coordination and regulation. It should be an open question whether the exact, actual degree of concentration of power is roughly proportional to the real needs for coordination and regulation or is grossly excessive with reference to such needs—either in the sense of overreacting to real needs or making what are otherwise real needs unnecessarily strong. I doubt it can plausibly be denied that China's unique circumstances require an exceptionally strong state of *some* form. But what is equally not in doubt is that this *form* must be democratic in order to create the plausible appearance of a *public* monopoly that makes for the legitimacy of a modern state.

Elias gives us reason to conclude, then, that an exceptionally strong state itself need not be a problem. Only such a state that acts like a private monopoly is, but there is no reason to think that a strong state cannot acquire a reasonably public character and find the democratic means to make this public character credible. Thus China's democratic project has its work cut out for it by the country's unique circumstances (as well as tradition), but the project itself is perfectly coherent and feasible—and, by the same token, urgently necessary.

Why China Must Be Flexible in How It Designs Its Democracy

On account of these unique circumstances (as well as more widely applicable considerations), I believe we should mean by *democracy* something reasonably general: a political regime broadly defined in terms of its fittingness for—and its conduciveness to stability and governability under—equality of conditions. Under such conditions, the avowable principle of a legitimate regime can only be sovereignty of the people—in order to let there be no doubt that the regime understands itself and intends to conduct itself as a public monopoly. It is only by virtue of its public character that the state can be representative of society and its authority can command the latter's consent. But a regime's claim to these characteristics—publicness, representativeness, consent—will only be an empty claim until a way is found of making it credible to the general public. A so-called free and fair electoral system is one way of generating such credibility. But while it seems the most intuitively or immediately convincing way, it need not be the only one. Credibility is what counts, and how it is achieved is best left open to accommodate different national circumstances and allow for experimentation. Let me suggest, then, that a regime can reasonably be considered democratic if, or to the degree that, it can satisfy the credibility condition over time with regard to the three characteristics just mentioned. In other words, a sustainably credible claim to publicness, representativeness, and consent makes a regime democratic.[18]

The publicness that is part of this characterization of democracy was implicit (how could it not be, since it is a truism?) in my discussion of representation and consent in Chapter 3. It is worth saying more about it—and about its relation to representation and consent—now that I have made it explicit. In doing so, however, I will make a small digression in order to shed further light on performance legitimacy in terms of publicness. The basic point is that performance legitimacy does not qualify as legitimacy because it lacks publicness in its rationale and in the nature of its effectiveness. It does not speak to the publicness Elias shows to be the defining feature of a legitimate nation-state. This is not to deny that performance legitimacy can effectively enhance a regime's ability to win the conditional support of masses of people. But such support is not, strictly speaking, *public* support—support for the regime qua public institution for reasons bearing on its public character as distinct from its contingent effects on purely private interests. Such effects are not produced *by* rulers who have a credible claim to public office that precedes and authorizes their performance, and they are not produced *for* citizens who have a properly public say in what performance they want, whom they consider to have the title to deliver the performance, and what counts as good performance. In the absence of publicness at both the giving and receiving ends, performance legitimacy is nothing but an ongoing chain of private transactions—between a de facto ruling group that has not acquired a credible public character, on the one hand, and members of society who react to the performance of this ruling group entirely in their capacity as private individuals, on the other. What passes for legitimacy is therefore not the affirmation of public interests but only the satisfaction of private ones. If enough private interests are sufficiently satisfied, then somehow this can give the beneficiaries good enough reasons to accept their rulers. This indeed often happens, but no amount of private interest satisfaction can by itself turn a private monopoly into a public one. It thus could not be more obvious that de facto acceptance of a regime solely on the grounds of its private role (its public role being in question) and of its performance in this role does not translate into legitimacy, the latter deriving its meaning from publicness alone.

This does not mean that the satisfaction of private interests is unimportant or unrelated to the public function of government. But what matters for legitimacy is not the satisfaction of private interests per se but the satisfaction of such interests in ways and by agents that are publicly determined. A legitimate modern state is in this sense a unique conjoining of the public and the private. Members of such a state are more bourgeois than citizens, to be sure, and, as such, are more preoccupied with private interests than public ones, and with the latter mostly as conditions for the former. Thus what counts as public and therefore stands in a direct relation to legitimacy is the public determination of how (mostly) private interests, including liberties, opportunities, and resources, are to be satisfied in accordance with some public notion of justice and then of what public goods are necessary to this end. Publicness, representation, and consent all find their meaning here. Small wonder, then, that performance legitimacy can win and keep support for a regime— as long as the performance is good enough and lasting enough—and can thereby create some semblance of real legitimacy. After all, modern publicness itself is *about* mostly private interests, and it rises above the private to the level of the public only through the democratic production of social justice—by people in their public capacity as citizens for the benefit of the same people qua private members of bourgeois society. This is why Elias says that the modern democratic nation-state results from the "struggle for the control of [the] yields of [monopolies], for the plan according to which their burdens and benefits are to be divided up, in a word, for the keys to distribution," and that "distribution itself [is] the task of the monopoly ruler and administration."

Thus publicness is both the essence of the modern state as a monopoly formation and the feature that legitimates its all-important distributive function. Representation (or representativeness) is but a different way of stating this essence of the state as a public function, the execution of which means taking care of (being representative of) all interests in society, all private interests, in accordance with some public notion of justice. Consent is representation viewed from the side of society, of the represented, of private interests, and, through its institutionalization, it serves as a marker of the presence of publicness or representativeness. As the latter, consent can be literally productive of "representatives" and hence representativeness of one degree or another, and it thereby functions as an institutionalized attempt to ensure publicness and make its existence credible to all concerned.

These, then, are the general features a regime must have in order to govern with fittingness and stability under modern equality of conditions. Such a regime qualifies as a democratic one in the reasonably strong sense of a regime that is able to sustain a credible claim to publicness, representativeness, and consent over time. Yet this standard is also reasonably open and flexible: anything weaker would simply be too weak. As long as some such standard is satisfied, it is advisable to leave the form of government, as well as the manner of choosing it, open and variable in order to avoid the dogma that the only genuine form or method of democracy is the one that prevails in its many variations in contemporary Western societies.[19] It is especially necessary to do so in order to leave room for due consideration of China's special need for a strong state with exceptional centripetal force.

It bears repeating that the most important and daunting challenge in pursuing democratic progress in China is precisely how to take care of this need under a democratic regime. What should not be in doubt is that the need for a strong central authority will be left unaltered by a change in regime type. For those factors responsible for this need, such as the sheer size and ethnic complexity of the population and all the attendant problems of cohesion and administration, will remain the same; if anything, they may well become even more intractable, even with democracy as a new and more effective source of legitimacy. As far as China is concerned, then, a viable democracy must be broadly conceived in terms of whatever credible form of publicness, representativeness, and popular consent, along with such discursive public will formation as is (minimally) presupposed by these, is capable of making China stable and governable under equality of conditions.

This may well mean, in practice, that a democratic China, at least in its early stages, will need the CCP at the helm no less badly than the so-called authoritarian China does now. After all, the party is the only political force in China that boasts any experience of governing the country since 1949. It has given no other political entity the slightest chance to emerge, let alone establish itself, except as a compliant minor ally of the CCP. One can take issue with this state of affairs all one wants, for good reason, but the fact remains that there is no other centripetal political force to turn to than the CCP.[20] We will be stuck with this fact—this politically created fact—for quite some time to come and, like it or not, we must fully realize what it means if we are to think realistically about how China could make orderly progress toward a democratic arrangement. With its monopolistic yet in many ways positive experience of governing China for seven decades, the CCP, by its own claim uniquely capable of saving China in an earlier time, may now be the only political force that can steer China safely toward democracy—if it sees fit to do so.

It must be expected, however, that, in the propitious event that the party does see fit to do so, it will favor a democratic arrangement that caters to China's need for a strong central authority and at the same time no less to its own desire to play the role of this central authority for as long as possible. One need not be squeamish about the merging of these two considerations (on the part of the CCP) as long as it happens in a broadly and sustainably democratic setting.

It would be premature, indeed risible, to try to stipulate what that setting must be like, beyond the requirement that it must give substantial and credible expression to publicness, representativeness, and popular consent, with the attendant rights and freedoms for citizens. If the CCP will predictably shape the democratic setting to its own advantage, it will also be true that the democratic setting itself, as long as it is a substantially democratic one, will, in turn, shape the party, if slowly then also surely, until the latter becomes an organization that is used to operating under the principles and constraints of a democratic polity. By then, the democratic arrangement tailor-made by and for the CCP will have become delinked from any specific beneficiary—depersonalized, as it were—leaving only a certain structure of institutions and values that are themselves to be judged and adjusted in terms of how well they serve the general need that China, as a uniquely complex social and political entity, has for cohesion and stability under equality of conditions.

That democracy is feasible and desirable in China rests on the premise, and hope, that it can take a form capable of generating a strong enough central authority to hold the vast and complex society together in a peaceful and stable order while at the same time satisfying the need, itself a matter of governability, for publicness, representativeness, and popular consent. This dual requirement is the only fixed point of reference flexible and realistic enough for appraising democracy in China.

Thus, as far as the scheme of institutions and values is concerned, all one could say is, first, that, insofar as the institutions are designed to make possible a strong central authority (by which we must mean an *exceptionally* strong central authority) that is at the same time subject to the requirements of publicness, representativeness, and popular consent, they may be expected to leave less room for freedoms, such as the freedom to substantially challenge and destabilize a government after it is duly put in office through free and fair elections or otherwise appropriate methods. Second, although a strong central authority is needed for the rather generic purposes of cohesion and stability, that central authority will be able to serve these purposes well only if it goes about doing so in furtherance of some conception of public goods—say, harmony and equity—that commands very broad public approbation and support. The strong central authority is thus defined—and simultaneously enabled and limited—by two factors. An extensive set of rights and freedoms for citizens, as required by publicness, representativeness, and popular consent compatible with a strong central authority, will allow citizens to realize and value their agency, both individual and political, and thus to willingly accept such limits as are necessary to create a sufficiently strong central authority. At the same time, a popularly endorsed conception of public goods will make it possible for citizens, on the one hand, to identify with the central authority and thereby help make it strong and, on the other, to appraise the central authority and hold it to account in substantial and critical yet prudent ways.

The second factor will require a lot more of what Jane Mansbridge calls unitary, as distinct from adversary, democracy than is typically found in the modern democratic state, and, of course, genuine unitary democracy must rest on the creation of shared ends and values rather than the suppression of conflicting interests.[21] Since we are talking about unitary democracy on the scale of an entire state rather than some organization within it, this is a very tall order indeed. But while size matters, what can make almost as big a difference is how we approach the balancing of unitary and adversary democracy. "One cannot," writes Mansbridge, "like most contemporary political scientists, throw away the half of human experience that values unitary goods and judge a polity solely on adversary criteria. One must judge the pros and cons of sizes and forms of government according to the often competing claims of unitary and adversary democracy." It is also worth emphasizing the obvious point that both unitary and adversary democracy are made rather than simply found, although they cannot simply be created at will or from scratch. And this means that the making of democracy is a project that is social as well as political, involving the shaping of interests as much as the designing of political institutions. This makes both easier and more difficult the challenge of "how to articulate the entire complex of unitary values with those of adversary democracy."[22] I would say that this is especially the challenge faced by a country like China that must make a virtue of the necessity of a strong central authority while trying to build a democracy of genuine substance.

Since this is an extremely tall order, one must not expect too much, especially at the beginning. For better or worse, the arrangement likely to emerge in China will definitely not conform to the priority of the right over the good that is the heart and soul of modern Western liberal democracy. What we may expect to find instead, in keeping with China's inherent need for a larger proportion of unitary democracy than is typical, will be closer to the priority of the good, as explained in Chapter 5, with the degree of priority corresponding to how strong the central authority needs to be. But this will not be anything like the standard, traditional priority of the good, in that it is meant to coexist, in dialectical tension, with extensive rights and freedoms, as well as the democratic prerogative of citizens to publicly appraise the central authority and, if necessary, hold it accountable.

Still, this arrangement may be expected to place more limits on democracy than one is accustomed to in the dominant understanding of how democracy is supposed to work. But one must not exaggerate how far it falls short—even apart from the need to avoid unrealistic expectations. Let's face it: it is true of almost every existing liberal democracy in the world that it is a combination of oligarchy and popular consent (polyarchy, as Robert Dahl calls it, meaning a democracy of sorts made possible by a plurality of mutually constraining hierarchies of power that prevents not so much political domination as monopoly of such domination);[23] that its orderly operation rests in large part on the cohesion and stability of the more or less informal oligarchic component;[24] that oligarchic cohesion and stability derives, in turn, from a seamless alliance of liberal democracy and capitalism, of a political class and a corporate elite; and that, therefore, popular political participation, while shifting the balance of power somewhat toward the demos, is confronted with a paucity of real political options.[25] It is indeed just these features that characterize what is commonly considered an "advanced" democracy.

It will be a long time, if then, before China is able to give its democracy, supposing its orderly arrival, such an "advanced" form. Until then, in the absence of the requisite informal oligarchic cohesion and stability, the imperative to hold the country together in peace and good order has to be met chiefly through a strong formal central authority.[26] And the need for such authority is made all the stronger by the exceptional scale and complexity of Chinese society, the legacy in part of that unique cultural-political entity called the Middle Kingdom, which was always, not least during the Yuan and Qing dynasties, more an empire than a state. Given the geopolitical circumstances it faces today, China already finds it an increasingly difficult challenge to keep certain separatist forces at bay, a challenge all too easy to render even more intractable by ill-considered policies. Any democratic development, however necessary for its own reasons, must rise to this additional challenge if it is to enjoy popular support; otherwise, it would run the serious risk of being rejected, all things considered, or else contributing to the partial breakup of China and dooming democracy at the same time. As things stand in China and in the world at large, the typical Western combination of political elite and plutocracy would simply not do the trick for China. There is no formula for preventing what may be called democratic disintegration other than an exceptionally strong central authority, just as there is no effective way of maintaining any such authority today except by laying it on a reasonably democratic foundation.[27] A successful democracy in China must learn to create a central authority with sustainable centripetal force and make it compatible with such publicness, representativeness, and popular consent as are fitting under equality of conditions.

It is only after the completion of this daunting task that China may grow in strength and maturity as a democracy. One may then look forward to the day when the challenges just noted will recede and perhaps cease to exist as the result of a significant further rise in power both hard and soft. Only then will China be able to afford to be a liberal democracy. Since a liberal democracy is either liberal democratic capitalism or, as yet only in theory, liberal democratic socialism, it may be possible to imagine and to try to bring about a realistic utopia of a kind of liberal democracy, coupled with a different kind of socialism, neither of which has ever been realized.[28] Should China opt for liberal democratic socialism and make a reasonable success of it, it would derive from its increased power not a new threat advantage vis-à-vis the rest of the world but the ability to present to other nations an example of a socialism that is for the first time worthy of its name. But as the reader will have realized, I am getting way beyond anything that can now be considered realistically utopian by my own standard.

China Urgently Needs Democratic Preparation

Let me return to the path of realistic utopia and address what must now be the first order of business for China's democratic progress: democratic preparation. It will have become clear from all the realistic elements of our realistic utopia that China is not yet ready for democracy—that is, for *political* democracy, for completing the passage from democratic society to democratic polity. Since the lack of readiness does not in any way reduce the urgency of the need for this passage, what China desperately needs now and for some time to come is democratic preparation.

By *democratic preparation* I do not mean, or at least do not chiefly mean, what usually goes by the name of political reform. For any political reform truly worthy of the name must amount to the initiation of political changes whose express aim is to effect a transition from the present regime to a democratic one, at least a much more democratic one. Thus understood, political reform is not exactly democratic preparation but rather the beginning of the completion of democracy. If we nevertheless want to treat political reform as part of democratic preparation because it is, after all, only the beginning of what could be a protracted process, it must come last among all the steps of democratic preparation. And it is of crucial importance that these steps are taken in the right order.

Having named the last step *political reform,* I will characterize the other steps as reforms as well. To begin with, *moral reform* is badly needed in order to overcome the rampant moral crisis in the reform era and make possible a reasonably mature citizenry and civil society, which will give China a shot at the orderly passage to political democracy. Central to this reform is the valorization of freedom as a condition for individual and societal maturity.

This broad objective can also be promoted in another, complementary way, in the shape of a *legal reform* designed to enhance individual and societal agency through stronger and more effectively protected legal rights. Moral reform and legal reform may thus be expected to work in tandem and be mutually reinforcing. Since legal reform, as conceived in a more "technical" way than is possible with moral reform, can be effective yet also politically safe, prudence may suggest giving it some tactical priority, depending on other relevant circumstances.

Another reform is badly needed as well, and that is because the current level of economic (or quantitative) inequality in China, with its divisiveness and unceasing production of resentment, is clearly inimical to any reasonably healthy democratic development. In response to this systemic inequality, China requires what may be called *social justice reform* both for its own sake and in the interest of democratic preparation. Such reform, involving but going beyond poverty reduction, cannot start soon enough if conducted with a combination of prudence and vision. It is needed all the more because it can serve the equally important purpose of preparing the CCP itself for democracy—by enhancing its popularity for the best of reasons and thereby improving its chances of a leadership role in a future democratic China. In addition, social justice is good for democracy not only for these kinds of reasons but also because the only effective way to make an exceptionally strong central authority benign, and no stronger than is strictly necessary, is to have a just and happy society that will not require the strong state to be repressive in order to keep resentment and discontent from disrupting the social order.

Thus legal, moral, and social justice reforms make up democratic preparation, only after which will political reform be able to accomplish its distinct mission and bring about political democracy as the final step of the democratization process. I will address each of these three reforms in turn, but first a few observations on the riskiness of premature political reform.

Forget Political Reform—for the Time Being

I do not think one can reasonably expect the CCP to undertake political reform right away, still less under the explicit rubric of political reform. Given the exclusively vertical structure of power through which Chinese society has always been held together and given the even greater reliance on purely political power that characterizes the modern, revolutionary version of this structure, the CCP simply cannot afford to appear weak. And, as every seasoned China observer, Chinese or foreign, knows, there is no surer way of appearing weak than by undertaking political reforms and thereby letting it be known, by unavoidable implication, that a regime lacks confidence in its moral and political high ground. In this regard, the lessons of Louis XVI and Mikhail Gorbachev have definitely been taken to heart in Beijing.[29] For the first time since Deng Xiaoping, we have a central leadership that has both fully absorbed these lessons and created for itself enough political authority, first and foremost within the CCP itself, to act on them. In the way it has secured this authority and in the high-profile uses it has made of it, the present leadership is acting not willfully but in strict accordance with the vertical logic of power that Mao and his comrades first established and that has not fundamentally changed despite the profound economic and social transformations in the reform era.

Until this logic is changed, no central leadership can be expected to act contrary to it, except by default, and, of course, the logic itself will not undergo real change unless the central leadership undertakes to make it happen. But no central leadership can easily *afford* to take such a step. For to initiate a fundamental change, and especially to be seen to be doing so, is bound to loosen the grip on the power of those undertaking it, and this at a time when such power is needed most. There is in China today not the remotest consensus, official or popular, regarding democracy, and no prospect of one. The long-standing and recently reinforced moratorium on discussion of the very topic (under the rubric not only of democracy but also of constitutionalism) is not the least cause of this confusing state of affairs, leaving everyone, including the CCP itself, largely in the dark about the real, rather than strenuously contrived, mood of the party and the country. The country's desperate objective and perhaps (for we cannot know for sure) deep subjective need for democracy is one thing, but its ability to form a unified political will to act on this need is quite another, the latter rendered almost impossible by the absence of unconstrained discussion just mentioned. In the absence of such a will and consensus, a leadership with the temerity to undertake major political form *without incontrovertible evidence of a dire necessity* might risk drawing more ire than appreciation. It could be blamed for betraying the legacy of the communist revolution in the eyes of some and for proceeding too slowly and too undemocratically in the eyes of others. It could become one of the first casualties of the process well before it was able to guide it to orderly and self-sustaining fruition.

Such dire necessity, as distinct from warning signs, does not quite exist in China today, not yet, and one would hate to see it arise before the country is in a better position to react to it. It would therefore be unrealistic to think that the present leadership is going to take even minor steps outside its familiar logic of power, especially given that it has rediscovered the way, which eluded its immediate predecessor, of acting effectively within it. Thus the moratorium on preparation for stormy political weather continues and does so as if it could last forever. For reasons I discussed earlier, however, it cannot last forever. Simply put, as long as the economic and social changes set in motion by the reform are not halted, their cumulative side effects will only deepen contradictions, in reality and in political consciousness, between a growing equality of conditions and an essentially unaltered vertical structure of power. The course of events in the foreseeable future will depend on, among other things, the legitimacy and performance of the central leadership, the shape of the economy, the state of social justice, the international political environment, and how well those countries fare that already have either a mature or a shaky democratic form of government. But the contradictions between social equality and political inequality have a momentum and causal potency of their own. Sooner or later, as long as the current economic and social dynamic is not fundamentally altered, such contradictions will grow to the breaking point or, before then, to a point where a central leadership much weaker than the present one would not be able to contain them.

China today is blessed in a way with the most authoritative and effective leadership in decades—authoritative and effective within its own vertical logic of power and by the corresponding standard. But because this leadership seems to use its authority and effectiveness to contain the contradictions rather than to find a way out of them, thereby at once ameliorating them and allowing them to accumulate and become more acute, this is a mixed blessing. It is a blessing nonetheless, for it buys time, even though the time thereby made available for what one hopes will be a learning process is, for now, being compromised by an enhanced moratorium—in the form of even more stringent restrictions on freedoms of speech (including academic speech) and of the press—on any semblance of democratic preparation.

Is there any plausible way out of this double bind?

Moral Reform as a Crucial Part of
Democratic Preparation

There can be no simple and straightforward answer. It is helpful, however, to start with an observation that could hardly be wrong—namely, that the CCP finds itself confronted with serious problems in its governing of China. These are problems the CCP itself recognizes as problems, which it has a vested interest in resolving or at least keeping from progressive deterioration. Chief among these, and of special relevance here, are rampant official corruption, willful and irresponsible use of political power, and grave shortfalls in social justice made even worse by corruption and abuse of power. For reasons already noted, however, one cannot expect the CCP to go about resolving problems such as these in ways that have the foreseeable prospect of weakening its power and hence its effectiveness. One should not therefore expect solutions in the shape of major political reform—reform that is political in substance, involving the fundamental power relations, and is presented and perceived as political.

How about *moral* reform? The need for moral reform arises from the fact that all of the problems just mentioned have their origin, at least part of their origin, in a moral crisis that has beset China in the era of reform and that the CCP itself is prepared to acknowledge and keen to resolve, both in its own right and as a root cause of other problems. The moral crisis presents a problem of a social-infrastructural kind: deeper, more basic, more pervasive, and more diffuse. While on account of these features it may be even more difficult to handle, both the pinpointing of the problem and the attempt to resolve it are less politically risky, which is not to say that no risk is involved. And I for one believe it is even more important than the question of democracy—more important in its own right and as one of the most essential preparations for democracy.

Since I have already discussed the moral crisis at length, a much briefer account will suffice here. As the reader will recall, by the moral crisis in postcommunist China I mean, first and foremost, a crisis of moral subjectivity. We can directly perceive this crisis only by observing its outward manifestations. Hence, in an earlier book, I devote a fair amount of space to the crisis of moral behavior.[30] But my main interest lies elsewhere: in the deeper, less readily observable crisis of moral subjectivity, or of the moral subject. Given its very nature, the crisis of moral subjectivity cannot be fixed simply by changing and improving behavior. Overcoming *this* moral crisis will require nothing less than the creation of favorable conditions for the birth of a new moral subject.

Because moral willingness, the disposition to act morally and to do so for what one understands as moral reasons, lies at the heart of moral subjectivity, a crisis of moral subjectivity must have its primary cause in the failure of society to produce and maintain this all-important willingness. To cut a long story short, the problem is that this moral willingness used, in prereform China, to be effectively produced in a way that has been rendered entirely useless by the reform. This is because the old reasons for acting morally, involving deference to moral authority and imitation of moral exemplars, no longer made sense once China abandoned the old collectivistic, totally organized way of life in favor of a much more individualistic one consisting largely of bourgeois pursuits. For this new way of life, whether one likes it or not, new reasons for moral behavior are needed, and, whatever these reasons may be, they must be fitting for a much more individuated kind of moral subject. Hence they must speak to the new moral subject's desire for moral initiative and leave sufficient room for such initiative. This means that the old reliance on compulsory deference and imitation must be replaced by a new respect for a moral agent's freedom as the primary perceived source of his or her moral willingness. In order for this to happen, freedom as a moral value, above and beyond mere de facto freedoms, must first be made available.

The crux of the problem is that this has not even begun to happen; the kind of freedom that is a necessary condition for the emergence of a new moral subject appropriate for today's China has not been created. Morally speaking, China today is between two worlds—one dead, the other yet to be born; the old moral subject obsolete and known to be so, a new one yet to make its urgently needed appearance in what is now a moral vacuum.

What is crucial in this causal nexus is that the necessary freedom, and hence the badly needed moral subject, has not been *allowed* to appear. This brings up a political complication of the moral crisis, especially of its possible solution. China has a distinctive political structure, one that gives sole political leadership to the CCP. So far it has been part of this dispensation that the monopoly of political leadership is treated as inseparable from a similar degree of monopoly of *moral* leadership. The latter monopoly has worked less well, as we all know by now, which is why China is saddled with a moral crisis. The frightening thought is that, as long as the political monopoly of moral leadership is not given up or at least significantly relaxed, it will prevent the rise of freedom as a moral value and this, in turn, will make impossible the birth of the desperately needed new moral subject. Thus the political complication of the moral crisis must be resolved if the moral crisis itself is to be resolved.

Is the CCP going to part with its monopoly of political leadership in the near future? Obvious not. Is it nevertheless possible for the party to maintain its hold on political power while loosening its grip on moral leadership and thereby allowing the rise of freedom as a moral value and, with it, the emergence of a new, freer, and more individuated kind of moral subject? I see no reason why the answer cannot be affirmative, in principle. But I also believe that making a positive answer come true would require political genius—that rare combination of foresight, daring, fortitude, prudence, and much else—operating under relatively favorable circumstances. For this reason, I want to be sympathetic and refrain from rushing to firm judgment about how well the present leadership is doing in a larger scheme of things yet to fully reveal itself; it has at least several more years to show what it is truly up to and capable of. At the same time, there is a place for legitimate criticism, because the moral crisis must be dealt with in one way or another, and there are shortsighted, expedient ways and relatively farsighted, durably effective ways of doing so, and Chinese citizens have every right and every responsibility to push for the latter.

While we are on the subject of the political dimension of the moral crisis, some readers may be wondering whether I have not exaggerated the seriousness of the moral crisis and its political intractability. If the moral crisis is as grave and consequential as I have made it out to be, how, you may ask, could China be doing so well on so many fronts, having already risen to become the world's second-largest economy and being poised to turn its economic prowess into global cultural and political clout? Why hasn't China suffered anything like a comprehensive breakdown despite the alleged moral crisis? Why, indeed, does it sometimes even seem, at least to some, that the moral crisis itself has been somewhat on the mend—at least in one of its forms, official corruption and its contagious effects on society at large—since the present leadership took over in 2012? The answer (aside from the difficulty of making an accurate assessment, as caused especially by the media blackout on negative aspects of the country's moral condition) is simple: it is political power that has mainly been responsible for these achievements, such as they are, and its stock in trade, not least in Xi Jinping's anticorruption campaign, is not so much credible moral exhortation as the effective projection of fear.[31] Not ordinary political power, to be sure, but *excessive* political power, as it has to be. For in the absence of reasonably well-formed moral subjects capable of acting with relative independence from political power, in the absence of a strong civil society, and hence in the absence of the power of civil society as a source of moral socialization and of cohesion, only political power can do the trick. And, to be effective, political power has to be excessive— excessive to the degree that moral subjectivity, civil society, and social power are lacking. If we look at the matter in this way, we can no longer simply blame political power for being excessive. We should rather criticize the conditions under which political power has no choice but to be excessive in order to be effective. And we can also criticize those factors, including agents and institutions, responsible for creating such conditions in the first place or for keeping such conditions alive beyond necessity. But such critique, necessary as it undoubtedly is, is a much more complicated affair.

Leaving this deeper, more complicated critique aside, the basic fact to bear in mind is that, as things stand, China can be held together, can be made to tick, only through a heavy reliance on political power, and hence only by a political power strong enough to support this heavy reliance. For this reason alone, and in the short run, the exceptionally strong leadership of Xi is at least partially good news for China. Chinese society was undergoing a profound transformation under Jiang Zemin, who led post-1989 China (especially after Deng's death) until 2002. Jiang obviously had other things on his mind than the elementary moral health of China, or of the CCP for that matter, and he used political power accordingly, leaving an ambiguous legacy of political liberalization and moral anarchy in almost equal measure. As Jiang's successor, Hu Jintao presided over a period of ten years when central political leadership (as distinct from state capacity) was at its weakest in the entire history of Chinese communist rule. It would not be inaccurate to say that for the better part of that decade the central leadership was neither loved nor feared, even by the party's own standard. It is only natural that, despite the less dramatic character of economic and social transformation compared with the previous ten years, the moral crisis spun out of control in a way that few could foresee, notwithstanding the gradual return of conspicuous political repression in the later phase of Hu's rule. Xi's current leadership is definitely more feared, including within the ranks of the party itself, and, among a large part of the population, it seems to be more loved. Political power is working with a level of authority (and repressiveness) we have not seen for a long time. The present leadership seems to mean business, and it has put an impressive amount of business on its agenda. There is no doubt about the success of some of its efforts so far, especially where authority and determination, as distinct from vision or humility, may be expected to make a big difference. The campaign against official corruption is a case in point, although much remains to be done and no one knows whether, and how, the daunting remainder will be done.

This is reason enough to breathe a sigh of relief, but it is also a cause for concern, even apart from the cost in increased political repression as such. For it is clear that such success (if one happens to support the ends) as the present leadership has achieved is due almost entirely to the effective use of political power. The result is that while the crisis of moral behavior may have abated in some respects, the crisis of moral subjectivity remains as acute as ever. Whatever improvement in moral behavior we have seen in the past few years is the result of more effective political leadership, rather than of the coming into being of a new moral subject. But my concern here goes beyond the moral crisis as *moral* crisis. It extends, via the effect of political power on the moral crisis, to the consequences of an intractable moral crisis for China's political development—an interaction with the distinct potential to create a vicious circle that draws us ever closer to a more comprehensive crisis. It is the latter concern I want now to foreground.

Because China is held together almost by political power alone, whatever weakens political power will cause problems that are bound to profoundly affect Chinese society on every level, including the moral. A breakdown in political power will mean the breakdown of the entire society.[32] I do not think this is quite true of societies in general. Even if we grant, for the sake of argument, that this is a matter of degree, I would still maintain this is true of China to an extraordinary degree. China today is arguably closer than it has ever been, in its relatively brief modern experience, to Ferdinand Tönnies's definition of *Gesellschaft*—that is, a society (as distinct from a community) in which people are "essentially detached" and "remain separate in spite of everything that unites them"[33]—except, it is important to add, that it has precious little to unite them, in the first place, but political power. This will continue to be the case until Chinese society is cemented by reasonably well-formed moral subjects who can muster enough agency to play a more or less independent part in holding society together. When that happens, Chinese society will be able to depend for its stability and vitality on two forms of power instead of one, with a healthy measure of independence from the vicissitudes of political power.

It is only then that China will be able to afford to take major steps toward democracy, as it will need to do in the foreseeable future. Alexis de Tocqueville is largely correct, in my view, that democracy is marked, above all, by an equality of conditions that prevails in the social state. In such a social state, people are, ideally speaking, not only equal but also free. I would only add that it is only as reasonably well-formed moral subjects that members of a society can be free and equal. Otherwise they would need a vastly superior political force to hold them together as a society and give them the semblance of a moral life, in which case they would be neither free nor equal, not even approximately. In this light (I am not exactly invoking the social contract), democracy is a truly dangerous experiment with the normative ordering of collective human life, for it is, in the limit case, about horizontally, hence only loosely, connected individuals voluntarily coming together to form a cohesive society and a durable political order, and there is no guarantee that they can bring this off. Failure in such an experiment invites the most excessive of excessive political power, which is why what Tocqueville calls despotism (of a distinctively modern kind) is always only one step away from democracy.[34] It is also why a society made up of reasonably well-formed moral subjects is so essential for democracy, with democracy, in turn, capable of strengthening civil society in a virtuous circle. A society made up of reasonably well-formed moral subjects has at least a decent chance of succeeding in the experiment, always an ongoing experiment, with democracy.

So, to be perfectly honest, I do not think China is remotely ready yet for *political* democracy, for taking the last step to formally complete the democratizing process. This will remain the case until a way is found of creating reasonably well-formed moral subjects capable of bringing a significant measure of stability and cohesion to society independently of political power. And yet, as I have suggested, in another sense China is already ripe for democracy—nay, it is already a substantially democratic society—in that it is already characterized, to a substantial and ever-increasing degree, by equality of conditions.

This, then, is our current situation. Thanks to the equality of conditions that has arisen as a result of the quasi-democratic leveling under Mao and the quasi-liberal neutralization in the era of reform, China has within its present social circumstances a natural momentum toward political democracy. Yet, because of its crisis of moral subjectivity, China cannot afford to let this momentum run its natural course and must instead hold it back; in comparison with this, the existence of vested interests standing in the way of democracy represents a lesser menace, in that overcoming them would be a more localized operation. This creates an internal contradiction—between the systemic necessity of democracy and the equally systemic inability to make it work. And it is a contradiction that cannot be resolved but only contained—through economic growth, through improvements in governance and in social justice, or by intensifying identification with rising national power, and so on. Each of these measures is a tall order, and there is no guarantee that these ways of containing the contradiction will always be available or effective. Indeed, if truth be told, even the sustained accomplishment of all these feats would not be able to halt the quickening steps of democracy as the political capital of the communist revolution dwindles inexorably with each passing year.

In this context, I would venture to suggest that the most desirable change that could happen to China, and hence the greatest service the CCP could perform for it, is for the CCP to begin to create favorable conditions for the emergence of a new moral subject and an autonomous civil society. It is worth noting that in this regard China no longer belongs to the category of "totalitarian societies of bureaucratic socialism," of which Jürgen Habermas observes that "here a panoptic state not only directly controls the bureaucratically desiccated public sphere, it also undermines the private basis of this public sphere," with the result that "communicative rationality is . . . destroyed *simultaneously* in both public and private contexts of communication."[35] Thanks to its plentiful de facto individual freedoms, China already has a more or less integral private sphere, which Habermas rightly sees as tightly connected to an autonomous civil society. In the Chinese private sphere today, communicative rationality is no longer severely limited, let alone destroyed. What has yet to happen is for the de facto freedoms to be valorized and protected by law and for an autonomous civil society to be allowed to rise on the basis of an already existing integral private sphere. Once this occurs, once the new moral subject and an autonomous civil society are formed, political power's impact on society in general and on its moral ecology in particular will weaken. Political power will still be of foremost importance, perhaps necessarily so in a country as big and complex as China, but its stakes will no longer be so unbearably high that major political change, especially democratic change, becomes almost unthinkable. Precisely when political power becomes less powerful or less excessive, it will be more powerful or dynamic in another way. It will have more room for maneuver, for change, for deliberation, for popular involvement, even for intense contestation, without threatening to unleash chaos on society, including on its moral life. Only in this way can China come to afford politics for the first time, for political change, however sweeping, and political contestation, however intense, will be taking place in a setting where it can be expected that a healthy measure of stability and cohesion is independently provided by reasonably well-formed moral subjects sustained by a reasonably autonomous civil society.

Legal Reform and Its Positive Political and Moral Consequences

To argue that moral reform is essential is not to suggest that such reform is in the offing. It is only to show that it would make both normative and prudential sense for the CCP to undertake it, with whatever level of risk involved outweighed by the risk of doing nothing. After all, while the breakdown of moral order is all too visible, the crisis of moral subjectivity underlying it requires for its correct diagnosis and proper response a way of approaching moral matters—with freedom and maturity (moral adulthood) at the center of it all—that is rather foreign to the CCP's entrenched paternalistic and propagandist instincts. Such instincts, along with the practices they spawn, will have to change before the party has any chance of seeing the moral crisis for what it is and developing an adequate sense of crisis in response to it. That progress in this regard does not have insurmountable prudential obstacles in its way can give us no more than modest hope that it will actually happen. But one could not try hard enough or often enough to show that moral reform is essential *and* can in principle be pulled off with benefit rather than damage to the CCP.

I rather doubt, however, that the *near future* will see anything like moral reform in its own right, a moral reform of the requisite kind and one that is conceived and conducted as such. But it is just possible that moral reform may happen as a by-product, intended or not, of another undertaking. Because that other effort has to do with the law, with the line between political and legal power, I shall dub it legal reform, although this is not how it is officially designated. Much as in the case of economic power, even as legal power becomes more independent, if and when it does, it will remain under the overarching control of the CCP. But a functional separation, accompanied by clear recognition and institutionalization of the distinct nature and operation of legal power and further supported by a corresponding professional ethos, could go a long way toward reducing the sheer presence of political power *as* political power and thereby reducing its negative effects, including on the moral crisis and its potential solution. Here again, however, one would be well advised to limit oneself, for the most part, to spelling out the inner logic of a certain possibility rather than speculating about the sheer empirical likelihood of its coming true. To show that something is necessary, beneficial, doable, and without undue risk is as far as an intellectual contribution to such matters can go in its effort to be realistic (as part of a realistic utopia).

It is revealing, and perhaps moderately encouraging, in this connection, that the CCP is placing unprecedented emphasis on the role of law in improving governance of the country, including in its fight against official corruption and the abuse of power. This is a matter not of the replacement of bad laws *(erfa)* with good ones *(shanfa),* nor even of the more effective implementation of good laws, although both are important, but of governing the country in a different, more transparently rule-based way. The new way, amounting to nothing less than a basic orientation and blueprint *(jiben fanglüe),* was inaugurated at the CCP's eighteenth national congress in 2012 and finds its most authoritative and detailed expression in a set of guidelines and measures adopted at its fourth plenum in 2014 to "govern the country in accordance with the law" *(yifa zhiguo).*[36] Whether, strictly speaking, this is rule of law or rule by law, one charitable reading is that the enhanced role of law is meant in one way or another to counter the willfulness *(renxing,* as the once red-hot term has it) of political power.[37] Even if the target is such willfulness on the part of local and central-government officials at levels well below the apex of power, the experiment with pitting the law against the willfulness of political power is of the utmost importance. It is still too early to say how effective it is likely to be, other than that it would be more likely to succeed if it could be conducted without posing any serious challenge to the leadership of the CCP, including its leadership over the law. Thus the experiment has limits placed on it from the outset.

Even so, the experiment could have extremely far-reaching consequences if it could lead, as it is meant to do in its openly stated rationale, to a systemically reduced reliance on the largely unhampered will of political power as distinct from the authority of the law. Should this come to pass, it may bring with it, whether by way of intended or unintended consequences, a *gradual* but profound change in political culture and in the scope of societal initiative and independence, however constricted the scope may be at the beginning or at any other point in time. Once the law sets publicly known parameters for the exercise of political power (in principle at all levels but in likely reality at all but the highest level), everyday life in society will be able to unfold with a different kind of freedom—beyond the de facto freedoms that now may exist in abundance and yet are always highly vulnerable to the willfulness of political power. When the arbitrary will of political power recedes from the routines of everyday life, even with the top leadership retaining its political prerogatives above the law, it will be possible for ordinary members of society under ordinary circumstances to exercise their agency under the relatively reliable protection of the law. Over time, as may reasonably be expected, they will evolve into agents or subjects more accustomed to initiative and discretion and more jealously protective themselves of the legally demarcated space that makes such initiative and discretion possible.

Moreover, any real improvement of transparency in the creation and implementation of laws will be part of the progress in the broader publicness of public matters. In law as in any other public matter, publicness is conducive *over time* (regardless of how good or how bad things are at the start, or at present) to rational justification on the part of officials and the production of rational motives on the part of the public. This means also that, with regard to the actual scope of societal initiative and independence permitted by law, even if the scope is relatively narrow at the start (or even narrower than before), one has reason to count on the great cumulatively transformative power of transparency and publicness to expand that scope over time. This is regardless of the short-term intention of those who set the legal reform in motion. The only thing that matters is whether the reform brings a real increase in the transparency of the entire legal process and, more generally, in the publicness of public matters.

If and when such an increase occurs, the problems noted earlier as requiring urgent action by the CCP will be much more amenable to resolution than they are now. To begin with, the law, with its newfound transparency and gradually improved rationality, in addition to actual ordinances becoming better as well as better implemented (over time), will stand more effectively and reliably as a barrier against the willfulness of political power that has been such a big cause of so many of China's social and political problems. But even more crucially, the positive socializing impact of the law's being just, respected, and followed and of the incremental change in political culture will help produce better-formed citizens. It is ultimately from such citizens that all officials, including top officials, will be recruited, and so one may expect a corresponding improvement in the integrity and performance of officials—the more so under the watchful eye of citizens more aware of what they have the right to expect. By this point a virtuous circle will have been formed.

I need not go further with this line of thought, as I do not mean to speculate on the future but only to suggest a plausible scenario that might get China out of the double bind in which it now appears to be trapped. With this scenario, I intend to bring out the following considerations. First, it is one thing to openly and directly prepare for democracy right away, which is implausible for reasons already noted, and something else altogether for the CCP to deal with urgent problems that it both recognizes and has the incentive to resolve. Second, and this is not a negligible fact, among the measures adopted by the CCP for dealing with these problems is an increased role of law, along with a conception that unequivocally pits respect for the law against the willfulness of political power. Third, such a measure, if successful, will have the far-reaching consequence, whether intended or not, of creating favorable conditions for a new, more public, and more rational political culture; a society more independent of political power; and a new, freer kind of citizen more capable of exercising initiative in society. Fourth, and just as important, all of this could happen—and this is why it could conceivably be allowed to happen—without having in principle to pose an unmanageable challenge to the political leadership of the CCP. These considerations add up to the distinct possibility of a virtuous circle.

Some such virtuous circle need not entail or require the rule of law in the modern Western sense. In any case, it is far from clear what the rule of law in the Western sense actually is, or ought to be. Is it the rule of law based on private law as advocated by Friedrich von Hayek, a bulwark not only against despotism and the police state (in the manner of *Rechtsstaat*)[38] but also against a social democratic state interfering with a supposedly spontaneous market order?[39] Or is it the rule of law informed by communicative rationality as proposed by Habermas, making the rule of law almost synonymous with democracy and democracy itself synonymous with unhampered and undistorted communicative action regarding public matters?[40] The former, very much alive in the theory and practice of neoliberalism today, is antidemocratic. The latter, boasting impeccable democratic credentials, is largely utopian even in the most advanced Western societies, and I daresay it shall remain so at least for the foreseeable future. Then there are an indefinite number of possibilities between these poles.

The very complexity of this picture ought to give us pause and serve as a warning against dogmatism. Just as I have argued for an open and flexible understanding of what democracy requires, so I shall do the same with the rule of law. And one of the considerations that defines democracy ought to be treated as central to the rule of law as well: publicness. We know that the CCP is not going, anytime soon, to give up its prerogative when it comes to deciding what the content of the law should be. Whether this is a case of the CCP being "above the law" in an unarguably bad sense depends on whether the law determined in this way possesses a credibly public character, being equally in the interest of all in its intent and impartial in its implementation. After all, the modern rule of law and indeed the modern state itself—both manifestly bourgeois institutions—have their fundamental rationale in the establishment and protection of the equal rights of all, such that departures from this rationale invite contestation, including ideology critique of the (bourgeois) rule of law itself. It is undeniable that the CCP's very prerogative with regard to the law makes it vulnerable to such contestation, to the charge of being above the law in the unarguably bad sense of acting to one degree or another as a private monopoly (to use Elias's term). And there can be no doubt that this charge is validated by the sheer gravity and scale of *official* corruption. Thus, as long as the CCP maintains its double-edged prerogative, it must bend over backward to avoid using it, and being seen to use it, in the interest of a private monopoly masquerading as a public one. China will have achieved the rule of law in a credible sense when the link between this prerogative (being above the law in an arguably formal, neutral sense) and the tendency toward private monopoly (being above the law in an unarguably bad sense) is cut and seen to be cut, and when publicness has become the generally acknowledged character of the law in its intent and execution. It will be a daunting challenge to bring this feat off, to put it mildly, but as it wages its unprecedented campaign against official corruption, the CCP deserves more benefit of the doubt than it usually receives. We will know it has succeeded if and when it proves able to create the virtuous circle mentioned earlier. Only through such success will it also be able to convince critics and skeptics that *yifa zhiguo* (governing the country in accordance with the law) is not merely a strategy for strengthening *dangde lingdao* (leadership of the party), with *renmin dangjia zuozhu* (the people as masters of the country) thrown in for propagandist effect.[41]

In this light, the worst obstacle to the rule of law in practice is the corruption of the legal system, especially of the courts. As long as the CCP is able to make and keep the legal system clean, it will rid the latter of the worst kind of political interference that has plagued the system in recent decades. After all, the vast majority of cases handled by the courts are not themselves political matters, and the constitutional principle that places the law under the CCP's leadership does not in and of itself require or warrant political interference in such cases. It does not therefore seem implausible to suggest that once corruption is largely cleansed from the legal system, the strength of the claim that the party is above the law will be weakened in the eyes of ordinary, law-abiding citizens going about their everyday lives. What remains objectionable will then be confined more or less to a subset of cases that are politically sensitive in one way or another. The important point is that it may not be necessary to wait for significant progress in this subset of especially challenging cases in order to reap major benefits of legal reform. Some recent developments, such as the exclusion of coerced testimony and the significantly expanded role of people's assessors in the trial process (the Chinese near equivalent of the jury system), are cases in point. As far as democratic preparation is concerned, success in rendering more plausible and visible the publicness of the law in its intent and execution—by improving the quality of laws, ensuring their corruption-free implementation, raising respect for the law as the embodiment of the equal rights of all citizens, and so on—will be enough to land China in a virtuous circle. In this regard, what is most to be feared is not the CCP's leadership of the law but the ineffectiveness of such leadership—that is, its inability to rid the law of the corruption that damages the party and the country alike.

Suppose a virtuous circle does materialize, perhaps even with a moral reform added thereafter. What then? Will the CCP have unwittingly prepared for full-fledged democracy in China and, in so doing, paved the way for its own exit from the political stage? No, by no means. In this scenario, we know that the CCP will have brought into being an improved China, one whose society is more independent of the state and more truly stable, whose citizens are freer and more self-reliant, and hence a society that would be better able to handle the move to a more democratic form of government. One should hasten to add that the party will have done all of this not by way of indulging in a normative fantasy but under the very real pressure of having to resolve social and political problems in order precisely to maintain its legitimacy and ensure its survival. Balanced against the increased momentum toward democracy as a result of these developments, then, will be the party's enhanced legitimacy. There is no telling exactly what this new balance of factors will be like and how it will evolve. But it is entirely possible that in guiding China to this more benign point in its political evolution, the CCP will have accumulated an unprecedented (in its own history) amount of positive experience in working with a stronger society and a more mature citizenry. Thus it will have learned how to govern effectively and maintain its legitimacy in a progressively more democratic setting and will itself have become more democratic in its own principles, spirit, and mode of operation. And it may even have developed a way of reconciling the overwhelming imperative to hold Chinese society together in peace and prosperity with the irresistible necessity of adopting a form of government that accords with the irreversible equality of conditions. If so, it will have made good for the first time its long-professed belief in "democratic centralism," along with all the other undeniably genuine democratic aspirations it had cherished and fought for until not long after its conquest of power in 1949.[42] It may even be able to convince a sizable portion of a more mature and more responsible citizenry that "democratic centralism"—a genuinely *democratic* centralism—is the form of democracy likely to work best for China.

Moral and Legal Reforms Converge on Enhancing Freedom

It will have become obvious that what I have called moral reform and legal reform have one important aim and, if successful, one important outcome in common, and that is substantially enhanced freedom—whether achieved via more independent moral agency or better-protected legal rights. It is absolutely essential for the success of these reforms—indeed even for getting them off the ground—that the freedom expected to grow out of them be so understood and exercised as not to immediately challenge and be seen to challenge the leadership of the CCP. When I earlier expressed caution regarding the empirical likelihood of moral reform, I did so partly with this worry in mind. It so happens that there is a way to allay this worry, thereby reducing, in principle, the political risk of moral reform, and of legal reform as well, and increasing the likelihood of their being taken up, other things being equal. The key, I would suggest, lies in distinguishing between the use of freedom as a condition for individual and societal maturity, on the one hand, and its use for political purposes, on the other, and, on this basis, in going about moral and legal reforms without the immediate aim of creating political liberty.

I noted earlier that the road leading from equality of conditions to political democracy in China is likely to be a lot more tortuous than Tocqueville found to be the case in America. While equality of conditions is undoubtedly already strongly present in China, another essential condition for democracy is as yet largely missing, a condition that Tocqueville understandably did not write about, presumably because it could be taken for granted in the context of America. The condition I have in mind is individual and societal maturity, a condition that naturally comes to the fore when the prior condition—that is, equality of conditions—is already largely established. Taken together, these two conditions are so much a part of the very meaning of democracy that they may be considered democracy's *metaconditions*. The second of these conditions, individual and societal maturity, deserves a careful look.

Equality of conditions is a matter of degree, and what is most important in determining its degree is how much freedom is present in a particular instance of equality of conditions. Here again Tocqueville is instructive, although he does not directly talk about the maturity for which freedom serves as a necessary condition. Operating at the level of what Max Weber was later to call ideal types, Tocqueville wrote that "men will be completely free because they will be entirely equal; they will all be completely equal because they will be entirely free" and that therefore "democratic nations aim for this ideal."[43] There is thus a sense in which equality of conditions is not complete until freedom is fully realized and equally enjoyed. Imagine a situation in which the ends and goods of human life are so conceived and society so constituted that it no longer makes sense to consider any subset of human beings fundamentally superior to the rest and yet in which it is nevertheless the case that people are prevented from becoming fully free by a political regime rooted in an earlier, less equal state of society and hence from being fully equal. Such a situation is what we find in China today, and we can say this situation is marked by an equality of conditions that is not allowed to run its natural course because it is not permitted to be completed by a corresponding measure of freedom.

I am *not* talking here about political liberty, which is part and parcel of political democracy. The precise sense in which freedom is to be understood in the present context is best captured in terms of what Immanuel Kant thinks of as a certain intellectual and moral maturity, as already briefly described. Taking some liberties for my own purposes with Kant's classic text on the meaning of enlightenment, and thus letting my case stand or fall entirely on its own merit, I would say that such maturity is the condition for the completion of equality of conditions *short of political democracy*. Exercise independence of thought, seek such freedom as is necessary for the public use of reason, and thereby give up self-imposed immaturity, Kant enjoins, but do so in such a way as is fully compatible with political obedience and hence public order. The realization of freedom thus conceived and justified depends on political power being able to say, with a ruler like Frederick II who "has at hand a well-disciplined and numerous army to guarantee public security," *"Argue as much as you like and about whatever you like, but obey!"* If the people too are prepared to fulfill their part of the bargain, drawing a clear line between the public and private uses of reason and keeping the public use of reason (for the time being, as Kant hints at) from spilling over into political action, they will have shown, to use Kant's words, "how freedom may exist without in the least jeopardizing public concord and the unity of the commonwealth."[44] They will have shown that they can usefully avail themselves of freedom for the sake of maturity without necessarily demanding democracy.[45]

The context in which Kant thus reflected on the meaning of enlightenment is different from ours, and Kant's reasons for not taking the leap from freedom for the sake of maturity to freedom in the sense of political liberty, with their intriguing ambiguity and openness, are not necessarily of a kind one need endorse in the abstract.[46] And, of course, no one is so naïve as to mistake today's China for the Prussia of Kant's time. But I see no reason why we cannot draw valuable lessons from Kant's line of thinking, and I find nothing in the circumstances of China that would render such lessons inapplicable.

By drawing on Kant's reasoning, admittedly with some license, I believe we will be able to identify *a locus of freedom short of democracy* and hence a place where it is possible to make a case for freedom as a condition for maturity, as Kant does in his own scheme of things. On this basis we can then take a step beyond Kant and construct an argument for freedom, along with the maturity it makes possible, as an essential second condition for democracy standing next to the first one, equality of conditions. To appreciate and preserve the usefulness of this argument, it is absolutely essential to understand it as distinct from an argument for democracy itself. It is independently important to create this condition for democracy given equality of conditions, whether or not it is desirable, all things considered, to make an immediate and comprehensive move from the readiness of conditions for democracy to democracy itself.

Before proceeding further with this argument, I should hasten to preempt a potential misunderstanding and distraction. By *intellectual and moral maturity* I do not mean a high level of achievement but—in a somewhat Kantian, regulative sense—only what it takes to be a cognitive and moral subject to the normal or minimal degree that is expected of a properly socialized modern individual. Basic as it is, such maturity deserves its name in a distinctive and important sense. It requires freedoms commensurate with the responsibilities that modern individuals typically have to assume, and thus it requires extensive freedoms, roughly speaking what Benjamin Constant calls liberties of the moderns. Although one has no reason to expect the exercise of such freedoms and the discharge of such responsibilities to be occasions for the cultivation and display of excellences or great virtues, one may count on them over time to produce citizens who have what it takes to make democracy minimally workable. And it is for this reason that I treat intellectual and moral maturity as an essential condition of democracy.

What is of inestimable value is that once this essential condition of democracy is available, along with equality of conditions, democracy becomes a live option that no longer undermines its own normative appeal with a lack of political prudence. For once individual members of a society have become mature agents, cognitively and morally, the society constituted by them will likewise become mature through their use of public reason in thinking and acting together (in nonpolitical ways, at least initially). And it will come to be stable, independently stable as a society as distinct from a political entity, to the degree that it is mature. Once maturity is achieved through freedom and its exercise in society, then, people will be able to take care of themselves without tutelage either as individuals or as society. Thus, whatever else it may be and whatever other purposes it may serve, the kind of maturity Kant so eloquently pleads for is an essential condition for civil society, a society capable of supporting itself as society. It is only as mature individuals and members of society that people will have a reasonably good chance of making a success of democracy, at least to the extent of rendering democracy—with its absence of absolute or near-absolute power as a guarantee of stability—compatible with public order. Only then will a society be ready for democracy, after the latter is rendered fitting and necessary by equality of conditions. Individual and societal maturity as made possible by liberty in the exercise of public reason may thus be said to serve as the pivot of democracy, linking equality of conditions and a political regime best befitting it, and supporting a country's orderly movement from the one to the other.

Thus I believe that the crucial place where the case, both prudential and moral, can be most compellingly and consequentially made for democracy, at least in China, is one step away from democracy. It directly concerns not democracy itself but the second of its essential conditions—that is, intellectual and moral maturity. I say this not because the first essential condition for democracy, equality of conditions, is less important but because this condition, which is also a condition for the very need for and entitlement to maturity, is one that presents itself to members of modern societies as already more or less a fact of life that is neither possible nor, on the whole, desirable to change. Under the relative equality of conditions that surrounds us, then, once the case for maturity is made, and once it is put into practice, I believe the rest can be allowed to run its natural course through the gradual expansion of the public use of reason to include the public *political* use of reason[47] and through the employment of the latter in response to the circumstances of a society. At least this much will have been accomplished: freedom, as an even more important good than democracy under modern conditions of life, is provided for, and the individual and societal maturity made possible by freedom will, in turn, put a society within reach of adopting democracy in a way compatible with social stability. Should such freedom turn out to be fragile without political rights as its best guarantee, the case for democracy would only become stronger. And this too would be part of the natural course that a free society would run under the actual circumstances in which it finds itself.

Given equality of conditions, then, the first order of business in getting a society ready for democracy is to create conditions for individual and societal maturity, and chief among such conditions is an extensive set of freedoms—needless to say, not merely de facto freedoms but publicly valorized ones. The problem is that these freedoms can easily be exercised in such a way as to pose a serious threat to a regime that has yet to become democratic, as is the case in China today. Predictably, the regime will not allow such freedoms in anticipation of their subversive uses or, having allowed some of them by design or default, will withdraw them in response to such uses. As a result, an emergent equality of conditions, even if well under way and irreversible, is not allowed to be complemented by the introduction of freedoms necessary for intellectual and moral maturity. A society is thus trapped in a situation in which an advancing equality of conditions makes democracy increasingly fitting and necessary and yet the regime understandably cannot afford to facilitate the growth of maturity that is indispensable for the orderly establishment of democracy.

China today finds itself exactly in this trap, and it badly needs to find a way out of it. It is in this context that Kant provides an extremely valuable clue for a way out when he shows how freedom in the public use of reason can be made compatible with public order. From this clue it is only a short step to entertaining the possibility that freedom as a condition for maturity can be established independently of and before freedom in the sense of political liberty. And thus we can plausibly imagine meeting the two metaconditions for democracy—equality of conditions and individual and societal maturity—without the immediate replacement of the regime presiding over the achievement of such conditions by a fully democratic one.

There is no reason why the present Chinese leadership, the strongest in more than two decades and almost impossible to duplicate in the future, cannot in principle undertake, gradually and prudently, the kind of reforms a ruler like Frederick the Great was able to carry through—with regard, say, to censorship, freedom of expression, and religious tolerance.[48] It will be motivated to do so only if it is fully cognizant of the drastic worsening of the legitimation crisis that looms in the foreseeable future and, on this basis, makes the historic decision to choose a broadly democratic solution as the only one consistent with China's already irreversible equality of conditions. But this is not enough. For the citizenry, especially the politically active, must be prepared to abide by their part of the Kantian compromise, as it were. This means drawing a reasonably clear line between freedom as a condition for maturity and freedom in the sense of full-fledged political liberty and, over an extended period of time, carefully (even obediently, as Kant says) refraining from the political, especially subversive, use of freedom.

Under China's special circumstances, some such compromise is what it takes to make substantial yet prudent progress toward democracy: given the strong equality of conditions already present and irreversible in China, it is in the rational interest of all Chinese, including the CCP no less than those most eager to replace it with a democratic regime, to promote individual and societal maturity and, to this end, to support the prudent and gradual enlargement of freedoms short of political liberty and democracy. For a long time the CCP has governed China according to a logic that makes it imperative to keep freedoms at bay and keep the vast majority of Chinese from achieving the maturity they need and deserve under an increasing equality of conditions. It cannot go on doing so indefinitely, because the unstoppable progress in equality of conditions will make the country less and less governable as it renders any regime other than one based on popular consent less and less fitting. China's greatest danger is the persistence of a systemic lack of individual and societal maturity if and when democracy comes insistently knocking on the door and catches the country with no time left and no strong central leadership available to prepare the citizenry for its orderly arrival. The time for such preparation is now, and the leadership strong enough to undertake it is the present one. But it is a delicate task that requires steady and deft hands not only from the CCP but also from the populace, not least the politically active intellectuals.

While it would be too much to expect anything remotely like a smooth and well-coordinated execution even in the best of scenarios, it is not irrational to hope that the most enlightened and powerful within the CCP leadership and the most enlightened and influential among the public will learn to exercise the comprehensive political virtue that Weber aptly calls the ethic of responsibility. Unless they do so, and soon, China may well be doomed to the miserable choice between a barely governable authoritarian state and a chaotic democratic one, if not worse.

How the CCP Can Prepare Itself and the Country for Democracy through Social Justice Reform

This is an eventuality the CCP has a rational interest in preventing for its own sake and on behalf of China at large—provided, of course, that it develops a clear vision of the danger lurking just beyond the horizon. Few in China would stand to benefit from either scenario. But this is only about disaster prevention, and there is no telling whether a successful strategy to this end will, beyond averting the worst, also leave the party with a positive future in a democratic China. I believe that there could be such a future and, even more importantly, that this very possibility, if properly appreciated and explored by the CCP, would stand China in good stead like nothing else in its democratic development in the crucial ten to twenty years to come.

The potential for this positive future lies in the CCP demonstrating its willingness and ability to accomplish two things at the same time. The first is to prepare the citizenry for democracy through moral and legal reforms aimed at the gradual and prudent expansion of freedoms as a condition for individual and societal maturity. The second, dependent on the first and, in turn, supporting it, is to massively improve social justice—none other than what Karl Polanyi calls the self-protection of society—so that all members of Chinese society will more equitably benefit from economic and social development than they have done so far in the reform era.[49] It is difficult to believe that success on these two fronts combined would not give the CCP a positive role, even a sustained leading role, in a future democratic China, given also its unique mastery of the formidable art of governing a country as large and complicated as China. Having already spelled out what the first task involves, I will now address the second.

It is a commonplace that, as a result of the economic reform in the past four decades, China has become an oddly hybrid society, with an economy, now the world's second largest, well integrated into the global capitalist order yet led by a political party that is still calling itself communist and shows no sign of wanting to part with its ostensible socialist credentials. If one is not dogmatic about it, there is little doubt that the dynamic and ethos that make China tick today—the do's, as it were, as distinct from the don'ts, which boil down to *not* undermining the rule of the CCP—are informed by essentially capitalist values and goals. This is especially the case with Chinese *society* insofar as it is distinct from the political state. But even the political state, and this means the party above all, is happily operating in a global capitalist order whose core logic and orientation, as distinct from the current balance of power and pecking order, it has shown little desire to resist or challenge. At the same time, the CCP has reformed China's domestic economy, and will continue to do so, with a view to maximizing its competitiveness in just such a capitalist order. It goes without saying that the CCP has another agenda distinct from and even more important than success in its capitalist endeavors. It is determined to maintain its exclusive hold on state power, and therefore it unsurprisingly adapts the structure and operation of China's economy to this supreme end, with the predictable result that China's economy and society are not capitalist in the same way Western or Western-style liberal democratic capitalist systems are. Hence, for example, the formal distinction between the economic and political domains cannot be drawn as strictly as under democratic capitalism, and the state-owned enterprises, for all their problems, will continue to play an indispensable role in the overall political economy.

So we are talking about a hybrid China, and the CCP responsible for creating it could not be any less hybrid. It would be an understatement to say that it will not be easy for the party as we now find it to make truly significant progress in social justice (beyond poverty reduction)—a goal associated with social democracy rather than communism—and to live up to its putative socialist credentials. What are its socialist credentials anyway, other than its organizational continuity with Mao's CCP?[50] Is there indeed still a communist party to speak of, given the inextricable links of the higher levels of its personnel and their relatives to the most powerful domestic capital and capitalists, and given the way it has been treating working people in terms of welfare provision, factor income distribution, and protection against the worst ravages of capitalist exploitation? The CCP of today is not the CCP of old, but if it is to have a future as a party with up-to-date socialist credentials, it must find a way to promote social justice in a largely capitalist domestic economy embedded in a global capitalist order still under the sway of neoliberalism.

It is worth noting that social justice is not only a matter of poverty reduction, social welfare, factor income distribution, the prevention of extreme concentration of wealth, and the like but also a moral imperative stemming from the supposedly public character of the state, particularly of a state that considers itself socialist, as China does. Indeed, the latter, moral aspect of social justice is more basic than the former, policy aspect and is what informs and warrants it. It is in my view the lack of this animating moral impulse and its institutional embodiment that presents by far the deeper and more daunting challenge to the CCP with respect to social justice reform. For, given its track record in recent decades and its current practices, it is difficult not to view the Chinese party-state as, in no small part, a massive apparatus for *private* appropriation. The principal basis for this view is not only, indeed not even chiefly, systemic official corruption but also the perfectly legal entitlements enjoyed by officialdom, especially at the higher levels, and a corresponding, irrepressible sense of entitlement. Many of the privileges—with respect to such things as housing, medical care, and transportation—benefit the officials' immediate families as well, while the arrogance born of a culturally ingrained sense of privilege unfailingly rubs off on the offspring of officials high and low. It remains true today, for all the positive effects of the antigraft campaign and of the reintroduction of the so-called mass line (that is, better communication with and service for ordinary people), that higher officialdom, inclusive of immediate family and offspring, lives as a species apart. Unsurprisingly, politically based and hence highly conspicuous privileges are increasingly being converted into advantages associated with wealth and, in the latter form, better hidden from scrutiny. Just consider how many of the sons and daughters of the higher officials have, quietly and with freedom from public oversight, enriched themselves in financial and other highly profitable sectors or at least as highly paid employees of domestic or global capital.

Whether or not the party-state under Mao also worked in this way, at least partly, is debatable, but there can be no doubt that private appropriation was severely constrained by scarcity and especially by the abolition of private ownership of the means of production. Now that private property rights have been reestablished, the operation of the party-state as partly an apparatus of private appropriation takes on dramatically new dimensions and a new meaning. This is what political grievances against one-party rule, the moral hatred of official corruption, and social resentment of state-owned enterprises have in common: the underlying perception of the extent to which, and the hypocrisy with which, the public institutions of a nominally communist party-state are used as an apparatus for private appropriation. Correspondingly, the call for democracy is, at the deepest level, the demand for an end to the sources of this perception, rather than the fetishizing of the formal mechanisms of democratic elections and decisionmaking. In this sense, the call for democracy and the demand for social justice are one and the same.

Some may think, not without reason, that the CCP is too far gone, too much prey to powerful vested interests within its own ranks, to attempt or even think of attempting social justice reform thus understood, or even as less ambitiously conceived.[51] But this cannot be a completely foregone conclusion. What is both an exceptional strength and weakness of the CCP is that there are times when it is possible for a central leadership equipped with authority and imbued with vision to turn the party and the country in a new direction, good or bad. The present may well be among such times, and the present leadership may well have it in them to undertake a major change of direction. This would not be easy, to be sure, given the unholy alliance of powerful political and corporate interests enriching and aggrandizing themselves at the expense of the weak and vulnerable, which has been an important part of the story of China's economic reform. The difficulty is made all the more acute by a global environment in which new growth and distribution patterns, as shaped by the dominance of financial capital and information technology, have dampened egalitarian aspirations throughout the world. And, needless to say, with its heavy dependence on exports and its ever-expanding finance and IT industries, China has shown itself to be both attracted and vulnerable to these patterns, not least in the wake of the 2008 financial crisis.

Such formidable odds against progress in social justice are balanced by the unusually large room for maneuver that China enjoys because of the size of its economy, combined with a degree of bona fide political independence (not least from American influence) available to few of the world's leading economic powers. This room affords the CCP the possibility of making substantial progress in social justice if it is really determined to do so—the more so if and as it increases its share of the global economy and elevates its status in the global value chain. But considering that the global value chain is itself a morally ambiguous arrangement at best, and that today's finance-dominated, consumerism-driven model of capitalism is bringing unprecedented levels of risk and waste to economies, human lives, and the natural environment, must China single-mindedly try to play the same game and, indeed, aim to improve social justice only in terms determined by this game? Constrained by the realism of a self-imposed realistic utopia for China, I will hold back from a confident "no." But surely it is not too much to expect a country with China's economic and political possibilities to demand of itself at least a serious effort to responsibly imagine better things than today's capitalism has to offer and to experiment accordingly where it is feasible. Surely it is possible to give the Chinese Dream a bit more dreaminess than is to be found in becoming as powerful and respected a global capitalist hegemon as it could be.

No one knows for sure whether the present CCP leadership will seize such opportunities, afforded it by the size of China's economy and its political independence, among other things. But what is not in doubt is that, as things stand in China, there is a great deal of congruence between a moral interest in promoting social justice and the CCP's own prudential or rational interest in readying China for democracy and readying itself for a leading role within it. A proven track record in advancing the cause of social justice[52]—say, in education, health care, social security, and, not least, the household registration *(hukou)* system involving the urban-rural divide, within the next ten years or so—combined with the successful execution of the moral and legal reforms, will endear the CCP to the majority of Chinese even as it may create new yet benign problems by raising expectations and may alienate powerful vested interests, not least within the CCP's own ranks. If the party is able and motivated, as it should be, to establish a positive track record in all-around democratic preparation while maintaining even a moderate level of growth, it will have every reason to be confident that it will be rewarded by a sizable part of the citizenry in a democratic China it can proudly take credit for having helped establish in the first place.

It is definitely not beyond the realm of feasibility that, if the CCP cares about its own future and the future of China and acts with a proper combination of vision and prudence, it may succeed in creating a future for China that is open to democracy and in bringing about positive conditions for a well-functioning democracy that is open to the party playing an important, even leading, role in it. While democracy must mean the cessation of one-party rule, it need not entail the end of the CCP as a major, positive political force—with or without the prospect of one-party democracy (as is essentially the case, say, in democratic Japan and somewhat less democratic Singapore). I would venture to suggest that this congruence of the CCP's interest and the country's interest, with its objective basis in the present-day reality of China, is a far from negligible ground for rational hope.

Excursus on Confucianism with Regard to Democratic Preparation

I want to conclude this chapter on democratic preparation with some brief reflections on Confucianism to complement those made toward the end of Chapter 3. It seems natural to do so, as the CCP is showing signs that it has some interest, however guarded, in drawing on Confucianism as a source of ideological power. It is appropriate to do so in this chapter because Confucianism could come to the aid of the CCP if and when the latter decides to undertake democratic change, not least at the stage of democratic preparation. And there is a way to do so that is not too farfetched if we try to identify potential links not so much between Confucianism and democracy as between it and republicanism. For Confucianism seems substantially closer to republicanism (on a certain understanding of it) than to democracy, while republicanism, in turn, is not too far removed from democracy and could be conceived as a more elitist version of it. Thus I will explore, in a brief and schematic way, some potential affinities between Confucianism and republicanism—affinities that may serve as *part* of China's bridge to democracy.

Much of the argument for Confucianism in the modern setting seems to rest on the belief that Confucianism has a certain flexibility with regard to regime type. Traditionally, of course, Confucianism went together with monarchy and only with monarchy. Contemporary proponents of Confucianism, however, seldom favor monarchy, and some of them find Confucianism, duly revised, eminently suitable for democracy. A blanket denial of Confucianism's claim to regime flexibility would obviously be premature. Yet there is little doubt that Confucianism is more suited to some regime types than to others. If we approach this fact in terms of the distinction between Confucianism playing a major, structural role and its playing only a relatively minor, subsidiary role in a regime, it is plausible to advance the hypothesis that Confucianism can play a major, structural role only in certain regime types.

Take liberal democracy as a regime type (to use *regime* in a loose sense to be explained presently). In a liberal democracy the constitutional essentials revolve around majority rule and the protection of individual rights and liberties. Given such constitutional essentials, the most that Confucianism can do is twofold: first, to keep alive Confucian ideals and values in civil society and thereby serve as part of the informal background of a democratic political culture; and, second, to contribute one comprehensive doctrine to a liberal society where no single comprehensive doctrine is supposed to hold sway. Within a liberal democracy, then, there is no room for Confucianism to play more than a subsidiary, nonstructural role. It is not always clear what contemporary Confucians of a broadly liberal democratic persuasion (as discussed in Chapter 3) are up to. Are they happy to accept a subsidiary role for Confucianism within the structural parameters of liberal democracy? Or are they, by virtue of the revisions they propose to liberal democracy, aiming for a regime type that is no longer liberal democracy, strictly speaking? If so, what exactly is the regime they prefer? More important, is such a regime possible under modern conditions?

It is against this background that I want to raise the question of Confucianism's regime flexibility, but I can do no more than lay out some terminological and conceptual preliminaries. First, by *regime types* I roughly mean distinctive political arrangements differing in such factors as who rules, over what kind of society, under what principles, and so on, and what results therefrom in terms of distinctive configurations and potential contradictions. This deliberately loose and mixed characterization is meant to be neutral as between, say, Aristotle's and Montesquieu's accounts and classifications (though perhaps actually somewhat closer to the latter), and it allows me to speak of liberal democracy as a regime as my purpose requires. Let me now introduce a complication. It arises from the idea, as treated in Chapter 3, that the socioeconomic condition of a community has an important bearing on what regime is suitable for it. Instead of starting again with Protagoras, I will this time briefly invoke Aristotle, who too hinted that *social* conditions play a role in the functioning of a *political* regime, saying, for example, that the strong presence of what we would today call the middle class is conducive to a stable democracy.[53] This is an insight the likes of which we have come to associate especially with Tocqueville when it comes to *modern* democracy, as discussed at length in Chapter 3. For Tocqueville, as we have seen, democracy is not merely a regime type but, first and foremost, a certain type of society marked by what he calls equality of conditions—that is, equality of *social* conditions. I am bringing in Tocqueville again because his understanding of democracy as covering both regime and society is a conceptual innovation that is exceptionally useful for my present purposes. In the light of this innovation, I must recast the question of what I earlier called Confucianism's regime flexibility. To be more precise, then, what is at issue is Confucianism's flexibility with regard not so much to regime types as to society types—especially if we pair a society type with its corresponding regime type, in which case we can speak of a *society-regime* type.

Tocqueville has a further value for my present exercise in that he has performed an illuminating simplification by reducing all society-regime types into two. One of these is democracy, whose defining feature is equality of conditions. The other is aristocracy, based as it is on inequality of conditions. Aristocracy in this deliberately broad sense covers all nondemocratic ways of organizing social and political relations, including monarchy. This allows Tocqueville to pit democracy in the broad sense against aristocracy in an equally broad sense and to speak of them as marking "two distinct kinds of humanity."[54]

What are we to say of Confucianism if we try to place it in Tocqueville's binary scheme of society-regime types, bearing in mind the distinction between a structural role and a subsidiary role? We can, I think, make three fairly straightforward observations: first, that Confucianism can play a structural role only in an aristocracy; second, that it can at best play a subsidiary role in a democracy; and, third, that since aristocracy is a thing of the past, the most that Confucianism can aspire to in the modern world is to play a subsidiary role in a democracy if the latter happens to have a living Confucian tradition.

This is plainly not good enough for those contemporary Confucians who entertain higher hopes for Confucianism. Small wonder, then, that their thought contains traces, sometimes more than traces, of republicanism—not so much republicanism's valorization of political liberty and nondomination as its emphasis on checks and balances, on the common good, and on civic virtue in both active and passive forms; in other words, on what seems a more even balance between the good and virtue, on the one hand, and right and freedom, on the other. Such traces seem to be informed by the intuition that, if Confucianism is to play a structural role in a modern setting, there must be a third possibility in addition to aristocracy and democracy. This third possibility is republicanism—as an intermediate type and, especially for our purposes, as a *transitional* type.

I doubt that those Confucians who are drawn to republicanism think of it as a society type—that is, as more than just a regime type. It may indeed appear odd to speak of republicanism as a society type at all. But there need be nothing incoherent about the idea of a republican society in the following sense: a society whose conditions favor the establishment and flourishing of a republican regime, which, in turn, promotes and helps give political shape to those conditions. It so happens that this usage finds some support from the American historian Gordon Wood, who conceives of the general conditions surrounding the American Revolution in terms of the succession of monarchy (before the revolution), republicanism (in the wake of the revolution), and democracy (two to three decades after the revolution).[55] By *monarchy, republicanism,* and *democracy,* Wood clearly means what I am calling society-regime types.

Two things are worth noting. The first is the affinity between the burgeoning Confucian republicanism of our time (in thought more than in reality so far) and the political mentality of what Wood describes as the republican phase of American history. The second is Wood's observation that by the early nineteenth century, republicanism was decisively and irrevocably replaced by democracy. In this regard, Wood shows far greater sensitivity to the intimate relation between society type and regime type than does the common run of republicanism's contemporary advocates, who seem to have less awareness that civic republicanism is rendered utopian by the thoroughly democratic character of American society today.

I am not implying that, by the same token, Confucian republicanism is nothing but an unrealistically utopian doctrine. For societal conditions are not uniform in the modern world. If republicanism has little chance in America, the same need not apply to China, at least today. The least one could say on behalf of Confucian republicanism is that in republicanism Confucianism finds an option that, while being normatively more congenial to it than democracy, is at the same time more realistic than aristocracy. For, on the one hand, the Chinese social imaginary still contains substantial space for a relatively thick conception of the common good, a relatively prominent place for virtue on the part of leaders and citizens, and a residual hankering for political meritocracy in terms of promotion of the common good led by those with supposedly exceptional civic and instrumental virtues. On the other hand, China is fast creating its own versions of atomistic individualism, value pluralism, postmodern irony, and rampant capitalism. As long as this mixed *societal* condition lasts, there seems—just seems—to be some room for a mixed *political* regime comprising the Few (aristocracy, or what the Confucians prefer to call meritocracy, emphasizing *natural* aristocracy) and the Many (democracy), if not—to judge by the more or less democratically inclined Confucian theorists' own pronouncements—the One, although the latter perhaps should not be ruled out outright, if only to accommodate what might become of the leading role of the CCP. Such room seems to exist in the same way that the societal condition of America in the decades immediately following 1776 permitted, indeed encouraged, its own distinctive brand of mixed government.[56]

Thus Confucian republicans definitely have their work cut out for them, with a mixture of daunting challenges and tantalizing possibilities. The challenges arise from the complex character of Chinese society today. The possibilities come from the more old-fashioned part of Chinese society, as it were, and, equally important, from the CCP's urgent need for sources of ideological power to augment its fast-declining old, communist one. There are few more obvious or promising candidates than Confucianism, and a suitably revived and revised Confucianism could conceivably lend the CCP an ideological hand in its possible attempt to set China on a democratic course that is not too fast or too radical. But before Confucianism could play such a role, if and when the time comes, Confucian intellectuals active today must first come up with some fully developed conception of Confucian republicanism as a normative political doctrine. This conception, in turn, must be predicated on a plausible demonstration that a Confucian republican (mixed) regime is a realistic prospect on account of China's present societal conditions. Short of this, Confucianism will be caught between the binary options of aristocracy and democracy. Of these, one (standing by itself) is a thing of the past, and the other—more precisely called liberal democracy—allows only a minor, subsidiary role for Confucianism.

PART THREE

The International and Hong Kong Dimensions

Democracy at Home and Legitimacy around the World

THE RISE OF CHINA in economic power and geopolitical influence has not been matched by a corresponding enhancement of its legitimacy on the world stage. The resulting gap between China's so-called hard and soft power is one of the most prominent features of this rise and the strongest proof, if proof is needed, of its radical incompleteness. To the degree that China is not yet respected, it is perceived as a threat and a source of destabilization in proportion to its power. Whatever benefits China's rising power may have brought it, the lopsidedness of this power has become a liability—a rallying point against China whenever there is a significant convergence of interests, economic or geopolitical, uniting a group of nations. This explains the ebb and flow of anti-China (though not necessarily anti-Chinese) sentiment in much of the world.

Whether this sentiment is just or unjust, and whatever the proportion, those who hold it are undoubtedly responding to the lopsidedness of China's rise and its resulting power. This is a matter of perception, of course, but this does not make it any less a psychological reality, a political and geopolitical psychological reality. As such, it is in part a manufactured reality and lends itself to constant, sometimes blatant manipulation by powerful governments and media in the context of international relations. That this is possible is enough to confirm the lopsidedness of China's rise—and its huge cost, geopolitical and economic, alongside the gains brought by the rise itself. The Chinese state has few true headaches involving geopolitical or international economic relations that do not have an important part of their source in this lopsidedness,

in a rising China's legitimacy deficit on the international stage. These headaches are not going away anytime soon, and exertions of hard power are
simply too blunt an instrument for handling them.

This is no less true of those domestic issues in which foreign powers happen
to take a special political or geopolitical interest. The intractability of separatist tendencies in Tibet, Xinjiang, Hong Kong, and Taiwan stands in a direct causal relation to the Chinese state's perceived lack of legitimacy, allowing
the internal separatists and their external supporters and sympathizers to
take the moral high ground. That high ground, varyingly articulated in terms
of human rights, religious freedom, democracy, or the rule of law, has the
miraculous effect of weakening the Chinese state's perceived legitimacy and
thereby, subtly yet undeniably, weakening whatever sovereignty claims the
state has against separatist challenges from within. Although this logic is
seldom made explicit, a legitimacy deficit has the distinct potential, in cases
of dispute, to turn into a sovereignty deficit that gives a morally plausible
opening to more or less tactful external meddling.

The Chinese leadership cannot but be painfully conscious of the headaches caused by the lopsidedness of the country's rise. However, they understand this lopsidedness in terms of a shortage of soft power rather than a legitimacy deficit. This is a big mistake, in that what is involved is not a lack of
soft power as such but, above all, a lack of soft power of a particular, political
kind. It is essential to think of this lack in terms of a legitimacy deficit
because much of it has to do with democracy and because, when it comes to
the nation-state as we know it today, nothing is more liable to create a cloud
over its legitimacy than a lack of democracy. China's deficit in soft power is
a legitimacy deficit, which is, in turn, a democracy deficit.[1]

Not everyone will accept this conclusion, naturally, so let us take a step
back from democracy and treat as our point of departure the more easily acceptable idea that China cannot hope to enjoy full legitimacy abroad unless
it enjoys full legitimacy at home, leaving it open whether the latter legitimacy
is, in turn, dependent on democracy. I believe there are those who will readily
agree with this idea and yet think that domestic legitimacy can be achieved
while bypassing democracy and that once domestic legitimacy is secured,
with or without democracy, this ought to suffice for international legitimacy
as well. However one may approach the issue normatively, the fact of the
matter is that given the way the global political value space is currently con-

stituted, no country can enjoy full legitimacy on the international stage without being a democracy at home.

To decide how one ought to react to this fact, it is necessary to return to the question of legitimacy at home, the question of whether democracy is an essential condition of domestic legitimacy—as an empirical matter. An answer is readily suggested by the fact, just noted, that the global political value space is so constituted as to place democracy at the center of conditions for international legitimacy. Obviously, it is impossible for this to be the case without it also being the case for most domestic regimes. China is clearly not an exception, and there is no better proof than its own refusal to accept any designation as a nondemocracy and then proceed to mount a self-defense in terms of such a designation. In fact, democracy is treated in China as—and in this crucial sense *is*—a crucial condition of legitimacy at home. However, since democracy is an essentially contested concept and what is at issue is domestic legitimacy, we need an appropriately flexible concept of democracy as a condition of legitimacy. It should be reasonable to suggest, then, that it is a sufficient condition for domestic legitimacy that China is regarded (under appropriate conditions of freedom, equality, and information) by a majority of its own citizens as a democracy. We can now revisit my earlier statement about the relation between internal and external legitimacy and fill in the part that was left open. Thus we have reason to hold that China cannot hope to enjoy full legitimacy internationally unless it enjoys full legitimacy at home, and that it cannot enjoy full legitimacy at home unless it is a democracy, *in the sense that* it is perceived by a majority of its own citizens as reasonably democratic.

This way of viewing the matter has an extremely important consequence. Suppose, hypothetically, that things are otherwise, that the external pressure on China to enhance its legitimacy through democracy does not coincide with an internal pressure for democracy. Under this supposition, it is a tricky question whether China ought to respond to the external pressure—tricky because there is something both imprudent and undemocratic about bowing to external pressure on an issue bearing on legitimacy when domestic public opinion points in a different direction. In other words, ex hypothesi what is conducive to greater legitimacy abroad is detrimental to legitimacy at home, and vice versa. Now lift the hypothetical supposition and matters will become much more straightforward, at least in principle: China ought, for both prudential and normative reasons, to respond to *internal* pressure for legitimacy enhancement—if such pressure exists, as it clearly does—through democratization. In so doing, China will also be responding positively to the external pressure, but, crucially, doing so for internal and hence better reasons. Consistent with this reasoning, one might put the point differently and say that China ought to respond to external pressure for democracy to the degree that it coincides with an internal one.

The question that remains is whether the domestic legitimacy thus achieved will necessarily translate into legitimacy on the international stage—and whether it ought to even if in reality it does not. Without even attempting to answer this question, it is already clear that there is no bypassing democracy if China is to have any reasonable hope of gaining full legitimacy on the international stage. Since the Chinese state has yet to develop a political form that will convince enough of its own citizens that it is democratic, this much at least is the task that it must accomplish for purposes of both domestic and international legitimacy. Whether fulfillment of this task will be sufficient to achieve international legitimacy is a question whose answer we will know only when this task is accomplished. By then China will at least be able to lay a plausible claim to the essentially contested concept of democracy—that is, able not to bypass democracy but, as it were, to bypass only a particular, hitherto hegemonic interpretation of it.

As things stand, the relation between internal and external legitimacy also goes the other way, such that not only is it true that China cannot enjoy full legitimacy abroad unless it enjoys full legitimacy at home, it also seems true—to a degree and in ways not to be sneered at—that, the countervailing power of nationalism notwithstanding, the Chinese state cannot enjoy full legitimacy at home unless it enjoys full legitimacy abroad. The latter is, for example, at least partially the case with regard to large enough numbers of people in Tibet, Xinjiang, and Hong Kong to cause great worry for the Chinese state. If and when the Chinese state has successfully sorted out its domestic democracy deficit, it will also be in a much stronger moral position vis-à-vis those of its citizens who defer to so-called international standards when these happen to differ from China's own.

In the domestic case as in the global one, a further rise in China's hard power will undoubtedly help, as it always does, but the change that will ultimately matter is the one that happens to perceptions of legitimacy via perceptions of democracy. To achieve the latter change, China will first have to achieve full domestic legitimacy via democracy. Only then will it be able to plausibly contest the meaning of democracy at home and, especially, abroad. There is no telling what form political and geopolitical confrontation will take thereafter. What we know for sure is that until that point is reached, China can count on one extra challenge from its powerful democratic rivals, in the form of what I will call political-system hostility.

A Magnet for Political-System Hostility

I have argued that China's need for international legitimacy and its need for domestic legitimacy converge to make democratic development desirable and that this convergence gives China good reason to respond positively to the external pressure for democracy. It does not follow, however, that external pressure is invariably a good thing. It is one thing for such pressure to exist in the form of the logic that China will not gain full international legitimacy until it gains full domestic legitimacy by becoming what is (at least) internally regarded as a democracy. It is something else for this pressure to manifest itself in the form of political hostility, sometimes intense political hostility. Such hostility and the distinctive pressure that can go with it may or may not be advisable from a prudential point of view and may or may not be justified from a normative point of view. It is necessary to take a step back in order to reflect on the wisdom and rightness of such hostility. But, first, what does this hostility look like?

While the Cold War is officially over, one legacy of it that has proved especially potent and enduring for China is a widespread perception of its political system as morally inferior and hence in need of fundamental change. Such a perception is shared by all liberal democratic states and by those in China itself who wish to see their country become a liberal democracy. For the most part only implicit and seldom fully spelled out even when explicit, this perception is nevertheless extremely strong and consequential. It informs in ways blunt and subtle almost all the dealings with China by states and individuals alike that involve an element of negative moral-political judgment.

At the core of this perception is China's lack of democracy, with its human rights record thrown in for good measure. This lack is regarded as an incorrigible deficiency of China's political system. At the same time, it is perceived, sometimes with what seems a mixture of envy and revulsion, as a strength that compounds the deficiency and turns it into a unique menace. For, on the one hand, the disposition of power peculiar to China's political system is viewed as the source of the more serious of the country's domestic problems, as well as of the more controversial aspects of its conduct in international affairs. Yet, on the other, it is registered as a cause for alarm in view of its undeniably positive contribution to China's spectacular rise as an economic, and increasingly geopolitical, power.

Small wonder that Western democracies, especially the United States, and domestic liberal critics of China alike are wont to hold China to liberal democratic standards and profess, or at least imply, the desire to see China evolve into a polity more or less like the United States. (The true shock and scandal of June 4, 1989, from this perspective, was that this evolution was not going to happen smoothly or anytime soon.) This cannot but mean that they want to see a China that is no longer ruled by the Chinese Communist Party (CCP) in a one-party state. At least in this broad sense, they all desire "regime change" in China; whether, and to what degree, they take positive steps to help bring this about is another matter, a matter of prudence and feasibility rather than sheer desirability. While the European Union, not itself an empire and lately overwhelmed by problems of its own, is generally less vocal in its political criticisms of China, it does not fundamentally diverge from the American stance and is happy, for the most part, to let the leader of the free world do most of the moral-political lecturing, whenever so inclined. What is not in doubt, least of all from the Chinese perspective, is that as long as China keeps its current political system, it will not be left alone to take care of its political business according to its own standards, even under normal circumstances. In our increasingly globalized political world, whether a state is democratic seems to have become everyone's legitimate business and all states deemed nondemocratic are fair game, at least when it comes to moral judgment and, where feasible, political pressure. One has only to notice the almost complete absence of such judgment and pressure in the opposite direction, except in feeble protest or discursive tit-for-tat (such as China's annual white paper on human rights in the United States), to have some sense of the dominant international political sentiment that seems ever ready to be mobilized.

Against this background, China under the CCP naturally sees itself as facing a distinctive threat. The sense of threat comes in no uncertain manner from China's perception of an unmistakable will to democracy on the part of powerful Western liberal democracies, as well as supporters of liberal democracy at home. It is driven even more, not least because of the uncertainty and opacity involved, by the fear that this will to democracy is only waiting for opportunities to translate it into subversive action—in the form, say, of a "color revolution"—as it has done in not a few other parts of the world. It should come as no surprise, therefore, that the Chinese state registers the negative perception of its political system not only as an injury to its pride as an equal among the world's political systems. More importantly, it sees in this deep-seated and widespread perception a potentially lethal threat to its very existence with its current political identity. There can be no doubt, then, to the guardians of China's political system—indeed to the detached observer—that this system, if not China itself, is permanently under siege, warranting a permanent state of emergency. Even when the perceived threat is neither grave nor imminent or is outweighed by economic cooperation, there is an unmistakable hostility that lurks barely beneath the surface.

We need a name for this sentiment, and I deem it appropriate to call it *political-system hostility*. It is worth adding that this hostility is essentially one-sided, with manifestations of hostility on China's side being for the most part reactive and defensive. There is little doubt that this distinctive hostility, even when not particularly active, is sufficient to cause China to act, both domestically and in international relations, in ways it would otherwise not act. Likewise, those state and individual actors that deem China's political system hopelessly flawed are thereby disposed to treat China in ways they would otherwise not. This tense reciprocity, though often well contained in the interest of economic and other agendas, is a fundamental fact of the political relationship between China and Western liberal democracies, and between China and its liberal dissenters. And the two relations are inextricably intertwined—recent political developments in Hong Kong being a prominent case in point. It would be difficult to exaggerate the consequences, intended or not, that such reciprocity is likely to have for the action and reasoning of the Chinese state, which, in turn, will have important consequences of their own, both domestic and international.

The Stakes of Political-System Hostility

It is by no means a straightforward matter to determine what to make of political-system hostility in the context of advancing the cause of democracy in China, unless one starts from a pregiven vested political interest or from a purely moral position, itself probably questionable. I do not propose to start from either. What seems more worthwhile is an examination, in this section, of the stakes involved, and then, in the two sections that follow, of the factors that tend to render external involvement in China's democratic progress appropriate or otherwise.

There is little doubt that this political-system hostility has its principal meaning and function today in the context of the rise of China and the resulting rivalry between China and the United States. It is for this reason that political-system hostility toward China figures with much greater prominence in the United States than in Europe, at least at the level of governments. But the threat China may pose to American hegemony is by no means only political, still less a matter exclusively of relations of hard power. When Japan, America's ally and protégé, appeared to present what in some respects was a similar threat not so long ago, around the time of the Plaza Accord, the United States reacted with manifest hostility, going so far as to label Japan an "adversary."[2] This was despite the fact that although Japan was an Asian power, it was a liberal democratic capitalist state like the United States, indeed one it helped create on the debris of World War II. This time around, China, in addition to being an Eastern civilization, possesses the singularly provocative identity of a communist state, regardless of the amount of truth in this identity. This is an identity to which China shall be chained, both for its own purposes and in the eyes of the Western world, as long as it does not signal in action and rhetoric a fundamental shift to the liberal democratic system of government, its adoption of capitalist values and institutions notwithstanding. In this context, the rise of China cannot but present a rather unfamiliar challenge to the sense of *comprehensive* superiority that has long been part of the political self-understanding and self-confidence of liberal democracies, whether or not the challenge also contains a civilizational dimension. It is easy to imagine that the United States, the hegemon that it is and leader of the free world, must have felt this challenge most keenly.[3] But it is just as obvious that the identity from which, and on whose behalf, the

United States is reacting is one that European liberal democracies fully share.[4] This common identity remains a potent source of transatlantic ideological and political (not to mention military) unity, even as the inevitable divergence of economic and other interests between the United States and Europe, whether or not connected with China's growing clout in the global economy, has a far from negligible causality of its own. This state of affairs may be expected to keep political-system hostility alive, although it is impossible to predict how that hostility will express itself and with what effect over time.

While the existence of political-system hostility is not in doubt, it is by no means obvious what the Western liberal democracies, especially the United States, want from China or for China in professing or implying the desire for it to undertake major political reform with a view to eventually adopting the Western political model. It is one thing for them to prefer China to already be a liberal democracy—say, to have successfully become one in the wake of June 4, 1989, had events turned out differently. Such a preference is logically built into the strategic and normative thinking of the American political establishment, in particular, predicated as it is on the mostly correct assumption that the governments and citizens of democratic countries tend to be well disposed toward the world's most powerful democracy (President Donald Trump being a complicating factor rather than a game changer), just as a free-market economy anywhere in the world is more permeable to the immense influence of corporate America and global corporate power in general.

But it would be something very different for the United States and its democratic allies to want to see China, under such circumstances as exist today, take concrete and irrevocable steps toward regime self-transformation. For they must know full well that democratic change in China is a risky proposition, and they have no reason to count on China to succeed in such change and to continue performing as well or even better in the role it has been playing in the global capitalist *economic* order. After all, all the Western liberal democracies are at the same time capitalist economies and, in that capacity, have an extremely strong vested interest in China's continuing political stability and economic growth, even while, in their identity as liberal democracies, they may also see themselves as being under the most discomforting of threats. A bungled experiment with democracy in China, without adequate democratic preparation, could well spell disaster for the global capitalist economy, and possibly worse.

Could it be, then, that the United States, let alone Europe, is not really keen to have China embark on what could turn out to be a destabilizing and even dangerous path to democracy, at least for now? Perhaps, and if so, it would not be entirely farfetched to suggest that the United States is engaging in political-system hostility toward China precisely in the comforting knowledge that China will not listen or budge. This is, in other words, just part of an ideological game to prevent China from cementing its growth in hard power with a comparable rise in soft power, democracy being an indispensable component of political prestige in the world today. We cannot know for sure, however, and this is an aspect of the uncertainty and opacity I spoke of earlier. In the absence of the certainty of intentions, combined with the certainty of political-system hostility itself, the Chinese state must fear the worst and prepare for the worst. And it must, even in the relatively benign scenario of largely peaceful confrontation, be tempted to counter American assertiveness with a defensive assertiveness of its own, the latter with the distinct potential to acquire a momentum of its own.

None of this would matter so much, of course, were it not for the fact that the Chinese state is also beset by an internal vulnerability on account of its political system. Such vulnerability has been entirely foreign to Europe and North America since the end of the Cold War. In their mature liberal democracies, while the approval rates of governments (in the person of the top elected officials) may sometimes be embarrassingly low, popular allegiance to the liberal democratic political system is generally so firm as to escape everyday notice—even today. The political system (especially in the sense of democratic rule of law) simply is not a problem, so decisive and durable has been the victory of liberal democracy that ended the Cold War. In China things seem to be the other way around: the CCP and government may, on the strength of their performance, combined from time to time with subtly or not so subtly administered doses of nationalism, enjoy considerable popular support, and yet such support does not extend to the political system itself. It certainly cannot be taken to reflect such approval. The vulnerability of China's political system was first driven home in 1989, and the basic facts of the matter, along with the reactive sensibility of the CCP, have not changed since. That is why the official verdict on June 4 has not been overturned and will not be until the CCP is able to feel safe on the issue of democracy, either by making China so powerful as to be no longer afraid of democracy or by deciding to join its ranks. What is still called China's socialist system, which includes, by definition, the permanent leadership of the party, is something to be jealously guarded in the face of an irremovable uncertainty of allegiance (at best) or a patent lack of allegiance (at worst) on the part of China's own citizens. It is only in this context that the West's political-system hostility toward China touches a permanently raw nerve and lends itself to the perception of a foreign interference ever ready to pounce on a vulnerable political system with a color revolution.

Beyond understandable vigilance against such a prospect, it is not immediately obvious what it is that China is doing when it resists the pressure to evolve into a liberal democracy. Having given up its erstwhile socialism of sorts in favor of some of the defining values and institutions of capitalism, China no longer has the dictatorship of the proletariat and its vision of a communist future to defend in trying to ward off the so-called peaceful transformation of its socialist identity. It is very telling, in this connection, that none of the recent Chinese administrations seems to have been truly alarmed by Hollywood's massive conquest of the tastes and minds of the young, and not just the young. Through the seemingly innocuous exposure to American cultural and entertainment products, the peaceful transformation of China is taking place slowly but surely and in the most instinctual and embodied way possible. No matter, it seems, because what is really at stake is no longer the socialist system, with its own distinctive values and tastes, but only the place of the CCP in a quasi-capitalist China and China's place in a world still largely under American hegemony. The party will not relinquish its exclusive leadership over the Chinese state, whatever the latter's true identity may be, and it will not settle for the role that, say, Japan has played in the capitalist world-system vis-à-vis American hegemony. To defend China's current political system is to defend these two paramount claims.

Why Political-System Hostility Is Misguided

Turning to the normative pros and cons of external involvement, including political-system hostility, it seems unavoidable to use as one's point of reference some understanding of democracy's intrinsic value. But what exactly is this intrinsic value? In answering this question, the least we could do is not to go back to the "classical doctrine of democracy" that Joseph

Schumpeter has so effectively demolished. This means that we must give up the naïve idea that the intrinsic value of democracy lies in the realization of the common good through the faithful execution of the will of the people by their elected representatives. Schumpeter replaces this conception of democracy with one that features "the democratic method, viz., free competition among would-be leaders for the vote of the electorate. Now one aspect of this may be expressed by saying that democracy is the rule of the politician."[5] The problem is that "the rule of the politician," once divorced from the common good and the will of the people (and this is the *point* of Schumpeter's redefinition), cannot serve as a locus of the intrinsic value of democracy. And whatever substitute we find for Schumpeter's view in order to capture democracy's intrinsic value must not fall into the romantic naïveté for which the classical doctrine was substituted in the first place.

It seems to me that the best, if not the only, rationale for democracy that both satisfies this requirement and brings out democracy's intrinsic value is to be found in the argument from fittingness. According to a view derivable from this argument, democracy's intrinsic value as a *political* regime lies in its unique moral and psychological fittingness for an existing *social* situation— what Alexis de Tocqueville calls equality of conditions—a situation that is enduring because we affirm it and would be powerless to change it even if we wanted to. Thus understood, democracy's intrinsic value is at the same time its great prudential or instrumental value. For, other things being equal, a political regime (democracy) is more likely to be stable the more it is morally and psychologically fitting for the type of society in question (a society marked by equality of conditions). To put it negatively (and this time drawing on the argument from governability), there will come a point in the development of equality of conditions in a society at which any but a democratic political regime will be so lacking in moral and psychological fittingness that it will render the citizenry ungovernable.

Unlike the high-flown classical doctrine rightly rejected by Schumpeter, the modest view of democracy's intrinsic value just outlined makes a strong case for democracy and yet does not boast enough confidence in its own correctness, especially in practice, to place democracy on the moral high ground vis-à-vis other regime types. After all, fittingness is a matter of degree, in that equality of conditions is a matter of degree and so is democracy itself, and these nuanced judgments are best left to the citizens of each country themselves. These citizens are in the best position to make such judgments because they know the conditions of their country best and care most for its stability, and they are in the best position to decide whether external help is necessary or desirable. It is indeed their self-regarding concern for the enduring stability of their political order that alone is capable of producing that combination of moral vision and prudence which gives democratic change a reasonable chance of success. In other words, it is only to a country's own citizens that the purely prudential argument for democracy (from governability) can matter as desperately as the partially moral argument (from fittingness) does. In the real world, the ultimate test of whether a society is ripe for democracy is whether it will be able to accomplish the passage from social equality to political democracy while preserving and, over time, enhancing stability. Such passage recommends itself under a substantial equality of conditions only when other favorable or enabling conditions are present as well. That is why, as the reader will recall, having first argued for democracy in China in terms of fittingness and governability, I went on to make an equally insistent case for the view that democratic preparation is necessary before the passage from social equality to political democracy can safely take place. Here again, it is a country's own citizens who know best whether the other enabling conditions are met in addition to equality of conditions and who alone can undertake democratic preparation and judge when enough such preparation has been made.

Given complications such as these, which arise naturally from the modest conception of democracy's intrinsic value, it is quite unbecoming to feel and express political-system hostility to other regime types *purely and simply* on account of their not being democratic. If democracy's intrinsic value gives rise to a categorical imperative, as it were, it is a categorical imperative of such complexity that only a country's own citizens can best decide when and how to act on it—when, indeed, their country finds itself under sufficient equality of conditions to plausibly trigger the imperative in the first place. Democracy's prudential or instrumental value is, of course, even less a reason for political-system hostility, because it has the status only of a hypothetical imperative, making it discretionary in the light of an agent's desires.

When all is said and done, however, it may still appear odd that democracy's intrinsic value, as embodied in its unique fittingness—moral fittingness—does not qualify it for the moral high ground. Well, it does, and indeed this moral high ground is already implicit in my insistence throughout that democracy's intrinsic value does generate strong reasons to act and yet a country's own citizens are alone the qualified agents to assess such reasons and act on them. The moral high ground, or *higher* ground, exists unambiguously in democracy's greater fittingness than nondemocratic regimes can possibly achieve, under modern conditions of life. The important thing, however, is that this comparison is meaningful, relatively accurate, and usefully action guiding only when it is made among options available to the same country, not with other countries—that is, only when it is an internal comparison. Thus, if we find in this way and in no uncertain terms a moral high ground for democracy's intrinsic value as based on its fittingness, then just as surely this moral high ground is such that it properly directs one's normative gaze inward—to the goal of choosing the best political regime for one's own society given its distinctive and specific conditions, as one, along with other citizens, understands them. There is little room for the other-directed righteousness that leads to political-system hostility.

Political-system hostility is all the more unbecoming in view of a further consideration. As I have noted, in today's world the equality of conditions I am talking about finds its place—and is put in its place—in a capitalist order, and hence the second-most important raison d'être of democracy, after stability, is the self-protection of society against capitalism. Part of this protection is none other than the protection of equality of conditions. For under capitalism there is an ever-present possibility of (quantitative) economic inequality becoming so great that it undermines the (qualitative) equality of conditions itself. Whenever this possibility becomes a reality, as it is doing before our eyes in the leading democracies in the world today, it deprives equality of conditions and the political democracy based on it of much of their reality and spirit while leaving only their name and form intact. Given modern democracy's very (actual, not necessarily inherent) embeddedness in capitalism, the self-protection of society in general and the protection of equality of conditions in particular are always uphill struggles. There is no moral high ground that can be securely held. For the genuine egalitarian and democrat, there is simply no room for complacency and self-righteousness and hence no reason for the direction—that is, misdirection—of moral energy into political-system hostility.

One may go further and suggest that democracy is nothing but an uphill struggle—a two-pronged struggle against imperium (domination by state power) and dominium (in the modern world, domination by the capitalist class) and, in our time, against the imbrication of imperium and dominium in the form increasingly of capital's capture of the state. As a state form or regime type, democracy plays the crucial role of redressing the balance of power between ruler and ruled by giving the latter the right to demand representation and give or withhold consent, and between capital and the rest of society through social democracy and the welfare state. But when a society is capitalist, even when it is also democratic, hence democratic capitalist, the playing field can never be level. The capitalist class enjoys a huge advantage vis-à-vis the rest of society not only in the social domain itself but also in its ability to influence the actions and reasons of state power. Thus, while, as a state form or regime type, democracy can play an important, if necessarily severely limited, role in mitigating the worst excesses of imperium and dominium, that state form or regime type itself is nothing to be hugely proud of. There is something to be celebrated, but celebrated with a sense of proportion, only when this state form is put to sustained good uses for the self-protection of society. This is not happening, or happening nearly enough, anywhere in the world today. When this is the case, democracy as a state form can degenerate into little more than an ideological cover for a distinctively capitalist imperium-dominium—and the "opium of the people" in secular political life. It will be a double travesty if such an eviscerated democracy, instead of working to refill itself with democratic substance, turns around to channel what remains of its moral energy into political-system hostility against competitors or adversaries that happen to be nondemocratic.

It is worth emphasizing that the political-system hostility I am taking issue with is an ideological-strategic stance, which exists to motivate and sanction pressure and potentially active measures to bring about regime change in other countries in conformity with one's own interests and values. As such, political-system hostility in the name of democracy is distinct from what may be called a personal, instinctive (meaning not unreflective but stronger and deeper than reflective) normative preference for democracy. Such a preference, with its attendant moral discomfort in the presence of nondemocratic regimes or even the very idea thereof, is all too natural for members of modern societies to have. Indeed, it is unimpeachable, for it follows from the very fittingness of democracy under modern equality of conditions. One cannot feel this fittingness of democracy without also feeling the lack of fittingness of nondemocracy.

Thus I do not speak of the modern citizen's instinctive normative preference for democracy as something with little normative bearing, still less as something to be overcome. This preference is not any less worthy for being instinctive, for the instinct in question, instead of being purely subjective or only intersubjective, has a solid basis in reality. That reality is the relative equality of conditions in modern society that has put a definitive end in the more progressive parts of the world to any public, political, qualitative rank-ordering of people and their conceptions of the good life. Thus it is that any political power that behaves as if it had some title to rule that could bypass popular consent and any semblance of representativeness would come across as an affront to the modern citizen's moral and political sensibility. The same offense is caused, if often to a lesser degree than is warranted, whenever private, economic power visibly translates into public, political power. What I call the instinctive normative preference for democracy is nothing but this experientially and normatively well-grounded psychological reality. And it is a psychological reality that all members of modern societies share to one degree or another unless they fancy themselves belonging to the ruling class rather than the "people" or somehow identify with the ruling class.

There cannot, therefore, be anything amiss with entertaining a normative preference for democracy, nor with this preference being instinctive, nor with the consequent discomfort evoked by nondemocracy. But this natural instinctive preference and aversion is one thing, and a considered political stance toward other societies of whose conditions one can claim no intimate knowledge, still less knowledge attended by genuine solicitude, is quite another. The important thing is to keep this preference in a proper balance with awareness of the complexity and risks involved in the passage from social equality to political democracy. Moreover, since this passage is likely to present itself as a daunting *problem* precisely in the absence of assuredly favorable or enabling conditions, as is true of China today, the right approach needs to involve prudential considerations as much as normative ones. For a political project that is fraught with risk and promise in equal measure, it is imperative not to let one's instinctive normative preference for democracy serve as too automatic a substitute for the judicious weighing of values, the careful consideration of facts, and, finally, the making of what is bound to be a very difficult choice where the line between the normative and the prudential is blurred. If all of these considerations are necessary even for a country's own citizens, how much greater the pause they should give to those who are keen to make a positive contribution from the outside. Political-system hostility must be resisted lest it turn a complex political matter into a simple, black-and-white moral judgment and, in so doing, risk becoming a recipe for political tragedy, even political farce.

Appropriate and Inappropriate External Actions

It does not follow from my arguments against political-system hostility that all external actions and reactions designed to aid democratic progress in China are misguided, although the room for appropriate and constructive interventions is indeed small. More needs to be said about what kind of external involvement is conducive to China's democratic development and consistent with the spirit of democracy, and what kind is likely to be counterproductive and incompatible with the very nature of democratic development.

To this end, it is helpful to distinguish three stages in the process whereby a country such as China evolves into a political democracy. The first stage is the rise of equality of conditions in the social state, replacing a former inequality of conditions, as happened under Mao Zedong, or, broadening a hitherto rather narrowly conceived equality, as during the reform era. The second stage is the completion, itself a matter of degree, of equality of conditions by freedom, where freedom serves as a condition for the intellectual and moral maturity of individuals and of society as a whole, which, in turn, does more than anything else to make a society ready for democracy. The third and final stage is the adoption by such a society, a society properly readied for self-government, of a democratic political system, with all its inherent limitations and other, contingent imperfections.

It is fairly obvious that the first stage comes about, when it does, through such complicated causes that it would be naïve and perhaps counterproductive to try to bring it about through outside involvement. In any reasonably modern society, however, relative equality of conditions must already be a fact of life. For such a society, and China is undoubtedly one, it seems entirely appropriate for anyone, from within or without, to help make what is already relatively equal more fully equal, if they so desire. Such efforts need to be carried out sensibly and with due respect for the agency and complexity of the society in question, as well as in the spirit of mutual aid wherever appropriate. It is unlikely, therefore, that they will be marked by the urgency of problems and the moral superiority of the helping parties that typically justify talk of outside intervention.

The third and final stage, though obviously more amenable to outside involvement, should also be left to members of the society itself, for two reasons. Before I come to these reasons, however, I must first make something of a digression in order to bring up the issue of weighing the goods of democracy against other goods. The latter goods include, on a commonsense view, the secure provision of public order; social justice; economic development; the creation of an environment, social and natural, conducive to the good life, however conceived; and, last but not least, freedom roughly in the sense of what Benjamin Constant calls the liberties of the moderns. Of these goods, freedom is in a class of its own, as defined by a standard (modern, liberal democratic) conception of its relationship to democracy.[6] Next to freedom, only social justice (that is, the self-protection of society) arguably stands in some intrinsic relationship to democracy, but only as a stipulated requirement of democracy, which, however reasonable and indeed necessary, can all too easily fail in practice.[7] All the other goods are related to democracy in a more or less contingent way. For example, public order may be better provided for in a democratic society but only if certain conditions are met, and yet it is highly contingent whether these conditions are in fact met, and, if not, how difficult it will be to meet them (hence my argument for democratic preparation). It is also contingent whether economic development is promoted by democracy. As to whether human life flourishes better under democratic conditions, the answer will be widely open if the good life itself is left widely open, or else it will favor democracy via a circular argument if the good life is defined in terms that are themselves shaped by our modern democratic conditions.

In terms of relative importance, there can be little doubt that public order should carry no less weight than does democracy. The potential need for a difficult tradeoff between democracy and public order can be real, not merely ideological. As for social justice and economic development, their importance relative to democracy is a matter for debate, especially when it happens to be true of a society that democracy—such democracy as is realistic in the society at the time—does not contribute to social justice or economic development and may even stand in their way to one degree or another. When democracy is thus weighed against these other goods, what actually happens is, strictly speaking, not the comparison of democracy and these other goods in terms of urgency or importance but rather the assessment of democracy vis-à-vis an alternative political arrangement, say a nondemocratic one, in terms of which is better able to deliver these other goods. At least this is part of what is going on when we speak of weighing democracy against other goods. Regardless of how the weighing is conceived, however, the important thing is that some difficult weighing is necessary, and this necessity raises the question of what kind of agents it takes to carry out the weighing and who is in the morally and politically appropriate position to do it.

This leads naturally, then, to the first of my reasons why the third stage of democratic evolution should be left entirely to members of a domestic society: the good of a democratic political system must be weighed against other important goods, and this weighing can be done sensibly, indeed democratically, only by members of a society themselves once they have been allowed to part with their immaturity and become equal to the task of such weighing. Especially important in the case of China, for reasons discussed earlier, is the weighing of China's growing need for democracy against democracy's own need for stability in a country that relies so heavily on a strong central authority for the provision of national cohesion and social order. There is a further reason for leaving the third stage to a society itself, and this reason is internal to the very meaning of democracy. For we are here talking about progress from the second to the third stage of democracy, and thus we assume that members of the society in question, say, China (in due course), have already acquired a sufficient measure of maturity through the public use of reason made possible by individual liberty. Quite apart from prudential considerations, the very meaning and spirit of democracy dictates a principled deference to such cognitively and morally mature agents with regard to progress toward political democracy.

What about the second stage, the completion of equality of conditions through the valorization and institutionalization of nonpolitical liberty in the interest of moral maturity? There can be no doubt that, once this stage is reached, the case for democracy will be significantly enhanced, other things being equal, in that the scale for weighing democracy against other goods—or, more precisely, against an alternative political arrangement in terms of how well it can deliver these goods—is no longer tipped against democracy by democracy's internal lack of a pivotal condition (that is, individual and societal maturity). Thus, as I have noted, the reasons for moving from the first to the second stage are the most compelling along the entire trajectory of a society's democratic evolution. They are well-nigh morally irresistible, provided that intellectual and moral maturity can be introduced in a politically prudent manner, and there is no reason to think that the latter will not be achievable, especially when viewed as a matter of degree and hence incremental progress. Such reasons do not provide grounds for anything as strong as outside intervention, however, for not only is intervention unlikely to work but it is also contrary in spirit to the very aim of rendering people free from tutelage and the need for tutelage. But moral support, intellectual assistance, and transnational solidarity are entirely in order, although the worthiness and even nobility of those who provide such goods do not in any way dispense with the need to show moral modesty and political maturity.

A Positive External Influence That Is Sorely Lacking

It has turned out that the room for appropriate constructive assistance is indeed small, confined as it is for the most part to the second stage of China's journey to democracy. Intervention or tangible, practical aid is one thing, however, and influence quite another, and there is much greater room—I would say unlimited room—for positive external influence on China's democratic development. The prevalence of what I earlier called the instinctive normative preference for democracy in many parts of the world, especially in the advanced democracies, is itself an omnipresent source of moral influence—soft power of potentially the most bracing kind. But this influence is positive and credible only if the advanced democracies themselves are shining examples of the checking of imperium and dominium, and of the self-protection of society, by effectively representative government. This means that the most salutary and potent influence of all is positive example.

The example does not have to be perfect, or even nearly so, and it would be naïve for Chinese to look to Europe or North America for impeccable exemplars of democracy in the first place. But it needs to be uplifting enough to give democracy a deservedly good name despite all of its human, all too human, flaws. And part of being uplifting enough consists precisely in seeing and acknowledging these flaws and making such efforts to remedy them as are worthy of societies that claim to be founded on democratic principles and to be instantiations of the best political regime in the world.[8] New Deal America comes to mind as a positive example in this regard, if one is not too demanding (and one shouldn't be), as does Western Europe in the two decades or so after the inauguration of the Marshall Plan.

Western democracies have not been acquitting themselves in any remotely exemplary fashion since the Thatcher- and Reagan-led neoliberal revolt against democracy and equality—unless one means by *democracy* precisely the neoliberal taming of representative institutions into the handmaidens of deregulated, finance-dominated capitalism. There is no shortage of people who think that way, but they are hardly champions of democracy. When many Chinese, not least economists (by ideology as much as by profession), still look to the United States for positive lessons of governance, it is obvious that they are looking for ways of containing state power in favor of the market rather than ways of checking imperium and corporate dominium for the sake of democracy and the self-protection of society.

While it would nevertheless be a gross exaggeration to conclude that democracy is dead, there is little doubt that shining examples of democracy are hard to find. The United States of today is widely considered to have entered a New Gilded Age—a charge all the more credible when it comes from moderate, liberal domestic commentators rather than the more astringent and demanding radical Left.[9] And Europe has been plagued by its own worst democratic deficit, among other crises, since the formation of the European Union and the eurozone, if not further back. Worse, the bad name that some of the great powers have earned for democracy through warmongering and the militarization of diplomacy aided and abetted by an unsupervised military-industrial complex will take its rightful place as one of the most inexcusable crimes against both democracy and humanity.

It does not follow that China would be foolish and foolhardy even to contemplate having a go at democracy under such inauspicious global conditions.

For the reasons why China must attempt the passage from equality of conditions to political democracy are internal, and these reasons are not only normative but also, and especially, prudential, having to do, above all, with China's own need for enduring social and political stability.

To this end, China must wake up to the reality that, while democracy is worthy of its best efforts, it must make such efforts without the inestimable benefit of having shining examples to learn from and emulate. But no country owes this benefit to China anyway. For their part, those who set great store by democracy in Europe and North America need to form a more accurate, and hence more sobering and more humbling, assessment of the state of democracy in their own countries or regions, if they have not done so already and to a sufficient degree. Having done this, they will realize that in order to come to the effective aid of democratic progress in China (and other places), they must first put their own democratic house in order—that there is no better way of spreading democracy than by having a worthy, truly recommendable democracy to spread or, better still, to spread itself. Indeed, the quest for such democracy—for democracy as the unceasing and reasonably effective countermovement to imperium and dominium alike, especially to their symbiosis in the shape of neoliberal capitalism—is the common challenge of all countries in our time.

Almost all the themes just covered resonate in one way or another with Hong Kong. Hong Kong is part of China yet also stands apart from it in ways, cultural and political, that make it (in the shape of many of its citizens) look and behave almost as if it were part of the external, especially the Western democratic, world. This peculiarity of Hong Kong promises to shed much light on the intricacies and, for the most part, the counterproductiveness of political-system hostility; on the nature of the difficulties that a nondemocratic China is bound to face in its relations with the outside world; on the inadvisability of an overly moralized approach to democracy and democratic progress and on the corresponding need for normatively clear-sighted realism and prudence; and, above all, on the inextricable relation between China's legitimacy abroad and its legitimacy at home, as well as on democracy's role in this relation. So it is only fitting that I turn next to the topic of democracy in Hong Kong.

CHAPTER EIGHT

Two Systems, One Democratic Future

DEMOCRATIC MOVEMENTS ARE seldom simple, and one complexity arises when people who are trying to bring about democracy also have some other ax to grind. Discerning this ulterior motive can be a useful, even indispensable way of understanding the particular character and dynamic of a democratic movement. In the case of Hong Kong, the other ax to grind is to preserve a certain Hong Kong identity or, if we are not to mince words, an emphatic apartness from China. Apartness rather than (necessarily) independence, as the desire for apartness comes in many degrees, shading into the aspiration to independence only at the extreme. We will overlook what is at stake in the fight for democracy in Hong Kong if we fail to understand its relation to this broad and widespread desire for apartness. Everyone does not think and feel alike in a city of over seven million people and much internal diversity, of course, but there is little doubt that those who do set great store by apartness and are giving political expression to it in the form of democracy have reached a critical mass. What has happened?

Capitalism is definitely not under threat in Hong Kong. Nor are civil liberties and the rule of law, for the most part, as judged by real-world rather than textbook or imagined Western standards, although in jealously guarding these core values of Hong Kong, as they are now called, activists sometimes understandably and usefully exaggerate the threat. Symptomatic of the lack of a truly serious threat to civil liberties and the rule of law is the conspicuously low level of fear of the government and law enforcement in Hong Kong—both for good and for ill in terms of consequences. This phenomenon bears traces of the relative mildness of British colonial rule, but its continuation to this day is attributable in no small part also to the strategic restraint exercised by the Chinese Communist Party (CCP), although there are signs that this restraint is wearing thin. Equally intact is the Hong Kong way of life in its familiar everydayness, involving work and career, commerce, fashion and consumption, family and social life, enjoyment, and so on. The one feature of that way of life that is in danger of being gradually yet irrevocably eroded is Hong Kong's apartness from the mainland, itself ever more capitalist, consumerist, and fun-loving, just like Hong Kong, if as yet less well trained in middle-class sophistication and orderliness except in its first-tier and other advanced cities and among the well-to-do. It is in no small part as a response to this menacing reality that so many in Hong Kong have rallied around the banner of democracy.

This is not to imply that if Hong Kong were an independent jurisdiction, its members would not care about democracy, only to suggest that they would care about it in a different way. As it is, we all know for a fact that those who devote themselves to the cause of democracy in Hong Kong also set great store by an inviolable apartness from China and seem to do so with even greater passion.

This is not surprising, for apartness from China had been a defining feature of Hong Kong for a long time before the handover (that is, China's resumption of sovereignty) in 1997. The Hong Kong that was returned to the People's Republic of China was not the Hong Kong that had under military threats been ceded to Britain as a Crown Colony by the Qing dynasty over one and half centuries before. In between, especially after 1949, Hong Kong and its people had simply evolved apart from (mainland) China and its people. By 1997, this apartness from China, both outer and inner, had simply hardened into a fact about Hong Kong through no one's design but rather as a result of the initial severance and the great sweep of events thereafter.

But whence the desire to *keep* this apartness? Whence the passion invested in this desire? In a nutshell, and not to put too fine a point on it for now, China is not cool, the China that came to bring Hong Kong back into the national fold. This seemingly flippant characterization is accurate enough as a simple way of suggesting that China enjoys neither political legitimacy nor general prestige among a very sizable portion of the Hong Kong population. Mao Zedong's China, red and poor, was understandably an anathema to

Hong Kong, given the backgrounds and life stories of so many Chinese settlers in Hong Kong, and it still is. Today's China, already the second-largest economy in the world and no longer genuinely red despite its remaining under the leadership of a nominally communist party, has yet to turn its undoubted hard power into the ability to win admiration and allegiance, to bind with cultural spell and moral values rather than with sheer force or material inducement alone. This is as true of China's relation to Hong Kong, more than two decades after the handover, as it is of China's image in the international arena. People in Hong Kong may grudgingly accept that the territory is now part of China, but many of them lack the eagerness to belong, the pride of belonging; instead they are more eager to retain their apartness, prouder of being apart, despite China's rise.

As a matter of fact, China's rise is part of the problem, and this has to do with the nature and substance of Hong Kong's apartness from China. For it is an apartness that is at the same time defined against China and as superior to China. It is constructed and articulated as a multifaceted identity, a Hong Kong identity that is political (civil liberties, rule of law, anticommunism), economic (market capitalism with low taxes and a noninterventionist government), and cultural-linguistic (a mixture of the Cantonese and elements of the English, with a modicum of the traditionally Chinese thrown in for good measure). What is essential to this Hong Kong identity is that it is not simply a matter of *horizontal* uniqueness or diversity in relation to China, of being different but more or less equal. Rather, the Hong Kong identity is largely constituted by pitting itself against the mainland—that from which it constitutes an apartness—with the result that Hong Kong, in being different from the mainland, is either better (for example, Hong Kong culture being more cosmopolitan or more open to the West, or Hong Kong's average living standards being higher) or simply good where the mainland is bad (for example, Hong Kong's liberties and rule of law being good, while the mainland's lack of them is bad). For a considerable length of time, especially after Hong Kong's anointment as one of Asia's so-called minidragons, and stretching beyond the 1997 handover, this sense of superiority gave no small ego boost to the Hong Kong population, individual and collective, serving especially to reconcile the poor and downtrodden to their lot and to soften both class conflict and the conflict between colonized and colonizer. Memories of this period die hard, so constitutive have they been of the Hong

Kong identity, and they can be passed on to the younger generations in the form of a general Hong Kong consciousness of China. Even today the Hong Kong identity has no other essential foothold than in its hierarchically and largely antagonistically conceived apartness from China. This is the main reason why Hong Kong lives in mortal fear of mainlandization but has never had any comparable fear of Anglicization (which many instead treat as a proud part of their legacy).

It is easy to appreciate that an identity fashioned around this morally and hierarchically understood apartness is delicately poised and fragile and can be maintained without stridency only when both its distinctness and its superiority are at least implicitly acknowledged by mainland China. This was the case to one degree or another in the early years after the handover, when China was busy becoming more like Hong Kong, in many respects, rather than the other way around. In this process, mainland Chinese, including those in positions of power, wealth, and cultural prestige, naturally looked up to Hong Kong as an economically and culturally more advanced exemplar. As the balance of power between Hong Kong and the mainland has inexorably shifted, however, the Hong Kong identity, with its integral sense of superiority vis-à-vis China, has come under increasing strain. Although in terms of per capita gross domestic product, average standard of living, and much else, Hong Kong remains far ahead of China, as a locus of economic and cultural power it has in the past decade or so been completely eclipsed by mainland China.

In this context, one should not be surprised that China's economic and other achievements, in dwarfing Hong Kong's importance and puncturing its sense of superiority, are far from being a straightforward cause for celebration in Hong Kong. In particular, these achievements, led as they have been by what is still thought of as a communist regime, are definitely not worthy of reflected glory and unreserved identification in Hong Kong's densely anticommunist climate. As far as Hong Kong is concerned, it would be an understatement to say that the "rise of China" is not an unmixed blessing. "The great rejuvenation of the Chinese nation" has, for many, been anything but rejuvenating when it comes to Hong Kong.

But even when this complication of the Hong Kong–China relationship did not exist, back in 1997, the problem of Hong Kong's alienation from China was already challenging enough. For the main difficulty that China had with

Hong Kong back then, as it still does today, was its lack of legitimacy, political and otherwise. Had China enjoyed much greater legitimacy from the start or been able to acquire more legitimacy since, its growing importance in the world would only have added to its appeal and prestige in the eyes of the Hong Kong public. As it was, China's glaring lack of legitimacy was the single most important reason why the handover was so traumatic for so many people in Hong Kong. It does not seem implausible to hazard the guess that most people in Hong Kong would have preferred the handover not to happen, and, since it was bound to happen, the next best thing would be to maintain a high degree of apartness after and despite the handover. From the degree of their traumatization (by no means an exaggerated description) can be inferred the intensity of their fear of losing their apartness from China, what the central government unilaterally and rather ineffectually calls Hongkongers' motherland. Today, after the early years following the handover turned out to be less traumatic than originally feared, the worst nightmare for many Hongkongers—that of losing their apartness—is belatedly coming to pass and with a vengeance. It is sad to note that for many Hongkongers, perhaps the worst scourge after war and starvation is mainlandization.

It has thus become much clearer, in retrospect, on what implicit understanding the promise of "one country, two systems" was able to serve for a time as a palliative to the Hong Kong psyche. It is extremely important to realize that this magic formula did its work not merely in the legalistic and institutional sense of allowing Hong Kong to retain its capitalist *economic* system and to exercise a high degree of *political* or administrative autonomy but also in the much broader sense of making it possible for Hong Kong to remain *comprehensively* apart from China while being, as much as possible, only nominally a part of it. Apartness rather than independence (except for the recent rise of localism, especially among the young) to be sure, but apartness of a profound and bona fide kind. To many people in Hong Kong, if "one country, two systems" is to mean anything, it must be able to preserve enough apartness from China to ensure that Hong Kong does not become simply "another mainland city"—or, to be more precise, not *another* mainland city but *a* mainland city, period. In the final analysis, a high degree of political, legal, and economic autonomy is valued not so much for its own sake as for the high degree of all-around apartness, especially apartness of identity, it is expected to sustain.

Channeling the Desire for Apartness into the Democracy Movement

Unfortunately, the depth of this desire for apartness, with its constitutive animus against a supposedly still communist China, does not seem to have been properly factored in by those, both in the central government and in the Hong Kong administration, who have exerted the biggest political influence over the course of events in Hong Kong since the handover. But it must have become painfully obvious in the wake of the 2014–2015 civil disobedience movement (known as Occupy Central) that an admittedly considerable degree of political or administrative autonomy combined with the continuation of Hong Kong's distinctive kind of market capitalism—that is, a purely politico-economic arrangement—will not be enough to satisfy the desire for apartness.

It is just this unrequited desire that has come to the fore as both the substance and the motive of the democracy movement in Hong Kong—not the only substance and motive, to be sure, but by far the most important. And not surprisingly, it takes only half-effective mobilization to bring the rousing mixture—the desire for apartness and the passion for democracy—to the boiling point. When the desire for apartness was better satisfied or when it was milder because Hong Kong's sense of superiority to China was more self-assured, it did not need a democratic movement as its vehicle. Now that neither is any longer the case, the desire for apartness must take a new form and find a new expression, and nothing fits the purpose more handily than democracy's call to arms. With China hanging on to one-party rule, what better way is there for Hong Kong to assert its apartness and superiority than via the struggle for democracy? Where else could one find a more natural political affinity than between apartness and democracy: a democratic cause of apartness from a nondemocratic China?

It is not hard to imagine that had participants in the movement been pursuing democracy in a hypothetical Hong Kong that resembled, say, Singapore in its status as a city-state, they would have been involved—career politicians, those in the legal profession or the business sector, college students and faculty, some disadvantaged members of society, and so on—for very divergent reasons, some of which might be linked only through family resemblance. In Hong Kong as we actually find it, a Hong Kong that is grudgingly part of a powerful country still weak in legitimacy, we see an altogether different scenario. Those in the democracy movement all desire one thing, whatever else they may severally desire, and that, as we have seen, is apartness from China and from what China stands for. This gives the movement a special kind of emotional and motivational unity or cohesion, differences of opinion regarding strategy and much else notwithstanding, and, with it, a distinct kind of moral fervor and, on the part of some, of quasi-religious intransigence. The implacable desire for apartness from China may well be the only reason that all members of the movement have in common for joining the cause of what they call genuine democracy in Hong Kong. It may indeed be said that the democracy movement in Hong Kong is, above all, a movement for apartness, a democratic movement for democratic apartness.[1] Without the desire for apartness, it would be a totally different movement with a totally different mass psychology and political dynamic.

Freedom from an unwelcome and, as it were, externally imposed sovereign, rather than domestic civic equality, is what people want first and foremost from democracy in Hong Kong—and from the very experience of striving for democracy. This peculiarity partly explains why the manifest futility of pursuing democracy in the antagonistic spirit of apartness has not deterred the fighters from continuing the fight. For what is at stake is freedom from China more than democracy in its own right, and part of this stake is the very *feeling* of apartness as inner freedom. This is all the truer for those who support independence or at least self-determination (with an open outcome). It also explains why this fight, not least Occupy Central, looks less like the typical domestic political agitation than it does a national liberation movement. In this context, a component in the Hong Kong identity that had always been important became even more pronounced and charged. This is the political-system hostility toward communist China that I addressed in Chapter 7—in the case of Hong Kong, a deeply ingrained animosity toward post-1949 China, whose identity first as a totalitarian and then as an authoritarian communist regime has remained constant in the eyes of the Hong Kong public because of the uninterrupted leadership of the CCP.

Whatever reservations one may have about the postcolonial discourse in which a supposedly communist China figures as the new colonial power in Hong Kong, there is no doubting the psychological reality and ideological perception that such discourse conveys. That dominant and assertive Chinese other from which much of Hong Kong desperately seeks apartness comes across, at least analogically, as a colonial power, an imposition from the outside. What matters most in this perception is not race, of course, but legitimacy, and, as I have noted, China has a huge legitimacy deficit in Hong Kong. When some in Hong Kong call China a new colonial power, this is just another, deliberately provocative way of saying that China's sovereignty over Hong Kong or its way of exercising this sovereignty is not welcome, and its invocation of national identity and belonging does not help, either.

Much as in a national liberation movement, so in Hong Kong's struggle for democracy, the overwhelming concern is to free one's community from a dominant other, whether strictly colonial (as in the first case) or not (as in the second). In Hong Kong this all-consuming passion seems to have so crowded out all other preoccupations that it can sometimes look as if there were no other stake in the struggle for democracy, as if a citizenry famous for its pragmatism wanted nothing else from democracy—as if utilitarian, capitalist Hong Kong, of all places, had overturned Benjamin Constant's thesis regarding the priority, in our world, of the liberties of the moderns over that of the ancients. The upsurge in independence-seeking localism in the wake of Occupy Central is but the latest mutation of a more general political dynamic. And, not insignificantly, this happens to be a mutation that is not particularly costly on the part of those, still in high school or college, who do not yet have enough tangible material interests about which to exercise political prudence.

Speaking of material interests, there is little doubt that a huge amount of the oppositional energy that has been poured into the democracy movement stems from pent-up frustration, however unconscious or subconscious, with the city's scandalous level of inequality and, in step with the rest of the advanced capitalist world, the worsening of career prospects and chances of upward social mobility, especially for the young.[2] In this regard, Hong Kong is doing much worse than mainland China in terms of so-called performance legitimacy, with the almost predictable result that masses of ordinary citizens enjoying neither upward social mobility nor the (at least procedural) chance to improve their lot through democracy must find some way of venting their frustration. The objects of this frustration, in turn, must have a large part of their cause in a local political economy known for favoring real estate developers and big business in general and balking at more than the bare minimum of social welfare for the worst off. But why hasn't this frustration been mobilized on a society-wide scale in the name of, and for the sake of, greater social justice? Why hasn't the coexistence of huge wealth for the rich and manifestly undignified living conditions for the poor provoked much reflection on Hong Kong's distinctive capitalist system, accompanied by a public outcry to radically reform it?[3] Why, instead, is Hong Kong's market economy, often lauded as the "freest" in the world by neoliberal think tanks, still so effectively serving for so many in Hong Kong as an object of pride differentiating Hong Kong from China? And why has the central government's long-standing (though now somewhat, but only somewhat, weakened)[4] oligarchic alliance with Hong Kong's billionaire class seemed often to be the least of local complaints against China? The answer is simple: none of these descriptions of grievances or explanations of their causes has the remotest chance of resonating far and wide in ultraliberal, capitalist Hong Kong. Even more importantly, none of them speaks explicitly to the problematic of apartness and gives direct expression to the overwhelming desire for apartness, and therefore none of them is capable of eliciting political passion in a city where the issue of identity has all along eclipsed that of class.

We are thus led to the inescapable conclusion that the democracy movement in Hong Kong is not about the self-protection of society against capitalism (Karl Polanyi's rationale for democracy, as discussed in Chapter 4) but about the self-defense of Hong Kong's identity against mainland China. It is not about (distributive) social justice but about recognition; not about political participation as an exercise in collective power in the spirit of (European) social democracy but about political agitation as an expression of and vehicle for a distinct and separate identity. For those who care about democracy for the first reason in each of the foregoing distinctions, the most salient fact staring them in the face is the iron grip that the tycoon class has on Hong Kong's economy and society. This fact imposes a formidable constraint on the extent of social justice and welfare possible in Hong Kong and hence on the scope for effective democratic politics. Given this constraint, a democratic political structure of real substance would be a most improbable prospect, regardless of what the CCP wants to see in Hong Kong. For democracy, once formally instituted, would either be reduced to utter impotence, as long as the constraint is in place, or else be revolutionary and destabilizing, if it threatened to sweep away the constraint and, with it, what has so far given

Hong Kong the only stability and (highly unequal) prosperity in its recent experience.

If truth be told, the only semblance of democracy compatible with the avoidance of potential social upheaval would be a mixed regime à la Aristotle or Polybius (with the central government, along with its partial representative in Hong Kong in the person of the chief executive, being the One, as it were, the capitalist class or the tycoons the Few, and ordinary people the Many)—openly acknowledged as such, of course—leaving a more worthy democracy to the fullness of time. But this is beside the point as things stand. What the partisans of democracy want is "genuine democracy" right now, and this has little to do with protection against capitalism and everything to do with defense against China and its nominal communism. The Many whose sympathies rest with the democracy movement have chosen to side with the Few, the tycoon class, in defense of their shared Hong Kong identity, at least to the extent of not targeting the Few as their chief political adversary. In doing so, they have left unexplored the option of siding with the One, the central government in Beijing, in the interest of securing greater economic equality and social welfare. Had they contemplated that option, at a time when the central government badly needed their (moral) support for electoral reform, they might well have succeeded in wresting substantial concessions from the tycoon class—and from its representatives in the political establishment of the special administrative region (SAR)—with the help of pressure exerted by the central government. That nothing of the sort happened, or is likely to happen in the foreseeable future, speaks volumes about the thoroughly capitalist character of Hong Kong society, the preeminent role of identity politics in the democracy movement, and the resulting blind spots and limitations of the otherwise commendable democratic struggles.

Thus Occupy Central is a misleading name, because the movement was not at all directed against capitalism, financial or real estate, as Occupy Wall Street, its prototype, clearly had been. What the movement expressed instead, above all, was many Hongkongers' desire for apartness—the desire, that is, not so much to create a new (democratic) Hong Kong as to retain or restore what was once true of old Hong Kong—namely, its palpable and conspicuous difference and separateness from China. It is a coincidence at once understandable and potentially confusing that democracy thus presented itself as the chief vehicle for satisfying this desire.

This, it seems, is the fundamental fact about politics and political consciousness in Hong Kong today. Small wonder, then, that democracy—democracy for apartness and apartness as democracy—has become the single biggest public issue in Hong Kong. Politics, in other words, has come to revolve around apartness, with political differences among citizens defined largely in terms of how much apartness they want. Not everyone wants strong apartness, to be sure, and not everyone wants apartness with passion. But a substantial number want strong apartness and do so with passion, and it is they who have given the struggle for democracy in Hong Kong the distinctive meaning it has—a spectrum of meaning that has now been stretched to include more radical calls for independence or self-determination. Thanks to their impact, the division of Left and Right on economic and social issues has been almost entirely preempted, or displaced, by the politics of apartness. Even in the case of the democracy activists, one senses that most of them have gotten involved in the movement not so much because they care about specific public issues and seek through democratization a platform for pursuing them as because they passionately desire apartness and because, under Hong Kong's present circumstances, there is no more potent way of objectifying and voicing this desire than through the fight for democracy. The historically rather moderate desire for a comprehensive apartness has thus crystallized and escalated into a highly charged passion for *political* apartness: for a democratic Hong Kong versus an undemocratic China. One is thus left in little doubt that the current struggle for democracy in Hong Kong is political in a special sense—that is, in Carl Schmitt's sense of starkly and implacably pitting "us" against "them," "friends" against "enemies"—quite beyond the conflict of mere interests, or so it seems.[5] The unprecedentedly belligerent rhetoric that is often heard in the thick of Hong Kong's democracy movement, far from being merely juvenile or immature, mirrors the unprecedented politicization of Hong Kong in just this sense.

This does not mean, however, that democracy is an excuse or pretext merely playing the role of a polarizer. I have (in Chapter 3 and elsewhere) discussed at length the rise of equality of conditions in China and its profound impact on social and political psychology. There is a sense in which the most decisive and far-reaching transformation in Hong Kong brought about by China's resumption of sovereignty in 1997 was none other than the establishment of equality of conditions. This was comparable in the nature of its consequences for Hong Kong to the year of 1776 for America, for in Hong Kong until 1997, much as in America until 1776, inequality of conditions had prevailed by virtue of colonial rule. Whereas America established itself after independence as a republic and then a democracy,[6] post-1997 Hong Kong has not been able to match its newfound equality of conditions with a corresponding democracy. It is thus not surprising that Hong Kong has become progressively more ungovernable—after an initial period of relatively patient waiting for democracy's expected arrival. In this context, the argument concerning China as a whole (as made in Chapter 3) seems to apply to Hong Kong with special force, for the lifting of colonial rule and the ushering in of equality of conditions in a society that was already liberal have unleashed a dynamic toward democracy that is well-nigh impossible to argue against and to completely frustrate with success. The only thing standing in the way of this dynamic running its natural course is the fact that Hong Kong is not a sovereign state, as America was able to become with independence, while the sovereign state to whose jurisdiction it has returned is not a democracy. Democracy can happen in Hong Kong only at the sovereign's pleasure, yet Hong Kong's lack of universal, wholehearted identification with China naturally makes the sovereign balk at the prospect of a democratic Hong Kong asserting itself against the motherland.

Why Hong Kong Cannot Have a Separate Political System

Hong Kong *is* part of China, and, as long as China is able to keep things this way, any democratic movement with strong apartness from China as its twin objective is doomed to failure. It is precisely this desire for apartness, especially for political apartness, that the central government does not want to satisfy in any shape or form. What China with its sovereign's prerogative demands from Hong Kong is identification with, not apartness from, the motherland, and, accordingly, a high degree of autonomy is designed to secure such identification rather than an identity-constituting apartness. The limits imposed by this very sovereignty make up an even more fundamental fact about Hong Kong than its desire for apartness—an iron fact, one might say, that has framed a flesh-and-blood desire since the handover.

The bottom line is that Hong Kong cannot have a separate and independent political system and, ipso facto, a separate and independent *democratic* political system. In this sense, the very idea of democracy in Hong Kong *as a political system,* as a self-authorizing regime, is an odd proposition. Strictly speaking, it does not make sense, and, somewhat loosely construed, it could make only a kind of limited sense that many in Hong Kong consider worth very little. Yet this has not prevented democracy from becoming a hotly contested concept among the three main parties concerned—the central government in Beijing and, very broadly speaking, the two opposing sides in Hong Kong, one of which is politically very close to the central government. It is not surprising that the contest has heaped confusion upon confusion, yielding a lot of heat and almost no light. Yet plainly none of this is simply obtuseness and the parties involved seem to know perfectly well what they are doing, because each has studiously refused to be the first to utter the politically unutterable—namely, that democracy in Hong Kong, in the all-important sense just noted, is not a meaningful proposition.

It is a commonplace that democracy is, above all, a distinct type of sovereignty—namely, popular sovereignty or sovereignty of the people. What is usually left unsaid, because unnecessary, but not misunderstood is that this sovereignty is one that is exercised on itself. As far as Hong Kong is concerned, however, there is no getting around the fact that sovereignty resides not in itself but in the People's Republic of China. Hong Kong's basic political structure is not authorized by its own, selfsame sovereignty, popular or otherwise, because it does not have any (and has never had any), and therefore the idea of Hong Kong as a democratic system or polity does not make sense, strictly speaking. (By the same token, democracy in Hong Kong would have made no more sense under the British colonial government.) This has been reinforced by its designation since 1997 as an SAR subject to the formula "one country, two systems," which is meant to serve as the fundamental guideline for Hong Kong's affairs, including its relations with the central government. "One country" means precisely that sovereignty rests with China, not Hong Kong, and that what is imprecisely and misleadingly called Hong Kong's "system" must be authorized by China.

What the Chinese government has authorized for Hong Kong is a different way of conducting political and other affairs than applies to the mainland, including the method of choosing the chief executive and members of the legislature and, perhaps even more important, continuation of the colonial legacy of the rule of law with an independent judiciary. This different way is of sufficient independence, especially by virtue of a legal system vastly different from the mainland's, to be roughly called a separate "system"; and, with the addition of periodic elections to select public officials, elements of it can sufficiently resemble certain features of democratic sovereign states (or units of a democratic federal system) to be called "democratic." But whatever democracy is thereby made possible does not have its source in a selfsame sovereignty, let alone a selfsame popular sovereignty, and, for this reason, it cannot strictly be called a political system, any more than units of a democratic federal union can. This then is the limited sense that democracy in Hong Kong can have if loosely construed: not as a political system, still less as the expression of popular sovereignty, but only as *a democratic way of doing certain political things.*

It is only understandable that in granting Hong Kong a democratic way of doing things, the central government in Beijing wants to make sure, above all else, that the election that is part of this arrangement will not produce a chief executive who is unfavorably disposed toward the central government and may act on this disposition in his or her official capacity. It is this imperative, itself part of the CCP's general habit of insuring against any hint of political dissent, let alone instability, that lies behind the framework for the election of the chief executive laid down by the National People's Congress Standing Committee on August 31, 2014. We need not be detained here by the exact substance of this framework, as the proposal for electoral reform tabled by the Hong Kong SAR government within the framework was subsequently voted down in the legislature, so the framework itself is now history. As far as electoral reform is concerned, Hong Kong is back to square one—although being *back* to square one in matters like this never means exactly square one. The only thing that is worth noting in the present context is that under any electoral rules compatible with this framework, it would be next to impossible for the scenario feared by the central government to happen, which is precisely the purpose.

It is equally understandable, however, that the so-called pan-democrats cried foul upon hearing what they called the "restrictive" framework—understandable especially because the framework would effectively prevent anyone within their ranks from even being nominated as a candidate, let alone elected. Such complete disempowerment naturally left them unhappy and protesting in the name of "genuine universal suffrage," whose precise meaning therefore can be grasped only in this context. The framework does not allow genuine universal suffrage, according to their logic, because although the chief executive is to be elected on the basis of one person, one vote, and hence nominally universal suffrage, candidates of a certain political persuasion would be screened out by a pro-Beijing, unrepresentative nominating committee. This charge is no doubt correct and their reaction is completely understandable. But why, an observer might ask (in the interest of understanding what is going on), must they help bring about the restrictive framework of the National People's Congress by being so unfavorably disposed toward the central government in the first place?

The answer is simple and can be found in the mentality of apartness, especially political apartness, sketched earlier. They are staunch Western-style democrats (minus, in most cases, pronounced leanings toward *social* democracy), strong believers in the Western liberal values as universal values, and they cannot pretend to be otherwise. As such, they have trouble pledging unequivocal allegiance to the sovereignty of China because this sovereignty happens to be embodied by what they see as a communist party-state. In their eyes, the People's Republic of China is inseparable from the CCP—so inseparable that to express allegiance to the former is to imply political and ideological endorsement of or at least acquiescence in the latter, and this they cannot bring themselves to do as honest, conscientious liberal democrats.

Nor is this only a matter of conscience. Politically, their firm ideological stance raises the specter of divided loyalties. The pan-democrats are openly and uncompromisingly committed to Western-style liberal democratic values, and it is by no means certain that this *ideological* commitment would not translate into *political* ambivalence, which might even set them at loggerheads with the central government while making them unduly cozy with Western governments, should they one day take the reins of power in Hong Kong. There is a foretaste of this very possibility in the way that pan-democrats of all persuasions have been seeking the support of Western media and politicians as if they were part of an international democratic alliance pitted against the authoritarian Chinese state. Their attachment to Western-style democracy seems as instinctive as their animus against what they see as Chinese communist authoritarianism is irresistible.

This fact alone is enough to make the Chinese government apprehensive, in the same way that Western governments, not least the US political establishment during the McCarthy era, were worried about domestic communist subversion during the Cold War. Just as the communists in Western countries back then wanted to replace the capitalist system at home, so it is no secret that the pan-democrats in Hong Kong today—at least those, especially the older members of the camp, who still think of China as their motherland—harbor the fervent wish to see China turn into a Western-style democracy, and the sooner the better. How can they, given who they are, genuinely feel and unreservedly express allegiance to a sovereignty that is bound up with a political form to which they take the strongest exception? And yet, from the point of view of the Chinese government, how can the pan-democrats be trusted with the running of Hong Kong, with all that this entails, when in their hearts they desire regime change in China?

There is thus an unbridgeable ideological and political divide between the CCP in China and the pan-democrats in Hong Kong. Short of China as a whole turning into a Western-style democracy, the only way for Hong Kong, now a part of China, to become such a democracy is for Hong Kong to become independent, to become politically apart from China. It is a foregone conclusion that the Chinese government will never allow this to happen, which means that Hong Kong will have no chance of "genuine universal suffrage" until China as a whole sees fit to embrace it.

In the light of this logic, one should not be surprised that the more uncompromising members of the pan-democratic camp, very loosely construed (especially given the radicalization of those at its margins), want to see Hong Kong tear itself away from China and become independent. Although this desire is not realistic, it makes some sense that it exists, if only because democracy is such an important vehicle for asserting Hong Kong's apartness from China and yet even in principle there is no other way for Hong Kong to become a Western-style democracy than by separating itself from China. Even though mainstream members of the pan-democratic camp, particularly the career politicians, steer clear of any talk of independence, what can often be glimpsed beneath the politically prudent surface is a deep antipathy toward the People's Republic of China that is barely distinguishable from an indiscriminate contempt for communism and, via communism, for the only China that now exists.

Parochial as this hostility may seem, it is not incompatible with the democratic mentality, for democracy as one organizing principle of a cohesive, bounded political group presupposes, unlike liberalism as an individualistic and humanitarian-cosmopolitan doctrine, the relative homogeneity of the citizen body, and this homogeneity, however it may be conceived, is achieved through the exclusion of whoever does not belong to it. Mainland China, seen as an authoritarian communist party-state, is what does not belong to this democratic homogeneity, now being constructed in Hong Kong, and what must therefore be excluded. In this context, Hong Kong, or a big part of it, has become more political than ever before—political not only in the customary sense but also, as noted earlier, in Schmitt's distinctive sense. To be political in the latter sense is to think and act in terms of the friend-enemy distinction, and many in the pan-democratic camp have lived up to this understanding of the political by treating China / communism as the external enemy that helps define Hong Kong / democracy, which they sometimes, as during Occupy Central, seem ready to defend to the death.

This mentality, which expresses itself in a variety of ways, is not quite the same as the rejection of Chinese sovereignty over Hong Kong. It can be both stronger and weaker than such rejection. But there is one sense in which it goes deeper: it is, on the part of some, the rejection of being Chinese—or, in a more conditional and nuanced way, the rejection of being Chinese in the monolithic manner that mainland China today is taken to stand for, or of being Chinese as long as China remains under the leadership of the CCP. Yet it is obvious that this is more than rejection merely of the CCP, for it takes as its object, as fair game, mainland Chinese as such, regardless of their attitude toward the CCP, and despite the fact that few mainland Chinese seriously think of their society as communist.

It is difficult to know exactly what proportion of Hongkongers think and feel this way, and the numbers keep changing anyway. But there is no mistaking the profound transformation of the political mentality in Hong Kong over the past few years. "One country, two systems" has completely lost its consensus-building power, even its effect as a palliative, however little it may have had of either initially,[7] and we are seeing an SAR of China in which a far from negligible number of people are unhappy with "one country" and would not settle for "two systems" unless the latter comes close to meaning two sovereignties and two ideological and political allegiances.

In a way, the seeds of what is only now staring us in the face have been there from the beginning, in the application of an overly harmonious-sounding formula to a reality full of intractable divisions. "One country, two systems" may be an ingenious response to this reality, but its surface optimism makes light of a difficulty that is implicit in its very logic. For the notion of "two systems" unequivocally assigns Hong Kong to the category of the capitalist system, and yet, given the close political and ideological link in recent history between capitalism and liberal democracy (in the case of colonial Hong Kong, via the United Kingdom), this is almost tantamount to placing Hong Kong on the side of liberal democracy as well. Once Hong Kong was severed from the United Kingdom, its capitalism lost the semblance of ideological integrity that used to rest, however tenuously, on the liberal democratic character of its former colonial master. To make itself whole (again), post-1997 capitalist Hong Kong has naturally strained toward liberal democracy—at least toward liberalism and, democracy being liberty's natural guarantee, toward democracy via liberalism. (This is in addition to the struggle for democracy as apartness, and to the democratizing effect of the post-1997 equality of conditions, both discussed in the last section. All three factors must be taken into account in trying to understand the irrepressible pull of democracy in Hong Kong today.) In this light, the notion of "one country" turns out to be a lot more demanding than it is usually made out to be; for it expects of Hong Kong's citizens a patriotic loyalty—loyalty to a (nominally) communist China—that is at odds with their politico-ideological leanings toward liberal democracy. If "one country, two systems" is unique in its artful compromise, it is no less unique in its conflicting demands and in the competing impulses (unintentionally) unleashed in the post-1997 Hong Kong citizenry.[8]

One particularly ominous symptom of the inherently divisive character of Hong Kong's political situation has been the near impossibility of any chief executive of the Hong Kong SAR being able to remotely please for long both the populace and the central government. For "one country, two systems" to be credible and stable, what Hong Kong needs is an effective political leadership that is neither supplicant to the central government nor implacably opposed to it—that can work with and be, as it were, on the same side as the central government while having the integrity to disagree with it openly and, when the (rare) occasion calls for it, even strongly, but always deferentially and within the bounds of the Basic Law. If the room for such leadership has been uncertain at best ever since 1997, it has now almost completely disappeared, very visibly. The vassal-like daily behavior of the Hong Kong leadership vis-à-vis the central government sends an unmistakable message: when those who govern Hong Kong see their first imperative as that of not taking even a moderate stand that might remotely contradict the wishes of the central government, the ordinary citizens of Hong Kong can be forgiven for thinking that they are dominated twice over.

This means that Hong Kong is in for a prolonged confrontation, whether violent or relatively muted, until all the major tensions inherent in postcolonial Hong Kong have had a chance to straighten themselves out. By its very nature, and hence from its founding moment, post-1997 Hong Kong has not really lent itself to the harmony all too optimistically prefigured in "one country, two systems." The architects too must wake up to this reality and reexamine their presuppositions and expectations—and go back to the drawing board (at an opportune moment).

Sovereignty without Identification

The "one country" part of "one country, two systems" is not just about sovereignty—that is, the sovereignty of the People's Republic of China over the SAR of Hong Kong. It is also designed to achieve political *integration*: "one country" means oneness of country, with sovereignty made concrete and secure by integration. Since this integration is meant to accommodate "two systems" and the two systems differ politically (one supposedly socialist and the other capitalist), it is only natural that political integration must largely take the form of *prepolitical,* or *metapolitical,* integration. Thus hopes for the success of political integration are pinned on ethnic-cultural identification with China as a nation, an identification that was presumed to already exist in Hong Kong to a substantial degree at the time of the handover and that could be strengthened over time. In this context, "one country" means, more precisely, "one nation" or "one nation-state," where the nation, resting on deep ethnic and cultural bonds and a prepolitical national consciousness, is expected to transcend the shallower, political divide between "two systems." The result, if achieved, will be the integration of the Hong Kong SAR into the People's Republic of China, with the latter understood as a *nation*-state rather than a political system—a nonpolitical political integration, if you will, or political integration resting on ethnic-cultural rather than directly political identification. To this integration are meant to be added supporting economic measures, so that the solidarity of shared descent and tradition will be reinforced by the material benefits of shared economic and social advancement.

It would be an understatement to say that this is not how things have turned out. The strength of ethnic-cultural identification was overestimated, and what identification there was has not been protected or tapped effectively, in what may have been unfavorable circumstances to begin with. China's assertion of sovereignty over Hong Kong, to be successful, presupposes on the part of Hong Kong a Chinese identity supported in one way or another. Alas, this identity was not ready-made, at least for a very large portion of the Cantonese-speaking Hong Kong population (let alone the residents of non-Chinese origin), but had to be created. It could only be created on the basis of China becoming an attractive proposition with which Hongkongers would be eager or at least willing to identify. In this China has signally failed in the two decades since the handover, whatever the causes. The hoped-for political integration has consequently not materialized, and some of those who have not been adequately integrated are turning the de facto separation into a cause of separatism. This does not exactly mean that Chinese sovereignty is objectively under threat; far from it. But such sovereignty is increasingly reliant on power as distinct from authority. Insofar as power, the conspicuous threat or exertion of superior force, invites resistance, a cycle of mutual provocation has already been set in motion, with no clear first cause and, if truth be told, with no end in sight. Thus, strictly speaking, the crisis we are witnessing in Hong Kong is one of failed political integration conceived in terms of ethnic-cultural identification backed up with economic support. Yet, because national sovereignty is also at stake, the crisis has the potential to grow even bigger—to the point of inviting more openly political integration as a last resort, or next-to-last resort. This will not be good news, should it come to pass, for, under Hong Kong's present circumstances, any attempt at openly political integration would only further weaken ethnic-cultural identification, leading to a vicious circle.

The key to integration, and hence to sovereignty taking root, lies in fostering Hong Kong's identification with China. Ethnic-cultural identification is not the only relevant form of identification, but we would do well to consider it first. If we distinguish between ascribed identity and actual, active identification, there is little doubt that the latter is what is needed in this context and that all along there has been less of it in Hong Kong in relation to China than the central government must have hoped. This relative lack of active identification is hardly surprising in view of the highly divergent trajectories of mainland China and Hong Kong, not least since 1949. By the time of the 1997 handover, Hong Kong had developed a distinctive Sino-British form of life, thanks to what was widely regarded as a relatively benign colonial experience, hugely boosted by the city's economic takeoff in the 1980s and by its resulting superiority in wealth and prosperity to mainland China, which it was able to maintain until the latter's recent spectacular rise. It was with this mixed form of life that most Hongkongers identified, rather than with Chinese culture or tradition as such. If much of this hybrid form of everyday life was substantively more Chinese than British, especially for ordinary people, the framing of this life came from the colonial power and hence was more British than Chinese. This framing too—not least the civil liberties, rule of law, and small government—had become part of Hong Kong's culture, indeed its political culture. If we break national identification down into its ethnic and cultural components, it seems that culturally, especially with regard to political culture, a very large number of people in Hong Kong had developed a stronger identification with Britain, and the West at large, than with China, and that this mattered no less to them than their ascribed ethnic Chinese identity. When, after the handover, people describe themselves as Hongkongers rather than, or more than, Chinese, this is a way of expressing the bifurcation of ethnic identity and cultural identification and giving special weight to the latter, especially as far as political culture is concerned. This bifurcation cuts even deeper if we add, on the side of cultural identification, liberal capitalist Hong Kong's almost total lack of consciousness of a shared "historical destiny" with communist China. This legacy of the Cold War has continued to this day, despite China's profound transformation in the reform era. The writing was already on the wall in 1997, indeed much earlier when the anticipated handover had been greeted with more apprehension than celebration, and with little sense of the unification, at long last, of a nation torn apart through its former weakness.

With the passage of time, of course, the colonial experience has receded into the background, and what is immediately constitutive of much of Hong

Kong today is no longer identification with the United Kingdom but a dis-identification, or negative identification, with China. In this regard, one of the decisive events was undoubtedly June 4, 1989. Whatever dream of democracy may have existed up to that point must have turned in a matter of days or weeks into a desire at once moral and prudential and hence one to be actively pursued, as subsequent events have amply demonstrated. However else democracy may have been viewed before June 4, it definitely came to be regarded thereafter as Hong Kong's only antidote to the much-feared excesses of Chinese rule after the handover. Against this background, "one country, two systems" came to be viewed, by a sizable part of the Hong Kong population, not in terms of capitalism versus socialism, as meant by the Basic Law, but more and more in terms of democracy versus its opposite. Anyone pondering the implications of this change of political consciousness would be able to see, especially with the extended hindsight now available, that the project of political integration has been doomed from the start.

On the one hand, Hong Kong after the handover will not, after a period of more or less patient reorientation, be pacified until a broadly credited form of democracy is achieved. On the other hand, democracy in Hong Kong does not promise to promote political integration unless and until China as a whole embraces democracy as well. Until then, a Hong Kong proud of its democracy as its new political identity (supposing, counterfactually, it is granted its wish) would only grow further apart from a nondemocratic China—either through the gradual attenuation of concerns for the nation or, as would be more likely, through agitation for democratic change on the mainland, or even for independence. It is all but certain that, if achieved, democracy in Hong Kong would not serve as an alternative vehicle of identification with China where ethnic-cultural bonds have failed. It would perhaps be an exaggeration to suggest that the only Chinese patriotism acceptable to most people in Hong Kong has to be one based on identification with a constitution enshrining the democratic rule of law—the so-called constitutional patriotism.[9] But there can be little doubt that, short of such a constitutional transformation in China, it would be difficult to see Hongkongers as a whole brought back *wholeheartedly* into the national fold. Even in the best scenario (given the separatist tendencies to be reckoned with), just too many Hongkongers would embrace the motherland only in their capacity as citizens of a democratic state, and until then they would be increasingly unable and unwilling to make up for what is missing by identifying with China as a community of common descent. As things stand now, ethnic-cultural identification is either attenuated by the combination of colonial hybridization and antipathy toward communist China as the de facto center of Chinese ethnos or, where it is manifestly present, rendered politically impotent by a lack of civic identification.

There is thus no easy fix: if democracy is a recipe for the pacification of Hong Kong, it is no less a recipe for enhanced negative identification with China as long as the latter remains nondemocratic. This incompatibility of democracy in Hong Kong (even construed as only a democratic way of doing things) with Hong Kong's political integration with China is the most important political fact about Hong Kong today, and about the relationship between Hong Kong and the central government. Until this fact is changed, and it can only be changed or at least modified by tackling the deeper issue of apartness, we are not going to see any fundamental change in Hong Kong's political crisis.

Apartness as a Greater Challenge Than Democracy

In a realpolitik sense, however, all is not lost, for what appears to have been lost was never Hong Kong's to enjoy or to successfully struggle for in the first place. A chief executive who might be ideologically and politically ill disposed toward the central government in Beijing was never in the cards, therefore a method of election that might lead to such a result was never in the cards, and therefore so-called genuine universal suffrage, by which the pan-democrats mean precisely such a method, was never in the cards. Those Hongkongers who thought otherwise and thought unrealistically must, if they care to promote democracy with enough prudence to be effective, come to terms with the facts of the matter, which were there from the start and which recent events have served only to make explicit.

It is only when these facts of the matter have sunk in and are accepted politically, if not fully affirmed morally, that Hong Kong will be ready to make the best of the limited democracy that is realistic under "one country, two systems"—namely, a democratic (or more democratic) way of doing certain political things. Chief among the things that most Hongkongers prize and that can belong to this democratic way of doing things without giving the central government good reason to stand in the way are civil liberties and the rule of law. Indeed, such things are already well established in Hong Kong, and the central government would be foolish to try to undercut them if Hongkongers show themselves ready to exercise a correlative restraint (on which more later).

Ultimately, two concerns take precedence over everything else as far as the Chinese government is concerned in relation to Hong Kong. The first is China's sovereignty over Hong Kong, valued in its own right and as an example for Taiwan, and the second Hong Kong's stability, followed by a third that is of course very important but by no means absolutely essential in itself—that is, Hong Kong's continuing prosperity. As long as the first concern is fully satisfied and the second largely satisfied, and the third sufficiently satisfied not to affect the first two, the rest is negotiable. The realpolitik constraints thus leave substantial room for exploring and gradually improving the democratic way of doing things in Hong Kong—subject, one must hasten to add, to what normally are not (but should be) thought of as realpolitik constraints as well, the limits set by Hong Kong's tycoon-dominated capitalist system, which more than anything else is what is meant by "system" in "one country, two systems." How well this room is used, and how much the tycoon constraint can be loosened, is a test for the political realism and wisdom present in Hong Kong; how securely and unambiguously the room is guaranteed is a test for the confidence and prudence of the central government in Beijing.

It is another matter, however, whether the vast majority of Hong Kong's citizens will see enough value in this room, in what I have called the democratic way of doing certain political things, in the first place. In other words, it is a separate question whether they are *motivated* enough to be realistic.

A fast-shifting balance of power between two parties long separated and then reunited, with much reluctance on one side and with nothing less than identity and self-esteem at stake, cannot but present a nearly intractable problem. If the problem is to be overcome or even merely contained, it must be recognized for what it is: it goes beyond democracy, is larger than democracy, and must itself be resolved or at least brought under control if significant progress is to be made in democratization, rather than the other way around. What is decisive, then, is what will happen to Hong Kong's identity-constituting apartness from China, and hence the handling of this apartness is the biggest and toughest test for both Hong Kong and China. This apartness, deeper and wider even than the political divide, is the fundamental fact about Hong Kong in its relation to China, and bespeaks a stubborn psychological reality that borders on the instinct for (identity) survival, both individual and collective.

It would be foolish to moralize this fact, either pro or con, for the fact has behind it a complex genealogy comprising layer upon layer of estrangement laced with a strange, one might even say estranged, closeness. Estranged closeness, as it happens, inasmuch as Hong Kong has come to depend for its identity and self-esteem on comparison with a larger yet inferior China—a China that it neither can do without nor wants to be part of. Yet China, while looming as large as before, is no longer so inferior, and, as a collectivity, not at all, with the further complication that, while no longer inferior, China has not risen enough to be fully legitimate. Leaving aside this further complication for now, there is no denying that the old balance of economic and cultural power between Hong Kong and China once (and still somewhat) constitutive of the Hong Kong identity is receding irrevocably into the past, and the new balance of power created by the so-called rise of China requires drastic adjustment on the part of Hong Kong as well as China.

Over and above its struggle to achieve democracy, Hong Kong needs to fundamentally rethink its apartness from China and develop a different kind of apartness that is in keeping with the new reality on the ground and hence has to be more equal and less zero-sum, more composed and less hostile, even perhaps more self-referential and more truly self-reliant and less parasitic on comparative advantage. This is an extremely tall order, of course. But there is little doubt that a belligerent insistence on radical apartness, or any variation on the old apartness that is no longer viable, will not work for Hong Kong and will only provoke overreaction from China.

In addition to its concern with sovereignty, China for its part must understand Hong Kong's apartness and find ways of lessening its estrangement and antagonism over time. To this end, it must refrain from trying to reduce this apartness through useless, indeed counterproductive, propaganda. It must also learn how to make Hongkongers feel free, equal, and respected instead of laboring under the illusion that showering economic favors on Hong Kong from time to time, especially when they do not have broad and tangible effects on the lower social strata, will on its own do much to weaken a desire for apartness that goes far deeper than material benefits. Treating Hong Kong with miscomprehension and the haughtiness of a master, if only reactively, will not work and will only cause Hong Kong to grow even further apart.

In alluding to the ineffectiveness of economic measures, however, I do not mean to suggest that such measures per se are unimportant or are bound to be ineffective. This is true only of economic measures conceived with reactive short-termism instead of political imagination and not designed to produce reasonably equitable and widespread benefits. If anything, ambitious and wise economic measures have never been more indispensable to political integration than under Hong Kong's present circumstances. It is far from inconceivable that the much-needed progress in political integration that has failed to materialize on the basis of ethnic-cultural identification may take place with the help of equitable and prudent economic measures. Such measures must be so conceived as to help bring about two scenarios: first, the mainland interacting with Hong Kong's economy in ways that better benefit ordinary Hongkongers, and especially benefit them more widely and equitably, than has been the case so far; and, second, a gradual yet major restructuring and rebalancing of Hong Kong's economy in favor of the less advantaged, giving them a plausible basis for hope once this process is seen to be under way.

What is happening in Hong Kong today is not only stalled democratization but, simultaneously and even more consequentially, economic disenfranchisement. I have heard it said that Occupy Central is Hong Kong's version of Brexit—before Brexit, of course—and I think there is a more than a grain of truth to this analogy. What Hongkongers need is greater enfranchisement, both political and economic. Since political enfranchisement is not going to happen anytime soon (and in any case, given the current level of alienation from China, would be counterproductive with regard to political integration until China itself embarks on democratic transformation), economic enfranchisement alone is what may help ease the prevalent resentment and frustration until a more propitious time arrives for political empowerment.

The unyielding militancy of Hong Kong's democracy movement that is so uncharacteristic of Hong Kong's otherwise inveterate pragmatism is to a large extent a sublimation of two crises—an identity/identification crisis, occasioned by the handover and exacerbated by June 4, and a crisis of economic disenfranchisement. This sublimation is already showing signs of hardening into a political movement that does not care to understand itself in anything but purely political terms and that displaces onto democracy frustrations and hopes for which democracy is extremely unlikely to be an effective vehicle in today's world. If anything can begin to slow down and even undo this hardening in the absence of significant political progress, it is economic enfranchisement. If even such partial enfranchisement does not happen, if large numbers of people, especially young people, feel *comprehensively* left out or unintegrated—that is, both politically and economically—then we will have no excuse for being surprised if populism increases and Hong Kong sinks deeper into crisis.

And, of course, progress in economic enfranchisement can aid political integration only if both Hong Kong and the central government, especially the latter as the more powerful party, find the incentive and ability to develop a less reactive and confrontational approach to the deeper issue of apartness. Both sides acting artlessly and with excessive self-righteousness on this emotionally charged issue, as they have been doing much of the time, will only reinforce the vicious circle that already seems to require near political genius to break. If Hong Kong and China do not find their way out of this vicious circle soon enough, the years leading up to 2047 could well see the breaking of the camel's back, which means either driving Hong Kong's desire for apartness to truly explosive proportions or crushing that desire by crushing the very fact of Hong Kong's apartness. In either case, the Hong Kong that is prized by Hongkongers and Chinese at large alike, and many others as well, would be no more, and that, rather than the events of 1997, would mean the veritable "disappearance of Hong Kong" as Hong Kong.

Legitimacy Is the Key, Not Economic Power

The two disastrous scenarios just mentioned, if either comes to pass, will have as their cause not merely the ineptitude of Hong Kong and China in dealing with the challenge of apartness. Whether Hong Kong is willing to bend for its own good, as it were, and whether China is able to act with sufficient deftness not to break Hong Kong are matters not merely of political realism and skill but, fundamentally, of legitimacy—that is, of Hong Kong's perception of China's legitimacy. In other words, if Hong Kong is to successfully recalibrate its identity in response to the changing balance of power between it and China (in addition to its changed status after the handover), China for its part must match its rising power with a comparable enhancement of its legitimacy. In the world as we find it today, there is no way that China would be able to win over Hong Kong and dissolve the hostility animating its estrangement without sharply raising its legitimacy internationally. Further, there is no way that China could bring about this enhancement on the international stage without first noticeably improving its legitimacy at home. And, last, there is no way that China could greatly enhance its domestic legitimacy—as distinct from silencing and deactivating all dissent and opposition—without making significant strides in its democratic development.

My point is not that China lacks legitimacy in absolute terms, although it does in the eyes of many, but rather that it lacks the legitimacy to go with the undoubted rise in its economic and, to an increasingly conspicuous degree, its military power. Despite its status as the world's second-largest economy, and its corresponding impact on the global economy, China has yet to command true (as distinct from opportunistic) approval and admiration, and it will have achieved this only when others, including Hong Kong, want to become like it instead of merely taking from it and, in the case of Hong Kong, value the fact of being part of it. There is no shortage of countries in the world that are all too eager to benefit from China's rise as an economic powerhouse through trade and investment, but there are few whose populations are unreservedly drawn to what China is and what it stands for. Many in Hong Kong do not even seem to care to benefit from China in this way, as the latter's international business and trading partners (not least the US high-tech and financial elite) are so eager to do, and while this may be partly an illusion, there is no doubt that few in Hong Kong are exactly keen to have their city become like China. Small wonder, then, that no overwhelming majority in Hong Kong takes unqualified pride in a sense of belonging to China. Insofar as what is involved is identification rather than mere obedience, this is a battle that China has definitely lost so far, and there is no prospect of things becoming significantly better until China finds an effective way of improving its legitimacy.

If we leave aside the more intangible factors such as culture and tradition, we are left with a rough explanation of prestige in the world today in terms of the combination of economic prowess and political democracy. While democracy is less and less seen as the panacea it was once mistaken for and, in our current neoliberal order, is showing alarming vulnerability to oligarchic appropriation, its status as the paramount source of legitimacy remains largely intact, both within nations and internationally. To borrow Antonio Gramsci's terms for our purposes,[10] we can say that democracy alone is capable of elevating domination to the normative status called hegemony—that is, authority based on willingly accepted leadership—and it does so through the integrating force of consent rather than the use of violence or coercion.[11] It is worth noting that Gramsci uses the term *hegemony* in a largely descriptive sense, which allows him to speak of socialist as well as capitalist hegemony. Whatever one may think of democracy or, more precisely, representative democracy, one must concede to it, as perhaps both a sincere and a backhanded compliment, the unique ideological ability to produce consent in a modern setting, although not all of this consent is warranted on close intellectual scrutiny. This is the secret or not-so-secret key to liberal democratic capitalist hegemony for which so-called communist regimes, including China's, have yet to invent an equivalent in their quest for legitimacy. As Michel Foucault has observed, socialism lacks a governmental reason or governmentality of its own.[12] We can take this to mean, especially, that socialism has not been able to develop its own way of forming moral-political subjects who willingly identify with their government (hence known as self-government) in their capacity as citizens and willingly govern themselves in their private life. Insofar as Gramsci's notion of hegemony corresponds to what Michael Mann calls ideological (as distinct from political) power,[13] it might be said that communist regimes, though themselves a modern phenomenon, have not learned how to use ideological power in the modern way.

It is the governmental rationality inherent in liberal democracy—rather than, or more than, the role of so-called free and fair elections to produce a government—that China must learn if it is to enhance its legitimacy in the world at large and with respect to Hong Kong in particular. This means that the CCP, before learning how to bring democratic governmentality to the mainland, must first figure out how to deal with Hong Kong in ways that offer the reasonable prospect of consent from Hong Kong's populace. It must, that is, aim to achieve hegemony (in Gramsci's descriptive sense) in Hong Kong according to laws that govern the production of legitimacy as distinct from coerced obedience or opportunistic acquiescence.

Hegemony, as distinct from domination, is to be achieved through what Louis Althusser, carrying further Gramsci's insights, calls the Ideological State Apparatuses (ISAs), as distinct from the Repressive State Apparatus (RSA).[14] For my more limited purposes, it is especially worth emphasizing that the ISAs do not rely on what we commonsensically mean by *indoctrination* and *propaganda*. Instead of denying that indoctrination and propaganda are among ideology's stock-in-trade, let us grant, at least for the sake of argument, that this is indeed the case. What is useful in the present context, though, is not to pass moral judgment on indoctrination and propaganda but to reveal their distinct mode of operation, which constitutes their distinct integrity *as ideology*. Thus, when indoctrination and propaganda operate as they should—that is, as tools of the ISAs as distinct from the RSA—they will be treated in the present context as unproblematic; otherwise they are problematic, but that is only because they cease to operate in the manner of ideology and become barely distinguishable from the coercive methods of the RSA. How do we know when this happens? The answer is very simple: when indoctrination and propaganda are seen, or seen through, as such. This is because when they are brought to light as such, they become either useless as ideology or useful only as barely disguised violence.

What this shows is that the defining feature of ideology in a modern setting marked by equality of conditions has to be the (apparent) respect for the agency of those at the receiving end. After all, indoctrination and propaganda find their mode of operation and integrity in being directed at subjects worthy of persuasion, rather than mere objects fit for brute force, which is how human beings are treated by the RSA left to itself. Therefore, they have to come across as plausible—as true, right, good, and so on, as the case may be—and it must be left to those at whom they are aimed to decide whether they are plausible. This means, in turn, that all those subjected to the ISAs must nevertheless be treated as, or credibly as if they were, equal, free, and intelligent (hence deserving not to be lied to). The state cannot shape their subjectivity except by approaching them, in their adulthood or even earlier, as equal subjects—a necessary condition of successful ideology under modern equality of conditions. And the state cannot procure their consent and acquire legitimacy in their eyes if it does not leave them free to dissent as well as assent, to withhold as well as give consent, or if it is perceived as insulting their intelligence (by telling them lies, for example), in which case indoctrination and propaganda cease to be what they are supposed to be—persuasion or communication rather than just another, milder form of coercion or manipulation—and at once lose their ideological power. They lose this power because they are no longer properly addressed to subjects qua subjects and thus fail to satisfy the first and foremost condition of modern ideology—namely, the credible semblance of respect for agency. This happens whenever the ISAs are used clumsily, against their own distinct character and integrity, thereby becoming no different from the RSA.

Ideology's required respect for agency is not a matter of discourse and discursive attitude only. For the state cannot *credibly* treat people as equal, free, and intelligent at the level of discourse without backing up this treatment, and the very content of the discourse itself, with concrete measures to improve the people's standing and condition. Thus talk of social justice is made (more) credible by the welfare state, talk of freedom by the codification and protection of concrete liberties, talk of popular sovereignty by free and fair elections and universal suffrage, talk of (bourgeois) universalism by the introduction of formal or legal equality, and so on. This means that "real" concessions have to go with otherwise merely discursive gestures to make the latter credible. Universal suffrage and the welfare state are textbook examples of concessions made by the liberal capitalist state to the working class to bring the latter under the sway of the ISAs. Members of the working class were not simply duped by bourgeois indoctrination and propaganda; they were co-opted by a heightened level of discursive respect for their agency that was, in turn, made acceptably credible by concrete concessions in the shape of very considerable improvements. In this way modern ideology's mandatory respect for agency makes itself felt not only in a discursive but also in a material form.

Neither the discursive respect for agency nor the matching material concessions, however, change the fundamental character of the capitalist relations of production (in Marxist parlance) or of the unequal relations of power (in generic leftist terminology). Thus, even at its "best," ideology remains reprehensible in the sense of helping reproduce such relations by misrepresenting them and by creating moral-political subjects custom-designed for them. The sharper-eyed will always be able to peep into the workshop of ideology, where consent is "educated" and invariably "organized," as Gramsci says,[15] or otherwise manufactured. In the present context, though, I must resist the temptation to do this myself, for my aim is not to present the CCP with (misappropriated) reasons to stick to its current ways but rather to show what positive lessons the central government has to learn from democratic governmentality—which is surely not without merits—in its dealings especially with Hong Kong.

To this end, I will suggest that an extremely large number of Hong Kong's citizens today have a very strong sense of agency—especially by Chinese standards—that must be respected by the central government if it is to make any headway in raising Hong Kong's level of identification with the motherland. This sense of agency, with its possessors' demand for treatment as free and equal citizens, is sufficiently entrenched and widespread to constitute an important new addition to Hong Kong's political culture. It has come about in part on the basis of the liberal values carried over from British colonial rule; in part from the spontaneous upsurge in the demand for political equality stimulated by decolonization; in part from the intensification of self-consciousness caused by the identity / identification crisis surrounding, and lasting well beyond, the handover; in part from the politicization of apartness by the democracy movement; and, finally, to no small degree from the experience of democratic struggle itself, with, as it were, its own indoctrination and propaganda.

However this enhanced sense of agency may have made its irrepressible way into Hong Kong's political culture, there is no turning back the clock. Recognizing this fact is of the highest importance for the central government. Doing so means that, if identification rather than obedience is the object, then the central government must see to it that its ISAs work as they should, rather than as a barely disguised appendage of the RSA. The ISAs, that is, must studiously address themselves to the people of Hong Kong as equal, free, and intelligent citizens and, on top of this, back up the right kind of discourse with material—that is, real—concessions.

At this point I must make an important correction,[16] for it is inaccurate to refer to the central government's ISAs *in the plural*. I have borrowed the term from Althusser, of course, and, as is well known, he always speaks of the ISAs in the plural form. As he explains, "While there is *one* Repressive State Apparatus, there are several Ideological State Apparatuses. This difference is important."[17] But this is true only of a liberal state, such as France, which Althusser uses as the main empirical basis for his analysis. In France, as in liberal states in general, the ISAs (the church, schools, trade unions, the family, culture, entertainment, the media, and so on), being (mostly) private institutions and scattered in civil society, "are objectively distinct, relatively autonomous, and do not form an organized, centralized corps with a single, conscious leadership."[18] Unlike France or any other liberal state, China has not several ISAs but only one, for all the different institutions that perform an ideological function are centrally controlled and possess not even relative independence or autonomy. No wonder that China's ISA—now correctly referred to in the singular, with the result that it becomes a contradiction in terms by Althusser's entirely appropriate definition—finds it so hard to operate in ways that set it clearly apart from the RSA.

As things stand, then, the central government is not availing itself of any ISAs in its relation to Hong Kong, and, interestingly, this is so in a different sense from what is true of the situation on the mainland. For, on the one hand, all the media and cultural institutions in Hong Kong that are *firmly* and *consistently* supportive of the central government—that is, the Chinese state—are deemed the propaganda tools of the RSA, and correctly so. Hence they do not perform an ideological function: their support, however unswerving, makes no contribution to the central government (or the Hong Kong SAR government, for that matter) that is distinctively and properly ideological. On the other hand, there undoubtedly exist in Hong Kong's civil society a wide variety of institutions—media, cultural, educational, religious, and so on—that operate with sufficient autonomy from the RSA to count as ideological. Yet by and large they do not function as Ideological *State* Apparatuses, for they do not serve to procure consensus or consent on behalf of the Chinese state. If anything, almost all the ideological institutions in Hong Kong are, as it were, Ideological *Anti*state Apparatuses, to one degree or another. Independent of the RSA—that is, of the Chinese state—and in this (Althusserian) sense ideological, they are nevertheless not so independent in another sense, propagating as they do values that mostly originate in the ISAs of Western states. The result is truly peculiar and puts the Chinese state in an extremely awkward position. It would not be true to say that this is entirely of the Chinese state's own making. But as long as China features the ISA in the singular, which is to say that it is actually devoid of ISAs altogether, it will be inadvertently leaving the *state*-ideological vacuum in Hong Kong, as long as the SAR retains its liberties, to be filled by ideologies originating elsewhere, and thereby undermining itself in ways that only the Chinese state itself is capable of doing. There is no stronger proof of such self-undermining than precisely the central government's difficulty in procuring true identification rather than mere obedience.

Implications of Hong Kong's Development for China

I have for obvious reasons focused on China's impact on Hong Kong, but this is not to imply that the influence goes only one way. For what happens to Hong Kong's democratic development is bound to have a strong impact on the dynamic of China's political evolution. It would in my view not be an exaggeration to say that, politically, Hong Kong and China will sink or swim together. It is therefore entirely pertinent to consider the question of democracy in Hong Kong not only in its own right but also in terms of what is conducive to positive political development, including democracy, in China as a whole.

Recent events, as I have noted, have highlighted Hong Kong's long-standing political-system hostility toward Chinese communism. This hostility is understandable, even if somewhat unbalanced, in view of the family histories of a substantial part of the Hong Kong population. Traditionally somewhat low-key and devoid of effective mobilization (except at special times such as June 4, 1989), this political-system hostility has seen a dramatic escalation in the past few years. Although the exact consequences of this escalation are hard to predict, it is quite obvious that, generally speaking, political-system hostility toward the Chinese state will not help the democratic cause in Hong Kong. It will do so even less when it is seen to be supported, if only morally, by Western media and influential Western politicians. It is a political fact independent of anyone's normative preference that whatever political progress is to be made in Hong Kong must have the blessing or at least the acquiescence of the central government in Beijing. The appearance of an international democratic alliance directed at the Chinese government, however soft and informal, can almost be counted on to produce the opposite effect. It can only give the CCP ideas or reinforce ideas it already has.[19] Such ideas point in one clear direction: Chinese sovereignty is not fully respected; it is not fully respected on account of political-system hostility; and such hostility contains within it the unmistakable desire, as distinct from any concrete plan (all but ruled out by the continuing rise of China), for regime change. Against such hostility, with all that it entails, the Chinese government has no choice but to stand firm, or so it believes, and this means that it must not yield an inch to the pan-democrats in Hong Kong, lest it will create a slippery slope toward regime change.

One does not need much political astuteness to see that political-system hostility toward the Chinese government will not serve any useful purpose for Hong Kong. As expressed by the pan-democrats, it will serve only to marginalize them and undermine the central government's minimal trust. As expressed by Western governments, it will only lend credence to the idea that foreign forces are behind the democracy movement and that they will not let pass any opportunity to weaken the political respectability of the Chinese government. As expressed by Western media, it will only strengthen an already widespread political-system hostility toward China in some Western countries and put greater pressure on their governments and politicians to speak and even act accordingly. If the Chinese state happens to be extremely weak, it may well cave in to ideological and political pressure based on political-system hostility, but then this would have happened for other reasons, with or without such pressure. When the Chinese state is strong, as it is now, although it is far from invulnerable, it can be counted on to take the pressure as a reminder that it must act even more strongly and do all it can to reduce its vulnerability. This is happening right now.

This chain of causes and effects applies on the mainland as well, in its own right, except that there the stakes are much higher and the authorities react to perceived threats with a corresponding highhandedness. Because the same logic is at work in Hong Kong and yet Hong Kong is, deep down, a milder society compared with the mainland, what is happening in Hong Kong may acquire the importance of an ominous precedent. It may have done so already. If political-system hostility is so hard to contain in Hong Kong, how much more irresistibly must a similar hostility give vent to itself on the mainland if allowed half a chance? If Hongkongers, already blessed as they are with plentiful liberties, have so many among them who will not settle for the enjoyment of such liberties combined with a more democratic way of doing things, what reason is there to think that mainlanders, once granted the same liberties, will not immediately demand political democracy and thereby challenge the leadership of the CCP?

Fortunately, this is still an open question. Yet the answer to it that will be provided by future developments in Hong Kong may have an extremely important bearing on how the party thinks and acts in the rest of China. I sometimes wonder whether there isn't something we can learn from what Immanuel Kant has to say about nonpolitical freedom, on the one hand, and political obedience, on the other. I have already had occasion to explain and use Kant's insights in Chapter 6, but some of these insights bear repeating briefly here, especially because they have a different twist given Hong Kong's specific context. Exercise independence of thought, seek such freedom as is necessary for the public use of reason, and thereby give up self-imposed immaturity, Kant pleads, but do so in such a way as is fully compatible with political obedience and hence public order. The realization of freedom thus conceived and justified depends on those in power being able to say, with a ruler like Frederick II, *"Argue as much as you like and about whatever you like, but obey!"* because he "has at hand a well-disciplined and numerous army to guarantee public security."[20] One could be forgiven for wishing that the CCP, which is even more mightily equipped, were able to say something like this—and, of course, act accordingly, as Frederick did. And one might hope the people of Hong Kong could treat political *restraint*, short of political obedience, as a temporarily acceptable price to pay for the liberties they enjoy and, not least, for the numerous things, both public and private, that such liberties allow them to do if they make good and ample use of them.

Political restraint means, in Hong Kong's context, taking advantage of civil liberties and of the democratic way of doing things, limited as it is, in such a way as to show a reasonable measure of respect for the sovereignty of the Chinese state, and to show such respect by refraining from actions that can reasonably be perceived as stemming from political-system hostility. Think what you will about China's political system, and discuss it freely and, if possible, without overzealous prejudice, but do not oppose it, do not try to subvert it, and do not work for regime change. If the people of Hong Kong can do this, they will have shown, to use Kant's words, "how freedom may exist without in the least jeopardizing public concord and the unity of the commonwealth."[21]

This does not mean that the use of freedom will be public only in Kant's sense and hence entirely apolitical, and that is why I distinguish political restraint from political obedience and argue only for the former. For the argument for political restraint is itself political, and political restraint is meant precisely to make possible the most effective use of the limited democracy available to Hong Kong to safeguard civil liberties and the rule of law and to improve social justice.[22] These are worthy political purposes, and the last one in particular is as difficult to achieve as it is worthy. Rather than discourage such purposes, political restraint serves only to concentrate political energy on achieving them or preserving their achievement, uncompromisingly if necessary, and to caution against the futile and especially destructive pursuit of political goals—such as democracy *as a political system* (in the sense explained)—that are ruled out by "one country, two systems." Subject to the same proviso, civil liberties, too, can be put to political uses, just as they can serve as the training ground for the moral and intellectual independence that is presupposed by all effective democratic participation.

By exercising political restraint, then, and doing so in keeping with the reality of Hong Kong's relation to China, the people of Hong Kong will have shown, beyond the Kantian compatibility between nonpolitical liberty and political order, that they care about democracy and, being realistic, care just as much about the effective, just, and progressive uses of the limited yet considerable democracy that is in principle available to Hong Kong—that is, they care about democracy as a democratic way of doing things short of a political system. They will have shown, too, that valuing as they dearly do their historically given apartness and the individual and collective identity based on it, they are nevertheless prepared not to let their identity struggles escalate into defiance of China's political system and its sovereignty over Hong Kong.

If and when such a change of heart happens, and things needn't (and wouldn't) be perfect thereafter, Hong Kong will have created an invaluable precedent by making possible a better way of doing things, both freer and more democratic, without undermining the authority of the CCP and the sovereignty of the Chinese state. If this is shown to be possible in Hong Kong, in time it may also start to happen on the mainland—and further political evolution may follow that will gradually but surely take China, and Hong Kong with it, in an even more democratic direction. Otherwise, Hong Kong's failure today would be China's loss tomorrow.

Concluding Reflections

IF I WERE TO NAME ONE THING as the most formidable challenge to my prudential argument for democracy in China, it would have to be the potentially powerful countervailing pull of the Chinese Dream. To properly assess this challenge, one would need a closer look at the Chinese Dream than I have been able to provide. Since in the present context I am interested in the Chinese Dream not for its own sake but only in relation to democracy, I should note that the crucial question that needs to be answered is whether the Chinese Dream can do without democracy, whether the Chinese Dream can be considered complete, and felt as complete, in the absence of marked progress in meaningful democracy.

Democracy and the Chinese Dream

While the rise of China, as the core of the Chinese Dream, is not in doubt as event, its meaning is contentious and its future course uncertain. Key to fathoming its meaning and tracking its future course is the notion of universality. For China's rise has supposedly created a model—the China model, or the China approach *(zhongguo fang'an)*, as Xi Jinping calls it—that is either serviceable only to China itself and at most also to developing countries or exemplary for the world as a whole. A qualitative difference exists between the two scenarios: only the latter is of potentially world-historical significance and will, if it comes to pass, give America, and the West as a whole, cause for worry about its place in so-called universal history.

For this latter scenario to materialize, China must first show itself capable of escaping the so-called middle-income trap and surmounting other daunting challenges, including that of regime stability and perpetuation. But already China under Xi has shed much of its modesty about claiming universal impact and significance for what would otherwise be seen as only its own parochial achievements, however impressive on their own terms. The latter cannot be what "the great rejuvenation of the Chinese nation" *(zhonghua minzhu de weida fuxing)* is about. For Xi and the Chinese Communist Party (CCP), China's rise is obviously meant to occur as part of universal history; the rise itself is a rise to the level of universality.

This departure from Deng Xiaoping's dictum of "hiding one's light and biding one's time" *(taoguang yanghui)* may be tentative at this stage, yet its intent is unmistakable. We are witnessing China's rise, and hence its rise in universality, at its initial stage. While drawing from time to time on the universalist discourses of the Enlightenment and Marxism and of the Chinese tradition, the last with its time-honored concept of All under Heaven, the CCP is allowing its newfound zeal for universality to take largely the paradoxical form of a heightened confidence in exceptionalism. Chinese exceptionalism may be viewed as the initial stage (to borrow a standard CCP term) of universalism—a way of carving out a politico-economic space for China while subverting the West's monopoly on universal history.

Xi's eponymous thought—"socialism with Chinese characteristics for a new era"—is a case in point. If in the post–Cold War era (Marxian) socialism itself has been decisively relegated to the realm of the particular, indeed to the marginal and residual, "socialism with Chinese characteristics" is the further particularization of the particular. But what about "for a new era"? It turns out, upon a modicum of reflection, that what is new is precisely the dawning of China's newly recovered confidence in claiming its share of universal history. This reclaimed universality sets the Xi era apart from the entire "old" reform era stretching all the way from Deng through Jiang Zemin to Hu Jintao, the latter era marked by the plain loss of communist nerve and the veiled and somewhat hesitant and ambiguous desire to join Western capitalist universality while maintaining nominally communist one-party rule. No more blind worshiping of Western universality, no more naïve trust in the West's spurious assertion of universal values, Xi is saying or implying, and it is time for China to stake out its own claims to universality.

What is new about Xi's "new era" is thus the beginning of the end of all attempts to join Western universality. The new era is the era of China's reasserted universality.

There remains, however, a readily noticeable ambivalence between exceptionalism (as a challenge to universalism and hence to *Western* universalism) and universalism (in the guise of exceptionalism). Thus while China is no longer "hiding its light," it is still "biding its time," in that the time to couch China's new claims in the unabashed language of universality has not yet come. The result is an accentuated form of Chinese particularism reinforced by the universalization of particularism, by the insistence that Western claims to universality are no less particularistic for all their hegemonic status. At the same time, more or less explicit appeals to universality—for example, Xi's suggestion that the Chinese Dream has a close affinity with the dreams of all nations, and his proposal for building a shared future for all of humanity—are increasingly creeping into official CCP discourse.

What all this suggests is that, if things go well, it is only a matter of time before China feels self-assured enough to shed its particularism and lay explicit claims to universality. Indeed it is only then that we will know that China believes its rise to have been completed—but only provided that the validity of this belief is ungrudgingly accepted by other nations of the world. Whether this condition can be met will no doubt depend on how economically consequential, and, more generally, how materially powerful, China has become. For material power, or hard power, is a necessary vehicle of global influence, although it defies the unalloyed moral sense that this is how it is. Yet ideas and values are what make up the substance of all claims to universality. This is because in ideas and values alone can be found the highest and most inclusive common denominator among all humans qua humans, which is what we mean by universality. Universality is humanity, itself (as we know it today) an invention of the European Enlightenment, however complicated its subsequent uses and abuses. Since the rise of China is nothing but the ascendance to universality thus conceived (via Karl Marx's debts to the Enlightenment), it cannot be merely material but must also be, indeed chiefly be, ideational and moral. The Chinese Dream is the dream of such a rise of China, or the rise of such a China.

Hence arises the question, Can this happen without China finding its own path to meaningful democracy? I very much doubt it, for I find it almost inconceivable that any claim to universality will be found credible and worthy of acceptance if it does not plausibly and amply provide for that which lies at the core of humanity's highest common denominator—namely, freedom, or what Marx calls the "free, conscious activity [that] is man's species character."[1] I am invoking Marx here not only because I believe he is right but also in order to leave room for the objection that capitalist freedom is not real freedom and bourgeois democracy accomplishes only—to use Marx's terms[2]—political emancipation short of human emancipation. The point is that if the CCP takes exception to freedom and democracy as practiced in capitalist societies, it has its work cut out for it to create real freedom and real democracy. Simply rejecting Western instantiations of freedom and democracy is not enough. Doing that without offering meaningful alternatives of its own is not an option if China is to complete its rise as a rise to universality. And what will count as meaningful alternatives must be left to the free judgment of the international court of public opinion, and thus they must go substantially above the level of plausibility and credibility that China is today capable of achieving in such matters. Marxism provides no refuge, for, accurately understood, Marx is a thinker in the Enlightenment tradition who seeks to move beyond the bourgeois democratic revolution rather than block its progress and who attempts to complete what he calls political emancipation through human emancipation rather than take humanity back to the condition preceding political emancipation. Even for Marx, the founder of historical materialism, freedom has to be the goal of universal history[3]—freedom in the sense of nonalienated life activity of the species, and in the sense of a social arrangement that is supposed to make this possible, which Marx calls democracy, "democracy [as] the solved *riddle* of all constitutions."[4] For without some such postulation, historical materialism would lose its ethical point and cease to be the emancipatory project it claims to be.

Absent freedom and democracy, the Chinese Dream would be left offering only prosperity (albeit prosperity that is meant to become ever more civilized, harmonious, and beautiful—all adjectives used by the CCP), the de facto freedom to produce and enjoy the fruits of such prosperity, and the construction of a peaceful global politico-economic order (called the community of the shared future of humankind, *renlei mingyun gongtongti*) based on this conception of the good life. This vision is clearly not without its attractions, especially when it contains a well-tested formula for efficient execution, which China is perfecting as an exemplar to developing countries and, in some cases, perhaps even beyond. The China model is none other than this conception of the good life plus the formula for carrying it out. In a way it is not so different from Benjamin Constant's picture of the liberties of the moderns, although it is important for Constant that these liberties be guaranteed, the best guarantee being some form of the liberty of the ancients—that is, democracy.[5] But Constant's proviso makes a huge difference, and some may find even this view of liberties, equipped with the proviso, too earthbound, too much oriented to what Constant calls enterprises and pleasures, and lacking a spiritual dimension. Be that as it may, what is all but certain is that *without* Constant's proviso, the China model's conception of the good life will be found wanting even by the Chinese themselves as they become more prosperous and more used to prosperity and start to demand more.

I began this book with the observation that one crucial element is missing from the CCP's impressive list of recent achievements: a way to provide for—along with economic development—an ever-rising sense of agency among the Chinese people as individuals (freedom) and as citizens (democracy). That is, development *as freedom,* to borrow an expression from Amartya Sen, rather than development only as rising living standards.[6] To this kind of observation I have often encountered the response that a sense of agency—as realized through freedom and democracy—may not be so necessary if people have everything else they want—that is, individual prosperity, national power and prestige, and so on. My rejoinder is, Wait until they have gotten over the first excitement of "everything else." Chinese society as we find it today is populated by an ever-growing middle class—the bourgeois—and by even greater numbers animated by middle-class aspirations. I just cannot imagine, for reasons supported by Marx as much as by Alexis de Tocqueville, that the bourgeois will not desire bourgeois freedoms and bourgeois democracy and seek to obtain them, *given the chance.* So wait also until the political system and culture become milder and less repressive, as they are bound to become over time (if economic development continues), so that fear will no longer prevent actual preferences from being expressed and the lack of opportunity for fulfillment will no longer produce massively adaptive preferences.[7]

I believe this is exactly the kind of thing the CCP must be thinking (and worrying about), or else it would not be devoting such a superabundance of political energy and financial resources to the seamless monitoring and control of society. In this matter as in so many others of the same kind, one can do no better than defer to the (implicit) judgment of the party itself—not what it says but what it does. The dead serious measures taken to maintain social order, the extraordinary lengths gone to and the enormous costs incurred, both material and psychological, all point to one conclusion: the CCP is a good reader of the nature of the bourgeois and of bourgeois society, and the only reason it is not acting on this insight *positively* is that it wants to maintain its exclusive hold on power. All the repression aimed at arresting the *moral-political* evolution of Chinese bourgeois society only goes to prove the irrepressible desire for agency in bourgeois society, such that if the state represses this desire, then it must also repress all the expressions of frustration about and protest against the original repression. This is a costly project almost certain to fail at some point.

For now, things are held together by a combination of fear, displacement, and sublimation. The fear needs no further explanation. *Displacement* means that the desire for agency, thwarted in the moral and political domains, finds a compensating outlet in making money, seeking career advancement and social status, and chasing pleasures, especially that of consumption. This is the individualistic dimension of the Chinese Dream: a good life for oneself made possible by material abundance and enjoyed in the company of one's family and friends. If this is not satisfying enough—and it definitely is not in the absence of the greater sense of agency afforded by reasonably guaranteed freedoms and democracy—there is also the collective dimension of the Chinese Dream: the great rejuvenation of the Chinese nation. The mechanism at work here is also displacement or compensation, with one big difference, however—the intoxicating effect of being and feeling part of the largest cohesively organized human crowd, the nation. Insofar as members of this crowd feel uplifted, above their purely individual concerns and fortunes, by the shared glory of a rising fatherland, they undergo a *sublimation* of their everyday desires and aspirations, from the purely individual to the collective, from the merely exciting to the inspiring.

I do not intend to pass judgment, positive or negative, on the collective dimension of the Chinese Dream, or on sublimation as its correlate in collective psychology. What requires comment is only whether such sublimation can long serve as a displacement of the desire for democracy. I have already argued for the view that the bourgeois *will* be bourgeois—will act like the bourgeois—over time, given the chance. Since this view already covers the displacement of the desire both for individual freedom and for democracy, all I need to add is a simple thought pertaining to democracy. For an increasingly middle-class society, it would be hard to imagine collective, national *pride* being long sustained on the basis of the collective (and individual) *indignity* of not having the right to plausible and meaningful political participation—that is, democracy. Being *long* sustained means lasting much beyond the Xi era. Objectively speaking, Xi is an extraordinary leader and his era an extraordinary era—extraordinary, in both cases, in the descriptive sense that contradictions that under ordinary circumstances and ordinary leadership would produce an irresistible momentum toward fundamental change, or collapse, are being effectively kept in check. There is no reason to believe, however, that Xi will be followed by a successor equally extraordinary and therefore no reason to believe that things will not resume their ordinary course in a post-Xi China.

What *ordinary course* must mean is, above all, the appearance or reappearance of freedom and democracy (with plausible, meaningful, not merely Chinese, characteristics) on the list of normative things that the Chinese people can openly and knowingly care about. Only in this way can the Chinese Dream be achieved and be worthy of being a dream come true—and prove potentially attractive enough to win the free recognition of other peoples of the world and thereby ascend to the level of credible universality.

The most important question, then, is whether Xi will see fit and be able to get China ready, boldly yet prudently, for a return to the ordinary course of individual and national life *before* he leaves the political stage. The answer to this question will truly determine the future and fate of China.

Democracy in China, Democracy in America

I could not have written this book, then, dispassionate and analytical as I have tried to make it, without a certain trepidation. I fear that the looming legitimation crisis is not taken seriously enough, that China's urgent need for democracy is not sufficiently recognized, and that democratic preparation will not take place until it is too late. Too late because by then, with the crisis visibly brewing and those in power unable to keep it under control in a calm and peaceful way, and with no other seasoned political force to step into the breach, the country could descend into paralysis and even chaos. Should this happen, the earlier need for democracy could mutate into an emergent need for draconian measures, adopted by whoever is charge, just to keep a semblance of order and normality.

I have this fear because, for one thing, those running the country are understandably absorbed in the endless challenges of the moment—economic, technological, political, military, international, and so on—which are enough to create at the very top the mentality of emergency and make statesmanlike foresight into rainy days ahead all but a luxury. This overwhelmingly distracting preoccupation with the present (and with the future largely as a continuation of, hopefully, the positive things of the present) is, equally understandably, compounded by the force of habit, in this case the CCP's habit formed over seven decades of ruling the country by taking only its own counsel and without the inconvenience of having to deal with the demos. It is easy to imagine how prohibitively difficult it would be to give up such a habit—the more so if, as seems to be the case, the current leadership has ambitious national goals to achieve to which democracy's inefficacies seem ill suited. Then, with or without such ambitious goals, there is the sheer confidence, arrogance, and blindness unfailingly fostered in those at the top by possession of great and barely challenged power, especially power still on the rise.

For these reasons among others, I do not think that mine is an ungrounded fear. Yet, given what is at stake, I cannot but *hope* that I will turn out to be wrong—wrong, that is, even if those who have the power to act now, when there is still time, fail to do so. Even in the event of their failure to act, I would not wish my prognosis to be proved true, and thus, by the same token, I must, even now, wish my diagnosis to be incorrect.

There is little point in imagining purely hypothetical circumstances that would fulfill my wish. I can imagine, however, two scenarios, neither totally unrealistic, in which things would turn out differently from what my present analysis leads me to expect. Unsurprisingly, both scenarios involve China's relationship and balance of power with the United States. As it happens, what is special about China vis-à-vis the United States is its dual status as the world's second-largest economy *and* the most powerful (nominally) communist country, the latter giving China a politico-ideological identity that, in turn, imparts an especially unsettling meaning to China's new economic might. This doubly tense relationship affects both China and the United States deeply, in different ways. For China's part, other things being equal, the democratic challenge confronting it is likely to wax and wane in response, first, to its balance of power, especially hard power, with the United States, and, second, as far as soft power is concerned, to America's performance and image as the world's leading democracy.

The first of the two scenarios, then, is one in which China catches up with or even surpasses the United States in economic power, and approaches the United States in military might, sooner than it is hit by the paralyzing legitimation crisis sketched in this book. It is almost as if there were a race between China's economic and military advance, on the one hand, and the CCP's progressively decreasing legitimacy, on the other. It is just possible that the very fact of such a race, as it were, and of its being registered by the CCP and the public at large, will by itself give the party more time. Should things turn out in China's favor in this regard, they could complicate the political dynamic in China—both positively, in ways I shall speculate on shortly, and negatively, if China were to acquire the ambitions of empire. I just do not see, however, the CCP succeeding in such ambitions, even if it were to entertain them, before it runs into domestic legitimation problems of a sufficient severity to overshadow everything else. If I am right, then, the complications resulting from China's relatively rapid further rise would *by themselves* be more likely to favor the cause of democracy than not, as I shall argue.

The second scenario bears some relation to the first, in that America's performance and image as a democracy are profoundly affected by its status as an empire (all but in name). Whether one likes it or not, the fortunes and reputation of democracy in the world today rise or fall largely (though by no means only) with the fortunes and reputation of democracy in America. There can be no doubt that America's performance as a democracy and as an empire is keenly watched in China, by democracy's supporters as much as by its detractors and skeptics. This is the single most important international factor affecting the prospect of democracy in China. American democracy, instead of offering a fixed formula fit to serve as an unquestioned model, has always been a project in the making. It makes a world of difference whether we are talking about American democracy in the Gilded Age or in the Progressive Era—or, closer to our time, American democracy in the decades of the New Deal or in the New Gilded Age, which has coincided with the unprecedented ambition and reach of the American empire, declining or not. And it is not too farfetched to hypothesize that if the New Gilded Age roars on domestically and in the form of new military misadventures abroad in the mode of the (second) Iraq War and the Libya intervention, this may well cause at least temporarily irreparable damage to the reputation of democracy and, in so doing, dramatically alter the perception, and hence the prospect, of democracy in China.

What if the first scenario materializes but the second does not—with China succeeding in the nationalist dimension of the Chinese Dream (short of superseding the United States as the new global hegemon) and America somehow thriving as a democracy? Well, at least this much would be relatively certain: first, that China would be better able to accomplish an orderly passage to democracy, given its enhanced self-confidence and its greatly reduced vulnerability to potential interference from foreign powers in the democratizing process; and, second, that America's very success (at that point) in its ongoing democratic project would in and of itself constitute enormous moral and ideological pressure on China, however otherwise powerful, to acquire the ultimate legitimacy that only democracy could confer in the modern setting of equality of conditions. This pressure, in turn, would be reinforced by what is almost certain to be a third fact—namely, that China itself would have advanced much further in its progress toward equality of conditions, the most powerful domestic cause of democratic transformation. Taking these three factors together, I cannot see how, or why, China would long find it either necessary or possible to resist the pressure, both domestic and international, to take the final step toward democracy. Indeed I can well imagine that pressure becoming rather a temptation, because only by taking this (for itself) unprecedented step could China *fully* accomplish its rejuvenation—in the *modern* world—and acquire the legitimacy at home and abroad that is commensurate with its new capabilities and its better ambitions.

The moral of this speculative exercise is that what will stand in the way of China's democratic progress is not its further rise but rather this fact conjoined with democracy's further decline, especially in the United States. By itself, China's further rise, if (a big "if") reasonably smooth and rapid, could conceivably give the CCP more time, but it would not change China's basic sociopolitical dynamic. If anything, it would help rather than hinder China's democratic progress. It is only given the *combination* of the two scenarios— China's further rise and democracy's further decline—that all bets would be off. But in that case, all bets would be off with regard to America as well, and the world at large.

Absent this conjunction of scenarios, I cannot quite bring myself to *believe* (as opposed to wishing) that my diagnosis is incorrect in its essentials. Let it, then, along with the prognosis based on it, stand as a warning that will do no harm if it turns out to be wrong and that could do some good if it is credited with a reasonable chance of being right.

Notes

Index

Notes

Introduction

1. See Manuel Castells, *The Information Age: Economy, Society, and Culture,* vol. 2, *The Power of Identity,* 2nd ed. (Oxford: Wiley-Blackwell, 2010), chap. 6.

2. Louis Althusser, *On the Reproduction of Capitalism: Ideology and Ideological State Apparatuses,* trans. G. M. Goshgarian (London: Verso, 2014), 135–36, emphasis in original.

3. Ibid., 137.

4. Ibid.

5. As used, say, by General Secretary Xi Jinping at the news conference immediately after the nineteenth party congress.

6. This notion was first proposed by W. B. Gallie in two articles, one of them being "Essentially Contested Concepts," *Proceedings of the Aristotelian Society* 56 (1956): 167–98. Democracy is among the examples given in this article of an essentially contested concept—a concept of something totally or largely positive yet with its best interpretation subject to contestation. Robert A. Dahl recognizes a similar status for democracy when he writes, "Today, this idea of democracy is universally popular. Most regimes stake out some sort of claim to the title of 'democracy'; and those that do not often insist that their particular instance of nondemocratic rule is a necessary stage along the road to ultimate 'democracy.' In our times, even dictators appear to believe that an indispensable ingredient for their legitimacy is a dash or two of the language of democracy." Robert A. Dahl, *Democracy and Its Critics* (New Haven, CT: Yale University Press, 1989), 2.

7. John Dunn does as good a job as anyone of pinpointing what is deeply good and attractive about democracy without being misled by its surface charms; see his *Democracy: A History* (New York: Atlantic Monthly Press, 2005), 130–47, 164, 174, 185. Another judicious account of the strengths and limits of democracy is Adam Przeworski, *Democracy and the Limits of Self-Government* (New York: Cambridge

University Press, 2014). Przeworski sees the test for democracy in its ability to rise to four challenges: "(1) the incapacity to generate equality in the socioeconomic realm, (2) the incapacity to make people feel that their political participation is effective, (3) the incapacity to ensure that governments do what they are supposed to do and not do what they are not mandated to do, and (4) the incapacity to balance order and liberty" (1–2). Przeworski makes a plausible case against holding democracy to unreasonable standards in these four regards, and for believing that even when democracy is not at its possible best, it tends under relatively favorable conditions to do better than nondemocratic regimes. There is little doubt that, even by Przeworski's sober standard for democracy, the typical advanced democracies in the world today fall a long way short, with regard to all four challenges.

8. There is an academic and journalistic industry devoted to showing the discontents of democracy in our time. See, for example, Christopher H. Achen and Larry M. Bartels, *Democracy for Realists: Why Elections Do Not Produce Responsive Government*, rev. ed. (Princeton, NJ: Princeton University Press, 2017); and Jacob S. Hacker and Paul Pierson, *Winner-Take-All Politics: How Washington Made the Rich Richer—and Turned Its Back on the Middle Class* (New York: Simon and Schuster, 2011). In many ways, C. B. Macpherson's *The Life and Times of Liberal Democracy* (Oxford: Oxford University Press, 1977), in outlining the normative credentials and vicissitudes of four models of democracy, remains a good conceptual basis for forming a sober assessment of democracy's moral potential and the prospect of its coming to fruition. That the "developmental model" has dropped out of mainstream discussion altogether since Macpherson and the "participatory model" has turned out to be more utopian than ever is enough to dent any high-flown normative case for democracy.

9. John Dunn, preface to *Democracy: The Unfinished Journey, 508 BC to AD 1993* (Oxford: Oxford University Press, 1993), ed. John Dunn, vii, emphasis added.

10. I have in mind, for example, Jason Stanley, *How Propaganda Works* (Princeton, NJ: Princeton University Press, 2015); and Jason Brennan, *Against Democracy* (Princeton, NJ: Princeton University Press, 2016)—both otherwise highly salutary in their warnings about the ideological distortion (Stanley) and even ethical-psychological harms (Brennan) of democracy.

11. Niccolò Machiavelli, *The Prince,* trans. Harvey C. Mansfield (Chicago: University of Chicago Press, 1998): "But since my intent is to write something useful to whoever understands it, it has appeared to me more fitting to go directly to the effectual truth of the thing than to the imagination of it. And many have imagined republics and principalities that have never been seen or known to exist in truth; for it is so far from how one lives to how one should that he who lets go of what is done for what should be done learns his ruin rather than his preservation" (61).

12. John Dunn makes a strong case for "placing the value of prudence at the center of modern political theory" (198) in "Reconceiving the Content and Character of Modern Political Community," in *Interpreting Political Responsibility* (Princeton, NJ: Princeton University Press, 1990), 193–215. Although not specifically

related to China, Dunn's argument is especially salutary in urging "a large measure of objectivity: a deliberate distancing from the contingencies of our own desires and sentiments" (193) and the special importance for political theory of "the causally adequate analysis of the human world in terms of its openness to human betterment (or even human preservation)" (196). Dunn writes, "History, if anything, can tell us how we have come hither; moral philosophy, perhaps, what to make of the fact that this is where we now are. But political theory has no choice but to tell us how to act, given that this indeed is where we now are" (196).

13. See John Dunn, *Breaking Democracy's Spell* (New Haven, CT: Yale University Press, 2014).

14. See, for example, Max Tegmark, *Life 3.0: Being Human in the Age of Artificial Intelligence* (New York: Knopf, 2017).

15. I know of no more impressive snapshot of such performance than Graham Allison's racy account of the rise of China in his *Destined for War: Can America and China Escape Thucydides's Trap?* (New York: Houghton Mifflin Harcourt, 2017), chap. 1. All positives, no negatives, which is understandable given the author's purpose in this part of his book. One can imagine the Chinese leaders being (before the trade war) intoxicated by just some such account, as much as their American counterparts would, as Allison presumably hoped, be alarmed by it. It is striking that an astute scholar and experienced national security expert such as Allison should find the idea of performance legitimacy plausible (143), although even he cautions that such legitimacy depends, empirically, on "sustaining the unsustainable" (123).

16. Charles S. Maier, "Democracy since the French Revolution," in Dunn, *Democracy*, 125–53, at 126–27, emphasis added.

17. What I am calling democratic epistemology receives perhaps the most influential account in our day in Jürgen Habermas, *The Theory of Communicative Action,* trans. Thomas McCarthy, 2 vols. (Boston: Beacon, 1984, 1987). It can indeed be said that Habermas presents democracy as first and foremost a matter of democratic epistemology, as in Jürgen Habermas, "Legitimation Problems in the Modern State," in *Communication and the Evolution of Society,* trans. Thomas McCarthy (Boston: Beacon, 1979), 178–205. One representative formulation is as follows: "I can imagine the attempt to arrange a society democratically only as a self-controlled learning process. It is a question of finding arrangements which can ground the presumption that the basic institutions of the society and the basic political decisions would meet with the unforced agreement of all those involved, if they could participate, as free and equal, in discursive will-formation. Democratization cannot mean an a priori preference for a specific type of organization, for example, for so-called direct democracy" (186). See also Jürgen Habermas, "Popular Sovereignty as Procedure," appendix 1 of *Between Facts and Norms: Contributions to a Discourse Theory of Law and Democracy,* trans. William Rehg (Cambridge, MA: MIT Press, 1998), 463–90.

18. As these are variously documented in, say, François Guizot, *The History of the Origins of Representative Government in Europe,* trans. Andrew R. Scoble

(Indianapolis: Liberty Fund, 2002); Barrington Moore Jr., *Social Origins of Dictatorship and Democracy: Lord and Peasant in the Making of the Modern World* (Boston: Beacon, 1993); Dunn, *Democracy;* and Pierre Manent, *Metamorphoses of the City: The Western Dynamic,* trans. Marc LePain (Cambridge, MA: Harvard University Press, 2013).

19. As distressingly documented in the Oxfam reports, among others.

1. Legitimacy and Performance

1. This time frame allows for the impact of such contingent factors as President Xi Jinping's health, his ability to maintain his currently unchallenged grip on power, potential major setbacks in the Chinese economy, and unpredictable events on the international scene.

2. To call this type of legitimacy communist teleological-revolutionary is to suggest that its form is teleological, its teleological substance is communism, and its means of execution is revolution. For simplicity and convenience, I will for the most part refer to this type of legitimacy as teleological-revolutionary, or communist revolutionary, or, simply, revolutionary—in all cases as a stand-in for all three features.

3. For reasonably comprehensive analyses of the multiple vulnerabilities faced by China as part of the global capitalist order, see Ho-fung Hung, *The China Boom: Why China Will Not Rule the World* (New York: Columbia University Press, 2016); and George Magnus, *Red Flags: Why Xi's China Is in Jeopardy* (New Haven, CT: Yale University Press, 2018). For equally solid assessments by foreign observers who seem somewhat more positively disposed toward China, or more detached, see William H. Overholt, *China's Crisis of Success* (Cambridge: Cambridge University Press, 2018); and Arthur R. Kroeber, *China's Economy: What Everyone Needs to Know* (Oxford: Oxford University Press, 2016).

4. "The Chinese Dream" is a translation of *Zhongguo meng,* which is sometimes rendered as "the China Dream." There is a subtle, or perhaps not-so-subtle, difference between these two renderings, with the China Dream hinting at some collective project (e.g., national rejuvenation) as the dream's main object. The Chinese Dream, on the other hand, is more neutral, as it is also open to a more generic and mundane interpretation in terms of prosperity and happiness as ordinary people understand such things. Such an interpretation makes the Chinese Dream rather similar to the American Dream, as no less an authority than Xi Jinping once suggested, in his speech at the press conference after his meeting with President Barack Obama at the former Annenberg Estate in California in 2013. This speech is included, under the title "Goujian Zhongmei xinxing daguo guanxi" [Build a new type of major-country relationship between China and the United States], in *Shibada yilai zhongyao wenxian xuanbian* [Selections of important documents since the eighteenth party congress] (Beijing: Zhongyang wenxian chubanshe, 2014), 305–6. The reference to the comparability of the Chinese Dream and the

American Dream is on 305. It is also worth noting that the meaning of the Chinese Dream has evolved since 2013, recently (as in Xi's speech at the CCP's nineteenth national congress, on October 18, 2017) seeing a much stronger emphasis placed on the collective, national dimension, but never to the exclusion of the earlier, more generic meaning. Thus "the Chinese Dream" remains a more suitable translation for its elasticity, although "the China Dream" is clearly more apt when applied to "the great rejuvenation of the Chinese nation." It is surely significant that Xi's speech at the CCP's nineteenth national congress ends with the juxtaposition of these two dimensions of the Chinese Dream. See Xi Jinping, *Juesheng quanmian jiancheng xiaokang shehui duoqu xinshidai Zhongguo tese shehui zhuyi weida shengli* [Secure a decisive victory in building a moderately prosperous society in all respects and strive for the great success of socialism with Chinese characteristics for a New Era] (Hong Kong: Sinminchu, 2017), 71.

5. To borrow a concise formulation from Jürgen Habermas, *Between Facts and Norms: Contributions to a Discourse Theory of Law and Democracy,* trans. William Rehg (Cambridge, MA: MIT Press, 1998), 441.

6. See ibid., 333; and Jürgen Habermas, *Legitimation Crisis,* trans. Thomas McCarthy (Boston: Beacon, 1975), pt. 2.

7. "When we speak, in the present day, of a public power, of that which we call the rights of sovereignty, the right of giving laws, taxing, and punishing, we all think that those rights belong to no one, that no one has, on his own account, a right to punish others, and to impose upon them a charge, a law. Those are rights which belong only to *society in the mass,* rights which are exercised in its name. . . . Thus, when an individual comes before the powers invested with these rights, the sentiment which, perhaps without his consciousness, reigns in him is, that he is in the presence of a public and legitimate power, which possesses a mission for commanding him, and he is submissive beforehand and internally." François Guizot, *The History of Civilization in Europe,* trans. William Hazlitt (Indianapolis: Liberty Fund, 1997), 84.

8. The goal for the first one hundred years, by 2020, is a "moderately prosperous society" *(xiaokang shehui)*—still a developing country in per capita terms but one that is comprehensively free from poverty—and the goal for the second, by 2050, a society affluent enough to join the ranks of the developed nations while supposedly retaining its socialist identity.

9. Something like this was consciously at work, for example, as far back as in the ancient Roman Republic. Cicero seems to mean something very close to performance legitimacy when he writes of "the methods by which we can acquire the ability to embrace and retain the support of other men." Marcus Tullius Cicero, *On Duties,* ed. M. T. Griffin and E. M. Atkins (Cambridge: Cambridge University Press, 1991), 2.19. Those methods closest to performance legitimacy today involve "liberality by service to the community at large" (heading in the synopsis for 2.72–85), such as "to increase the republic in power, in land and in revenues," with the result that "men who pursue these kinds of duties will win, along with the utmost benefit

to the republic, both great gratitude and great glory for themselves" (2.85). For what is service but performance and what is gratitude and glory earned by service (and honor) but performance *legitimacy?*

10. Max Weber, *Economy and Society: An Outline of Interpretive Sociology,* ed. Guenther Roth and Claus Wittich, 2 vols. (Berkeley: University of California Press, 1978), 1:31, emphasis added. In the well-known passage from which the quote is taken, Weber also identifies an order based on custom or habit, which lies between the other two in terms of stability.

11. See Daniel A. Bell, *The China Model: Political Meritocracy and the Limits of Democracy* (Princeton, NJ: Princeton University Press, 2015).

12. Ibid., 8.

13. The fundamental relation between legitimacy and the realization of a society's ends and values is well expressed by Habermas: "By *legitimacy* I understand the worthiness of a political order to be recognized. The *claim to legitimacy* is related to the social-integrative preservation of a normatively determined social identity. *Legitimations* serve to make good this claim, that is, to show how and why existing (or recommended) institutions are fit to employ political power in such a way that the values constitutive for the identity of the society will be realized." Jürgen Habermas, "Legitimation Problems in the Modern State," in *Communication and the Evolution of Society,* trans. Thomas McCarthy (Boston: Beacon, 1979), 178–205, at 182–83, emphasis in original.

14. I chart the unfolding of this legitimation crisis in *Dialectic of the Chinese Revolution: From Utopianism to Hedonism* (Stanford, CA: Stanford University Press, 1994).

15. Habermas, *Between Facts and Norms,* 441.

16. John Dunn, *Democracy: A History* (New York: Atlantic Monthly Press, 2005), 19.

2. The Question of Regime Perpetuation

1. I am using "June 4" as shorthand for a major outbreak of social or political unrest, not necessarily one spearheaded by students, which seems much less likely today.

2. On these concepts of power (along with economic and military power), see Michael Mann, *The Sources of Social Power,* vol. 1, *History of Power from the Beginning to AD 1760,* new ed. (Cambridge: Cambridge University Press, 2012), chap. 1. Following Mann, I am here using the term *ideology* in a sense that is different from and broader than Althusser's, as invoked in the Introduction and Chapter 1.

3. On this Machiavelli remains pertinent: "One should take it as a general rule that rarely, if ever, does it happen that a state, whether it be a republic or a kingdom, is either well-ordered at the outset or radically transformed *vis-à-vis* its old institutions unless this be done by one person. It is likewise essential that there should be but one person upon whose mind and method depends any similar process of

organization. Wherefore the prudent organizer of a state whose intention it is to govern not in his own interests but for the common good, and not in the interest of his successors but for the sake of that fatherland which is common to all, should contrive to be alone in his authority." Niccolò Machiavelli, *The Discourses,* trans. Leslie Walker with revisions by Brian Richardson (London: Penguin, 2003), 1.9, p. 132.

4. As Machiavelli says (almost immediately after the passage quoted in the previous note), "Though but one person suffices for the purpose of organization, what he has organized will not last long if it continues to rest on the shoulders of one man, but may well last if many remain in charge and many look to its maintenance" (ibid.).

3. The Case for Democracy

1. See Edward Schiappa, *Protagoras and Logos: A Study in Greek Philosophy and Rhetoric,* 2nd ed. (Columbia: University of South Carolina Press, 2003), 13. See also ibid., chap. 9.

2. The pragmatists arguably have their more immediate precursor in the anti-Federalists, philosophically if not politically. Gordon S. Wood, in *The Radicalism of the American Revolution* (New York: Vintage Books, 1991), 256–59, provides an intriguing reading of the anti-Federalists (in the person of William Findley rather than the better-known "Brutus") that puts one in mind of Protagoras. In contrast with Findley, the Federalists almost come across as following in the footsteps of Socrates. Wood does not make this comparison, but he draws, in the context of the American Revolution, a very apt distinction between republicanism and democracy, placing the Federalists in the category of republicanism, with a tinge of aristocracy thrown in for good measure, and only the anti-Federalists in that of democracy.

3. I single out Dewey and Rorty here in large part because they present, among other things, third-person, observer accounts that capture well the spirit and ethos of our democratic age, whether or not one likes the spirit and ethos in question. The first-person, participant perspective is equally important, however, and always unavoidable. For the latter, we would do well to turn not to Rorty but to Jürgen Habermas, as detailed in note 17 in the Introduction; T. M. Scanlon, *What We Owe to Each Other* (Cambridge, MA: Harvard University Press, 1998); and Bernard Williams, *Truth and Truthfulness: An Essay in Genealogy* (Princeton, NJ: Princeton University Press, 2002).

4. See Plato, *Protagoras,* trans. C. C. W. Taylor (Oxford: Clarendon, 1976), 321d–23a.

5. My treatment of Protagoras is much indebted to the bold and illuminating discussion in Ellen Meiksins Wood, *Citizens to Lords: A Social History of Western Political Thought from Antiquity to the Late Middle Ages* (London: Verso, 2011), chap. 2. See also the translator's helpful commentary on Protagoras in *The First Philosophers: The Presocratics and the Sophists,* trans. Robin Waterfield (Oxford:

Oxford University Press, 2000), 205–20; and Laurence Lampert, *How Philosophy Became Socratic: A Study of Plato's* Protagoras, Charmides, *and* Republic (Chicago: University of Chicago Press, 2010), 50–55, 68–69. Given how little is known about Protagoras, my discussion aims only to convey the drift of Protagoras's thought and, especially, to tease out from it a distinctive way of thinking about democracy that proceeds from the character of a society to the type of regime befitting it.

6. Niccolò Machiavelli, *The Discourses*, trans. Leslie Walker with revisions by Brian Richardson (London: Penguin, 2003), 1.55, p. 248.

7. Aristocracy in a broad sense, as contrasted with democracy in an equally broad sense. With aristocracy and democracy thus understood, all (Western) political thought may be considered an endless refutation or defense of (the Socratic / Platonic view of) aristocracy as against democracy, plus the equally endless search for compromise formulas in between. Since the fall of the Qing dynasty, Chinese political thought has increasingly joined this history, bringing with it its Marxist and Confucian influences.

8. "Xi Leads Top Leadership to Meet Press," *China Daily,* November 15, 2012, http://www.chinadaily.com.cn/video/2012-11/15/content_15933043.htm.

9. That is why all such traces have migrated into certain reconstructions of Confucianism, which the CCP has so far been reluctant to fully and openly endorse.

10. The "rectification of names" *(zhengming)* is an idea proposed by Confucius, according to whom, "If names are not rectified, then language will not be in accord with truth. If language is not in accord with truth, then things cannot be accomplished." *The Analects,* 13.3, trans. Wing-Tsit Chan, in *A Source Book in Chinese Philosophy* (Princeton, NJ: Princeton University Press, 1963), 40.

11. See Ronald Coase and Ning Wang, *How China Became Capitalist* (New York: Palgrave, 2013). This book makes a good case for calling today's China capitalist by giving an account of the process—a complex and fraught one—whereby China has moved further and further away from its socialist past even if it still falls some way short of the textbook version of capitalism.

12. See Jiwei Ci, *Moral China in the Age of Reform* (New York: Cambridge University Press, 2014), 165–66.

13. One must not overemphasize the nationalist dimension of the Chinese Dream. This is how President Xi explains the connection between the two dimensions: "History tells us that the future and fate of every individual is closely bound up with the future and fate of the country and the nation. Only if the country does well and the nation does well can all the individuals [*dajia*] do well" (my translation). This is from a speech titled "Shixian zhonghua minzu weida fuxing shi zhonghua minzu jindai yilai zuiweida de mengxiang" [Accomplishing the rejuvenation of the Chinese nation is the greatest dream of the Chinese nation in modern times], in *Xi Jinping tan zhiguo lizheng* [Xi Jinping on governing the country and handling public affairs] (Beijing: Waiwen chubanshe, 2014), 35–37, at 36. This is the most authoritative official statement of the connection. Nowhere in it, nor in the speech as a whole, can be found any suggestion that the well-being of the

nation is the be-all and end-all of the well-being of individuals. If anything, the well-being of individuals—every individual or all individuals *(dajia)*—almost comes across as the main goal, with the well-being of the nation treated as a necessary condition, though not reduced to a mere means. Unlike in the communist project under Mao, it is as an individual person pursuing his or her own prosperity and happiness, not only as a proud member of a collective, that the average Chinese is able to respond positively to "the great rejuvenation of the Chinese nation." How much difference in this regard is there between the Chinese and, say, the Americans?

14. All the more so in that Chinese society today, thanks to the profound effects of its reform, shows a significant resemblance to America in the early, democratizing decades after the revolution, and Tocqueville bore the most illuminating witness to the culmination of these decades in a democratic society.

15. Also worth noting is François Guizot's profound influence on Tocqueville's approach to democracy. It suffices to quote one important passage on method from Guizot's *History of France:* "It would have been wiser to study first the society itself in order to understand its political institutions. Before becoming a cause, political institutions are an effect; a society produces them before being modified by them. Thus, instead of looking to the system or forms of government in order to understand the state of the people, it is the state of the people that must be examined first in order to know what must have been, what could have been its government. . . . Society, its composition, the manner of life of individuals according to their social position, the relations of the different classes, the condition [*l'état*] of persons especially—that is the first question which demands attention from . . . the inquirer who seeks to understand how a people are governed. . . . In order to understand the political institutions, it is necessary to understand the different social conditions (classes) and their relations." Quoted in Larry Siedentop, introduction to François Guizot, *The History of Civilization in Europe,* trans. William Hazlitt (Indianapolis: Liberty Fund, 1997), xxi.

16. That the equality of conditions in question is social, in the first instance, rather than (necessarily) political is clear from passages such as the following: "Equality can take root in civil society without having any sway in the world of politics. A man may have the right to enjoy the same pleasures, enter the same professions, meet in the same places; in a word, to live in the same way and to seek wealth by the same means, without all men taking the same part in the government." Alexis de Tocqueville, *Democracy in America,* trans. Gerald E. Bevan (London: Penguin, 2003), 584.

17. Ibid., 704.

18. As Tocqueville wrote, "There are just as many wealthy people in the United States as elsewhere; I am not even aware of a country where the love of money has a larger place in men's hearts or where they express a deeper scorn for the theory of permanent equality of possessions" (ibid., 64). Admittedly, Tocqueville was, or would today be, on less firm ground when he immediately went on to say, "But

wealth circulates with an astonishing speed and experience shows that rarely do two succeeding generations benefit from its favors" (ibid.).

19. For an interpretation of equality in terms of a shared fundamental status—an interpretation that is continuous with Tocqueville's notion of equality of conditions—see Danielle Allen, *Our Declaration: A Reading of the Declaration of Independence in Defense of Equality* (New York: Liveright, 2014), esp. chaps. 29–31, 49.

20. In terms of historical sociology, the formation and institutionalization of equality of conditions thus understood took place through a process involving competition; monopoly formation, especially in the form of nationalization (responsible for the modern nation-state); and the central regulation of the drive economy and the superego—from social constraint to self-constraint. See Norbert Elias, *The Civilizing Process*, vol. 2, *Power and Civility*, trans. Edmund Jephcott (New York: Pantheon Books, 1982). For Elias's illuminating discussion of democracy in particular, see 316, 332.

21. Norbert Elias, *What Is Sociology?*, trans. Stephen Mennell and Grace Morrissey (New York: Columbia University Press, 1978), 68, emphasis added.

22. Tocqueville, *Democracy in America*, 66. Tocqueville also writes in the same book, "The condition of society is normally the result of circumstances, sometimes of laws, more often than not a combination of these two causes; but once it is established, we can consider it as the fundamental source of most of the laws, customs, and ideas which regulate the conduct of nations; whatever it does not produce, it modifies" (58).

23. See Jürgen Habermas, *Between Facts and Norms: Contributions to a Discourse Theory of Law and Democracy*, trans. William Rehg (Cambridge, MA: MIT Press, 1998).

24. Although not concerned with political matters per se in general or democracy in particular, Scanlon's contractualist account of morality can serve as the basis for an even more powerful, because more substantive, reason in favor of democracy—a *moral* reason in favor of democracy. See Scanlon, *What We Owe to Each Other*, esp. introduction and chap. 4. On Scanlon's contractualist view—according to which morality (or a part thereof) consists in "the reason we have to live with others on terms that they could not reasonably reject" (154)—it is difficult to conceive how democracy, understood as political participation by free and equal citizens, can be morally denied. Scanlon is right to claim that contractualism is "phenomenologically accurate" (155). I would add, for my purposes, that *empirically* the contractualist account becomes all the more phenomenologically compelling under modern equality of conditions—resulting, in the case of democracy's preferability, for example, in an extremely high probability of coincidence of hypothetical and actual agreement.

25. See Joseph Schumpeter, *Capitalism, Socialism and Democracy* (New York: Harper Perennial, 2008), chaps. 12–13.

26. See Tocqueville, *Democracy in America*, 775–76.

27. Elias, *What Is Sociology?*, 67.

28. "*The normative fault line that appears with this ability to say no* marks the finite freedom of persons who have to be *convinced* whenever sheer force is not supposed to intervene." Habermas, *Between Facts and Norms,* 324, emphasis in original.

29. Karl Marx, *A Contribution to the Critique of Political Economy,* in *The Marx-Engels Reader,* 2nd ed., ed. Robert C. Tucker (New York: Norton, 1978), 4, emphasis added.

30. Friedrich Engels's preface to Karl Marx and Friedrich Engels, *The Communist Manifesto,* in Tucker, *Marx-Engels Reader,* 472, emphasis added.

31. See, for example, G. A. Cohen, *Karl Marx's Theory of History: A Defence* (Princeton, NJ: Princeton University Press, 1978); and Jürgen Habermas, *Communication and the Evolution of Society,* trans. Thomas McCarthy (Boston: Beacon, 1979), chaps. 3–4.

32. Friedrich Engels, *Socialism: Utopian and Scientific,* in Tucker, *Marx-Engels Reader,* 683–717, at 702.

33. Jon Elster, *Political Psychology* (Cambridge: Cambridge University Press, 1993), 3.

34. Ibid., 184; see also 188.

35. Tocqueville, *Democracy in America,* 66.

36. Elster, *Political Psychology,* 184; see also 188.

37. Ibid., 184.

38. Another factor working against democratic pride is the lingering timidity of citizens who view themselves more as subjects than as masters—like the burghers in twelfth-century Europe as described by Guizot: "I mean the prodigious timidity of the citizens, their humility, the excessive modesty of their pretensions as to the government of the country, and the facility with which they contented themselves. Nothing is seen among them of the true political spirit, which aspires to influence, reform, and govern; nothing which gives proof of boldness of thought, or grandeur of ambition: one might call them sensible-minded, honest, freed men." *History of Civilization in Europe,* 145–46.

39. See Xi Jinping, "Goujian Zhongmei xinxing daguo guanxi" [Build a new type of major-country relationship between China and the United States], in *Shibada yilai zhongyao wenxian xuanbian* [Selections of important documents since the eighteenth party congress] (Beijing: Zhongyang wenxian chubanshe, 2014), 305–6, at 305; and "Shixian zhongguomeng bujin zaofu zhongguo renmin erqie zaofu shijie renmin" [Realizing the Chinese Dream promotes not only the well-being of the Chinese people but also the well-being of people the world over], in *Xi Jinping tan zhiguo lizheng,* 56–57. The idea of a "community of the shared future of humankind" appears in Xi's speech at the CCP's nineteenth national congress, *Juesheng quanmian jiancheng xiaokang shehui duoqu xinshidai Zhongguo tese shehui zhuyi weida shengli* [Secure a decisive victory in building a moderately prosperous society in all respects and strive for the great success of socialism with Chinese

characteristics for a New Era] (Hong Kong: Sinminchu, 2017), 25. In spelling out this idea, Xi reiterates the affinity of the Chinese Dream with the dreams of other nations (25).

40. The first crucial impetus was provided by the New Culture Movement of the mid-1910s to 1920s and the May 4 Movement of 1919. But there is no denying the radical nature and enduring effects of Mao's antipatriarchal efforts.

41. See Jean Hampton, *Political Philosophy* (Boulder, CO: Westview, 1997), 94–97.

42. Ibid., 109, emphasis in original.

43. Norbert Elias, *The Society of Individuals*, ed. Michael Schröter, trans. Edmund Jephcott (New York: Continuum, 2001), 15. On the formation of self-constraint, as distinct from social constraint, see Elias, *Power and Civility*, pt. 2.

44. See Michael J. Glennon, *National Security and Double Government* (New York: Oxford University Press, 2015); and Mike Lofgren, *The Deep State: The Fall of the Constitution and the Rise of a Shadow Government* (New York: Penguin, 2016).

45. Whether or not one continues to call it endorsement consent despite its falling short of justice. For convenience, I will, as this serves my purposes well enough.

46. See John Dunn, *Democracy: A History* (New York: Atlantic Monthly Press, 2005), 19.

47. Ibid.

48. See Jiwei Ci, "Political Agency in Liberal Democracy," *Journal of Political Philosophy* 14 (2006): 144–62.

49. For one promising approach to addressing this problem that combines realism and normative ambition, see Mark E. Warren and Jane Mansbridge, et al., "Deliberative Negotiation," chap. 5 of *Political Negotiation: A Handbook,* ed. Jane Mansbridge and Cathie Jo Martin (Washington, DC: Brookings Institution, 2015), 141–96. The entire volume is highly relevant.

50. One useful common denominator for comparing China (e.g., the National People's Congress and the Chinese People's Political Consultative Conference) with, say, the United States (e.g., Congress) is Warren and Mansbridge's notion of "deliberative negotiation" cited in the preceding note. While these authors do not reject elections, their focus is on a realistic yet normatively suitably demanding notion of deliberative negotiation, and this raises the possibility that China *could* in principle do better than, say, the United States with regard to representativeness via deliberative negotiation even if, short of free and fair elections, it will always do less well than the United States in terms of *actual* consent. Should China be able to make good use of the normative potential of deliberative negotiation, an interesting question would arise as to whether the lack of actual consent would still matter, and, if so, how much. Another, related question is whether the achievement of a high degree of representativeness through deliberative negotiation can realistically happen without the pressure of an electorate—that is, whether free and fair elections may be an enabling, if not strictly necessary, condition of well-functioning deliberative

negotiation. The answer to these questions may depend, in turn, on how flexibly the normative notion of deliberative negotiation is conceived in the first place. A comparison between China and the United States in terms of Warren and Mansbridge's standard may help make that standard itself more general or abstract in an appropriate way.

51. At least one that is good enough to dispel a suspicion well expressed by Guizot: "The introduction of an elective, that is, moveable element, into government, is as necessary as a division of forces to prevent the sovereignty from degenerating in the hands of those who exercise it into a full and permanent sovereignty of inherent right. It is therefore the necessary result of a representative government, and one of its principal characteristics. Accordingly we see that actual governments which have aimed at becoming absolute, have always endeavoured to destroy the elective principle." *The History of the Origins of Representative Government in Europe,* trans. Andrew R. Scoble (Indianapolis: Liberty Fund, 2002), 69.

52. See Baogang He and Mark E. Warren, "Authoritarian Deliberation: The Deliberative Turn in Chinese Political Development," *Perspectives on Politics* 9 (2011): 269–89. Especially interesting is the authors' idea of "deliberation-led democratization" as one possible trajectory of the developmental logic of authoritarian deliberation; the other, less positive trajectory being "deliberative authoritarianism." Events since the publication of this article seem to have favored the latter trajectory, although this does not mean that things cannot change in the future.

53. See Sungmoon Kim, *Confucian Democracy in East Asia* (New York: Cambridge University Press, 2014), chap. 8 and 280–84; and Sungmoon Kim, *Public Reason Confucianism: Democratic Perfectionism and Constitutionalism in East Asia* (New York: Cambridge University Press, 2016), chaps. 3–4.

54. See Sungmoon Kim, *Democracy after Virtue: Toward Pragmatic Confucian Democracy* (New York: Oxford University Press, 2018).

55. On Confucian democracy, see Kim, *Confucian Democracy.* For Confucian political perfectionism, see Joseph Chan, *Confucian Perfectionism: A Political Philosophy for Modern Times* (Princeton, NJ: Princeton University Press, 2014). See also Jiwei Ci, "Review of *Confucian Perfectionism: A Political Philosophy for Modern Times,*" Dao: A Journal of Comparative Philosophy 14 (2015): 289–93.

56. It is worth noting an interesting twist to the original demise of *tian,* as intriguingly discussed in the work of Billy K. L. So (Su Jilang) with reference to the fate of the idea of rule of law in modern China. So has noted an important twofold development in this regard. On the one hand, the traditional Chinese notion of *tian* had been largely discredited and, where *tian* continued to make an occasional appearance, it did so as an evolutionary concept that was at best amoral and, from the traditional Chinese point of view, even immoral. This evolutionary turn was due less to Darwin's influence than to that of Yan Fu, who, as translator of Thomas Huxley's *Evolution and Ethics,* played fast and loose with the text, including its title. On the other hand, when Chinese legal thinkers brought the idea of rule of law to China from the West, they—partly under the impact of Yan's enormously influential

dissolution of the notion of *tian* as a source of justice—did so without due cognizance of the natural law tradition behind it and of the Christian theological background at large. So argues that the traditional Chinese *tian* has a greater affinity with the Western rule of law, the latter with its original transcendent underpinning, than is commonly appreciated, including among legal scholars. Matters are complicated, however, by the fact that the original Christian, transcendent foundation for the Western rule of law has since receded so much from view that the rule of law has acquired a secular, (at least seemingly) independent identity. By contrast, nothing like this has happened with the Chinese notion of *tian,* which has simply been eliminated, resulting in a net loss. See Su Jilang, "Yan Fu yi *Tianyan lun* dui ershi shijichu Zhongguo falü de yingxiang" [The influence of Yan Fu's translation of *Evolution and Ethics* on Chinese law at the beginning of the twentieth century], *Tsinghua Law Journal* 6 (2012): 1–24; and Su Jilang and Sushou Fumei [Sufumi So], "Wu Jingxiong de xianfa ziran zhuyi—jianlun qi yu jiateng hongzhi de yitong" [John Ching-hsiung Wu's constitutional naturalism—with comparative reflections on Katō Hiroyuki], in *Guojia jiangou yu falü wenming* [Nation-building and legal civilization], ed. Xu Zhangrun, Tu Kai, and Li Yida (Beijing: Falü chubanshe, 2016), 256–79.

57. See Daniel A. Bell, *The China Model: Political Meritocracy and the Limits of Democracy* (Princeton, NJ: Princeton University Press, 2015).

58. See Jiang Qing, *A Confucian Constitutional Order: How China's Ancient Past Can Shape Its Political Future,* ed. Daniel A. Bell and Ruiping Fan, trans. Edmund Ryden (Princeton, NJ: Princeton University Press, 2013), chap. 1.

59. See, for an example, Cao Jinqing, "Bainian fuxing: Zhongguo gongchandang de shidai xushi yu lishi shiming" [One-hundred-year-long rejuvenation: The contemporary narrative and historical mission of the Chinese Communist Party], in *Daolu zixin: Zhongguo weishenme neng* [Confidence in one's own chosen path: Why China can], ed. Ma Ya (Beijing: Beijing lianhe chubanshe, 2013), 338–68, at 350.

60. Interestingly, Lee Kuan Yew, the founder of Singapore, did not make such a claim either yet came close to making the admission. See Haig Patapan, "Modern Philosopher Kings: Lee Kuan Yew and the Limits of Confucian 'Idealistic' Leadership," *European Journal of East Asian Studies* 12 (2013): 217–41. Two complementary lessons emerge from this illuminating case study: that performance legitimacy is not enough, and that a modern state whose original founding was unconnected to Confucianism is unlikely to subsequently succeed in resting legitimacy proper on Confucian foundations.

61. Democracy figured even more prominently in the CCP's agenda and ideology when it sought to drive the Kuomintang from power before 1949. See Lü Xiaobo, *Jindai Zhongguo minzhu guannian zhi shengcheng yu liubian: Yixiang guannianshi de kaocha* [The rise and evolution of the idea of democracy in modern China: An exercise in the history of ideas] (Nanjing: Jiangsu renmin chubanshe, 2012), chap. 10.

4. Democracy and the Self-Protection of Society

1. As Tocqueville puts it, in his typical dialectical fashion, "I think that the industrial aristocracy which we see rising before our eyes is one of the most harsh ever to appear on the earth; but at the same time, it is one of the *most restrained and least dangerous.*" He then immediately goes on to write, "However, this is the direction in which the friends of democracy should constantly fix their anxious gaze; for if ever aristocracy and the permanent inequality of social conditions were to infiltrate the world once again, it is predictable that this is the door by which they would enter." Alexis de Tocqueville, *Democracy in America,* trans. Gerald E. Bevan (London: Penguin, 2003), 648, emphasis added. How right he was!

2. Tocqueville's ideological preferences in this regard become very clear in comparison with, say, Gracchus Babeuf's or Filippo Buonarroti's radically different interpretation of equality of conditions. See John Dunn, *Democracy: A History* (New York: Atlantic Monthly Press, 2005), 126.

3. Ellen Meiksins Wood, *Democracy against Capitalism: Renewing Historical Materialism* (Cambridge: Cambridge University Press, 1995).

4. Joseph Schumpeter, *Capitalism, Socialism and Democracy* (New York: Harper Perennial, 2008), 296–97.

5. Ibid., 297.

6. Or "capitalist democracy," of which John Dunn offers a sobering analysis in "Capitalist Democracy: Elective Affinity or Beguiling Illusion?," *Daedalus* 136 (2007): 5–13. Especially worth noting is Dunn's distinction between "political authorization" and "the formatting of public deliberation" (12), along with the tendency within capitalist democracy to treat the market as a "perfect proxy for deliberative rationality all on its own" (13).

7. Karl Polanyi, *The Great Transformation: The Political and Economic Origins of Our Time* (Boston: Beacon, 2001), 234, emphasis added.

8. Ibid., 242.

9. Ibid.

10. It is utopian in an extra, distinctive sense with respect to China, in that China, despite the "republican" overthrow of the Qing dynasty in 1911 and the "communist" victory in 1949, cannot really be said to have accomplished the bourgeois democratic revolution—any more than, say, Soviet Russia did. Far ahead of the bourgeois democratic revolution in its own rhetoric and apparent self-understanding, and arguably even in some aspects of reality, China under the Chinese Communist Party nevertheless has the source of its main political difficulties precisely in the general lack of such a revolution combined with its inability to acknowledge this fact and to make up for lost time. The reform of the past four decades is a capitalist market revolution more than a bourgeois democratic one. Under these confused circumstances, it is perhaps small wonder that many on the Left turn a blind eye to China's missed bourgeois democratic revolution while those on the Right look to such a revolution as nothing short of a panacea, with little inkling

of its limitations. So much for the influence of Marx in a country supposedly guided by his ideas!

11. Polanyi, *Great Transformation*, 76–77, emphasis in original.

12. Ibid., 233.

13. Ibid., 234.

14. In this regard, Jacques Rancière goes even further than Polanyi, insisting that democracy is an always necessary, because never fully successful, countermovement against the oligarchic constitution of society and its infiltration into the polity, democracy included. In our time, of course, the oligarchy takes the form of the capitalist class's conquest of political power. See Jacques Rancière, *Hatred of Democracy*, trans. Steve Corcoran (London: Verso, 2006), esp. chaps. 3–4.

15. See Wolfgang Streeck, *Buying Time: The Delayed Crisis of Democratic Capitalism*, trans. Patrick Camiller (London: Verso, 2014), 20–26.

16. There is a sense in which China is less advanced in terms of what is diagnosed as "colonization of the lifeworld" by Jürgen Habermas, *The Theory of Communicative Action*, vol. 2, *Lifeworld and System: A Critique of Functionalist Reason*, trans. Thomas McCarthy (Boston: Beacon, 1987). Some may object that colonization of the lifeworld only takes a special form in China—more politically than legally engineered compared with Western societies—but produces most of the ill effects on the lifeworld nevertheless.

17. For no better model exists in reality. Just as no actually existing socialism has succeeded in aligning itself with democracy, thereby producing "liberal democratic socialism," so no actually existing capitalism has found a way to evolve into a higher form than the democratic welfare state, thereby giving rise to, say, "property-owning democracy" as advocated by James Meade and John Rawls. On the concepts of "liberal (democratic) socialism" and "property-owning democracy," see John Rawls, *Justice as Fairness: A Restatement*, ed. Erin Kelly (Cambridge, MA: Harvard University Press, 2001), pt. 4. Meade's proposal on "property-owning democracy" is developed in James Meade, *Efficiency, Equality and the Ownership of Property* (London: George Allen and Unwin, 1964).

18. The so-called tripartite social pact in Europe also existed in the United States, during what Reich calls "the Not Quite Golden Age." See Robert B. Reich, *Supercapitalism: The Transformation of Business, Democracy, and Everyday Life* (New York: Vintage Books, 2007), 6, 46–49.

19. Wolfgang Streeck, *How Will Capitalism End?* (London: Verso, 2016), 2.

20. Streeck, *Buying Time*, 23, emphasis in original.

21. Ibid., 21, emphasis in original.

22. Ibid., 61, emphasis in original.

23. Ibid., 4–5; Streeck, *How Will Capitalism End?*, 20.

24. Streeck, *Buying Time*, 19, emphasis added.

25. Wolfgang Streeck, "The Crisis in Context: Democratic Capitalism and Its Contradictions," in *Politics in the Age of Austerity*, ed. Armin Schäfer and Wolfgang Streeck (Cambridge, UK: Polity, 2013), 262–86, at 263. The precise

meaning of these brief quotes becomes clear in the context of Streeck's chapter as a whole.

26. See Streeck, *Buying Time,* chap. 1; Streeck, *How Will Capitalism End?,* chap. 2; and Streeck, "Crisis in Context." Writing with particular reference to the United States, Reich charts the replacement of democratic capitalism by supercapitalism (*Supercapitalism,* 7).

27. Walter Scheidel, *The Great Leveler: Violence and the History of Inequality from the Stone Age to the Twenty-First Century* (Princeton, NJ: Princeton University Press, 2017), 365. See also Streeck, *How Will Capitalism End?,* 74.

28. Streeck, *Buying Time,* 5.

29. Jacob S. Hacker and Paul Pierson, *Winner-Take-All Politics: How Washington Made the Rich Richer—and Turned Its Back on the Middle Class* (New York: Simon and Schuster, 2011). The book has the great merit, however, of capturing the process of the oligarchic shift on the level of what the authors call the politics of organized combat.

30. "[To the question] whether democracy *can be made* compatible with *contemporary* capitalism, my answer is: only by building a Chinese Wall between the two—by sterilizing the redistributive potential of democratic politics while continuing to rely on electoral competition to produce legitimacy for the outcomes of free markets shielded from egalitarian distortion. Hayekian democracy serves the function of making a capitalist market society appear to be 'the people's choice' even though it has long been removed from democratic control." Streeck, *How Will Capitalism End?,* 188, emphasis in original.

31. To be sure, all of this still adds up to a state of crisis, not least in the form of the so-called democratic deficit of an increasingly fragile-looking European Union. See Peter Mair, *Ruling the Void: The Hollowing of Western Democracy* (London: Verso, 2013), chap. 4; Yanis Varoufakis, *And the Weak Suffer What They Must? Europe's Crisis and America's Economic Future* (New York: Nation Books, 2016); and Andreas Follesdal and Simon Hix, "Why There Is a Democratic Deficit in the EU: Response to Majone and Moravcsik," *Journal of Common Market Studies* 44 (2006): 533–62. For all the problems detailed in accounts such as these, however, it looks as if this is going to be a protracted yet only simmering crisis, especially if the European Union is able to hold itself together.

32. See Ernst Bloch, *The Principle of Hope,* 3 vols., trans. Neville Plaice, Stephen Plaice, and Paul Knight (Cambridge, MA: MIT Press, 1986), vol. 1, 75–76.

33. See André Gorz, *The Immaterial: Knowledge, Value and Capital,* trans. Chris Turner (London: Seagull Books, 2010); and David Harvey, *Seventeen Contradictions and the End of Capitalism* (Oxford: Oxford University Press, 2014), chap.12.

34. See Steve Fraser, *The Age of Acquiescence: The Life and Death of American Resistance to Organized Wealth and Power* (New York: Basic Books, 2015), chap. 12; Hacker and Pierson, *Winner-Take-All Politics,* 56–61, 127–32, 139–43; and Paul Mason, *Postcapitalism: A Guide to Our Future* (New York: Farrar, Straus and Giroux, 2015), 91–94.

35. See Streeck, *How Will Capitalism End?*, 15–17, 79.

36. Mason, *Postcapitalism*, 73.

37. F. A. Hayek being the outstanding example; see his *The Constitution of Liberty* (Chicago: University of Chicago Press, 1978). As Hayek once said, "Personally I prefer a liberal dictator to democratic government lacking liberalism." Quoted in Pierre Dardot and Christian Laval, *The New Way of the World: On Neo-liberal Society,* trans. Gregory Elliott (London: Verso, 2013), 142. Obviously, "democratic government lacking liberalism" means, chiefly, a democratic government that does not balk at pursuing goals of social justice.

38. Barrington Moore Jr., *Social Origins of Dictatorship and Democracy: Lord and Peasant in the Making of the Modern World* (Boston: Beacon, 1993), 418.

39. An apt phrase taken from Jürgen Habermas, *Between Facts and Norms: Contributions to a Discourse Theory of Law and Democracy,* trans. William Rehg (Cambridge, MA: MIT Press, 1998), 483.

40. See Streeck, *How Will Capitalism End?*, 17.

41. Armin Schäfer and Wolfgang Streeck, "Introduction: Politics in the Age of Austerity," in Schäfer and Streeck, *Politics in the Age of Austerity*, 1–25, at 9.

42. See the sobering account in Shoshana Zuboff, *The Age of Surveillance Capitalism: The Fight for a Human Future at the New Frontier of Power* (London: Profile Books, 2019).

43. See Streeck, *How Will Capitalism End?*; and Immanuel Wallerstein et al., *Does Capitalism Have a Future?* (Oxford: Oxford University Press, 2013).

44. Colin Crouch, *The Strange Non-death of Neoliberalism* (Cambridge, UK: Polity, 2011), 7.

45. Mason, *Postcapitalism*, 91–92; see also 93–94, 105.

46. On Marktvolk versus Staatsvolk, see Streeck, *Buying Time*, 81.

47. It is revealing, in this connection, that President Xi Jinping has gone out of his way to dispel a confusion of China's current supply-side structural reform (*gongjice jiegouxing gaige*) with the supply-side economics of neoliberalism. Xi describes China's current reform as focused on structural adjustment and reduction of overcapacity and emphasizes that it has nothing to do with neoliberalism, which he mentions and rejects by name.

48. Jürgen Habermas, *Legitimation Crisis*, trans. Thomas McCarthy (Boston: Beacon, 1975), 22.

49. *Pace* Stein Ringen, *The Perfect Dictatorship: China in the 21st Century* (Hong Kong: Hong Kong University Press, 2016), 3, 136.

50. Habermas, *Legitimation Crisis*, 22.

51. Unlike during the Great Depression, when communism was a viable threat.

52. Streeck, *Buying Time*, 61, emphasis added.

53. This revolt is illuminatingly analyzed in Streeck, *Buying Time.*

54. On American-style crony capitalism, see Hacker and Pierson, *Winner-Take-All Politics*; and Luigi Zingales, *A Capitalism for the People: Recapturing the Lost Genius of American Prosperity* (New York: Basic Books, 2012), chaps. 3–4.

55. See Colin Crouch, *Post-democracy* (Cambridge, UK: Polity, 2004); and Schäfer and Streeck, *Politics in the Age of Austerity*. In their introduction to the volume, Schäfer and Streeck go so far as to speak of "rich democratic-capitalist countries co-governed by global capital markets" (23). Streeck, in chap. 10 of the same volume, describes the Eurozone as the site of "the drama of democratic states being turned into debt-collecting agencies on behalf of a global oligarchy of investors" ("Crisis in Context," 284). In both cases, it would be difficult to argue against the authors.

56. See Karl Marx, "Contribution to the Critique of Hegel's *Philosophy of Right*," in *The Marx-Engels Reader*, 2nd ed., ed. Robert C. Tucker (New York: Norton, 1978), 16–25.

57. See ibid., 21.

58. Karl Marx, "On the Jewish Question," in Tucker, *Marx-Engels Reader*, 26–52, at 32, emphasis in original.

59. See Karl Marx, "Contribution to the Critique of Hegel's *Philosophy of Right: Introduction*," in Tucker, *Marx-Engels Reader*, 53–65; and Marx, "On the Jewish Question."

60. Marx, "On the Jewish Question," 35, emphasis in original.

61. If one has reason to abandon belief in the prospect of "human emancipation" yet to maintain the ethical impulses informing such emancipation (while also rejecting the logic of Marxist science with its division between the knowing and the ignorant), one will end up with a view on democracy best set out by Jacques Rancière in, say, *Disagreement: Politics and Philosophy,* trans. Julie Rose (Minneapolis: University of Minnesota Press, 1999). On this view, democracy is the permanent and never completely successful struggle to pit the political method of equality against the inherently oligarchic character of society.

62. As reflected in improvements in society, in the enhanced credibility of the Ideological State Apparatuses and hence the rise in ideological legitimacy, and in the relatively enduring appearance of consensus and consent.

63. Democratic pride too is both expressed and thwarted by this fundamental ambivalence of the bourgeois democratic state form. It is thus bound to fall short of full democratic agency, and yet it will not settle for mere bourgeois prosperity.

5. Contradictions and Arrested Transitions

1. As expounded, for example, in John Rawls, *Justice as Fairness: A Restatement,* ed. Erin Kelly (Cambridge, MA: Harvard University Press, 2001), 44–45.

2. Benjamin Constant, "The Liberty of the Ancients Compared with That of the Moderns," in *Political Writings,* trans. and ed. Biancamaria Fontana (Cambridge: Cambridge University Press, 1988), 309–28, at 316.

3. Ibid., 317, emphasis added.

4. Ibid., 323.

5. John Dunn, *Democracy: A History* (New York: Atlantic Monthly Press, 2005), 146.

6. As subtly described, for example, in terms of certain religious institutions and activities being neither permitted nor banned (i.e., limited and fragile de facto liberties), in Ian Johnson, *The Souls of China: The Return of Religion after Mao* (New York: Pantheon Books, 2017), chap. 4.

7. See Jiwei Ci, *Moral China in the Age of Reform* (New York: Cambridge University Press, 2014). The moral vacuum takes an additional, distinctive form in the countryside. See Wu Chongqing, *Wu zhuti shuren shehui ji shehui chongjian* [Decentered society of acquaintances and social reconstruction] (Beijing: Shehui kexue wenxian chubanshe, 2014).

8. See Zygmunt Bauman, *Consuming Life* (Cambridge, UK: Polity, 2007).

9. See Jiwei Ci, "Liberty Rights and the Limits of Liberal Democracy," in *Philosophical Foundations of Human Rights,* ed. Rowan Cruft, Matthew Liao, and Massimo Renzo (Oxford: Oxford University Press, 2015), 588–607, at 596–98.

10. See Bernard Williams, "Internal and External Reasons," in *Moral Luck* (Cambridge: Cambridge University Press, 1981), 101–13. Readers with a philosophical background will readily see that I am using Williams's term *internal reasons* in a loose and suggestive sense. On a more precise level, I am more than happy to have the sense of *internal* stretched in the way suggested by T. M. Scanlon in "Appendix: Williams on Internal and External Reasons," in *What We Owe to Each Other* (Cambridge, MA: Harvard University Press, 1998), 363–73, at 368–69. Obviously, my concerns in the present context, unlike those of Williams and Scanlon, are in general more sociological than philosophical, but Scanlon's discussion of Williams prompts me to consider the relation between the independent soundness of moral reasons and their durable internalizability. In examining this relation with special reference to the peculiarities of the Chinese moral scene, it strikes me that the durable internalizability of a moral reason as a moral reason may be a mark or symptom of its reasonableness, both in an empirical sense and possibly in Scanlon's deeper, hypothetical sense. Empirically, what China's moral culture lacks today is a system of moral reasons that lend themselves to durable internalization in the new, postcommunist society.

11. When Guizot speaks of freedom as a crucial part of morality, his reasoning applies especially to *modern* morality. As far as the latter is concerned, he states the rationale for freedom with exceptional eloquence: "This [religions] have often overlooked; they have considered liberty as an obstacle, not as a means; they have forgotten the nature of the force to which they address themselves, and have treated the human soul as they would a material force. It is in following this error that they have almost always been led to range themselves on the side of power and despotism against human liberty, regarding it only as an adversary, and taking more pains to subdue than to secure it. . . . It is necessary to guarantee liberty in order to regulate it morally." François Guizot, *The History of Civilization in Europe,* trans. William Hazlitt (Indianapolis: Liberty Fund, 1997), 123.

12. In Tocqueville's sense, as set out in Chapter 3.

13. Alexis de Tocqueville, *Democracy in America,* trans. Gerald E. Bevan (London: Penguin, 2003), 66.

14. The converse is also the case—namely, formal political equality cannot be fully substantive as long as domination persists in the social or private sphere. See the last section of Chapter 4; and Karl Marx, "On the Jewish Question," in *The Marx-Engels Reader,* 2nd ed., ed. Robert C. Tucker (New York: Norton, 1978), 26–52.

15. *The Book of Mencius,* 7B.14, translation by Wing-Tsit Chan, *A Source Book in Chinese Philosophy* (Princeton, NJ: Princeton University Press, 1963), 81.

16. This situation of social equality without political equality could be alternatively described as (not yet valorized) private autonomy without public autonomy, as the latter terms are used in Jürgen Habermas, *Between Facts and Norms: Contributions to a Discourse Theory of Law and Democracy,* trans. William Rehg (Cambridge, MA: MIT Press, 1998).

17. Tocqueville, *Democracy in America,* 502. This idea of democratic social power is found especially in what Tocqueville has to say about the power of the majority over thought (297–300) and is distinct from what he means by the tendency for political power to expand under equality of conditions (vol. 2, pt. 4, chaps. 6–7). For an illuminating discussion of democratic social power, see Pierre Manent, *Tocqueville and the Nature of Democracy,* trans. John Waggoner (Lanham, MD: Rowman and Littlefield, 1996), chap. 4.

18. Manuel Castells, *The Internet Galaxy: Reflections on the Internet, Business, and Society* (Oxford: Oxford University Press, 2001), 1.

19. See John Rawls, *A Theory of Justice,* rev. ed. (Cambridge, MA: Harvard University Press, 1999), 441–47.

20. See Jacques Rancière, *Hatred of Democracy,* trans. Steve Corcoran (London: Verso, 2006). What Rancière has to say on this subject is highly salutary, even if one does not entirely agree with him. Oligarchy, or what may be called pure oligarchy, is marked by the "logic of indistinction of the public and the private" (55). From this Rancière distinguishes what he calls "oligarchic State of law" (74), which features the carving out of a public sphere and hence the constant opposition between the private and the public. Such a state, usually called a democracy, is prone to reprivatize the public, and it does so in two ways: first through the public-private distinction, whereby wealth dominates through the liberties of all in the private sphere, and second through the effective monopoly of the public sphere by the wealthy. For Rancière, democracy is nothing but the constant struggle against both of these tendencies.

21. Long-term incumbency is one prima facie indication of inequality of influence, or oligarchy. For a list of criteria for long-term incumbencies that conform more or less to democratic norms, see Mark E. Warren and Jane Mansbridge, et al., "Deliberative Negotiation," chap. 5 of *Political Negotiation: A Handbook,* ed. Jane Mansbridge and Cathie Jo Martin (Washington, DC: Brookings Institution, 2015), 141–96, at 173–74. The question is how often such criteria are met, especially today.

22. See Maurizio Lazzarato, *The Making of the Indebted Man* (Los Angeles: Semiotext(e), 2012).

23. See Pierre Manent, *A World beyond Politics? A Defense of the Nation-State,* trans. Marc LePain (Princeton, NJ: Princeton University Press, 2006), 13.

24. Ibid., 16.

25. Ibid., 16–17, emphasis in original. This is essentially Montesquieu's idea of liberty, as Manent makes clear in *An Intellectual History of Liberalism,* trans. Rebecca Balinski (Princeton, NJ: Princeton University Press, 1995), 60.

26. See Louis Dumont, *Essays on Individualism: Modern Ideology in Anthropological Perspective* (Chicago: University of Chicago Press, 1986), 106–7; and Ellen Meiksins Wood, *Democracy against Capitalism: Renewing Historical Materialism* (Cambridge: Cambridge University Press, 1995), chap. 1.

27. See Manent, *World beyond Politics?,* 13.

28. Perry Anderson, *Passages from Antiquity to Feudalism* (London: Verso, 2013), 148.

29. See Zhang Fentian, *Zhongguo diwang guannian* [The idea of the imperial ruler in China] (Beijing: Zhongguo renmin daxue chubanshe, 2004), 129–44.

30. On the concepts of ideological and political power, see Michael Mann, *The Sources of Social Power,* vol. 1, *History of Power from the Beginning to AD 1760,* new ed. (Cambridge: Cambridge University Press, 2012), chap. 1.

31. See Chenyang Li, *The Confucian Philosophy of Harmony* (London: Routledge, 2014), 72–73.

32. As Fairbank rightly says, "The sequence of dynasties was due to the inveterate Chinese impulse during a dynastic interregnum toward political reunification. Unity was so strong an ideal because it promised stability, peace, and prosperity." John King Fairbank and Merle Goldman, *China: A New History,* 2nd enlarged ed. (Cambridge, MA: Harvard University Press, 2006), 47.

33. Immanuel Kant, *The Metaphysics of Morals,* trans. Mary Gregor (Cambridge: Cambridge University Press, 1996), 146, emphasis in original.

34. See Immanuel Kant, "On the Common Saying: 'This May Be True in Theory, but It Does Not Apply in Practice,'" in *Kant: Political Writings,* ed. H. S. Reiss, trans. H. B. Nisbet (Cambridge: Cambridge University Press, 1970), 61–92, at 73–74.

35. See John Rawls, *Political Liberalism* (New York: Columbia University Press, 1996).

36. Pierre Manent, "The Modern State," in *New French Thought: Political Philosophy,* ed. Mark Lilla (Princeton, NJ: Princeton University Press, 1994), 123–33, at 131. See also Pierre Manent, *The City of Man,* trans. Marc A. LePain (Princeton, NJ: Princeton University Press, 1998), 180–81.

37. See Iris Murdoch, *The Sovereignty of Good* (London: Routledge, 2013). In her only reference to "political liberalism," she writes, "It must be said in its favour that this image of human nature [in terms of sovereignty of the concept of freedom] has been the inspiration of political liberalism. However, as Hume once wisely observed, good political philosophy is not necessarily good moral philosophy" (79).

38. See John Skorupski, *Ethical Explorations* (Oxford: Oxford University Press, 1999), chaps. 9–11. The discussion of permissive and persuasive neutrality is in chap. 10.

39. See Guizot, *History of Civilization in Europe*; and Ellen Meiksins Wood, *Liberty and Property: A Social History of Western Political Thought from Renaissance to Enlightenment* (London: Verso, 2012).

6. Democratic Preparation

1. For an illuminating account of the factors that necessitated this form of social and political organization—with its distinctive centralization and family-state homology—and gave Confucianism a central place in it, see Ray Huang, *China: A Macro History* (Armonk, NY: M. E. Sharpe, 1990), chap. 3.

2. *The Analects,* 1.2, with the translation here and hereafter taken from Wing-tsit Chan, *A Source Book in Chinese Philosophy* (Princeton, NJ: Princeton University Press, 1963), 20.

3. *Mencius,* 4A.27, translation by Chan, *Source Book in Chinese Philosophy,* 76.

4. *Mencius,* 3A.5, in Chan, *Source Book in Chinese Philosophy,* 71.

5. Dong Zhongshu [Tung Chung-shu], *Chunqiu Fanlu* [Luxuriant gems of the *Spring and Autumn Annals*], chap. 42, translation by Chan, *Source Book in Chinese Philosophy,* 279.

6. Strictly speaking, although the goal of harmony (within the ranks of the proletariat and its allies) was actively pursued, the term itself was dropped for a long period of time because of its perceived inconsistency with the idea of class struggle. The term regained its positive status in official discourse only during the reform era.

7. As Fei Xiaotong observes, in traditional China the tendency toward *zhuanzhi* (despotism) was balanced by the emperor's actual *wuwei* (hands-off) approach. See his *Xiangtu Zhongguo* [From the soil: The foundations of Chinese society] (Beijing: Beijing daxue chubanshe, 1998), chap. 10.

8. This partly explains its greater strength and durability compared with the fate of the same formula in otherwise similar regimes in the former Soviet Bloc.

9. On the importance for democratization of "a liberal political culture supported by corresponding patterns of political socialization," see Jürgen Habermas, *Between Facts and Norms: Contributions to a Discourse Theory of Law and Democracy,* trans. William Rehg (Cambridge, MA: MIT Press, 1998), 316–17.

10. Mark Elvin, *The Pattern of the Chinese Past* (Stanford, CA: Stanford University Press, 1973), chap. 1.

11. See Jin Guantao and Liu Qingfeng, *Xingsheng yu weiji: Lun Zhongguo shehui chao wending jiegou* [The cycle of growth and decline: On the ultrastable structure of Chinese society] (Shatin, Hong Kong: Chinese University Press, 1992), chap. 2; and Dingxin Zhao, *The Confucian-Legalist State: A New Theory of Chinese History* (Oxford: Oxford University Press, 2015), chap. 9.

12. John Dunn, *Breaking Democracy's Spell* (New Haven, CT: Yale University Press, 2014), 73.

13. See Baogang He, *Governing Taiwan and Tibet: Democratic Approaches* (Edinburgh: Edinburgh University Press, 2015), chap. 3, for an excellent discussion of the "empire thesis," and for the author's own counterproposal—the "anti-empire thesis"—suggesting that democratization need not threaten China's national unity and territorial integrity.

14. In this regard, it is even possible to partly concur with Samuel Huntington's view that "the most important political distinction among countries concerns not their form of government but their degree of government. The differences between democracy and dictatorship are less than differences between those countries whose politics embodies consensus, community, legitimacy, organization, effectiveness, stability, and those countries whose politics is deficient in these qualities." *Political Order in Changing Societies* (New Haven, CT: Yale University Press, 1968), 1. Where I differ with Huntington is in thinking that democracy matters more than he allows for, inasmuch as democracy may be indispensable, though not sufficient by itself, precisely for achieving or maintaining the positive qualities he speaks of, as in today's China. But Huntington is surely correct in his useful reminder that democratic change has little to be said for it if it fails to be consistent with those positive qualities associated with a proper degree of government.

15. Norbert Elias, *The Civilizing Process*, vol. 2, *Power and Civility*, trans. Edmund Jephcott (New York: Pantheon Books, 1982), 114–15.

16. Ibid., 115.

17. Ibid., 165.

18. As noted in Chapter 3, representativeness and consent can diverge. Considering this, it makes sense to define democracy in terms of a regime's credible claim to representativeness *and/or* consent. There is also the option of insisting on both representativeness and consent. Although I prefer the first, weaker option, I want to leave the matter open.

19. As John Dunn writes, "Democracy in itself ... does not specify any clear and definite structure of rule." *Democracy: A History* (New York: Atlantic Monthly Press, 2005), 149.

20. This fact is well recognized by sober and perceptive Western observers. John Dunn, for example, puts it this way: other than the CCP now ruling China, "there is no independent surviving source of order and no external basis on which they or anyone else could readily set out to construct one. To choose to jeopardize that already highly imperfect and conspicuously vulnerable order would be, in the classic phrase of Edmund Burke, 'to play a most desperate game.'" *Breaking Democracy's Spell*, 81.

21. See Jane J. Mansbridge, *Beyond Adversary Democracy* (Chicago: University of Chicago Press, 1983), pt. 1.

22. Ibid., 288–89.

23. See Robert A. Dahl, *Polyarchy: Participation and Opposition* (New Haven, CT: Yale University Press, 1971); and Robert A. Dahl, *Democracy and Its Critics* (New

Haven, CT: Yale University Press, 1989), pt. 5. Dahl sounds only mildly defensive in comparison with the utterly unabashed apologia that only a nineteenth-century thinker such as James Mill was capable of: "Our opinion, therefore, is that the business of government is properly the business of the rich, and that they will always obtain it, either by bad means, or good. Upon this every thing depends. If they obtain it by bad means, the government is bad. If they obtain it by good means, the government is sure to be good. The only good means of obtaining it are, the free suffrage of the people." James Mill, "On the Ballot," as quoted in C. B. Macpherson, *The Life and Times of Liberal Democracy* (Oxford: Oxford University Press, 1977), 42.

24. Leo Strauss puts it well when he says, encapsulating the view of Machiavelli, "Every so-called democracy is in fact an oligarchy *unless it verges on anarchy.*" Leo Strauss, *Thoughts on Machiavelli* (Chicago: University of Chicago Press, 1978), 127, emphasis added.

25. This is increasingly reflected in "gold-plating." See Richard Sennett, *The Culture of the New Capitalism* (New Haven, CT: Yale University Press, 2006), 164–68.

26. There are signs that the elite cohesion that has served as a condition for the relatively smooth functioning of democracy in the United States and Europe is being significantly weakened by the ending of the Cold War and the subsequent globalization. One result, unsurprisingly, is a weakening of democracy itself and a turn toward a species of authoritarianism. See Wendy Brown, Peter E. Gordon, and Max Pensky, *Authoritarianism: Three Inquiries in Critical Theory* (Chicago: University of Chicago Press, 2018); and Cass R. Sunstein, ed., *Can It Happen Here?: Authoritarianism in America* (New York: Dey Street Books, 2018).

27. On the causes of democratic breakdown, see Bao Shenggang, *Minzhu bengkui de zhengzhixue* [The politics of democratic breakdown] (Beijing: Shangwu yinshuguan, 2014).

28. On the idea of liberal democratic socialism (and the kindred notion of property-owning democracy), see John Rawls, *Justice as Fairness: A Restatement,* ed. Erin Kelly (Cambridge, MA: Harvard University Press, 2001), pt. 4.

29. As Tocqueville famously says, only a great genius has any chance of pulling off this kind of reform. See Alexis de Tocqueville, *The Ancien Régime and the Revolution,* trans. Gerald Bevan (London: Penguin, 2008), 175. It is no accident that this book was not very long ago recommended reading within the CCP. Elsewhere, Tocqueville reminds us that "there can be no doubt that the moment of granting political rights to a nation hitherto deprived of them is a time of crisis, one that is often necessary but always perilous." *Democracy in America,* trans. Gerald E. Bevan (London: Penguin, 2003), 280.

30. Jiwei Ci, *Moral China in the Age of Reform* (New York: Cambridge University Press, 2014).

31. Thus the anticorruption campaign has been more effective in changing behavior than in improving morality—i.e., moral subjectivity. This is not to underestimate the effectiveness of the campaign but only to suggest that, given the very

nature of its effectiveness, no *inner, moral* transformation has taken place, either within the CCP or in the country at large. For such a transformation, something else—a true moral reform—is needed.

32. What Tocqueville says of France at the point of the revolution—"A nation so poorly prepared to act independently could not attempt a total reform without total destruction. An absolute monarch would have been a less dangerous innovator" (*Ancien Régime,* 166; see also 201–2)—is not without applicability to China today. In terms of the tightness of political control and its likely consequences, China's situation today definitely bears greater resemblance to the absolute monarchical rule in prerevolutionary France than to, say, English political life during the same period.

33. See Ferdinand Tönnies, *Community and Civil Society,* trans. Jose Harris and Margaret Hollis (Cambridge: Cambridge University Press, 2001), bk. 1, sec. 2; the quotes are from p. 52.

34. Indeed, Tocqueville speaks of a "democratic despotism." See Tocqueville, *Ancien Régime,* 162–63. See also Tocqueville, *Democracy in America,* 591–92.

35. Habermas, *Between Facts and Norms,* 369, emphasis in original.

36. For an illuminating attempt to make sense of this development, see Liang Zhiping, "Lun fazhi yu dezhi: Dui Zhongguo dangdai fazhi de yige neizai guancha" [On rule of law and rule of virtue: An immanent reading of rule of law in contemporary China], *Zhongguo wenhua* 41 (Spring 2015): 23–43.

37. Ronald Coase and Ning Wang, in *How China Became Capitalist* (New York: Palgrave, 2013), 102, are right to regard even rule by law as a significant improvement.

38. See Michel Foucault, *The Birth of Biopolitics: Lectures at the Collège de France,* ed. Michel Senellart, trans. Graham Burchell (New York: Picador, 2004), 168–69.

39. F. A. Hayek, *The Constitution of Liberty* (Chicago: University of Chicago Press, 1978).

40. Habermas, *Between Facts and Norms.*

41. These three phrases were joined together, as forming an "organic unity" *(youji tongyi),* by Xi Jinping at the CCP's nineteenth national congress. See Xi Jinping, *Juesheng quanmian jiancheng xiaokang shehui duoqu xinshidai Zhongguo tese shehui zhuyi weida shengli* [Secure a decisive victory in building a moderately prosperous society in all respects and strive for the great success of socialism with Chinese characteristics for a New Era] (Hong Kong: Sinminchu, 2017), 36.

42. On the evolution of the CCP's understanding of democracy, see Lü Xiaobo, *Jindai Zhongguo minzhu guannian zhi shengcheng yu liubian* [The formation and transformation of the idea of democracy in modern China] (Nanjing: Jiangsu renmin chubanshe, 2012), chap. 10.

43. Tocqueville, *Democracy in America,* 583.

44. Immanuel Kant, "An Answer to the Question: 'What Is Enlightenment?,'" in *Kant: Political Writings,* ed. H. S. Reiss, trans. H. B. Nisbet (Cambridge: Cambridge University Press, 1970), 54–60, at 59, emphasis in original. Kant published this essay in 1784, when Frederick the Great was still alive and king of Prussia.

45. It is worth noting, however, that Kant by no means rules out the *political* consequences of intellectual enlightenment, for he says, "Once the germ on which nature has lavished most care—man's inclination and vocation to think *freely*—has developed within this hard shell, it gradually reacts upon the mentality of the people, who thus gradually become increasingly able to *act freely*. Eventually, it even influences the principles of governments, which find that they can themselves profit by treating man, who is *more than a machine*, in a manner appropriate to his dignity." "Answer to the Question," 59–60, emphasis in original. It is clear from the text immediately before the quote that Kant even sees this as a paradoxical advantage that an enlightened monarchy has over a republic.

46. For the larger historical context that helps explain what might otherwise appear baffling in Kant's approach to liberty of thought, see François Guizot, *The History of Civilization in Europe,* trans. William Hazlitt (Indianapolis: Liberty Fund, 1997), twelfth lecture. In this context, Kant has a great forerunner in Spinoza, who claimed to have shown in chapter 20 of his *Theologico-Political Treatise,* "I. That it is impossible to deprive men of the liberty of saying what they think. II. That such liberty can be conceded to every man without injury to the rights and authority of the sovereign power, and that every man may retain it without injury to such rights, provided that he does not presume upon it to the extent of introducing any new rights into the state, or acting in any way contrary to the existing laws. III. That every man may enjoy this liberty without detriment to the public peace, and that no inconveniences arise therefrom which cannot easily be checked. IV. That every man may enjoy it without injury to his allegiance. V. That laws dealing with speculative problems are entirely useless. VI. Lastly, that not only may such liberty be granted without prejudice to the public peace, to loyalty, and to the rights of rulers, but that it is even necessary for their preservation." Benedict de Spinoza, *A Theologico-Political Treatise* and *A Political Treatise,* trans. R. H. M. Elwes (New York: Dover, 2004), 264–65.

47. Today this typically goes by the name of *public reason.*

48. The rationale for religious freedom and tolerance is well expressed by Frederick the Great himself, along lines not so different from Kant's. See the selection from Frederick's *Essay on Forms of Government* in *The Portable Enlightenment Reader,* ed. Isaac Kramnick (New York: Penguin, 1995), 452–59, at 457. The same rationale is largely applicable to censorship and freedom of expression.

49. One of the clearest calls for China to shift its emphasis from economic success to social justice goals comes from Sun Liping, "Cong gaige dao jianshe gongping zhengyi shehui" [From reform to building a fair and just society], *Jingji guancha bao,* March 1, 2013.

50. It is food for thought, in this connection, that even the first-generation revolutionaries, those who outlived Mao, failed to be disappointed with how China turned capitalist in the era of reform—in comparison with, say, America's founding fathers. On the latter's reactions to the upshot of the American Revolution within their lifetime, see Gordon S. Wood, *The Radicalism of the American Revolution* (New York: Vintage Books, 1991), 365–68.

51. On the obstacles to any potential social justice reform posed by powerful interest groups, see William H. Overholt, *China's Crisis of Success* (Cambridge: Cambridge University Press, 2018).

52. As outlined, for example, in Xi Jinping's speech at the CCP's nineteenth national congress, Xi, *Juesheng quanmian jiancheng xiaokang shehui.* Much of section 8 of this speech—points 1–4 (pp. 45–48)—is devoted to matters of social justice.

53. Aristotle, *The Politics,* trans. Carnes Lord, 2nd ed. (Chicago: University of Chicago Press, 2013), 1295b25–29, 1295b35–96a6.

54. Tocqueville, *Democracy in America,* 704.

55. Wood, *Radicalism of the American Revolution.*

56. See Gordon S. Wood, "Democracy and the American Revolution," in *Democracy: The Unfinished Journey, 508 BC to AD 1993,* ed. John Dunn (Oxford: Oxford University Press, 1993), 91–105.

7. Democracy at Home and Legitimacy around the World

1. I use the term *democracy deficit* to mean a deficit caused by nondemocracy, not a relative lack of democracy in what is already a democratic polity. For the latter, the term is *democratic deficit.*

2. See Peter Gowan, *The Global Gamble: Washington's Faustian Bid for World Dominance* (London: Verso, 1999), 69, 100.

3. See Graham Allison, *Destined for War: Can America and China Escape Thucydides's Trap?* (New York: Houghton Mifflin Harcourt, 2017), 139–40.

4. On Europe's attitude toward China, see Martin Jacques, *When China Rules the World: The End of the Western World and the Birth of a New Global Order,* 2nd ed. (New York: Penguin, 2012), 450–58.

5. Joseph Schumpeter, *Capitalism, Socialism and Democracy* (New York: Harper Perennial, 2008), 285.

6. In this standard conception there is little doubt that freedom takes precedence over democracy, and the liberties of the moderns over that of the ancients. Constant is essentially correct about this, although the details of the balance vary from one liberal democratic society to another. In addition to this relationship of priority, Constant is also largely correct in taking democracy to offer the best protection for freedom. Having pronounced "individual liberty" to be "the true modern liberty," he famously goes on to emphasize that "political liberty is its guarantee, consequently political liberty is indispensable," before cautioning, "But to ask people of our day to sacrifice, like those of the past, the whole of their individual liberty to political liberty, is the surest means of detaching them from the former and, once this result has been achieved, it would be only too easy to deprive them of the latter." Benjamin Constant, "The Liberty of the Ancients Compared with That of the Moderns," in *Political Writings,* trans. and ed. Biancamaria Fontana (Cambridge: Cambridge University Press, 1988), 309–28, at 323. It may be added,

in the light of the discussion of maturity and freedom in Chapter 6, that freedom is an essential condition for any reasonably well-functioning democracy. More importantly, once we realize that freedom, via its promotion of maturity, is one of democracy's essential conditions, this suggests an additional reason why, and an additional sense in which, freedom must take precedence over democracy. It is for these reasons that, among all the goods against which democracy needs to be weighed, freedom may be thought to stand in a relatively easy and straightforward relationship to it.

7. John Dunn, *Democracy: A History* (New York: Atlantic Monthly Press, 2005), 149: "Even as an idea (let alone as a practical expedient) it wholly fails to ensure any regular and reassuring relation to just outcomes over any issue at all. As a structure of rule, within any actual society at any time, it makes it overwhelmingly probable that many particular outcomes will turn out flagrantly unjust. The idea of justice and the idea of democracy fit very precariously together." See also 182–83.

8. The idea of democracy being the least bad regime, often associated with Winston Churchill, is simply not good enough for this purpose. Interestingly, this idea, whether correct or not, is also too modest to justify strong outside intervention.

9. It is, for example, part of the subtitle of an influential book, Larry M. Bartels, *Unequal Democracy: The Political Economy of the New Gilded Age* (Princeton, NJ: Princeton University Press, 2008). See also Joseph E. Stiglitz, *The Price of Inequality: How Today's Divided Society Endangers Our Future* (New York: Norton, 2013).

8. Two Systems, One Democratic Future

1. This is also one reason why the mainstream pan-democrats are still sometimes lumped together with the independence-seeking localists *(dupai)* and those favoring self-determination *(zijuepai)* as one broad political camp, despite great differences among them in aim, philosophy, and strategy.

2. See Leo F. Goodstadt, *Poverty in the Midst of Affluence: How Hong Kong Mismanaged Its Prosperity,* rev. ed. (Hong Kong: Hong Kong University Press, 2014).

3. On the high level of (conscious) tolerance of inequality and lack of social justice, even on the part of the less well off in Hong Kong, see ibid., 78–79, 82. Such conscious tolerance is perfectly compatible with the more or less unconscious accumulation of negative energy.

4. Thanks to the decisively altered balance of power between the mainland and Hong Kong, and to the political liability—which a more powerful Beijing can now afford to take proper notice of and do something about—of the central government having visibly cozy ties with the local tycoon class.

5. See Carl Schmitt, *The Concept of the Political,* trans. George Schwab (Chicago: University of Chicago Press, 2007), 26–27.

6. See Gordon S. Wood, *The Radicalism of the American Revolution* (New York: Vintage Books, 1991), for the difference between republic and democracy in this context.

7. On the contestation over democracy before 1997, see Alvin Y. So, "The Tiananmen Incident, Patten's Electoral Reforms, and the Roots of Contested Democracy in Hong Kong," in *The Challenge of Hong Kong's Reintegration with China,* ed. Ming K. Chan (Hong Kong: Hong Kong University Press, 1997), 49–83.

8. Under normal circumstances, "the loyalty demanded from every citizen is not mere loyalty to the bare country, to the country irrespective of the regime, but to the country informed by the regime, by the Constitution." Leo Strauss, *The City and Man* (Chicago: University of Chicago Press, 1978), 47–48.

9. See Jürgen Habermas, "Citizenship and National Identity," appendix 2 of *Between Facts and Norms: Contributions to a Discourse Theory of Law and Democracy,* trans. William Rehg (Cambridge, MA: MIT Press, 1998), 491–515.

10. Though not his exact idea, because Gramsci associates the exercise of leadership and the production of consent with civil society rather than the state, of which democracy is a feature.

11. See Antonio Gramsci, *Selections from the Prison Notebooks,* ed. and trans. Quintin Hoare and Geoffrey Nowell Smith (New York: International Publishers, 1971), 12, 57–58, 80f, 239, 263.

12. See Michel Foucault, *The Birth of Biopolitics: Lectures at the Collège de France,* ed. Michel Senellart, trans. Graham Burchell (New York: Picador, 2004), 91–92.

13. Michael Mann, *The Sources of Social Power: Volume 1: History of Power from the Beginning to AD 1760,* new ed. (Cambridge: Cambridge University Press, 2012), chap. 1.

14. See Louis Althusser, "Ideology and Ideological State Apparatuses," appendix 2 of *On the Reproduction of Capitalism: Ideology and Ideological State Apparatuses,* trans. G. M. Goshgarian (London: Verso, 2014), 232–72. It is a matter of some theoretical importance that, in a major departure from Gramsci, Althusser rejects the notion of civil society, preferring to see ideology too as part of the bourgeois state rather than as part of a distinct and independent civil society. On this, see Perry Anderson, *The Antinomies of Antonio Gramsci* (London: Verso, 2017), 77–79. Although Althusser may well be mistaken with regard to bourgeois democracy, at least partly, it is not by accident that his view of the matter lends itself particularly well to understanding how ideology operates, or fails to operate, in CCP-led China. After all, China is not a liberal democracy and does not feature a strong civil society.

15. Gramsci, *Selections from the Prison Notebooks,* 259.

16. Which is unnecessary, of course, if the reader recalls what was said on this subject in the Introduction.

17. Althusser, *On the Reproduction of Capitalism,* 135, emphasis in original.

18. Ibid., 137.

19. See John Dunn, *Breaking Democracy's Spell* (New Haven, CT: Yale University Press, 2014), 73.

20. Immanuel Kant, "An Answer to the Question: 'What Is Enlightenment?,'" in *Kant: Political Writings,* ed. H. S. Reiss, trans. H. B. Nisbet (Cambridge: Cambridge University Press, 1970), 54–60, at 59, emphasis in original.

21. Ibid., 59.

22. Unsurprisingly, the Basic Law, Hong Kong's so-called miniconstitution, is tilted in favor of business interests, seen as essential to Hong Kong's prosperity and stability. Thus it gives less priority to social justice than is desirable—less, presumably, than might be the case had the Basic Law been enacted in the rather different ethos prevailing in China today on matters of social welfare and economic inequality. Even so, the Basic Law leaves substantial scope for improvements in social justice. Article 145, for example, although a far cry from social democracy, is sufficiently ambiguous and flexible in this regard—if there is enough public interest in pursuing such improvements.

Concluding Reflections

1. Karl Marx, *Economic and Philosophic Manuscripts of 1844,* in *The Marx-Engels Reader,* 2nd ed., ed. Robert C. Tucker (New York: Norton, 1978), 66–125, at 76.

2. Karl Marx, "On the Jewish Question," in Tucker, *Marx-Engels Reader,* 26–52.

3. If history is to have a goal.

4. Karl Marx, "Contribution to the Critique of Hegel's *Philosophy of Right,*" in Tucker, *Marx-Engels Reader,* 16–25, at 20, emphasis in original.

5. See Benjamin Constant, "The Liberty of the Ancients Compared with That of the Moderns," in *Political Writings,* trans. and ed. Biancamaria Fontana (Cambridge: Cambridge University Press, 1988), 309–28.

6. Amartya Sen, *Development as Freedom* (New York: Anchor Books, 2000).

7. When wanting what the party does not let you want is not a live or actionable option, and when continuing nevertheless to maintain the useless wants, even in the sheltered space of one's consciousness, would tend only to worsen one's state of mind, all surveys of preferences (and approval ratings) must be taken with an even larger grain of salt than normal.

Index

Adaptive preference, 131, 373
All under Heaven, 147, 150, 234, 236, 371
Althusser, Louis, 4–5, 65, 68, 69, 362, 364–365
Altruism, 207, 208, 210
American Dream, 127, 208, 217
Analects, 257
Ancien régime, 226, 235
Anquangan, 7
Anticorruption campaign, 44, 80, 84–87, 89, 90; as purge, 86–87, 89, 92
Arendt, Hannah, 106
Aristocracy, as defined by Tocqueville, 114, 149, 152, 216, 304
Aristotle, 57, 105, 121, 304, 342
Asceticism, 207, 210

Beijing, 199
Bell, Daniel A., 55–58
Blake, William, 163
Bloch, Ernst, 170
Bo, Xilai, 78
Bourgeois democratic revolution, 8, 35, 123, 373
Buwang chuxin, 42, 77

Chartist movement, 162, 163
China model, 3, 55, 370, 374
Chinese Dream: affinity with American Dream, 127, 208; affinity with dreams of all nations, 127, 372; apolitical content of, 112; collective, nationalist dimension of, 375, 379; and communism, 82, 83, 217; as distinctively modern dream, 199–200; as ideology, 153; individualistic dimension of, 375; as new telos, 41–42, 60, 61, 76; relation to freedom and democracy, 370, 373, 376; and universalism, 208, 372
Chinese People's Political Consultative Conference, 220
Christianity, 73, 150
Citizens United, 138
Civil society: compatible with Communist Party's political leadership, 246; Confucianism in, 303; expanded under Jiang Zemin, 89; and functioning of ideology in Hong Kong, 365; Gramsci on, 68; as locus of freedom and agency, 8, 25; as locus of ideology, 365; Marx on, 122; necessary for democratic transition, 273, 282; political consequences of presence or absence of, 280, 283–284; requiring maturity, 294; requiring moral independence from state, 237–240, 241; silenced, 4; as source of moral leadership, 239; views of Marx and Tocqueville compared, 188–192
Color revolution, 96–97, 317, 321
Command-obedience relation, 232, 233, 257, 258
Communicative action, 104, 117, 288
Communism: absence of from Chinese Dream, 82–83; compared with Chinese Dream, 200; hostility toward in Hong Kong, 348, 366; and morality, 207–208, 209; no longer effective as ideology, 111; no longer plausible as discourse, 75–76;

Communism (*continued*)
  nominal, 199, 342; as original aspiration, 77;
  as part of revolutionary legitimation
  discourse, 72; and performance legitimacy,
  61; as substitute for *tian* as basis of rule, 148
Community of shared future of humankind,
  127, 372, 373
Compensation effect, 124, 125, 126
Conformism, 229, 230, 231, 234
Confucian democracy, 150, 152
Confucianism: as cosmology, 150, 151, 153,
  154, 155; flexibility with regard to regime
  and society types, 303, 304; as ideological
  power, 236, 261, 302; and republicanism,
  302–307; role in aristocracy, 303; role in
  democracy, 149, 150, 152–153, 303, 305;
  role in republican regime, 306–307
Confucian-Legalist state, 151, 235, 261
Confucian tradition, 3, 128, 149, 305
Consent. *See* Endorsement consent
Constant, Benjamin, 106, 200–201, 205,
  294, 328, 374
Constitutional amendment removing
  presidential term limits, 91, 92, 95
Constitutional patriotism, 154, 354
Consultative democracy, 220
Consumerism, 66, 67, 163, 207, 301
Convention consent, 136–137
Creditor-debtor relation, 221–223
Crisis of revolutionary spirit, 75–78
Crony capitalism, 89, 187, 188
Crouch, Colin, 175
Crowding-out effect, 124, 125, 126
Cultural Revolution, 87, 154, 221

Dahl, Robert, 271
Datong, 236
Dayitong, 235
Death of God, 154. *See also* Nihilism
Democracy: appropriate external involvement supporting, 328, 330; and capitalism, 2, 27–28, 157–165, 324, 325;
  challenges regarding in China, 22–29;
  China and West compared, 248–251;
  China's lack of cultural resources for, 26;
  contemporary condition of in West, 1–2,
  165–174, 330–331; devaluation of, 1–2;
  as essentially contested concept, 11, 12,
  155, 313, 314; flexibility as regards form,
  265–270; goods to be weighed against,
  328–329; inappropriate external involvement supporting, 328, 329; individual and

societal maturity as essential condition
  for, 294–295; intrinsic value of, 321–322,
  323–324; legitimation crisis of, 2, 164,
  170, 172–173; Marx and Tocqueville
  compared, 121–123, 188–194; and need
  for strong central authority in China,
  260–265, 268, 269, 270, 272; in society
  as distinct from polity, 1, 20–21, 113–117,
  120–121, 134, 135; in United States,
  144–145, 223–224, 378–379
Democracy, arguments for: argument for
  equality of conditions, 119–120; argument
  from fittingness, 22, 116–117; argument
  from governability, 22, 117–119; prudential
  argument for, 11–17, 101–121, 253–254,
  255, 291–297; as self-protection of society,
  156, 161–162, 164
Democratic centralism, 290–291
Democratic conception of virtue, 21, 103,
  104–105
Democratic culture, 248; democratic political
  culture, 248, 250, 251; democratic societal
  culture, 248, 249–250, 251
Democratic epistemology, 21, 103, 104–105
Democratic preparation, 25, 26, 29, 251, 260,
  319, 323, 328; components of, 273–274;
  legal reform as component of, 274, 285–291;
  moral reform as component of, 273, 274,
  277–285; social justice reform as compo-
  nent of, 274, 297–302
Democratic pride, 125–126
Democratic rule of law, 138, 140, 142,
  146, 147
Democratic social power, 223–231, 234
Democratic social state, 113, 114, 115
Democratization, functional, 115
Deng, Xiaoping, 39, 40, 61, 71, 76, 88–89, 111,
  175, 217, 371
Depoliticization, 82, 180–181
Dewey, John, 104
Dominium, 157, 162, 188, 325, 330, 331, 332
Dunn, John, 12, 17, 262

Economic inequality, 129, 193, 217, 324
Economy, party-state's role in, 110, 298
Elections, free and fair, 64, 141, 270;
  conducive to credibility of democracy,
  144, 146, 363; ideological function of, 142;
  liberal democratic governmentality deeper
  than, 361; not to be fetishized, 145;
  rationale for, 118; as vehicle of actual
  consent, 144

Elias, Norbert, 115, 118–119, 139, 257, 263–265, 267
Elster, Jon, 124
Elvin, Mark, 261
Emerging markets, 163
End of history, 194, 242, 243, 244
Endorsement consent, 137–140, 143, 267–268; abstract, 141, 142, 146; actual, 143, 144, 145; credibility of, 143–145, 266; hypothetical, 143
Engels, Friedrich, 122–123
Equality, passion for, 129, 218–219
Equality, qualitative versus quantitative, 217–218
Equality of conditions, defined, 114–115
Equality of opportunity, 115, 129, 218, 226, 230, 231
Essentially contested concept. See Democracy

Factionalism, 20, 42, 76, 80
Family, as site of authority in China, 128
Fear, role of in politics, 94–95
Filial piety, 128, 257
First Emperor, 90, 234
Foucault, Michel, 361
Frederick II, 292, 296, 368
Freedom: as condition for individual and societal maturity, as distinct from its use for political purposes, 291, 292; as condition for moral subjectivity, 203–205; de facto, 130, 202, 205–207, 283–284; priority of, 241, 245, 246; as value, 203, 205–207, 283–284
Freedom of press, 259, 276
Freedom of speech, 201, 259, 276
French Revolution, 114, 148
Friedman, Milton, 176

Globalization, 2, 12, 163, 174
Gorbachev, Mikhail, 275
Governmentality, 361, 364
Gramsci, Antonio, 68–69, 361, 363
Great rejuvenation of Chinese nation, 8, 37, 41, 50, 51, 77, 82, 178, 336, 371, 375
Guizot, François, 106, 121
Guo, Boxiong, 85

Habermas, Jürgen, 45, 117, 139, 283, 288
Hacker, Jacob, 169
Hampton, Jean, 136–137, 138–139
Han dynasty, 151, 235

Harmony, 236, 258–259, 270, 351
Hayek, Friedrich von, 173, 176, 288
Heavenly reign, 147, 148, 150
Hegemony, 13, 160, 164, 318, 321, 361, 362
Historical materialism, 121, 373
Historical nihilism, 111
Hobbes, Thomas, 125, 250
Hollywood, 321
Hong Kong: anticommunism, 335, 336, 339, 348, 355, 366; apartness from China, 333, 334, 336, 356–359; Basic Law, 351, 354; and capitalism, 333, 335, 338, 341–342, 350; China's legitimacy in, 334, 337, 340, 359–366; citizens' strong sense of agency, 364; civil liberties, 333, 335, 353, 356, 368, 369; democracy movement, 338–344, 358, 364, 367; democratic system ruled out by fact of sovereignty, 344–346; desire for apartness, 334, 337, 338–344, 347, 358, 359; identification with China, low, 351–355; impact of equality of conditions in, 343–344; impact on China's democratic development, 366–369; June 4, 1989, reaction to, 354, 358, 366; localism, 337, 340; mainlandization, fear of, 336, 337; Occupy Central, 338, 339, 340, 342, 349, 358; Occupy Central compared to Brexit, 358; one country, two systems, 337, 345, 349, 350, 351, 354, 355, 356, 369; pan-democrats, 346–347, 348, 355, 367; political culture, 353, 364; political integration with China, 351–355, 358; rise of China as problem for, 335, 336; rule of law, 333, 335, 346, 353, 354, 356, 369; sense of superiority to China, 335–336, 338; ungovernable, progressively, 344
Hu, Jintao, 84, 85, 87, 89, 280, 371
Hu, Yaobang, 38
Huodegan, 7, 82

Ideological power, 307, 361, 363; working in tandem with political power in communist China, 83–84; working in tandem with political power in Confucian China, 236, 261
Ideological State Apparatuses, 4–5, 65–69, 94, 211–212, 362–363, 364–365
Ideology critique, 65, 288
Imperium, 157, 162, 188, 325, 330, 331, 332
Industrial / manufacturing aristocracy, 157
Inequality of conditions, 114, 118, 119–120, 216, 304, 327

Internal reasons, 213
Iraq War, 2, 379

Japan, 302, 318
Jiang, Qing, 154
Jiang, Zemin, 84, 85, 89, 280
June 4, 1989, 38, 40, 42, 316, 320, 354, 358

Kant, Immanuel, 204, 292–293, 294, 296, 368, 369
Kuomintang, 149

Leadership succession, 20, 70, 88, 90, 96
Legalism, 150
Legal reform. See Democratic preparation
Legitimacy, conceptual analysis of: in de facto sense, 13; democratic inclusive, 64–65; exclusive, 63–65; ideological, 65–69; inclusive, 52, 59, 62; input versus output, 41; relation to performance, 49–55, 59–62. See also Right to rule
Legitimacy, empirical analysis of: China's international, 311–312; democracy as condition for China's domestic and international, 313, 314, 315; interaction between China's international and domestic, 313–315; intraparty, 39, 42–43, 76, 78, 79–81; revolutionary, 19, 36, 37, 40, 41, 42, 49, 70, 72–73, 93, 115, 129–130
Legitimation crisis: due to mismatch between society and polity, 17–22, 115–119; due to performance problems, 36–38, 60–62, 182–184; due to waning revolutionary legacy, 20, 36, 54–55, 70–71, 75–81, 95–96, 110–112; identity crisis as part of, 81–84; plausibility crisis as part of, 72–75
Liberal democratic socialism, 272–273
Liberalism: classical, 244, 245; political, 244, 245
Liberalization, 89, 90
Liberties of moderns, 105, 130, 172, 374; as common denominator for comparing China and United States, 196–197, 198–200, 201
Liberty, de facto. See Freedom: de facto
Liberty of ancients, 105, 130, 374
Liberty of conscience, 202
Ling, Jihua, 85
Louis XVI, 275
Lukács, Georg, 193

Ma, Jack, 165
Machiavelli, Niccolò, 13, 106–107

Maier, Charles, 21
Mandate of Heaven, 18, 36, 147, 151, 155, 235
Manent, Pierre, 232–233, 243, 244
Mann, Michael, 361
Mansbridge, Jane, 270–271
Mao Zedong, 18, 49, 61, 72, 88, 108, 258, 283, 327
Market, autonomous, 177, 178, 181, 182, 184, 186
Marx, Karl, 8, 35, 106, 108, 158, 373; compared with Tocqueville, 121–123, 188–194
Marxism, 49, 72, 155, 160, 371
Mason, Paul, 176
McCutcheon, 138
Mencius, 220, 250, 257
Meritocracy, 3, 4, 153, 306; Daniel A. Bell on, 55–58; not to be confused with legitimacy, 56–57
Migrant crisis, 2
Migrant workers, 218
Mill, J. S., 244
Mixed regime, 154, 220, 306, 307
Montesquieu, 304
Moore, Barrington, Jr., 172
Moral crisis, 24, 25, 212, 215–216, 237–238, 277–279; political dimension of, 278–284
Moral culture: communist, 207–208; current need for bourgeois, 208–210; outmodedness of communist, 208–212; Western influence on China's, 211
Morality, types of: morality based on freedom, 215; morality based on identification, 214
Moral reform. See Democratic preparation
Moral subject / subjectivity, nature and structure of, 213–215
Murdoch, Iris, 243, 244

Nationalism, 154, 320
Neoliberalism, 1, 28, 169, 171, 175, 176, 177, 299
Neopragmatism, 104
Network society, 2, 225
Neutrality: permissive, 244, 246; persuasive, 244, 246
New Deal, 28, 165, 166, 331, 379
New Gilded Age, 331, 379
Nihilism, 154, 243
Noble lie, 151

Obama, Barack, 208
Oligarchy, 2, 230, 271

One country, two systems. *See* Hong Kong
Opium War, 73, 258
Organized labor, 160, 171
Orientalism, political, 6

Patriotism, 69, 154, 354. *See also* Constitutional patriotism
Performance legitimacy, 18, 19, 38–43; as amelioration of lack of legitimacy, 19, 53–54, 56, 58–59, 71, 74; contrary to publicness, 266–267; as enhancement of legitimacy, 19, 53–54, 56, 58–59, 71, 74. *See also* Legitimacy, conceptual analysis of
Personality cult, 90
Perspectivism, 151
Pierson, Paul, 169
Plato, 103, 105, 107
Pluralism, 103, 151, 236, 306; reasonable, 203, 209, 242, 244
Polanyi, Karl, 159, 160, 161–164, 168, 169–170, 173, 193
Political agency, 142, 144–146, 250, 260
Political inequality, 219–220, 223, 228, 258, 276
Political reform, 4, 97, 254, 273, 274–276, 277
Political-system hostility, 317, 318–321, 323–325, 327, 366–367, 368
Polyarchy, 271
Polybius, 57, 342
Populism, 2, 359. *See also* Substantive populism
Pragmatism: as manifested by Deng Xiaoping, 128; as school of thought in America, 104; as trait of Hong Kong, 340, 358
Principle of Heaven, 147
Priority of good, 240, 243, 245, 246, 247
Priority of right, 241, 271
Private law, 288
Privileges, official, 299–300
Proletariat, 73. *See also* Working class
Propaganda, 82, 85, 176, 206, 209, 357; as distinct from ideology, 5, 69, 211, 362–365
Protagoras, 21, 103–105, 106, 107, 108
Publicness, 266–268, 286–287, 288; credibility of, 266, 268

Qing dynasty, 148, 272

Rancière, Jacques, 2
Rationalization of lifeworld, 117
Rawls, John, 203

Reagan, Ronald, 176, 331
Realistic utopia, 242, 253, 255, 273
Regime change, 316, 325, 348, 367, 368
Regime continuation. *See* Regime perpetuation
Regime perpetuation, 55, 70, 88, 136, 142, 194
Relativism, 103, 151
Religion, 202, 203, 212
Religious freedom, 202–203
Representation, 140–146, 268; credibility of, 143–145, 266, 267
Representativeness. *See* Representation
Repression, 89, 90, 201, 203, 281, 375
Repressive State Apparatus, 4–5, 6, 7, 65–69, 211, 212, 362–363, 364–365
Right to rule, 18, 44–49, 50, 51, 53, 62–63, 76, 77–78, 81, 234. *See also* Legitimacy, conceptual analysis of
Rise of China, 112, 318, 336, 357, 367, 370, 372; lopsided in terms of hard and soft power, 311–312
Rorty, Richard, 104
Rousseau, Jean-Jacques, 106, 201
Rule of law, 199, 201, 285, 312; corruption as obstacle to, 289; in Hong Kong, 333, 335, 346, 353, 356, 369; in modern Western sense, 288; need for flexible understanding of, 288; publicness as defining feature of, 288–289, 290. *See also* Democratic rule of law

Scheidel, Walter, 168, 169, 172–173
Schmitt, Carl, 343, 349
Schumpeter, Joseph, 13, 158–159, 321–322
Scientific socialism, 72, 237
Separation of church and state, 232, 237, 239
Separation of powers, 232, 235, 237, 238, 239, 247
Shanghai, 199, 201
Singapore, 302, 338
Skorupski, John, 244, 245, 246
Social democracy, 28, 165, 166, 168–173, 193, 299, 325, 341
Social integration, 179, 180
Socialism with Chinese characteristics for new era, 50, 237, 371
Socialist core values, 155
Socialist market economy, 42, 59, 180, 181
Social justice: and democratic preparation, 29, 274, 297–302; and Hong Kong's democracy movement, 341, 369; relation to democracy, 328–329; in social democracy, 164, 166–173, 185, 267

Social justice reform. *See* Democratic preparation
Social unrest, 81
Socrates, 103, 107
Son of Heaven, 147, 150, 151, 236
Sophists, 102, 103, 104
South Korea, 149, 150
Sovereign debt crisis, 168
Spillover effect, 124
State-owned enterprises, 109, 110, 165, 176, 180, 185, 298, 300
Streeck, Wolfgang, 164, 166, 167, 168, 169
Substantive populism, 112, 153
Surveillance capitalism, 174
System integration, 180

Taiwan, 149, 262, 312, 356
Territorial integrity, 26, 261, 263
Thatcher, Margaret, 2, 176, 331
Ti, 152, 153
Tian, 147–155
Tibet, 262, 312, 314
Tocqueville, Alexi de: argument for democracy, 105, 106, 219; argument for equality of conditions, 119–120; compared with Habermas, 117; compared with Marx, 121–122, 188–193; democracy and capitalism, 157; on democracy versus aristocracy, 114, 149, 152, 304; on democratic social power, 223–224, 227; on equality of conditions, 21, 114–115, 216, 230; on equality's connection to freedom, 292
Tönnies, Ferdinand, 281
Trickle-down economics, 179
Trump, Donald, 319

United States, the: compared with China, 196, 198–200, 201–202, 206; conformism in, 227, 231; and democratic social power, 223–224; effects on China's democratic development, 377–379; endorsement consent in, 137–140; Karl Polanyi on, 159; need for enemies, 6; New Gilded Age, 331; political-system hostility toward China, 316, 318–320; pushback against China's rise, 43; separation of economic and political spheres, 163
Unity, vertical, 256–260
Universalism, 127, 150, 208, 368, 371, 372
Urban-rural divide, 127, 217, 218, 302

Vanguard, 56, 72, 108, 153, 200, 258

Warring States, 234
Way of Heaven, 147, 151, 257
Weber, Max, 13, 72, 292, 297
Weiwen, 22
Welfare state, 158, 160, 163, 167, 170, 171, 190, 250, 325, 363
Western Zhou, 151
Williams, Bernard, 213
Working class, 163. *See also* Proletariat
World Trade Organization, 181, 248

Xi, Jinping, 28, 47, 78, 80, 84, 85, 88–97, 108, 208, 217, 371, 376
Xidan Democracy Wall, 113
Xingfugan, 7, 66, 82
Xinjiang, 262, 312, 314
Xu, Caihou, 85

Yifa zhiguo, 285, 289
Yong, 152, 153
Yuan dynasty, 272

Zhou, Enlai, 108
Zhou, Yongkang, 85
Zhutigan, 8